HEPTADIC STRUCTURE
OF SCRIPTURE

WITH A CHAPTER ON
SEVEN AND FOUR IN NATURE

BY

R. McCORMACK

Author of "Seven the Sacred Number"

MARSHALL BROTHERS, LIMITED

LONDON   EDINBURGH   NEW YORK

1923

Errata

Page 59, note 4, *for* 37   *read* XXXIV.

  „ 84,   „   3,   „   *simallu*   „   *samulli*

  „ 107, „   1,   „   *Hellene*   „   *Helene*

  „ 147, „   4,   „   *Ophik*   „   *Orphik*

  „ 172, line 3, „   Theocyeds „   Theocydes

  „ 261, last line, „   Ellis   „   Elis

  „ 273, third line from bottom, *for* the one merely God *read* the one only God

  „ 416, *for* Rilievo *read* Relievo

PREFACE

IN the year 1887 I published (under an assumed name) a book entitled *Seven the Sacred Number : its use in Scripture and its application to Biblical Criticism.* Since that date I have continued my study of the subject as opportunity allowed, and have been able to arrive at more definite and far-reaching results than were at that time attainable.

My position is that as the feathers in the wings of a bird are all numbered ; as the leaves of a plant are all numbered (phyllotaxis) ; as the rows of grain on a cob of maize are all numbered ; as the atoms in a molecule of every chemical compound are all numbered ; so the words and even the letters in the true text of Scripture are numbered.

Does this sound incredible ? There are many things once deemed incredible which are now acknowledged facts, instances of which will occur to every one.

As there is a harmony between the Works of God in Nature and the Word of God in Scripture, may we not expect that if Number pervades the one it will also pervade the other ?

The answer to this question is, of course, not a matter of argument but of fact, and it is therefore to facts I appeal.

I have said " the true text of Scripture," and as this has been to some extent obscured by copyists, the first and second chapters of this work are designed to show how the true text is to be recovered, and in so doing to supply facts which will bear out my statement and prove my position.

The chapter on Chronology has no necessary connection with the earlier chapters, so that the non-acceptance of the dates there given would not affect the argument as to the Text of Scripture.

The chapter on Nature is also extraneous to the main subject of the work ; it is designed to display the harmony between the Word and Works of God with regard to Number.

I should add that as the book above referred to on *The Number Seven* has long been out of print, some of it has been reproduced here, but revised and brought up to date. The more important parts of the present work are, however, entirely new.

In order that the subject may be intelligible to English readers, most Hebrew and Greek words have been translated or transliterated.

It is too much to hope that the work is entirely free from error. Let me earnestly beg that any errors (for which I crave indulgence) or differences of opinion on minor matters may not be allowed to divert attention from the main purpose of the work, which is to uphold the honour and purify the text of the Word of God.

LIVERPOOL,
April, 1923.

CONTENTS

7

LIST OF BOOKS AND ABBREVIATIONS

acc.=accusative.
Aram.=Aramaic.
art.=article.
AV=Authorized Version.
Barlow, Peter, "The Theory of Numbers."
Blackwood, Sir S. A., "The Number Seven in Scripture."
Blass, F., "Grammar of N.T. Greek," Eng. tr.
Bompass, Bp. W. C., "The Symmetry of Scripture."
Browne, Hy., "Ordo Sæclorum."
Bullinger, E. W., "Number in Scripture."
cent.=century.
ch., chh.=chapter, chapters.
"Chambers' Encyclopædia."
Ch. Q. Rev.="Church Quarterly Review."
Conder, Col. C. R., "The First Bible."
cf., cp.=compare.
Deismann, G. A., "Bible Studies," Eng. tr.
Driver, S. R., "Notes on Samuel ²."
Drummond, Hy., "Natural Law in the Spiritual World."
ed., edd.=editor, editors.
Enc. Brit.="Encyclopædia Britannica," 11th edn. 1910-11, and
　　12th edn. 1922.
Enc. Rel. Eth.="Encyclopædia of Religion and Ethics."
"Etymological Vocabulary of the N.T. Scriptures."
E.Vs.=English Versions (AV & RV).
"Expository Times."
Forbes, John, "Symmetrical Structure of Scripture."
Forbes, John, "Studies on the Book of Psalms."
Friend, J. N., "Inorganic Chemistry."
Garrison, J. F., "Symbolism of Numbers," (in "American Church
　　Review.")
Gillespie, G. K., "Greek Testament Roots."
Ginsburg, C. D., "Introduction to Hebrew Bible."
Girdlestone, R. B., "Outlines of Hebrew Chronology."
Grant, F. W., "Numerical Bible."
Grant, F. W., "Numerical Structure of Scripture."

Guinness, H. G., "The Approaching End of the Age," 9th ed., 1884.
Harris, Rendel, & V. Burch, "Testimonies."
Hastings' "Dictionary of the Bible."
Hastings' "Dictionary of Christ and the Gospels."
Hawkins, Sir J. C., "Horæ Synopticæ²."
Heb.=Hebrew.
Hellmuth, Bp. J., "Biblical Thesaurus: Genesis."
I.C.C.=International Critical Commentary.
Jones, F. A., "The Dates of Genesis."
J.T.S.="Journal of Theological Studies."
Jukes, Andrew, "The Types of Genesis."
Jukes, Andrew, "The New Man and the Eternal Life," etc.
Kitto's "Cyclopædia of Biblical Literature," ed. by W. L. Alexander.
La. or Lach.=Lachman (ed. of Greek Testament).
Lea & Bond, "The Cabala in Gnostic Books."
Lea & Bond, "The Apostolic Gnosis."
LXX or Sept.=Septuagint (O.T. in Greek).
Mahan, M., "Palmoni: Mystic Numbers."
McCook, Hy., "The Gospel in Nature."
Moulton, J. H., "Grammar of N.T. Greek."
Naville, Edouard, "Archæology of the O.T."
Naville, Edouard, "The Text of the O.T."
nom.=nominative.
N.T.=New Testament.
Old Lat.=Latin Versions before the Vulgate.
Old Syr. See Syr-cu. and Syr-sin.
O.T.=Old Testament.
"Oxford Hebrew Lexicon," by Brown, Driver & Briggs.
Panin, Ivan, "Bible Numerics," etc.
Pent.=Pentateuch.
Pesh.=The Peshitta Syriac Version.
R. or Rev.=Revisers' Greek Text of N.T.
R.V.=Revised Version.
rec. or rec. text=the "received text" of the N.T.
Robertson, A. T., "Grammar of the Greek N.T.³"
Roscoe & Schorlemmer, "Treatise on Chemistry."
Ryle, Bp. H. E., "Canon of the O.T."
Sam.=The Samaritan text of the Pentateuch.
SBOT.="Sacred Books of the O.T."
Smith, E. M., "The Mystery of Seven."
Smith, E. M., "The Mystery of Three."
Sod.=H. von Soden (ed. of Greek Test.).
Swete, H. B., "Introduction to O.T. in Greek."
Syr-cu.=Curetonian Syriac Version of the Gospels.
Syr-sin.=Sinaitic Syriac Verson of the Gospels.
Thackeray, H. St. J., "Grammar of the O.T. in Greek," v. i.
Thirtle, J. W., "The Titles of the Psalms."

Thomson, J. E. H., "The Samaritans."

Tilden, Sir W. A., "Introd. to Chemical Philosophy," 11th ed.

Tilden, Sir W. A., "Chemical Discovery and Invention in the 20th Century."

Ti. *or* Tisch.=Tischendorf (ed. of Greek Test.).

Tr. *or* Treg.=Tregelles (ed. of Greek Test.).

Vulg.=Latin Vulgate Version.

Waw Con.=The Hebrew Waw conversive or consecutive.

Westcott, Bp. B. F., "History of the Canon of the N.T."

WH.=Westcott & Hort, "The N.T. in the original Greek, Text and Introduction."

White, Malcolm, "Symbolical Numbers of Scripture."

Wright, Arthur, "Synopsis of the Gospels in Greek," 3rd ed.

Wright, G. F., "Origin and Antiquity of Man."

Wright, G. F., "Scientific Confirmations of O.T. History."

Figures in thick black type **(14)** denote numbers which are multiples of **7**.

" AND " in small capitals represents in the O.T. the Hebrew waw conversive or consecutive; but in the N.T. it represents the Greek καί.

" and " in ordinary type represents in the O.T. simple waw; and in the N.T. the Greek δέ.

THE HEPTADIC STRUCTURE OF SCRIPTURE

PART I

CHAPTER I

INTRODUCTORY : THE PRINCIPLE OUTLINED

IN the religion and philosophy of **ancient nations** Numbers occupied a far more important position than they do in our modern civilization, this being especially true of Eastern countries, as the records of Babylonia and Egypt, India and China, abundantly show. From this some may be led to suppose that the idea of sacredness attached to certain numbers in the Hebrew Scriptures is only in keeping with that found in other ancient writings. A little examination however will show that this is not so, but that the partiality of the Hebrews to those numbers was of a different origin and sprang from a higher source.

We should imagine that the number which would appeal to the minds of the ancients above all others would be the number Seven. For as they lifted their eyes upwards and searched the skies they found 7 radiant orbs whose movements differed from those of all the other heavenly bodies, and to them they gave the name of planets or wanderers, including under this designation the sun and moon. Then one of the most characteristic features in the northern sky is the constellation of **7** stars known as the Great Bear, with its **7**-starred companion the Little Bear, while another noteworthy object is the little group of the Pleiades or the Seven Sisters. The Rainbow was another striking celestial object with its **7** colours.

But it is the number Three (with its multiples) which is the outstanding number in the ancient religions and philosophies,[1] **7** having to take a lower place.

In **the Bible,** however, though not for the reasons just stated, **7** stands supreme.

This is evident even to the ordinary reader, but it is far more evident when the text of Scripture is studied closely, for then it will be found that, speaking generally, the number of sentences may usually be divided into paragraphs or sections of **7** each ; that in each of such sections the number of words and even the number of letters is usually a multiple of **7** ; that most words singly or in combination with others from the same root, or of similar meaning, occur a multiple of **7** times either in the same book or in the whole of the Old and New Testaments respectively, sometimes in both Testaments combined ; that even in the Parts of Speech, and often in the inflections the same heptadic influence may be traced.

This must be taken as a general statement, and not pressed too closely, for two reasons : (1) the number 10 is often employed, and occasionally other numbers, instead of **7**, there being usually a reason for the change ; (2) the text of Scripture, as it has come down to us, is not free from error ; and though the errors which have crept in from one cause or another are not of any moment as regards the meaning of the Divine message conveyed, they interfere with the arithmetical exactness which the pure text would show, and hide from our view the beautiful symmetry which the text would otherwise display.

It will be seen, then, what an extraordinarily valu-

---

[1] See *Encyc. of Religion and Ethics*, art. " Numbers."

able instrument is placed in our hands, for the restoration of the text, for the translation, the interpretation, and for other branches of Biblical study, when the true principles of the Heptadic Structure of Scripture are rightly understood.

Before entering upon the study which is the special object of this work, it may be well to spend just a few moments in naming some of the more obvious ways in which the number **7** is found in the Bible.

(1) The word " Seven " itself occurs quite an exceptionally large number of times, while multiples of **7** are also found frequently, e.g., **14, 42, 49, 70, 77, 700, 1260, 7000**, etc.[1]

(2) **7** words in a group : as Abram's " sheep and oxen and he-asses and menservants and maidservants, and she-asses and camels " (Gen. xii. 16) ; " thou, nor thy son, nor thy daughter, thy manservant, nor thy maidservant, nor thy cattle, nor thy stranger that is within thy gates " (Ex. xx. 10) ; " house, wife, manservant, maidservant, ox, ass, nor anything that is thy neighbour's " (Ex. xx. 17) ; " temptations, signs, wonders, war, a mighty hand, a stretched out arm and great terrors " (De. iv. 34) ; **7** blessings for obedience (De. vii. 13; **7** punishments for disobedience (De. xxviii. 22) ; " burnt offerings, sacrifices, tithes, heave offering, vows, freewill offerings, and firstlings " (De. xii. 6) ; " tithe of corn, wine, oil, firstlings, vows, freewill offerings, heave offering " (De. xii. 17) ; " bullocks, rams, lambs, wheat, salt, wine and oil " (Ezra vi. 9) ; **7** things which defile a man (Mt. xv. 19) ; **7**-fold ascriptions of praise (Re. v. 12 ; vii. 12) ; etc.

(3) **7** occurrences of Words : as the **7** " walks " in Ephesians ; **7** " *parousias* (comings) " in Thessalonians ; **7** " better " things in Hebrews ; **7** " precious " things in Peter ; **7** " blesseds " in Revelation; etc.

(4) Groups of **7** clauses or sentences : as **7** promises

---

[1] All numbers in thick type in this work are multiples of **7**.

to Abram (Gen. xii. 2, 3) ; **7** promises to Isaac (Gen. xxvi. 3, 4) ; **7** promises to Jacob (Gen. xxviii. 13-15) ; Isaac's **7**-fold blessing upon Jacob (Gen. xxvii. 28, 29) ; **7**-fold description of God's character (De. xxxii. 4 ; Dan. ii. 20-22) ; **7** kinds of false gods (Jud. x. 6) ; **7** things destroyed at Nob (1 Sam. xxii. 19) ; **7** occasions for prayer (1 K. viii. 31-46) ; **7** kinds of presents for Solomon (2 Ch. ix. 24) ; **7** blessings on him that considereth the poor (Ps. xli. 1-3) ; **7** promises to him that loves God (Ps. xci. 14-16) ; **7** acts of Wisdom (Pr. ix. 1-3) ; **7** invitations of Wisdom (Pr. ix. 4-6) ; **7** commands to Zion (Is. lii. 1, 2) ; **7** promises to the captives of Judah (Jer. xxiv. 6, 7) ; **7** things done by owner of vineyard (Mk. xii. 1, 2) ; **7** things done by good Samaritan (Lu. x. 33-35) ; **7** " gifts " of Romans xii. 6-8 ; **7** things unprofitable without love (1 Cor. xiii. 1-3) ; five series of **7**'s in 2 Cor. vi. (passive suffering, 4, 5a ; active service, 5b-6a ; means of endurance, 6b-8a ; result, 8b-10 ; promises, 16-18) ; **7** things Paul was as a Jew (Ph. iii. 5, 6) ; **7** things Paul desired as a Christian (Ph. iii. 8-11) ; **7**-fold armour of God (Eph. vi. 14-18) ; **7**-fold charge to the rich (1 Ti. vi. 17, 18) ; etc.

(5) **7** related things not joined together : as **7** utterances of God in Eden after the Fall ; Covenant given to Abram **7** times ; **7** weepings of Joseph ; **7** lists of furniture in the Tabernacle ; **7** weepings of the Israelites ; **7** servitudes of Israel and **7** deliverances by Judges ; **7** miracles of Elijah and **14** of Elisha ; **7** trials of Job ; **7** New Year's Days ; **7** prayers of our Lord in Luke ; **7** times Jesus spoke to woman of Samaria ; **7** " I am's " of John (two series) ; **7** miracles of Christ on the Sabbath ; **7** visions of Paul ; **7** " mysteries " of Paul ; **7** emblems of the Holy Ghost ; etc.

(6) Most of the Books of Scripture are capable of **7** Divisions, e.g., Genesis, Exodus, Job, Psalms, Proverbs, Sol. Song, Isaiah, Ezekiel, Daniel, Hosea, Joel, Obadiah, Jonah, Nahum, Zechariah, Malachi, Matthew,

John, Acts, Ephesians, Colossians, Hebrews, Revelation.[1]

These lie on the surface of Scripture, but we must penetrate below if we would see the Wondrous Things of God's Law, and explore its inexhaustible riches. We will now, therefore, proceed to the consideration of **heptads** of quite a different nature from the preceding, taking for our first example the well-known passage the **Magnificat.** It is too short, indeed, to display all the verbal wonders of the number **7**, but it will serve admirably for this introductory chapter, as it is fortunately not complicated by textual difficulties. The Greek text adopted by the Revisers can be shewn to be, not simply that current in the fourth century or the second century, but the actual text with the actual spelling as it left the hands of the writer of the Gospel ; in other words it is the exact Autograph Text. It is given below divided into the shortest possible grammatical sentences, with an attempt to represent it in English so as to shew the English reader the number of Sentences and Words and the Parts of Speech. A small circle above the line (°) represents the Greek article when it is not expressed in English, so must be counted in, but single words in parentheses ( ) must not, as they are understood but not expressed in the Greek. Words in *italics* also represent the Greek article. Words joined together must be counted as one.

LUKE i. 46–55.

1. Καὶ εἶπε Μαριάμ, Μεγαλύνει ἡ ψυχή μου τὸν Κύριον.

1. And Mary said, ° My soul magnifies the Lord.

2. καὶ ἠγαλλίασε τὸ πνεῦμά μου ἐπὶ τῷ Θεῷ τῷ σωτῆρί μου.

2. And ° my spirit rejoiced in ° God ° my Saviour.

3. ὅτι ἐπέβλεψεν ἐπὶ τὴν ταπείνωσιν τῆς δούλης αὐτοῦ.

3. For he-looked upon the lowliness *of* his handmaiden.

4. ἰδοὺ γάρ, ἀπὸ τοῦ νῦν μακαριοῦσί με πᾶσαι αἱ γενεαί.

4. For behold, from the present, all the generations shall-call-blessed me.

[1] See R. G. Moulton: *Literary Study of the Bible*; Sir S. A. Blackwood: *The Number Seven in Scripture*; etc.

5. ὅτι ἐποίησέ μοι μεγάλα ὁ δυνατός.

6. καὶ ἅγιον τὸ ὄνομα αὐτοῦ.

7. καὶ τὸ ἔλεος αὐτοῦ εἰς γενεὰς καὶ γενεὰς τοῖς φοβουμένοις αὐτόν.

1. ἐποίησε κράτος ἐν βραχίονι αὐτοῦ.

2. διεσκόρπισεν ὑπερηφάνους διανοίᾳ καρδίας αὐτῶν.

3. καθεῖλε δυνάστας ἀπὸ θρόνων.

4. καὶ ὕψωσε ταπεινούς.

5. πεινῶντας ἐνέπλησεν ἀγαθῶν.

6. καὶ πλουτοῦντας ἐξαπέστειλε κενούς.

7. ἀντελάβετο Ἰσραὴλ παιδὸς αὐτοῦ, μνησθῆναι ἐλέους (καθὼς ἐλάλησε πρὸς τοὺς πατέρας ἡμῶν) τῷ Ἀβραὰμ καὶ τῷ σπέρματι αὐτοῦ εἰς τὸν αἰῶνα.

5. For the Mighty-One did to-me great-things.

6. And holy (is) ° his name.

7. And ° his mercy (is) unto gen-erations and generations to-those fearing him.

1. He-shewed strength with his arm.

2. He-scattered proud in-their heart's imagination.

3. He-deposed princes from thrones.

4. And he-exalted lowly-ones.

5. Hungry he-filled with-good.

6. And rich he-sent-away empty.

7. He-helped Israel his servant, to-remember mercies, (as he-spake to ° our fathers) to Abraham and to his seed unto the age.

The Song, with the introductory words "And Mary said," which being Scripture must be taken along with it, contains **14** sentences, **105** words (7 × 3 × 5) and **546** letters $\left(\begin{array}{c}7 \times 77 + 7 \text{ or} \\ 7 \times 3 \times 13 \times 2\end{array}\right)$, numbers which taken to-gether are all divisible by **7**, *and by no other number*. There are two well-marked sections of **7** sentences each, and in each section the **7th** sentence is longer than any of the others, the last one containing **21** words and **112** letters. In the second section, vv. 51–55, **7** acts of the Lord are recited.

According to ancient Greek grammar there are 8 **Parts of Speech**: Noun, Pronoun, Verb, Participle, Article, Adverb, Conjunction, Preposition. It will be noticed that the Participle is separate from the Verb, while the Substantive and Adjective are classed together under the term Noun. There are no Adverbs in the Song, νῦν being here a Noun, preceded by an Article and governed by a Preposition. There are therefore

7 Parts of Speech used in the passage before us, the number of each being as follows :—

Noun (including νῦν)		**35**
Pronoun		**14**
Verb	16	
Conjunction	12	**28**
Article	17	
Preposition	8	
Participle	3	**28**
Total		**105**

Full lists in Greek and English will be found on the next two pages.

Of the Nouns, 7 are Sing. Masc. if we exclude the indeclinable proper names, 7 are Pl. Masc., and 7 are Sing. Neut. excluding the indeclinable νῦν. There are 7 Proper Names, if we may count Saviour and Mighty-One as such. 14 Nouns end in ς and 7 in ι. Names of God and things belonging to Him occur 7 (4 and 3) times (Lord, God, Saviour, Mighty-One, name, mercy, arm).

Of the Pronouns there are 7 different inflections used ; αὐτός (in its oblique cases) occurs 7 times in the Sing. (αὐτοῦ, αὐτόν, his, him), or 7 in the genitive (αὐτοῦ, αὐτῶν, his, their) ; 8 times in all.

Of the Verbs, 14 are in the Indicative Mood, and 14 (but not the same 14) in the Aorist tense ; 7 end with —σε(ν) and 7 begin with ε.

Of the Conjunctions, καί " and " occurs 7 times in the Song itself.

Of the Articles, 14 are in the Sing. and 14 begin with τ.

LUKE I. 46–55.

Nouns Subst. & Adj.	Verbs.	Pronouns.	Conjunctions.	Participles.
Μαριάμ	εἶπε	μου (3)	καί (8)	φοβουμένοις
ψυχή	μεγαλύνει	μοι	ὅτι (2)	πεινῶντας
Κύριον	ἠγαλλίασε	με	γάρ	πλουτοῦντας
πνεῦμα	ἐπέβλεψεν	ἡμῶν	καθώς	
Θεῷ	ἰδού	αὐτοῦ (6)		
σωτῆρι	μακαριοῦσι	αὐτόν		
ταπείνωσιν	ἐποίησε	αὐτῶν		
δούλης	ἐποίησε			
νῦν	διεσκόρπισεν			
πᾶσαι	καθεῖλε			
γενεαί	ὕψωσε			
μεγάλα	ἐνέπλησεν			
δυνατός	ἐξαπέστειλε			
ἅγιον	ἀντελάβετο			
ὄνομα	μνησθῆναι			
ἔλεος	ἐλάλησε			
γενεάς				
γενεάς			Prepositions.	Articles.
κράτος			ἐπί (2)	ὁ
βραχίονι			ἀπό (2)	ἡ
ὑπερηφάνους			εἰς (2)	τό (3)
διανοίᾳ			ἐν	τοῦ
καρδίας			πρός	τῆς
δυνάστας				τῷ (4)
θρόνων				τόν (2)
ταπεινούς				τήν
ἀγαθῶν				αἱ
κενούς				τοῖς
Ἰσραήλ				τούς
παιδός				
ἐλέους				
πατέρας				
Ἀβραάμ				
σπέρματι				
αἰῶνα				

LUKE I. 46–55.

Nouns Subs. & Adj.	Verbs.	Pronouns.	Conjunctions.	Participles.
Mary	said	my (3)	and (8)	fearing
soul	magnifies	to-me	for (3)	hungry
Lord	rejoiced	me	as	rich
Spirit	looked	our		
God	behold	his (6)		
Saviour	call-blessed	him		
lowliness	did	their		
handmaiden	shewed			
present	scattered			
all	deposed			
generations	exalted			
great-things	filled			
Mighty-One	sent-away			
holy	helped			
name	remember			
mercy	spake		*Prepositions.*	*The Article is translated*
generations			in	the (6)
generations			upon	of
strength			from (2)	to-those
arm			unto (2)	to (2)
proud			with	Untranslated(7)
imagination			to	
heart				
princes				
thrones				
lowly				
good				
empty				
Israel				
servant				
mercies				
fathers				
Abraham				
seed				
age				

Words. 7 words begin with π, 14 with ε (of which 7 are verbs) and 14 with κ; 7 end with ο and 28 with ι. 7 words have 7 letters each and 7 have 9. The only other number above the average is *four*, a number we shall meet with again.

105 (the number of words in the passage) is the " triangular number " of 14 (the number of sentence-divisions) ; i.e. it is the sum of the numbers 1 to 14, and if 105 units be arranged in regular lines in the form of an equilateral triangle, there will be 14 units in each side.

The **Letters** in the passage may be divided into 8 heptadic groups of 3 each.

α		70 }	3		ν	41	} Final	
ε		56 }	vowels		ϱ	16		Consonants.
ι		56 }	(separate).		ς	41	98 }	
ο	52		last 3		κ	16	} Contraction	
υ	38		} vowels		τ	38		for
ω	15	105 }	(together).		λ	16	70 }	etcetera.
ζ	0				β	5		
θ	6		1st }		π	22		
ξ	1	7 }	3 } Double		δ	8	35	
φ	2		} letters		η	16		
χ	2		last } and		γ	9		
ψ	3	7 }	3 } Aspirates.		μ	17	42	

Multiples of 4 are again frequent.

It will be seen that the letters which are used most frequently are the three vowels : α 70, ε 56, ι 56, while ζ, which as a numeral stands for 7, enjoys the distinction of being the only letter of the alphabet which is not found in the passage at all. The whole 7 vowels occur in all 303 times, which is not an heptadic number, but if we go by sound, then there are 173 single vowels and 65 diphthongs, total vowel sounds 238. The diphthongs are αι 14, ει 9, οι 6, ῳ 5, ᾳ 1 = 35 with ι; ου 21, αυ 8, ευ 1 = 30 with υ; total 65, of which 35 are in the first section, vv. 46–50, and 30 in the second, vv. 51–55.

The peculiar phrase ἀπό τοῦ νῦν lit (" from the now ")

= " henceforth," which occurs in the Song, is found **7** times in N.T. ; and " God my (or our) Saviour " **7** times ; καθελῶ, καθελεῖν " to put down, depose " is used as future and aorist to καθαιρέω **7** times ; μεγαλύνω is used in the sense of " magnify " **7** times, and is so translated in R.V., besides once " enlarge."

The Virgin is mentioned by name 19 times in N.T. : Μαρία **7** (acc. to WH[1] text) and Μαριάμ 12, of which **7** are in the nominative.

The Song is full of expressions taken from the O.T., indeed the greater part of it is so printed in WH text. In the Appendix to their Gk. Test. they give a list of 14 passages quoted in the Song.

Some of these items may be thought trivial and accidental. But there are far too many, and some are too striking, to be accidental. · In this short passage it is impossible for the number **7** to have full play *and yet remain hidden*, or to shew the marvellous results to be found in a longer passage such as John xvii. or Mt. i. ii.[2]

The bearing of all this upon the subject of Textual Criticism will be seen at once. The text adopted here by the Revisers, resting as it does upon the best authorities and *confirmed by the heptad test*, is correct. The rec. text differs slightly in two places, and is therefore wrong. WH have 9 letters more, owing to their adding ν at the end of certain words. This is simply a matter of spelling, and does not affect the sense.

Let us now turn to the OLD TESTAMENT, taking an equally familiar passage, " the psalm of psalms,"

---

[1] WH here and elsewhere = Westcott & Hort's *New Test. in Greek*. For other abbreviations, see List at commencement of volume.

[2] Some may think the following worthy of mention, at least in a footnote. There are 14 sentences
   105 words
   546 letters

   665 = 7 × 95. 9 + 5 = 14.

" the most beautiful of all the psalms," as it has been called, dividing it, as before, into the shortest grammatical sentences, of which it will be seen there are **14**, making two sections of **7** each.

PSALM XXIII.

1. The LORD (is) my shepherd.
2. I shall lack nothing.
3. He maketh me to lie down in green pastures.
4. He leadeth me beside waters of rest.
5. He restoreth my soul.
6. He guideth me in the paths of righteousness for his name's sake.
7. Yea, though I walk through the valley of the shadow of death I will fear no evil.

1. For thou (art) with me.
2. Thy rod and thy staff, they comfort me.
3. Thou preparest a table before me in the presence of mine enemies.
4. Thou hast anointed my head with oil.
5. My cup (is) overflowing.
6. Surely goodness and kindness shall follow me all the days of my life.
7. And I shall return into the house of the LORD for a length of days.

In the Hebrew text there are **56** words (or COMPOUND WORDS as I propose to call them), **84** SIMPLE WORDS (each prefix and suffix being reckoned a separate word) [1] and **210** letters, all heptadic numbers. In counting the words, *tsalmaveth*, "shadow of death" must be considered as two words, which it really is, just as much as "shadow" and "death" are two words in English, σκιὰ θανάτου in Greek, and *umbra mortis* in Latin. In the "simple words" we must count בְּ "in the" as two, for it is equivalent to בַּה.

There are **14** verbs in the Psalm, **28** common nouns, and **28** prefixes and suffixes.

Of the letters ו occurs **7** times as a consonant, and **7** as a vowel-letter. ר and ה also occur **7** times each.

---

[1] It might perhaps seem simpler to say **56** words, **28** prefixes and suffixes.

The two weak gutturals א ע occur **21** times and the two strong ones ה ח with ר which is often classed with the gutturals **28** ; total **49**. The three vowel-letters א י ו, representing the three original vowels *a i u*, occur **63** times.

Let us now see what help is afforded by the number **7** in the study of this Psalm in respect of the Text, Translation and Interpretation.

Text. We have seen that *tsalmaveth* must be treated as two words, *tsal*, construct of *tsēl*, " shadow of," and *maveth* " death," and as these words connote a single idea (not necessarily connected with death itself) they were not separated as they should have been. In ancient times it was the practice to write one word closely after another, without any division between, and when the words of this Psalm came to be written separately, these words should have been divided into two, instead of being written as one. They should probably not be joined by *makkeph*, as there are already **7** *makkephs* in the Psalm. Otherwise the present Hebrew text appears to be a faithful reproduction of the original writing. This proof by the heptad test is, however, presumptive, not absolute, for the results arrived at here and elsewhere should be largely accepted as provisional until the whole ground has been gone over.

Translation. In the Hebrew text as pointed, " I shall *return* into the house of the Lord for a length of days " is the correct translation, not " dwell in." The exact form of the word as pointed, and meaning " return " occurs **7** times in O.T. including this passage. Then there are in the Psalm **14** words which occur nowhere else in the same grammatical form, but if this word is to be derived from *Yashab* " to dwell," it would make a **15**th. Again *yashab*, " to dwell," occurs in Qal Perf. **126** times excluding it here, but **127** if it means " dwell " here. So that if we translate " return," we make three heptads, **7**, **14**, and **126**, while if we translate " dwèll " we spoil them, turning these numbers into 6, 15 and 127 respectively. But the translation of this word is influenced by the

Interpretation we place upon the Psalm, whether the figure of shepherd is continued throughout, or not. The consideration of this we will defer to the chapter on Interpretation.

The heptadic division in the middle of the 4th verse agrees, it will be seen, with the grammatical construction of the Psalm. In the 1st section the shepherd is spoken **of**, in the 3rd person—He. In the 2nd section he is spoken **to** in the 2nd person—Thou.

In the **Narrative** or **Historical** portions of Scripture a different method of marking the heptadic divisions is found. Even the most casual reader of the Bible can scarcely have failed to notice how very frequently the word " AND " is used at the commencement of sentences and clauses. In the Hebrew it is far more common than in the E.Vs, for our translators have tried to vary the monotonous repetition of the word by using " but," " then," " now," " therefore," and other words.[1] It comes as a surprise to find that this apparently insignificant word is the KEY to the whole system of heptadic divisions, and that therefore this little word possesses the greatest significance. As an illustration let us take the first two heptads in the Book of Jonah, rendering the Hebrew *waw* in every case by " and," joining it by a hyphen to the word to which it is prefixed in the Hebrew text. This necessitates the nominative being sometimes placed after the verb in the translation instead of before it, when it is not a simple pronoun. One alteration only is made in the text, viz. the insertion of " the cry of " in v. 2—one word of four letters in Hebrew. This has been carelessly omitted by Hebrew scribes, but is preserved in the Septuagint, and is required by the sense, cf. Gen. xviii. 20, 21 ; xix. 13.

[1] See Appendix A.

JONAH I. 1–5.

1. (*1*) AND-there-came the word of the LORD unto Jonah
2.   the son of Amittai, saying, Arise, go to Nineveh that great
        city.
   (*2*) And-proclaim against it, for (*or* that) [the cry of] their
        wickedness has ascended to my face.
3. (*3*) AND-rose-up Jonah to flee to Tarshish from the face of the
        LORD.
   (*4*) AND-he-went-down (to) Joppa.
   (*5*) AND-he-found a ship going (to) Tarshish.
   (*6*) AND-he-paid the fare thereof.
   (*7*) AND-he-went-down into it to go with them to Tarshish
        from the face of the LORD.

4. (*1*) And-the-LORD hurled a great wind into the sea.
   (*2*) AND-there-was a great tempest in the sea, and-the-ship
        was like to be broken.
5. (*3*) AND-were-afraid the mariners.
   (*4*) AND-they-cried every man unto his god.
   (*5*) AND-they-cast the wares that were in the ship into the sea,
        to lighten it unto them. And-Jonah had gone down into
        the innermost parts of the ship.
   (*6*) AND-he-lay-down.
   (*7*) AND-he-fell-fast-asleep.

Including the word זעקת " the-cry-of," there are
in the Hebrew in the

	Compound words.	Simple words.	Letters.
1st heptad	42	67	163
2nd heptad	35	59	145[1]
	—	—	—
	77	126	308

all heptadic numbers taking the two heptads together,
which is presumptive proof that the text is now correct,
though we may, again following the Septuagint, read
" its " for " their " in v. 2 without disturbing the
numbers.

There are 17 or 18 sentences, of which 16 begin with

[1] Some Heb. Bibles have one letter more, reading in v. 5 וישׂיל
with the marg. note "some copies read ויטלו." The shorter
spelling is adopted by Kittel and the *Oxf. Heb. Lex.*

waw, "and," which the E.Vs in order to avoid the constant repetition of the word, have in 7 cases rendered "but," "now," "then," "so," or "so that." In the first heptad there are 6 conversive or consecutive *waws* (printed above in SMALL CAPITALS) and one *waw* prefixed to a verb in the imperative. In the 2nd heptad the first division begins with *waw* prefixed to a noun, and the other six with *waw con.* The two remaining *waws* are prefixed to nouns and do not count here in the marking of divisions. Each division therefore in this passage begins with *waw* prefixed to a verb except the commencement of the 2nd heptad, which however is quite normal, as the first division of a heptad often differs from the rest in having simple (copulative) *waw*, or sometimes no *waw* at all.

We are here introduced to a remarkable peculiarity of Hebrew, which is found in no other language.[1]   The Heb. verb has only two tense-forms, Perfect (formerly called Preterite) and Imperfect (formerly known as Future), and in the narration of a series of connected events in past time, such as in Jonah above, Heb. employs a special and peculiar idiom. The *first* verb in the series, which marks the starting-point of the narration, may be (as in the 2nd heptad above) a Perfect, and the succeeding verbs Imperfects with the prefix ו *waw* "and." The *waw* which links the successive verbs into a single chain was termed *Vav* (or *Vau* or *Waw*) *Conversive* by the older grammarians from its apparent power to convert future into past and past into future, but is now usually called *Waw Consecutive*, from its use in consecutive narration. So also a series of events in *future* time may be described by an initial Imperfect, followed by Perfects with *Waw Con.*[2]

In the first heptad above, Jonah i. 1-3, all the *waws*

---

[1] The Phænician and Moabite are not really exceptions, as the languages are practically the same as Heb., from which they differ only dialectically. Similarly with the inscription of Zakkur.

[2] S. G. Green, *Handbk. to O.T. Heb.*, pp. 94, 96.

are consecutive except the one prefixed to a verb in the imperative, which does not admit of *waw con.* In the second heptad, vv. 4, 5, the first *waw* is the simple copulative joined to " the LORD," and all the others consecutive except two, " and-the-ship " and " and-Jonah." Why was not the *waw* joined to the verb instead of the noun in these cases also ? Because it would have made 9 divisions where only **7** were wanted.[1]

As this peculiar grammatical form has often a very important bearing upon the structure of the heptad, the word " AND," when it is the translation of *waw con.*, is printed above, and will be throughout this work in passages taken from the O.T., in SMALL CAPITALS.

When we consider how very frequently the word —or rather letter—occurs, and that in many cases it makes no difference to the sense whether it is inserted or omitted, we should not be surprised if occasionally it is wanting where it ought to be found, or *vice versa.* It says much for the general faithfulness and accuracy of Jewish scribes that instances of this nature are so comparatively rare. The *waw con.* is indeed in this respect a safeguard, for its omission would frequently alter the meaning of the verb.

Further remarks on the formation of heptads in the O.T. will be found at the end of this chapter.

When we turn to the Narrative or Historical portions of the NEW TESTAMENT we find that the word " and " occupies a similarly important position. But here we have to deal with an entirely different language from those in which the Old Testament is written, one in which there is nothing answering to the Hebrew *waw con.*, one which, indeed, in its general character- istics much more nearly resembles the English. Still, allowing for this difference in language, the same features mark the heptadic divisions. In the first

---

[1] The English reader may compare Dr. Robt. Young's *Literal Transl. of the Bible*, in which no regard is paid to the " conversive " power of " *waw.*"

three Gospels the rule is that a division must contain a grammatical sentence commencing with *and*; which is, therefore, practically the same as that which governs the division of the historical books of the Old Testament.   There is no one word, however, in Greek answering exactly to *waw* in the Hebrew, its place being supplied by the conjunctions καί and δέ.   The ordinary meaning of καί corresponds to the English *and*, though in certain circumstances it requires to be translated *even, both, also*, etc.   δέ is considered to be most properly adversative, and is therefore often rendered *but*; this adversative sense, however, cannot always be made out; and δέ may in many, perhaps in the majority of cases, be translated *and*, though very often *but* expresses its meaning more truly.[1]   It is not, however, necessary to go into the distinction between these two conjunctions, for I have not been able to trace any difference between them so far as their use in the formation of heptads is concerned; δέ, indeed, coming after a number of καί's, often marks the beginning of a new heptad, but this is not always the case.

In the remaining books of the New Testament the rule is usually the same as that which prevails in the poetical and prophetical books of the O.T.: every complete grammatical sentence forms a separate division of a heptad (or other section); dependent clauses whether relative, participial, infinitive, or connected by the particles *hina* "that," *kathōs* "according as," etc., do not form separate sentences, and are therefore not separate divisions.   However long the sentence may be (and there are some very long sentences in the N.T., notably in the Epistles of St. Paul and St. Peter), it must be continued to its full extent before a new divi-

---

[1] "The difference in meaning between the two conjunctions is practically [very] slight; for as Winer points out, '*Δέ* is often used when the writer merely subjoins something new, different and distinct from what precedes, but on that account not sharply opposed to it. . . . Hence in the Synoptic Gospels καί and δέ are sometimes parallel.'"—Hawkins' *Horae Synopticae*, ed. 2, p. 150.

sion may be commenced. *Amen*, when used as a prayer (= So be it), forms a separate division, but not when it occurs in the phrase " *Verily* I say unto you," nor of course in such texts as 1 Co. xiv. 16 ; 2 Co. i. 20 ; Re. iii. 14. In the Epistles, the superscription, and the salutation which immediately follows it (" Grace be to you, and peace, from," etc.), form separate divisions. Clauses commencing with *oudĕ*, *mēdĕ*, "neither" form separate divisions in places where they would do so if *ou*, *mē*, " not," were used simply.

It is only necessary to add further that where AND is the translation of *καί*, it is printed in SMALL CAPITALS, though it must be distinctly understood that this has no connection whatever with the *waw con.* of the Old Testament ; and that *δέ* is also generally translated " and," printed in ordinary type.

The structure will be best understood, however, by an example, and as the following verses are remarkably free from textual error they will serve our purpose admirably. They form two heptads or **14** divisions, of which 11 commence with *καί* (here printed " AND " in small capitals), while in the other 3 *δέ* is used, printed " and " in ordinary type.

LUKE I. 8–17.

8. (*1*) And it came to pass while he executed the priest's office
9.   before God in the order of his course, according to the custom of the priest's office his lot was to burn incense when he went into the temple of the Lord.
10. (*2*) AND the whole multitude of the people were praying without at the time of incense.
11. (*3*) And there appeared unto him an angel of the Lord standing on the right side of the altar of incense.
12. (*4*) AND when Zacharias saw him he was troubled.
    (*5*) AND fear fell upon him.
13. (*6*) And the angel said unto him, Fear not, Zacharias ; for thy prayer is heard.
    (*7*) AND thy wife Elizabeth shall bear thee a son.

    (*1*) AND thou shalt call his name John.
14. (*2*) AND thou shalt have joy AND gladness.
    (*3*) AND many shall rejoice at his birth,
15.   for he shall be great in the sight of the Lord.

(4) AND wine AND strong drink he shall not drink.
(5) AND he shall be filled with the Holy Ghost, even from his mother's womb.

16. (6) AND many of the children of Israel shall he turn to the Lord their God.

17. (7) AND he shall go before Him in the spirit AND power of Elias, to turn the hearts of the fathers to the children, AND the disobedient to the wisdom of the just ; to make ready a people prepared for the Lord.

There are, it will be seen, 14 clearly marked divisions, and in the Revisers' Greek text the passage contains **161** words **805** letters, both heptadic numbers (7 × 23 and 7 × 23 × 5). The rec. text and WH's are practically the same, the former containing one letter more, while WH's *margin* is the same as the Reviser's, but their *text* omits the article before "Lord" in v. 15, making 160 words 802 letters. We may therefore assume the Revisers' text to be correct.

It must not be supposed however that the heptadic divisions are so easily made out in all parts of Scripture as in the foregoing examples. Had this been the case the secret would doubtless have been discovered long ago.

In Part II a number of chapters are given from both Testaments with the divisions marked, but a few further examples are supplied below, taking the text as it stands, and showing the divisions only, in order to illustrate the Remarks on the formation of heptads at the end of the chapter. The translation of the A.V. is followed as closely as possible, and only departed from to show the occurrences of *waw* (" and ') in the Hebrew, and the words to which it is prefixed.

GENESIS XVII.

15   (1) AND-said God unto Abraham, As for Sarai thy wife, thou shalt not call her name Sarai, but Sarah shall her name be.

16 (2) AND-I-will-bless her, and-also give thee a son of her : (3) AND-I-will-bless-her, (4) AND-she-shall-be a mother of nations ;

17 kings of people shall be of her. (5) AND-fell Abraham upon his face, (6) AND-he-laughed, (7) AND-he-said in his heart, Shall a child be born unto him that is an hundred years old ? and shall Sarah, that is ninety years old, bear ?

There would be a difficulty in tracing the divisions
of this heptad in the English version of the passage, but
there is none whatever in the Hebrew when the key is
known.   And the key is simply this : *Every division of*
the heptad commences with what is called, by the older
Hebrew grammarians, *vau conversive*, now better
known, as explained above, as *waw consecutive*.   The
word "and," when it is the translation of *waw con.*
is printed above, and will be throughout this work,
in SMALL CAPITALS.

We will now go on to the consideration of the next
heptad :—

18   (*1*) AND-said Abraham unto God, O that Ishmael might
19   live before thee !   (*2*) AND-said God, Sarah thy wife shall bear
      thee a son indeed;   (*3*) AND-thou-shalt-call his name Isaac :
      (*4*) AND-I-will-establish my covenant with him for an ever-
20   lasting covenant, (and) with his seed after him.   (*5*) And-as-for-
      Ishmael, I have heard thee : Behold, I have blessed him, AND-I-
      will-make him fruitful, (*6*) AND-I-will-multiply him exceedingly ;
      twelve princes shall be beget, (*7*) AND-I-will-make-him a great
21   nation.   And my covenant will I establish with Isaac, which
      Sarah shall bear unto thee at this set time in the next year.

In this heptad, like the preceding, the **7** divisions are
each marked by *vau* conversive, with this difference—
that in the fifth division it is found, not at the beginning,
but in the middle of the division, but at the commencement of a grammatical sentence.

The next heptad is of a different character :—

22   (*1*) AND-he-left-off talking with him, (*2*) AND-went-up God
23   from Abraham.   (*3*) AND-took Abraham Ishmael his son, and
      all that were born in his house, and all that were bought with
      his money, every male among the men of Abraham's house ;
24   (*4*) AND-he-circumcised the flesh of their foreskin in the selfsame
25   day, as God had said unto him.   (*5*) And-Abraham was ninety
      years old and nine, when he was circumcised in the flesh of his
26   foreskin.   (*6*) And-Ishmael his son was thirteen years old,
      when he was circumcised in the flesh of his foreskin.   In the
      selfsame day was Abraham circumcised, and-Ishmael his son.
27   (*7*) And-all the men of his house, born in the house, and-bought
      with money of the stranger, were circumcised with him.

In this heptad the first four divisions commence with *waw con.*, and the other three with simple *waw*, but there is no difficulty in making them out, for they each contain a separate grammatical sentence commencing with *waw*. The sixth division indeed contains two sentences, but the second does not begin with *waw*.

We will now turn to the Book of Exodus, and transscribe the words immediately following the Ten Commandments.

EXODUS XX.

18 (*1*) And-all the people saw the thunderings, and the lightnings, and the noise of the trumpet, and the mountain smoking :
(*2*) AND-saw it the people, (*3*) AND-they-removed, (*4*) AND-they-
19 stood afar off. (*5*) AND-they-said unto Moses, Speak thou with us, and we will hear : and let not God speak with us, lest we
20 die. (*6*) AND-said Moses unto the people, Fear not : for God is come to prove you, and that his fear may be before your faces,
21 that ye sin not. (*7*) AND-stood the people afar off, and-Moses drew near unto the thick darkness where God was.

Each division here commences with *waw con.* except the first. " And " occurs 14 times in all.

The next heptad is of a different kind : of the ten grammatical sentences which it contains **7** commence with " and," not always prefixed to a verb, and not always at the beginning of a division, if we mark the divisions according to the sense of the passage :

22 (*1*) AND-said the LORD unto Moses, Thus thou shalt say unto the children of Israel, Ye have seen that I have talked
23 with you from heaven. (*2*) Ye shall not make with me gods of
24 silver, and-gods of gold shall ye not make unto you. (*3*) An altar of earth thou shalt make unto me, AND-thou-shalt-sacrifice thereon thy burnt offerings, and thy peace offerings, thy sheep, and thine oxen. (*4*) In all places where I record my name I
25 will come unto thee, AND-I-will-bless-thee. (*5*) And-if thou wilt make me an altar of stone, thou shalt not build it of hewn stone.
(*6*) For if thou lift up thy tool upon it, AND-thou-hast-polluted-
26 it. (*7*) And-not shalt thou go up by steps unto mine altar, that thy nakedness be not discovered thereon.

The position of *waw* in the sixth division seems

peculiar, but the form is common enough in the Hebrew. In the A.V. it is usually in such cases either left untranslated, as here, or rendered " then," as in Exod. xxi. 30 ; Lev. xii. 2, 5, 8.

The foregoing illustrations will for the present suffice ; we will now turn to another branch of the subject.

To treat of the **Symbolism of Numbers** is no necessary part of the plan of this work. We have to deal with facts rather than symbols, and with symbols only as they help to interpret the facts. So much has been said on this subject of a fanciful and even contradictory nature, both by the early Fathers of the church and by modern writers, that it can scarcely be wondered at that many have turned away from it as having no solid foundation to rest upon. But this is to fly to the opposite error. When we consider the peculiar significance which has always attached to certain numbers—notably the number 7—the enquiry suggests itself, Why do some numbers stand out from others, and why in particular does the number 7 occupy such a prominent place in Scripture, and occur so much more frequently than other numbers ? This question demands an answer, and an answer can only be given by tracing the ideas underlying those numbers and the symbolical meanings which may be attached to them.

" Numbers do not generally represent to Orientals the same ideas that they do to ourselves. With our highly trained, accurate, mathematical minds a number always represents a certain fixed quantity of units ; but it is not so with Orientals. To them numbers are and always have been symbolical rather than arithmetical : and this fact must always be borne in mind if we would intelligently study the Bible." [1]

" Among every ancient people, especially in the East, we find importance attached to numbers ; and this too in connection with religious worship. This instinctive apprehension of the heathen world involves a profound truth. Number and Proportion are essential and necessary attributes of the *Kosmos :* and God as a God of order, has arranged each several province of Creation—even to the minutest particle (" the very hairs of your head are all numbered,"

---

[1] Rev. Haskett Smith : *Patrollers of Palestine* (1906), p. 343.

Mt. x. 30)—according to definite numerical relations (Ps. cxlvii. 4, Isa. xl. 26, Ecclus. xvi. 26, 27). . . . Numbers, like words, are but the signs of ideas ; and if we can ascertain the idea corresponding to a particular sign, we have the meaning of that sign.   It is this underlying idea alone on which the numerical symbolism of Scripture depends." [1]

I do not propose to deal with numbers generally, but only, and that briefly, with such as will assist us to a right understanding of the number **7**.

It may seem a truism to say that **One** is the symbol of Unity.   So far as any symbolical idea seems to be attached to it in Scripture, it stands for the One Living and True God.   " Hear, O Israel, the LORD, our God, the LORD, (is) One." [2]   Again, " In that day shall the LORD be One, and his Name One." [3]

The ordinal **First** is also used as a name of the Deity in the phrase " the first and the last " (or " and with the last ").[4]

Three, however, is the more usual numerical symbol of God, not only in the Bible, but in ancient religions generally.   In the O.T. we have the 3-fold Blessing, Num. vi. 24–26, and the 3-fold Sanctus, Isa. vi. 3, each of which has its counterpart in the N.T. (2 Co. xiii. 14, Re. iv. 8).

Prof. Ed. Naville says, " The Jews from Elephantiné have taught us that the name of God was JaHU or JaHO.[5]   This was certainly the name of God used in Canaan. . . . The proof is in the proper names found with the name of God : in their complete form, when the name of God is at the end it is Jahu : Jeshaiahu (Isaiah), Jehiskiahu (Hezekiah) Uzziahu, Jeremiahu, Hilkiahu, Joshiahu (Josiah),

---

[1] Archdn. Lee in *Speaker's Comm., Intr. to Rev.,* pp. 472, 473.
[2] So Jewish translns., Dt. vi. 4, R.V. mg., Mk. xii. 29, R.V. text.
[3] Zec. xiv. 9 R.V.
[4] This phrase occurs 3 times in O.T., Isa. xli. 4, xliv. 6, xlviii. 12 ; and 3 times in N.T., Rev. i. 17, ii. 8, xxii. 13.   It is also found in the common text in Rev. i. 11, and one is tempted to regard this as genuine, making **7** occurrences in all.   But the emphasis here is on the number 3—God in his own Nature, rather than on 7—God in His relation to the World.
[5] In Hebrew יהו, 3 letters only, whose numerical value (See App. A) is 21 (3 × 7).

etc. . . . Where the name of God is at the beginning, there we find it complete: Jehoshua (Jaho is my helper), Jehonathan, Jehoram, Jehojakim, Jehohanan, Jehojada, etc. There is no transformation from JAHVEH, JAHO is the name of God, and there is no proper name found with JAHVEH complete."[1]

The number Three is dealt with more fully in App. B. It is sufficient to state here that all writers agree that Three is the number of the Triune God, especially as He has revealed Himself in His word and works.

Four is the number of the World.

"*Four*," says Archdeacon Lee, "is the signature of Nature, of the created, of the world:—not of the world as 'without form and void,' but as a *kosmos*, as the revelation of God, so far as Nature can reveal Him. Among the heathen, *Four* is the number of the elements, and of the regions of the earth."[2] "*Four*," says Professor Moses Stuart, "is the symbol of the creation, rational and irrational, but specially of the former. . . . Bähr states the matter thus:— '*Four*, considered in its arithmetical relation to *three*, obviously proceeds from three, and necessarily includes three in itself. If three, then, designates the true, the highest, and the most perfect Being, *four* must designate that which proceeds from Him, or is dependent on Him. If three designates God, four must consequently designate the world, or the universe ' (p. 155). . . . A better reason, as it seems to me," proceeds Professor Stuart, "can easily be given for the alleged signification of *four*. The created universe, according to general opinion among the ancients, resolves itself into four elements, fire, air, earth, and water. Four are the regions of the earth, viz. east, west, north, and south. In four different ways is the extension of all bodies conceived of; for they have length, breadth, height, and depth. Into four parts is circling time divided, morning, noon, evening, and midnight. Four are the seasons, winter, spring, sum-

---

[1] *The Text of the O.T.*, (1916), pp. 61, 62.
[2] *Speaker's Comm.*, Intr. to Rev., p. 474.

mer, and autumn.   Four are the marked variations of the lunar phases.   Four are the ages of man, infancy, youth, manhood, and old age. . . .   The Oupnekhat, a book of high authority among the Hindoos, says : ' There are four ways of production, from the egg, from the womb, by creation, and from the seed as of plants ' (Bähr, p. 157)."   After giving many other examples of the use of this number, both among the heathen and in Scripture, Professor Stuart asks, " Is it possible, now, to consider all this accord in the use of *four* as a thing merely *accidental* ?   This [he replies] will not be said, I apprehend, by any considerate man well versed in the knowledge of ancient symbols.   And if it is not accidental but symbolical, and as such is highly significant, then why should we reject so import- ant an aid in the interpretation of some parts of the Bible . . . ? " [1]   A most pertinent question, and one which may be asked with reference to many other numbers besides *four*.

Another writer says : " The number Four and the quadrifoil were held as sacred to the Supreme Spirit, as was the number Three. The potent Tetragrammaton was a four-lettered word, and almost all peoples of antiquity possessed a name for the Deity composed of four letters [Assyrian, Adad ; Egyptian, Amun ; Persian, Sire ; Greek, Θεός ; Latin Deus ; German, Gott ; French, Dieu ; Turkish, Esar ; Arabian, Allah : cf. *Numbers ; their Occult Power and Mystic Virtue*, by W. Wynn Westcott, p. 22].   Among the Gnostics, the Supreme Being was denoted by Four.   One reason for this reverence of the figure 4 was the perfect equality of the 4 sides of a square, none of the boundary lines exceeding the others by a single point." [2]

That there are four Gospels signifies that the gospel was to be preached in " all the world . . . to the whole creation " (Mk. xvi. 16 R.V.) and not confined to one nation.

As 7 is the predominant number in the Word of God, 4 is of equal prominence with 7 in the Works of

[1] *Commentary on the Apocalypse*, Excursus II. (2) and (3).
[2] H. Bayley : *The Lost Language of Symbolism*, i. 79.   See also Dr. C. F. Burney in *J.T.S.*, Oct. 1910, p. 118.

God, as will be seen when we come to deal with these numbers in Nature in a subsequent chapter.

The Number **Five** pertains to the Law, says St. Augustine, who also connects it with the 5 senses. But it is better to take 5 as the half of 10, and as 10 signifies completeness, 5 stands for incompleteness. Thus there are 5 books of the Law, but " the law made nothing perfect " (Heb. vii. 19). So the great sacrifices of the law were 5 in number—the burnt-, meal-, peace-, sin- and guilt- (or trespass-) offerings, but these sacrifices " cannot as touching the conscience make the worshipper perfect " (Heb. ix. 9 R.V.). The Urim and Thummim (by which God was enquired of) are mentioned together in the Hebrew text 5 times. They were an imperfect method of ascertaining the will of God, and ceased to be used even in O.T. times.[1] Five therefore is the symbol of Incompleteness.

Six is " man's number." Archdn. Lee calls it the " signature " of *human labour*, and " also a symbol of *human rule and power*."[2] But we have higher authority than this. " Let him that hath understanding count the number of the beast ; *for it is man's number* (ἀριθμὸς γὰρ ἀνθρώπου ἐστί) ; and his number (is) 666."[3] Now 666 is a very emphatic form of 6 ; not only is it 6 thrice repeated (or, as it is in the Greek 600 + 60 + 6) but it is the sum of the numbers from 1 to 36, i.e. it is the " triangular number " of 36, the square of 6. It is also the sum of the first *six* of the 7 Latin numerals—DCLXVI = 666. Further, man was made on the 6th day, and 6 days of the week were allotted to him for work.

We now come to the number **Seven,** the most im-

---

[1] The word Urim also occurs twice alone, making **7** times in all. The Septuagint however has both words in 1 Sam. xiv. 41, in a passage which many critics consider has dropped out of the Heb. text. But the Sept. omits Thummim in Neh. vii. 65, so that the words still occur together only 5 times even in that version.

[2] *Speaker's Comm. :* Intr. to Rev., p. 478.

[3] Rev. xiii. 18.

portant, the most wonderful of all. Even arithmetically it differs from other numbers in the denary scale as will be shewn in Chapter VII.[1] Its meaning is usually, and rightly, looked for as being the sum of 3 and 4, God and the world, and so, speaking generally, it has to do with God's dealings with the world. This is comprehensive, and will include many things of which it is sometimes called the sign or symbol. More briefly it may be called the Covenant Number.

Seven is associated in most Eastern nations with the formalities of an *oath* or covenant.

In the Oxford *Hebrew Lexicon*, the highest authority on the subject, the noun שֶׁבַע (*sheba'*) " seven " is given as a root (although in Hebrew the root is usually a verb), from which are derived the verb שָׁבַע *Shaba'*, " to swear," " prob. so to say, *Seven oneself*, or *bind oneself by seven things* "; and שבעה shebu'ah " oath "; while the meaning of the well-known place Beersheba is given as " *well of seven*, explained Gen. xxi. 30, 31, as place of *swearing by seven* lambs, or *well of oath*." Covenant is frequently associated with swearing in Scripture, e.g. " His covenant which He sware unto thy fathers," Dt. iv. 31, vii. 12, viii. 18, indeed covenant and oath are used as parallel or practically synonymous terms, 1 Ch. xvi. 15, 16 ; Ps. cv. 8, 9 ; Luke i. 72, 73. The occurrences of the word " covenant " form an interesting heptadic study.

The sign or token (same word in Heb.) of the covenant with Noah was the 7-hued rainbow, Gen. ix. 12, 13 ; of the covenant with Abraham, circumcision, which must be performed on the eighth day, or as we should reckon it, when the child was 7 days old, Gen. xvii. 11 ; of the Mosaic covenant, the Sabbath, or setting apart of every 7th day, Ex. xxxi. 13, 17 ; Ezk. xx. 12, 20.

Of the Christian covenant the sign is Christ himself, the name of 7 letters Χριστός, Messiah Μεσσίας :

---

[1] Page 216.   [2] Garrison, *Symbolism of Numbers*.

"this child is set . . . for a *sign* which is spoken against," Lu. ii. 34; "this is the *sign* unto you, ye shall find a babe," etc., ii. 12; "as Jonah became a *sign* unto the Ninevites, so shall also the Son of Man be to this generation," and no other sign should be given, Lu. xi. 29, 30. The number **7** is abundantly connected with our Lord and the events of His life. The "new covenant" is described in **7** terms:

(1) "I will put my laws into their mind,
(2) "On their heart also will I write them,
(3) "I will be to them a God,
(4) "They shall be to me a people,
(5) "They shall not teach, saying, know the Lord, for all shall know me,
(6) "I will be merciful to their iniquities,
(7) "Their sins will I remember no more."
     Heb. viii. 10–12, quoted from Jer. xxxi. 33, 34.

Christ defined his mission in **7** terms :—

(1) "The Spirit of the Lord is upon me,
(2) "Because he hath anointed me,
(3) ". To preach good tidings to the poor he hath sent me,
(4) "To proclaim release to the captives,
(5) "And recovering of sight to the blind,
(6) "To set at liberty them that are bruised,
(7) "To proclaim the acceptable year of the Lord."
     Luke iv. 18, 19 (true punctuation, see p 152.).

His answer to John the Baptist also consisted of **7** terms :—

(1) "The blind receive their sight,
(2) "The lame walk,
(3) "The lepers are cleansed,
(4) "The deaf hear,
(5) "The dead are raised up,
(6) "The poor have good tidings preached to them,
(7) "And blessed is he whosoever shall find none occasion of stumbling in me," Luke vii. 22, 23.

St. Peter also in the first great Christian sermon preached on the Day of Pentecost, summed up our Lord's career under **7** heads :—

(*1*) " Jesus of Nazareth, a man approved of God unto you by mighty works, etc.
(2) " Him, being delivered up by the determinate counsel and fore-knowledge of God,
(3) " Ye by the hand of lawless men did crucify and slay :
(4) " Whom God raised up . . . whereof we all are witnesses.
(5) " Being therefore by [*or* at] the right hand of God exalted,
(6) " And having received of the Father the promise of the Holy Ghost,
(7) " He hath poured forth this which ye see and hear." Acts ii. 22–33.

Bp. Hellmuth points out [1] that שֶׁבַע *sheba‘* " seven " is the sum total of שָׁ[לֹשׁ־אַר]בַּע " three " and " four," i.e. the Hebrew word for " three " is *shalosh* and for " four " *arba‘*, and if these are placed together and the middle letters eliminated, leaving three letters only, the usual number in a Hebrew root, thus sh* [losh–ar]ba‘, we have *sheba‘*.

" As 3 and 4 make one number in 7, (*a*) 7 is the note of union between God and the World (3 + 4), and therefore signifies union and harmony. (*b*) As the conceptions of God and the world are the conditions of every religion, so all systems which aim at union with God must include them. Being the symbol of this union, 7 is, in general, the " number" of religion ; (*c*) The end of religion being union with God, the number (7) which signifies this is the necessary " signature" of Salvation, Blessing, Peace, Perfection." [2]

Seven also = 1 + 6, God and man, but the usual divisions of 7 are 3 and 4, as e.g. in the Lord's Prayer, where the first three petitions are about God, and the last four about ourselves, and in the 7 words from the Cross, of which 3 (the first, middle and last) are addressed to God, and the other 4 are not ; 3 also referring to other persons and 4 to himself. For the first covenant named in Scripture was made, not with man alone, but with every living creature, with all the earth [3] And so 7 is the Covenant number as made up

[1] *Bib. Thesaurus* on Gen. ii. 2.
[2] Lee, *Intr. to Rev.*, in *Speaker's Comm.*, p. 475.
[3] Gen. ix. 12, 13.

of 3 and 4, God and the world, which of course includes mankind, and of which man is the head and representative.

Seven is also connected with *time*, for the great artificial division of time, as opposed to natural, is the week of **7** days. Some indeed suggest that the sacred signification of 7 probably originated with the week of **7** days and the Divine rest on the seventh. But the opposite is more probably the truth, that God stamped the number **7** on time because of the sacred signification of the number.

The word **Seven** and its derivatives occur altogether in the Old and New Testaments **931** times $= 7 \times 7 \times 19$. The squared 7 at once attracts attention, but has 19 any significance ? It may or may not have in such a case, but if a reasonable significance can be found, then doubtless it was intended. Now 19 has no special force in Scripture, but it has in Astronomy. Few persons probably have studied the Tables at the beginning of the Prayer Book, but few can have failed to notice the mysterious words " Golden Numbers," which run from I to 19, one of these Golden Numbers being assigned to each Calendar Year. It is one of the drawbacks to the study of Astronomy that the relations between the three natural divisions of time—the day, the lunar month and the year—cannot be stated without the use of intricate fractions. It would be so much easier if a lunar month were exactly 30 days and a year exactly 360 days. Now it was observed by Meton in the fifth century B.C. that the sun and moon always occupied the same relative position to each other which they had done on the same day 19 years before.[1] And so 19 years became known as a Metonic cycle, and was used in the computation of the Church's seasons. It seems reasonable to suppose, therefore, that the association of 7 and 19 in the number 981 was meant to indicate that there is a connection between **7** and time.

[1] Modern astronomers calculate that this 19 years is not exact, there being a difference of two hours.

Further investigation of this must be deferred until we come to the chapter on Chronology.

For the connection between 6 and 7, and between 7 and 8, see Appendices D and E.

Eight points to a new beginning, being the first after 7, and so is the symbol of regeneration and resurrection. See further in Appendix E.

Ten is the symbol of completeness. See Appendix C. Some give this meaning to the number **7**; but 10 stands on a higher plane than 7, as will be seen when the two numbers are contrasted.

For 7 and 10 contrasted see p. 167.

Twelve is the number of the Church or the people of God, both in the Old Testament and the New. It is usually considered as $=3 \times 4$. Thus in the camp of the Israelites in the wilderness there were 3 tribes on each of the 4 sides,[1] and to the New Jerusalem there are 12 gates, 3 on each of the 4 sides.[2]

Twelve furnishes, perhaps more clearly than any other number, proof that a number is sometimes taken as a token or symbol, and does not always stand for its exact numerical value. Thus in the O.T., Jacob had 12 sons, who were the progenitors of the 12 tribes. But Ephraim and Manasseh, the two sons of Joseph, each gave his name to a tribe, so that there were really 13 tribes in all. But they are never spoken of as 13, always as 12, and even when the names are enumerated (as they are about 24 times) only 12 names are given; for if Ephraim and Manasseh are both named, one of the others is omitted, usually Levi, but Dan three times and Simeon once. Even in the only list of the tribes given in the N.T. (Rev. vii. 5–8) Dan is omitted in order to preserve the number 12.

So in the N.T. Church the Apostles are always spoken of as 12 in number.[3] Thus our Lord said to them, " Ye shall sit upon 12 thrones, judging the 12 tribes

[1] Num. ii.
[2] Rev. xxi. 13.
[3] Or 11, but never 13 or 14, see Rev. xxi. 12, 14.

of Israel." "Where then shall Paul be?" asks St.
Augustine, "for Matthias was ordained in place of
Judas." And he replies, "To the 12 thrones not 12
men, but many belong. And why do all men everywhere belong to the number 12? Because the compass
of lands is contained in 4 quarters, E.W.S.N.: from
all these quarters they being called in the Trinity, and
made perfect in the faith and precept of the Trinity—
seeing that 3 × 4 = 12 ye perceive wherefore the saints
belong to the whole world; they that shall sit upon
12 thrones to judge the 12 tribes of Israel, i.e., the 12
tribes of the whole of Israel."[1] I quote this as an
example of the way in which Augustine deals with
numbers; but much that he says is very fanciful.

Those who think that Two stands for the Second
Person of the Trinity may prefer to consider 12 as=
6 × 2, Man as saved by Christ.

We will now turn to another branch of the subject—
the **Heptadic Occurrence of Words and Phrases.** It
occupies the first chapter of Part II of this work,
and is briefly noticed here in order that the reader may
understand the textual and other arguments which
are based upon it in this and the following chapters.

I. That there are many **Words** which occur in Scripture **7** or a multiple of **7** times is of course natural;
the same may be said of any other of the nine digits.
But here as elsewhere it is the large number of instances
that tells.

(a) *In O.T.*: "Cherub" **91** including **7** without
prefix or affix and **7** in Exod. xxv. 18–22; "Haran"
7; "Jephthah," **28** in Jud.; "Jezebel," **7** in 2 Kings
(ch. ix.); "Lebanon," **7** in Cant. and **7** in Minor Prophets; "Satan," **14** in Job; *Shaddai,* "Almighty,"
used in Job **7** times by Eliphaz and **14** by Job; *taph,*
"children," etc., **7** in Deut., **21** rest of Pent., **14** rest
O.T., total **42**; *l'bonah,* "frankincense," **7** in Lev., **14**
elsewhere, total **21**; *path,* "a morsel," **7** in simple

[1] On Ps. l. § 9, 10.

form, **7** with suffixes, total **14** ; *saraph,* " fiery serpent, seraph," **7.**

(*b*) *In N.T.: eisphero,* " to bring," **7** ; *enistemi,* " to be present," **7** ; *makarios,* " blessed," **7** in Paul, **7** in Rev., **28** spoken by Christ (incldg. Ac. xx. 35) of which **7** in Matt. and **7** in Luke are parallels ; *prepei,* "it becometh," **7**; *potapos,* " what manner of," **7** ; *hupsistos,* " Most High," **7** in Luke and Acts ; *psalmos,* " psalm," **7.**

Many more instances are given in Part II, but their number could be very largely increased.

More remarkable however than single words are **Words in Combination,** and of these there are several varieties.

II. **Phrases.**   (*a*) *In O.T.*[1]

1. " A new song," **7.**
2. " After his kind," **14.**
3. " All the days of thy life," **7.**
4. " All the souls that were therein," **7** (in Jos. x. 28–39).
5. " An abomination to the LORD," **14,** besides **7** with wording slightly different.
6. " Blessed is the man," **14** (four different Heb. words are used for " man ").
7. " Dwelleth between the cherubim," **7.**
8. " From Dan even unto Beersheba," **7** (*also* " from Beersheba even unto Dan," **2**).
9. " God Almighty," *El Shaddai,* **7.**
10. " In all the land of Egypt," **7** in Gen., **14** elsewhere, total **21.**
11. " In the selfsame day," **14.**
12. " Let the King live for ever " (Heb.) **2** : " O King live for ever " (Aram.) **5,** total **7.**
13. " LORD God " (*Jehovah Elohim*) **21** in Pent., **14** elsewhere, total **35.**
14. " LORD God of Israel," **14** in Jos., **7** in Jud., **21** in 2 Ch., **14** in Jer., **49** in other books to 1 Ch., **14** in

[1] See also Part II, Class II.

other books from Ezra to Mal., total in O.T., **119.**

15. " Stranger . . . fatherless . . . widow " (in this order), **14.**
16. " The glory of the Lord " **35** (7 with "and" prefixed).
17. " The kingdom of Og," **7.**
18. " The place which (the LORD thy God) shall choose to cause (his) name to dwell there," **7.**
19. " (And) the word of the LORD came unto me, saying," **49** in Ezek.
20. " Under the whole heaven," **7.**
21. " Who keepeth covenant and mercy," **7.**
22. " With all thy heart and with all thy soul," **7.**
23. "   „   „   {his / their}   „   „   „   {his / their}   „   „ **7.**

(b) *In N.T.*

1. Barnabas is mentioned by name 29 times in A.V., but (omitting Ac. xi. 25) **28** times in R.V., which may be divided as follows :
   " Barnabas and Saul," 4 ; " Barnabas and Paul," 3 = **7.**
   " Paul and Barnabas," **7.**
   Barnabas connected directly with Paul (other than above), **7.**
   Barnabas not connected directly with Paul, **7.**
2. *Dei pathein,* " must suffer " (of Christ) 4 } **7.**
   Edei „ " must have suffered " (of Christ) 3 }
3. *Doulos* and *eleutheros,* " bond " and " free " contrasted **7.**
4. (*En*) *tē eschatē hēmerā,* " in the last day," **7** (all in John).
5. *Hē genea hautē,* " this generation," **21.**
6. *Karpos* with *phero,* " bear fruit," **7** in John xv.
7. *Kat' idian,* " privately," **7** in Mark.
8. *Kata* (*tēn*) *sarka,* " after the flesh," physically or historically **7,** figuratively or ethically **7,** total **14.**
9. *Tēreo, tērēsias,* " keep(-ing) " with *entolē* " commandment(s)," **14.**

10. *Hupo (tou) Theou,* "by *or* of God," **14** (R is right in Rom. xiii. 1, xv. 15).

11. *Hōra erchetai,* "the hour cometh," **7** in John; also "hour" with "come" referring to our Lord's appointed hour, **7** in John.

12. "Day of judgment," **7**.

13. "God $\begin{Bmatrix} \text{my } 1 \\ \text{our } 6 \end{Bmatrix}$ Saviour," **7**.

14. "He that hath ears (to hear) let him hear," **7** (with slight variations) in Gospels. Also **7** (an ear) in Re. ii., iii., and an 8th slightly different in Re. xiii. 9.

15. "Jesus of Nazareth *or* the Nazarene" **21** (**7** in Matt., Mk., **7** in Luke, John, **7** in Acts; **7** nom., **14** oblique cases).

16. "Living God," **14**, including *Theou zōntos,* without art. **7**. In Re. xv. 7, the phrase is different. In John vi. 69, 1 Tim. vi. 17 R.V. is right in omitting "living."

17. "Lord God Almighty," **7** (including Re. i. 8 R.V.).

18. "My   Father which is   in heaven," **7**.

19. $\begin{Bmatrix} \text{" Our } 1 \\ \text{" Your } 6 \end{Bmatrix}$ „   „ $\begin{Bmatrix} \text{art} \\ \text{is} \end{Bmatrix}$ „   „   „ (R.V.) **7**.

20. "Peoples, $\begin{Bmatrix} \text{tribes,} \\ \text{multitudes,} \\ \text{kings,} \end{Bmatrix}$ tongues, nations." **7**, all in Re., no two exactly alike.

21. "Son of Man shall come $\begin{Bmatrix} \text{in} \\ \text{with} \end{Bmatrix}$ glory," **7**.

22. $\begin{Bmatrix} \text{" An} \\ \text{" O} \end{Bmatrix}$ evil (faithless, perverse, etc.) generation," **7**, besides 3 with "this" (included in No. 5 above) making 10 in all, perhaps indicating that the iniquity of that generation was now full.

III. In many cases, again too many to be accidental, if the occurrences of all the **Words from the same Root** are added together, they form an heptadic number.[1]

[1] See also Part II, Class III.

a In O.T.

1. נמר *namer*, Heb. "a leopard," 6 ; *n'mar*, Aram. id.
    1 ; total **7**.
2. פתר *pathar*, "to interpret," 9 ; פתרון *pithrōn*,
    "interpretation," 5 ; total **14.**
3. צפיר *tsaphir*, Heb. "a he-goat," 6 ; *ts'phir*, Aram.
    id. 1 ; total **7.**
4. קרס *qaras*, "to stoop," 2 ; *qeres*, "hook," 10 ;
    קרסל *qarsōl*, "ankle," 2 ; total **14.**
5. שלג *shalag*, "to be like snow," 1 ; שלג *sheleg*,
    "snow," 20 ; total **21.**

b. In N.T.

1. *Agros*, "a field," 36 ; *agrios*, "wild," 3 ; *agrauleo*,
    "to abide in the field," 1 ; *agri-elaios*, "wild
    olive tree," 2 ; total **42.**
2. *Aspazomai*, "to salute," 59 ; *aspasmos*, "saluta-
    tion," 10 ; *apaspazomai*, "to salute," 1 (Ac.
    xv. 6) ; total **70.**
3. *Dia-legomai*, "to reason with," 13 ; *dialektos*,
    "language," 6 ; *dialogizomai*, "to reason," 16 ;
    dialogismos, "reasoning," **14** ; total **49** ; of
    which 28 are in Luke and Acts.
4. Ephesus, 16 ; Ephesian, 5 ; total **21.**
5. *Tharsos*, "courage," 1 ; *tharreo*, "to be of good
    courage," 6 ; *tharseo*, "to be of good cheer,"
    7, omitting Luke viii. 48, with R. ; total **14.**
6. Israel, 68 (omitting Ac. iv. 8, Rom. x. 1, with R.)
    Israelite, 9 ; total **77**, of which **7** are in John and
    Rev.
7. *Kalupto*, "to cover," 8 ; *Kalumma*, "a veil,"
    4 ; *anakalupto*, "to unveil," 2 ; *apokalupto*, "to
    reveal," 26 ; *apokalupsis*, "revelation," 18 ;
    epikalupto, "to cover," 1 ; *epikalumma*, "a
    cloak," 1 ; *katakaluptomai*, "to be veiled," 3 ;
    akatakaluptos, "unveiled," 2 ; *parakalupto*, "to
    conceal," 1 ; *perikalupto*, "to cover," 3 ; *sug-
    kalupto*, "to cover up," 1 ; total **70.**
8. *Krupto, apokrupto* and *egkrupto*, "to hide," 24 ;

kruptos, kruptē and *kruphaios,* " hidden," 20 ; *kruphē,* " in secret," 1 ; *apokruphos,* " hidden," 3 ; *perikrupto,* " to hide," 1 ; total **49.**

9. Laodicea, 6 ; Laodicean, 1 ; total **7.**

IV. Words from Different Roots, but of similar or allied meaning.[1]

a. In O.T.

1. חמץ *chamets,* meaning "to be leavened," 5 ; *chamēts,* "leaven," 11 ; שאר *sōr,* "leaven," 5 ; total **21.**

2. מטה יהודה *matteh Yehudah,* "tribe of Judah," 10 ; שבט יהודה *shebet Yehudah,* id. 4 ; total **14.**

3. There are **7** names of God in Hebrew : (*1*) *El,* (*2*) *Eloah,* (*3*) *Elohim,* "God," ; (*4*) *Jehovah,* (*5*) *Jah,* (*6*) *Adōn,* (*7*) *Adōnai,* "Lord."

4. **7** kinds of Offerings : 4 with blood, (*1*) Burnt-offering, (*2*) Peace-offering, (*3*) Sin-offering, (*4*) Guilt *or* Trespass-offering ; and 3 without blood ; (*5*) Meal *or* Meat-offering, (*6*) Drink-offering, (*7*) Incense-offering.

5. **7** words rendered "river" in A.V.[2] (*1*) אובל *ubal,* 3 ; (*2*) אפיק *aphiq,* 16 ; (*3*) יאור *y'ōr,* 65 ; (*4*) יובל *yubal,* 1 ; (*5*) נהר *nahar,* **119** ; *n'har,* Aram., 15 ; (*6*) נחל *nachal,* 139, נחלה *nachlah,* 1 ; (*7*) פלג *peleg* 10, פלגה *p'laggah,* 3 ; total 372, less Hab. iii. 8, where נהר should be הר, = **871.**

6. **7** Metals mentioned in O.T. (*1*) Gold, (*2*) silver, (*3*) copper, brass or bronze, (*4*) iron, (*5*) lead, (*6*) tin, (*7*) *chashmal,* A.V. "amber," but evidently a metal of some kind, R.V. mg. "electron," American Revisers "glowing metal."

7. **7** Measures of length : (*1*) Finger's breadth, Jer. lii. 21, (*2*) handbreadth, (*3*) span, (*4*) cubit, (*5*) gomed, Jud. iii. 16, (*6*) reed, Ezk. xl. 5, (*7*) measuring line (of flax), Ezk. xl. 3.

[1] See also Part II, Class IV.
[2] Kitto's *Cyc. Bib. Lit.,* art. " River."

8. **7 Measures of Capacity** : (*1*) Log, (*2*) cab, (*3*) omer, (*4*) hin, (*5*) seah, (*6*) ephah *or* bath, (*7*) homer *or* cor.

9. " The number of animals mentioned in the Bible is considerable. No less than **42** Heb. names of mammals, **35** of birds, **14** of reptiles, and **26** [**28** ?] of invertebrate animals occur " (Tristram in *Variorum Bible*, p. 42).

10. **14** Perfumes : Aloe, bdellium, calamus, cassia, cinnamon, frankincense, galbanum, ladanum, myrrh, saffron, spicery, spikenard, stacte, sweetcane (Hooker & Tristram in *Var. Bible*, p. 41).

b. In N.T.

1. *Kapnos*, " smoke," **13** ; *tuphomenon*, " smoking," **1** ; total **14.**

2. *Lampo*, " to shine," **7** ; *lampas*, " a lamp," " torch," **9** ; *lampros*, " bright," **9** ; *lamprōs*, " sumptuously," **1** ; *lamprotēs*, " brightness," **1** ; *eklampo*, " to shine forth," **1** ; *perilampo*, " to shine round about," **2** ; total from root, **30** ; *Luchnos*, " a lamp," **14** ; *luchnia*, " lampstand," **12** ; total **26**. Total from both roots **56.**

3. " Kingdom of God," and " Kingdom of heaven," **14** in Mark, **70** in other Gospels, **14** in Acts and Paul. Total in N.T. **98.**

4. There are **7** words for " Servant " in N.T. : (*1*) *doulos*, " slave " ; (*2*) *hupēretes*, " servant " ; (*3*) *diakonos*, " minister " ; (*4*) *therapōn*, " attendant " ; (*5*) *oiketes* and (*6*) *pais*, " household servant " ; (*7*) *misthōtos*, " hired servant."

5. **7** Kinds of Birds : (*1*) Cock, (*2*) hen, (*3*) eagle), (*4*) raven, (*5*) dove (=pigeon, Lu. ii. 24), (*6*) turtledove, (*7*) sparrow.

6. **7** words denoting Colours : (*1*) White, (*2*) black, (*3*) red, (*4*) green, (*5*) scarlet, (*6*) *porphura*, and (*7*) *porphureos*, purple.

7. Bp. Westcott points out that our Lord is spoken of in the Epistle to the Hebrews by **7** different

names : (*1*) Jesus, (*2*) Christ, (*3*) Jesus Christ, (*4*) Son, (*5*) Son of God, (*6*) Jesus the Son of God, (*7*) The Lord.[1] These names occur **35** times in all.

These lists, and the similar ones in Part II refer to the whole of the Old and New Testaments respectively, except where otherwise stated, and they might be easily extended. They form a very remarkable series, which it is impossible to conceive of as being accidental. Three other classes will be found in Part II of which it is not necessary to give examples here, and I pass on to what is perhaps the most remarkable series of all, viz. :

Words and Phrases used 7 or a multiple of 7 times in the Old and New Testaments combined.

Owing to the difference of language, it is not to be expected that many Words will be found, and even in Phrases there may be in some cases slight verbal differences, but in the lists given below and in Part II the practical identity of the phrases in the two languages will be admitted.

1. " Abraham, Isaac and Jacob "—in this order, with or without other words—O.T., **21** (including **7** in Deut.) N.T., **7** ; total **28.**

2. " The God of Abraham, the God of Isaac, and the God of Jacob," O.T., 3 ; N.T., 4 ; total **7.**[2]

3. " The Lord, the God of Abraham . . . Isaac and . . . {Jacob / Israel}," O.T., 6 ; N.T., 1 ; total **7.**[3]

4. " The God of (thy, your, etc.) father(s) Abraham . . . Isaac and . . . {Jacob / Israel}," O.T., 5 ; N.T., 2 ; total **7.**[4]

[1] *Ep. Hebrews*, p. 33 f.

[2] Ex. iii. 6, 15 ; iv. 5 ; Mt. xxii. 32 ; Mk. xii. 26 ; Lu. xx. 37 ; Ac. iii. 13 (so א ACD, La, Ti, Sod).

[3] Ex. iii. 15, 16 ; iv. 5 ; 1 K. xviii. 36 ; 1 Ch. xxix. 18 ; 2 Ch. xxx. 6 ; Lu. xx. 37.

[4] Ex. iii. 6, 15, 16 ; iv. 5 ; 1 Ch. xxix. 18 ; Ac. iii. 13, vii. 32.

5. " Blessed is he that cometh in the name of the Lord," O.T., 1 ; N.T., 6 ; total **7.**[1]

6. " Candlestick " (of the candlestick in the Tabernacle only), O.T., 27 (all in Pent.) ; N.T., 1 (Heb. ix. 2) ; total **28.**

7. " Covenant (with) Abraham," O.T., 6 ; N.T., 1 ; total **7.**[2]

8. " Remember (his, my, etc.) covenant," (of God's covenant with Israel), O.T., 13 ; N.T., 1 ; total **14.**[3]

9. " David," O.T., 1075 ; N.T., 59 ; total **1134.**[4]

10. " Moses," O.T., 767 ; N.T., 80 ; total **847.**[4]

11. " Generations " (*tōledōth* without prefix or suffix) always in the phrase " These are the generations of . . ." or " The book of the generations of . . ." followed by proper name, O.T., 13 ; " The book of the generation of Jesus Christ," N.T., 1 (Mat. i. 1) ; total **14.**

12. " Holy City " (= Jerusalem), O.T., 5 ; N.T., 2 ; total **7.**[5]

13. " I will be to (you, them, etc.) a God, and (ye, they) shall be to me a people," [in this order], O.T., 5 ; N.T., 2 ; total **7.**[6]

14. " To me, etc., a people . . . to you, etc., a God " [or with clauses reversed], O.T., 19 (including 7 in Jer.), N.T., 2 ; total **21.**[7]

[1] Ps. cxviii. 26 ; Mt. xxi. 9 ; xxiii. 39 ; Mk. x. 19 ; Lu. xiii. 35, xix. 38 ; Jno. xii. 13.

[2] Ex. ii. 24 ; Le. xxvi. 42 ; 2 K. xiii. 23 ; 1 Ch. xvi. 15 ; Neh. ix. 7, 8 ; Ps. cv. 8 ; Lu. i. 72, 73.

[3] Ge. ix. 15, 16 ; Ex. ii. 24 ; vi. 5 ; Le. xxvi. 42, 42, 45 ; 1 Ch. xvi. 15 ; Ps. cv. 8, cvi. 45, cxi. 5 ; Jer. xiv. 21 ; Ezk. xvi. 60 ; Lu. i. 72. (Am. i. 9 is excluded.)

[4] I. Panin, *Scientific Demonstrations*, p. 16.

[5] Neh. xi. 1, 18 ; Isa. xlviii. 2, lii. 1 ; Dan. ix. 24 ; Mt. iv. 5 ; xxvii. 53. It is used also symbolically in Rev. xi. 2, xxi. 2, xxii. 19, making a total of 10. " Holy cities " occurs in Isa. lxiv. 10.

[6] Lev. xxvi. 12 ; Jer. vii. 23, xxxi. 1, 33 ; Ezk. xxxvii. 27 ; 2 Cor. vi. 16 ; Heb. viii. 10.

[7] Ex. vi. 7 ; Lev. xxvi. 12 ; Dt. xxvi. 17, xxix. 13 ; 2 S. vii. 24 ; 1 Ch. xvii, 22 ; Jer. vii. 23, xi. 4, xxiv. 7, xxx. 22, xxxi. 1, 33, xxxii. 38 ; Ezk. xi. 20, xiv. 11, xxxvi. 28, xxxvii. 23, 27 ; Zec. viii. 8 ; 2 Cor. vi. 16 ; Heb. viii. 10.

15. "I will not forsake thee," (אעזבך with negative), (sometimes translated "leave "), O.T., 6 ; N.T., 1 ; total **7.**[1]

16. "I will not fail thee, neither forsake thee " (with slight differences), O.T., 6 ; N.T. 1 ; total **7.**[2]

17. "In (thee, him) $\begin{Bmatrix} \text{and} \\ \text{or} \end{Bmatrix}$ and in thy seed, shall all the $\begin{Bmatrix} \text{families} \\ \text{nations} \end{Bmatrix}$ (of the earth) be blessed," O.T., 5 ; N.T., 2 ; total **7.**[3]

18. "Lest they should see with their eyes, and hear with their ears," etc., O.T., 1 ; quoted wholly or in part 6 times in N.T., total **7.**[4]

19. "Mercy-seat," O.T., 27 ; N.T., 1 ; total **28.**

20. "Shadow of death," 18 in Heb. common text + Ps. lxxxviii. 6, where the Septuagint and Syriac versions read " shadow of death," but Heb. text has במצלות " in the deeps," the same letters as בצלמות " in the shadow of death," but transposed in error by some early scribe. It is there associated with darkness or dark places, as " shadow of death " very frequently is. This makes O.T., 19 ; N.T., 2 ; total **21.**

21. (Sin-offering) "burned without the camp," O.T., 6 ; N.T., 1 ; total **7.**[5]

22. "Thou shalt not steal," O.T., 3 ; N.T., 4 ; total **7.**[6]

---

[1] Ge. xxviii. 15 ; Jos. i. 5 ; 2 K. ii. 2, 4, 6, iv. 30 ; Heb. xiii. 5.

[2] Dt. xxxi. 6, 8 ; Jos. i. 5 ; 1 K. viii. 57 ; 1 Ch. xxviii. 20 ; Ps. xxvii. 9 ; Heb. xiii. 5. The following have one clause only : Ge. xxviii. 15 ; 1 S. xii. 22 ; 1 K. vii. 13.

[3] Ge. xii. 3, xviii. 18, xxii. 18, xxvi. 4, xxviii. 14 ; Ac. iii. 25 ; Gal. iii. 8.

[4] Isa. vi. 9, 10 ; Mt. xiii 14 ; Mk. iv. 12 ; Lu. viii. 10 ; Jno. xii. 40 ; Ac. xxviii. 26 ; Rom. xi. 8.

[5] Ex. xxix. 14 ; Lev. iv. 12, 21, viii. 17, ix. 11, xvi. 27 ; Heb. xiii. 11. (Also of red heifer, Num. xix. 3–5).

[6] Ex. xx. 15 ; Lev. xix. 11 (ye) ; Dt. v. 19 ; Mt. xix. 18 ; Mk. x. 19 ; Lu. xviii. 20 ; Rom. xiii. 9.

23. " Thy salvation," O.T., 27 ; N.T., 1 ; total **28.**[1]
24. " Tribe (*matteh*) of Judah," 10 ; " tribe of the children of Judah," 5 ; " tribe (*shebet*) of Judah," 4 = 19 O.T. ; " tribe of Judah," N.T., 2 ; total **21.**
25. " Ye shall be holy, for I . . . am holy " (with slight variations), O.T., 6 ; N.T., 1 ; total **7.**[2]

Subjoined are a few

REMARKS ON THE FORMATION OF HEPTADS IN THE PROSE PORTIONS OF THE OLD TESTAMENT.

I. In many cases the heptad is plainly marked by each division of it containing a *waw consecutive*, as Gen. xvii. 15–17. (Note.—The *waw con.* is generally found at the commencement of the clause or sentence, but not invariably, as Gen. xxii. 24 ; and frequently the first division commences with simple *waw*, as Ex. xx. 18, Jonah i. 4, or none at all, as 2 Ch. i. 7.   There should not be two *waws con.* in the same division.)

II. In other heptads each division commences with (or contains) a verb with *waw* prefixed, but not necessarily consecutive, as 2 Ki. xii. 9, 14.   As the Heb. Imperative has only one tense, it does not admit of *waw con.*

III. In others, each division contains a sentence commencing with *waw*, which is not, however, necessarily prefixed to a verb, as Gen. xvii. 22–27.

IV. Sometimes a small heptad is found within a larger one, as Gen. i. 26, i. 28, xii. 2, 3 ; Exod. xxi. 18, 19.

V. Sometimes a passage contains fourteen clauses, though it is not easily divisible into sevens, as Lev. i. 1–9.

---

[1] יֵשׁ 5 masc. 2 fem. = 7 ; יֵשׁוּה 14 masc. 1 fem. ; תְּשׁוּ 5 = O.T. 27 + Lu. ii. 30 = total 28.

[2] Lev. xi. 44, 45, xix. 2, xx. 7, 26, xxi. 8 ; 1 Pe. i. 16.   In Lev. xx. 7 the second " holy " has dropped out of the common Heb. text.   It is found in 4 Heb. MSS, the Samaritan and the Septuagint.

VI. Where a single heptad embraces two subjects, or naturally divides itself into two parts, one part usually contains four divisions, and the other three. Sometimes the three occupy the first place, as Num. i. 1–19; but more often the four, as Gen. xxii. 19–24. (Divisions into five and two, and into six and one, are also found; so also are ternary divisions, such as 3, 1, 3, like the Golden Candlestick; 3, 3, 1; and quaternary, as 2, 2, 2, 1; 1, 2, 2, 2; but these are only subdivisions of 3 and 4.)

VII. In all cases the division must be natural and easy, and assist rather than obscure the sense of the passage.

Hebrew POETRY, which forms so large a portion of the O.T., is divided much more simply, each grammatical sentence forming an heptadic division, whether commencing with *waw*, " and," or not.

Having thus sketched in this introductory chapter some of the chief ways in which a right understanding of the use of the Number Seven is of service in the study of the Bible, I propose in the succeeding chapters to go into the matter more fully and in greater detail, taking the different branches of the subject in the following order :—

> Textual Criticism.
> The Canon of Scripture.
> Translation.
> Interpretation.
> Sacred Chronology.
> The numbers Seven and Four in Nature.

The concluding chapter will deal with the Inspiration of the Bible.

The proper treatment of almost each one of these matters might well fill a volume, instead of a chapter ; they will therefore be dealt with as briefly as possible, yet with sufficient fullness to illustrate thoroughly the principles laid down.

CHAPTER II

TEXTUAL CRITICISM

IT is in the department of textual criticism that a knowledge of the principles which underlie the septenary structure of Scripture will probably be deemed to be of the greatest value ; and in the present chapter it is proposed to illustrate and apply those principles more fully than has been done in the previous chapter, and to show that they provide a positive TEST whereby the true original text of Scripture may be ascertained almost, if not altogether, beyond the possibility of doubt.

The Revised Version has made English Bible-readers acquainted with the fact that there are certain words, phrases, and even whole verses which have hitherto been commonly accepted as part of the Word of God, which, in the opinion of the greatest scholars of the present day, have no just title or claim to such a place. The text of Holy Scripture has come down to modern times in manuscripts, which, either through careless copying or intentional alteration, differ more or less from one another. These differences are for the most part very slight, and in no case affect a single doctrine which we have been accustomed to receive as founded upon the Word of God. Still, nothing which concerns the sacred text can be deemed unimportant, and the attention of scholars has therefore been rightly directed to its purification from textual error. To this end ancient manuscripts have been examined, their testimony carefully ascertained and duly weighed, and the attempt made to find out what were the exact words set down by the original writers.   This constitutes the science of Textual Criticism as applied to the Holy Scriptures.

In treating of this subject it will be desirable to depart from the natural order, and to take the New Testament first.   For whereas the revision of the text of the Greek New Testament has largely occupied the attention of scholars for many years, and materials have been at great labour collected and arranged so as to afford almost every possible aid to the study of the subject, in the case of the Old Testament " the state of knowledge on the subject is not at present such as to justify any attempt at an entire reconstruction of the text."[1]   It will be well, therefore, first to familiarize ourselves with the processes of proof in the New Testament, and then to apply the same processes to the study of the Old.

New Testament

The authorities made use of for determining the original text of the New Testament are usually divided into three classes : (1) *Greek manuscripts*, some of which were written in the fourth and fifth centuries,[2] (2) *Versions* of a still earlier date in different languages, and (3) *Quotations* by Christian writers of the second and following centuries.[3]

The following is a brief description of the chief of these authorities :—

(1) Greek Manuscripts were anciently written entirely in UNCIAL or CAPITAL letters, with no spaces whatever between the words, a plan which has been the cause of many errors in copying.   For convenience of reference most of the Uncial manuscripts are designated by the capital letters of the Roman alphabet, others by Greek capitals, and others by

[1] Revised Version : Preface to O.T.
[2] A few fragments of papyrus, going back probably to the third century, have recently been found.
[3] Revised Version : Preface to N.T.

letters of the Hebrew alphabet. The oldest manuscripts now known to be in existence are the following :—

B (Codex Vaticanus), written in the fourth century ; considered by most critics to be the most valuable manuscript we have. " A most careful examination of B," says Bp. Westcott, " leaves it in possession of the title to supreme excellence."[1] It is only of late years that the exact text of this manuscript has been permitted to be made known.[2]

א *Aleph* (Codex Sinaiticus), also of the fourth century ; considered to be second in authority only to B. This manuscript was only brought to light so recently as the year 1859.

A (Codex Alexandrinus), written about the middle of the fifth century. Of much less authority in the Gospels than in the rest of the New Testament.

C (Codex Ephræmi), of about the same age as A, and perhaps equal in authority, in the Gospels superior. Unfortunately much of the original MS—over one-third of the whole N.T.—has perished.

D (Codex Bezæ or Cantabrigiensis), written in the fifth or sixth century. A most peculiar manuscript, containing many readings not found in any other Greek authority, some of which, however, there can be no doubt, represent the true original text. It is frequently supported in these readings by one or more of the ancient versions. This manuscript contains only the Gospels and Acts.

D₂ (Codex Claromontanus) containing the Epistles of St. Paul. Of about the same age and authority as the preceding.

[1] Introduction to St. John, in *Speaker's Commentary*, p. lxxxix.

[2] Scrivener pointed out years ago the many errors in B, some of them very serious ones, and in 1914 H. C. Hoskier published two volumes entitled, *Codex B and its Allies*, the first words in the Preface to which are " It is high time that the bubble of Codex B should be pricked." Still, though no doubt Westcott and Hort rated it too highly, it is generally placed at the head of our authorities for the N.T. text,

W (the Washington MS) was only brought to light so recently as 1906. It contains the four Gospels and was written about the fourth or fifth century. It sometimes supports one type of text and sometimes another.

(2) The oldest VERSIONS are the Latin, Syriac and Egyptian.

Latin (*a*) The term *Old Latin* is applied to a Version or Versions originally made in the second century and now existing in various forms, which are usually divided into two groups, the African and the European ; the oldest MSS extant belong to the fourth and fifth centuries. (*b*) The Old Latin was revised by Jerome with the help of Greek manuscripts, A.D. 383–385 ; the oldest MSS are of the sixth century. This revision, with a few changes of later date, is the Authorized Text of the Roman Catholic Church, and is known as the *Vulgate*.

Syriac. (*a*) The *Diatessaron* of Tatian is a Harmony of the Gospels made in the second century, only extant in an Arabic, and (partially) an Armenian version.

(*b*) What is now known as the *Old Syriac* was also made in the second century, but unfortunately only two manuscripts of this version, written probably in the fourth and fifth centuries, each containing considerable fragments of the Gospels, are known to exist, the *Sinaitic* or *Lewisian* (discovered by Mrs. Lewis in 1892) and the *Curetonian* (discovered by Dr. Cureton in 1842).

(*c*) The *Peshitta Syriac* is apparently a revised form of the above, made not later than the beginning of the fifth century. Its oldest extant manuscript is of the fifth century.

Egyptian. These include (*a*) the Sahidic (or Thebaic) in the dialect of Upper Egypt, made probably in the third or fourth century, or earlier ; and (*b*) the Bohairic (formerly called Coptic and Memphitic) in the dialect of Lower Egypt, somewhat later. Fragments of other Egyptian versions have also been found.

The only other Versions possessing any critical value are the *Gothic* (fourth century), *Armenian* (fifth century), *Ethiopic* (about the fifth century), and two later Syriac versions (sixth and seventh centuries).

(3) Among the early Christian writers, or FATHERS, whose works have come down to us, Irenæus (second century), Origen (third century), Jerome, Augustine, and Chrysostom (fourth century), are a few of the more important.

The Authorized Version of 1611, so familiar and so dear to the English people, was not founded upon these ancient authorities, but was made from the printed editions of the Greek Text, which had appeared in the sixteenth century. These, it must ever be remembered, had no claim to *authority* ; they were simply the work of individual scholars. " They were founded for the most part on manuscripts of late date, few in number, and used with little critical skill. But in those days it could hardly have been otherwise. Nearly all the more ancient of the documentary authorities have become known only within the last two centuries ; some of the most important of them, indeed, within the last few years. Their publication has called forth improved editions of the Greek Text," [1] still the work of individual scholars, chief among whom are Lachmann and Tischendorf on the Continent, and Tregelles, and Westcott and Hort, in our own country.

In 1913 appeared H. von Soden's edition of the Greek Testament with Apparatus. This work is a distinct disappointment to students, for instead of following in the steps of his predecessors he has scrapped the system of notation of MSS with which we are familiar, and invented an entirely new and very intricate one. With ample funds and plenty of assistants, he might have produced a book which would have been a real help, for so much new material has accumulated since Tregelles' and Tischendorf's time that a new Apparatus was greatly needed. Hoskier calls von Soden's work a step backward, and says the apparatus is positively honeycombed with errors.[2] . Similarly, Sir F. G. Kenyon remarks that the new

---

[1] Revised Version ; Preface to N.T.   [2] *J.T.S.*, April, 1914, p. 307.

numeration has been received with almost universal disfavour, and that von Soden has put every possible obstacle in the way of his disciples.[1] It is to be hoped that some English or American scholar or group of scholars will take the matter in hand, and give us a really full and reliable Apparatus in a convenient and intelligible form. It is an up-to-date Apparatus that is needed just now, not a new Text.

The English Revisers (1881) did not themselves publish a revised Greek text. They say : " A revision of the Greek text was the necessary foundation of our work ; but it did not fall within our province to construct a continuous and complete Greek text. In many cases the English rendering was considered to represent correctly either of two competing readings in the Greek, and then the question of the text was usually not raised."[2] But one of their number, Archdeacon Palmer, was authorized, in conjunction with Dr. Scrivener, to prepare a continuous Greek text incorporating the Revisers' readings. He took R. Stephens' edition of 1550 as his basis, and adhered closely to the text and orthography of Stephens in all cases in which the Revisers did not express a preference for other readings. This must be carefully borne in mind, as it explains why the Revisers' text (as we may call it) differs in some small matters (e.g., the omission or insertion of the Article) where the English translation is not affected, from other editors where the latter are undoubtedly right. A new edition of the Revisers' text by Prof. A. Souter was published in 1910, with the double advantage of showing the authorities for and against the more important variants, and giving a long list of MSS., etc., exhibiting both the old numeration as revised by Gregory, and that of von Soden.

In the examination of texts upon which we are now about to enter, I do not propose to give long lists of " authorities," nor to refer to other critical editions than those of the scholars just named. Where the

---

[1] *Ch. Q. Rev.*, October, 1914, pp. 60, 62.
[2] Preface to N.T.

HEPTAD TEST confirms the text followed in the Revised Version, it will be sufficient to state the fact; only where the Revisers are shown to have erred in their judgment will it be necessary to give the authorities against them.

The following notes are based upon the received Greek text, as followed by the A.V.

1. Matt. xviii. 11 : " For the Son of man is come to save that which was lost ; " omitted in R.V. Matt. xxv. 13 : " Watch, therefore, for ye know neither the day nor the hour *wherein the Son of man cometh ;*" R.V. omits the words in italics. Luke ix. 56 : " For the Son of man is not come to destroy men's lives, but to save them ; " omitted in R.V. The phrase " Son of man " occurs in the received text of the N.T. as applied to Christ 87 times, but with these three omissions, **84.** The R.V. is, therefore, correct. Of these 84, **14** are in Mark, and **14** in John and Revelation, while the phrase occurs in the nominative case 21 times in Matthew.[1]

2. Matt. xviii. 24 : for *prosēnechthē* (from *prosphērō*), which is read by rec. text, and also by the Revisers and von Soden on the authority of א, etc., Lach.,

[1] St. Luke, therefore, is the only Evangelist with whose writings this title cannot be heptadically connected. It occurs in his Gospel 15 times in the nominative case—a number strongly suggestive of **14.** There are two various readings, but both poorly supported. (1) In ch. xvii. 30 D and some manuscripts of the Old Latin have the genitive case. (2) In ch. vi. 5 one manuscript of the eighth century (Codex *Λ*) omits the title altogether ("And he said unto them that he is Lord of the Sabbath "), while in the leading authorities it is variously placed—a common sign of spuriousness. In the heptad to which this verse belongs (Lu. vi. 1–5) if we take out ὁ υἱὸς τοῦ ἀνθρώπου, "the Son of Man," and read *Δαυείδ* (the correct spelling) for *Δαβίδ*, the Revisers' text contains **91** words, **484** letters. To strike it out would reduce our 84 to 83, but the heptadic number might be restored in two ways: (1) by adding Heb. ii. 6, where "son of man " occurs, but not with reference to Christ ; (2) by adding Dan. vii. 13, the only passage in the Old Testament where the Messiah is called the Son of man. The matter requires further investigation.

Tisch., Treg., and WH. read *prosēchthē* (from *prosagō*), with B, D. *Prosagō*, and its derivative *prosagōgē*, already occur **7** times in rec. text, and to add the former here would make 8, and so spoil the heptad. *Prosphērō*, and its derivative *prosphora*, occur together **57** times, from which must be deducted Luke xii. 11, where the true reading is *eisphērō*, leaving **56.** So that to follow the critics in Matt. xviii. 24, would spoil the heptad here, too. They are therefore wrong. (There is no material difference in the meaning of the two words; both mean "was brought unto.")

3. Matt. xix. 29 : " And every one that hath forsaken (1) houses, (2) or brethren, (3) or sisters, (4) or father, (5) or mother, (6) *or wife*, (7) or children, (8) or lands, for my name's sake, shall receive an hundredfold, and shall inherit everlasting life." Mark x. 29 : " There is no man that hath left (1) house, (2) or brethren, (3) or sisters, (4) or father, (5) or mother, (6) *or wife*, (7) or children, (8) or lands, for my sake," etc. In both places (though in Matt. doubtfully) the Revisers omit " or wife," so making heptads. They need have had no doubt on the subject ; their text is quite correct. The words are interpolated from Luke xviii. 29, the assimilation to parallel passages being a very frequent cause of corruption in the Gospels.

4. Mark vi. 11 : " Verily I say unto you, It shall be more tolerable for Sodom and Gomorrha in the day of judgment, than for that city ; " omitted in R.V. Luke xiii. 35 : " Verily I say unto you ; " R.V. omits " Verily." The phrase " Verily I say unto you," or " unto thee," occurs **51** times in the received text of the first three Gospels ; these two omissions make **49** ; R.V. is therefore correct in both places.[1]

5. Mark vii. 5 : for " unwashen " here, R.V. reads

---

[1] In Matt. xviii. 19, B and a great many other authorities insert " verily," reading, " Again verily I say unto you," but rec. text is supported by ℵ, which here, as in many other places, shows itself a more trustworthy guide than B. So, too, apparently, thought the Revisers.

" defiled *or* common." The root *niptō*, "to wash," occurs 17 times, and its derivatives *niptēr*, " a basin," 1 ; *aponiptō*, " to wash," 1 ; *aniptos*, " unwashen," 3 : total, 22 ; but if we follow the Revisers this is reduced to **21**, which is the correct number.

6. Luke i. 50 : for " from generation to generation," R.V. reads "unto generations and generations," so making **7** occurrences of *kai*, " and," in Mary's song, as there are **7** in the song of Zacharias in the same chapter.

7. Luke ii. 40 : "And the child grew, and waxed strong *in spirit;*" R.V. omits "in spirit." Luke x. 21 : for " Jesus rejoiced in spirit," R.V. reads " he rejoiced in the Holy Spirit." Apart from these two passages there are **7** places in the Gospels where the (human) spirit of Jesus is mentioned, viz. Matt. xxvii. 50 ; Mark ii. 8 ; viii. 12 ; Luke xxiii. 46 ; John xi. 33 ; xiii. 21 ; xix. 30. (In Mark xv. 37, 39 ; Luke xxiii. 46, *last clause*, the Greek is different.) The R.V. is, therefore, correct in these two passages.

8. Luke iii. 33 : to insert " the son of Admin " (with R.V. marg., Tisch., Alford & von Soden) would make 78 names in our Lord's genealogy. The **77** of the common text is correct. The blunder is not difficult to account for.

9. Luke iv. 8 : " Get thee behind me, Satan, for," omitted in R.V. correctly. *Satanas*, " Satan," occurs 36 times, but with this alteration, **35**.

10. Luke xx. 14 : R.V. reads correctly " let us kill him," omitting " come." *Deuro*, " come," occurs 9 times, and *deute*, " come ye," 13 ; total, 22, but with this omission, **21**.

11. Luke xxiii. 34 : " Then said Jesus, Father, forgive them, for they know not what they do." Westcott and Hort believed that the Evangelists only recorded *six* words from the Cross, and that the above, the first of the **7**, is " a later insertion," coming from " an extraneous source." And the Revisers introduce here a marginal note, "Some ancient authorities

E

omit " the words.   What then ?   It only shows to us that some ancient authorities are wrong, even when they include a manuscript so ancient and so authoritative as Codex B.· Lachmann brackets the words (but probably would not have done so had he been acquainted with א) ;   all other editors consider them genuine.   *Seven* Words from the Cross were spoken, as even Westcott and Hort did not go so far as to deny, and *Seven* Words from the Cross we must have in our Bibles, and that without any qualifying remarks whatever.   If we take the parallel Greek and English edition of the R.V. we find that the paragraph Luke xxiii. 33–38 contains 7 sentences each beginning with " and " in English, and with καί or δέ in the Greek. The Revisers' Greek text gives 98 words, 474 letters. But they made one slight error in altering ἀπῆλθον of rec. to ἦλθον.   Tisch. saw that ἀπῆλθον was the more difficult reading, and therefore likely to be the true one, and that ἦλθον had been adopted by scribes from Matt. xxvii. 33 as seeming more appropriate, and so he deserted his favourite א and placed ἀπῆλθον in his text.   Von Soden has done the same, the case for the longer word having meanwhile been strengthened by the discovery of Cod. W.   The Revisers' text then, with this slight alteration, contains 98 words 476 letters, a proof that the words in question are genuine.

To discuss this passage further seems waste of time, but as we cannot afford to allow even the smallest possibility of doubt to rest on this loving utterance of our dying Lord, here is further proof.   Of 10 only of the prayers of Jesus are the actual words recorded, the 10 being divided, as 10 so often is, into 7 and 3.   The 3 are not strictly " prayers ; " two of them are thanksgivings (Matt. xi. 25, 26 ; John xi. 41, 42) ; and the other is the last of the Seven Words :   " Father, into thy hands I commend my spirit."   The 7 all contain petitions, and are therefore prayers in the stricter sense of the word ; they are Matt. xxvi. 39, 42, 44 (" the same words ") ; xxvii. 46 ; John xii. 27–28 ; xvii. 1–26 ; and the passage before us. Then as to the verbal test, *oidasi*, "they know," occurs **7** times in N.T., including this passage. And while it is true that *aphes*, "forgive," occurs 15 times, yet *aphes* followed by a pronoun occurs **7**, including the verse before us.   The other verbal proofs are complicated by various readings elsewhere, but two more may be given.   *Oida*, "to know," is found in conjunction with *ou* (*ouk, oudeis*, etc.), and *mē*, "not," **105** times in rec.   Two more must be added (Luke xii. 56 ; Rev. ii. 17), and two subtracted (1 Cor. ii. 11 ; 1 Pet. i. 8), still leaving **105**.[1]   *Aphiēmi* bears the meaning "to forgive" in **49** places, including Mark xi. 26, a verse which curiously illustrates the misplaced confidence which is placed in B and א. They both omit the whole verse, along with several other authorities, and they are followed unhesitatingly by Tisch., Treg., WH., Rev. and Sod., who all appear to be of opinion that the verse is an interpolation from Matt. vi. 15. As a matter of fact the very opposite is the case, for in א and other authorities Matt. vi. 15 is corrupted from Mark xi. 26 by the omission of the words "their trespasses," yet א is followed by Tisch. and Sod., while WH. were not able to decide which of their two favourite manuscripts, here at variance, gives the true reading. The rec. text is undoubtedly correct both in Matt. and Mark, and Tisch., WH and Sod. are therefore wrong.   Lach. only, amongst the great critical editors, appears to have seen that an early scribe of the passage in Mark, after copying the words "your trespasses" at the end of ver. 25, allowed his eye to fall on the *same words* at the end of ver. 26, and went on copying, utterly oblivious of the fact that he had omitted an entire verse. This species of error, called *homœoteleuton*, or "similar ending," is very common in manu-

---

[1] In 1 Cor. ii. 2, "not" is connected in the Greek with "determined," not with "know."   The sense is not exactly "I determined not to know," but rather "I did not determine to know anything among you, save Jesus Christ and him crucified."   So Alford, Ellicott, *I.C.C., al.*

scripts, א being a great offender in this respect.[1]

12. Luke xxiii. 38 : " In letters of Greek and Latin and Hebrew ; " rightly omitted by the Revisers as an interpolation from John xix. 20, on the authority of B, C, etc. ; the other great manuscripts, א*, A, D, wrongly inserting them. The test works out thus : " Rome " occurs 8 times in the New Testament ; *Rōmaios*, " Roman," 12 ; and *Rōmaïsti*, " in Latin," 1 : total 21 occurrences of " Rome " and its derivatives. To add *Rōmaïkos*, " of Latin " here, therefore, would spoil the heptad. *Hebraïs*, " Hebrew," occurs 3 times ; *Hebraios*, " Hebrew," 4 ; and *Hebraïsti*, " in Hebrew," 7, including John xx. 16 (see R.V.) : total 14 occurrences of " Hebrew " and its derivatives. To add, therefore, *Hebraïkos*, " of Hebrew," here would spoil the heptad. Again, *gramma*, " a letter," occurs 15 times in rec. text ; strike it out here, and we have 14. The test from the word " Greek " is complicated by various readings elsewhere, but the above are sufficient.

13. Acts xvii. 5 : " But the Jews *which believed not ;* " R.V. rightly omits the words in italics. *Apeithēs*, " disobedient," occurs 6 times ; *apeitheia*, " disobedience," 7 ; and *apeitheō*, " to disobey *or* disbelieve," 16 : total 29. Strike out *apeitheō* here, and we have 28.

14. Acts xx. 24 : " So that I might finish my course *with joy ;* " R.V. rightly omits the words " with joy." *Chairō*, " to rejoice," occurs 74 times ; *chara*, " joy," 60 (including Philem. 7) ; *sugchairō*, " to rejoice with," 7 : total 141 ; which is reduced to the heptadic number 140 by striking out *chara* here.

15. 2 Cor. xi. 3 : " The simplicity ; " R.V. adds, " and the purity." It is not often the rec. text errs on the side of omission, but it does so here, homœoteleuton being doubtless the cause of the error. *Hagnos*,

---

[1] It should be borne in mind that when Lachmann's text was published א had not been discovered. So also when Tregelles formed his text of the Gospels.

"pure," occurs 8 times; *hagneia*, "purity," 2; *hagnizō*, "to purify," **7**; *hagnismos*, "purification," 1; *hagnōs*, "sincerely," 1; *hagnotēs*, "pureness," 1: total 20, to which add *hagnotēs* here, making **21.** Most singularly, WH hesitate to follow their favourites here, although they are both right.

16. James iii. 8 : for "it is an *unruly* evil" R.V. reads, "it is a *restless* evil," rightly. *Akatastasia*, "tumult," etc., occurs 5 times, and *akatastatos*, "restless," twice, including this passage : total **7.**

17. Rev. xvii. 8 : for "that was, and is not, and *yet is*," R.V. rightly reads, "that he was, and is not, and *shall come* [marg. *shall be present*]." *Pareimi*, "to be present," occurs 23 times ; *parousia*, "presence," 24 ; *sumpareimi*, "to be present with," 1 : total 48, to which add *pareimi* here, making **49.**

18. Rev. xxii. 19 : for "*book* of life," R.V. reads, "*tree* of life." "Book of life" occurs in N.T. **7** times without this passage, and an examination of the phrase "tree of life" leads to the same result (see Part II., p. 305). R.V. therefore is correct.

We will now take two passages in which "the evidence is decidedly preponderating," but, unfortunately, preponderating on the wrong side.

19. 1 Cor. xiii. 3 : "Though I give my body *to be burned.*" So read C, D₂, and other authorities, and they are followed by rec. text, R.V. (doubtfully), and all editors except WH, who consider that the weight of manuscript evidence binds them to accept the singular reading, "though I give my body *that I may glory.*" This differs from the other in the Greek by *one letter* only, and is supported by א, A, B, one cursive MS, the Bohairic and Sahidic Versions, the margin of the Gothic, some MSS of the Ethiopic, and by some of the early Fathers. *Kauchaomai*, "to glory," occurs 38 times, but must be struck out in 2 Cor. xii. 11, leaving 37 ; *kauchēma*, "glorying," 11 ; *kauchēsis*, "glorying," 12, but must be struck out in 2 Cor. ix. 4, leaving 11 ; *katakauchaomai*, "to glory," 4 : total **63** ; to

read *kauchēsōmai* here, therefore, in place of *kauthēsō-mai*, would spoil the heptad.

20. Heb. vii. 21 : " Thou art a priest for ever *after the order of Melchizedek ;* " so A, D₂, and other MSS, and the Syriac, Bohairic, and Ethiopic Versions, which are followed by rec. text and Lachmann. The Revisers and other editors, however, omit the words in italics, following B, C, (א ?), and the Vulgate, Armenian, (Sahidic ?), and a third Egyptian version (א has not much weight here, as it also omits the preceding words ; nor the Sahidic, which is fragmentary and *may* have contained the clause). " After the order of Melchizedek " occurs 6 times in rec. text of N.T., and once in the O.T. : total 7. " After the *similitude* of Melchizedek " occurs once in N.T., which, added to the above-named 6, again makes 7. " After the order " occurs 7 times in N.T., being found once in the phrase, " after the order of Aaron." The other derivatives of *Tasso* " to order " occur 7 times in this Ep., making 14 in all from the root. *Kata,* " after," occurs 42 times in the Ep. to the Hebrews, including this passage. Thus, if we follow the critics and strike the words out, as the Revisers have done, we spoil five different heptads. The error is doubtless again due to homœote-leuton.

The above examples will be sufficient to show the usefulness of the HEPTAD TEST in the criticism of the text of the N.T., and the various ways in which it may be applied. They are a fair sample of the various readings found in MSS, having been chosen almost haphazard, and not (with one exception) on account of their importance.

There are still, however, many differences between the rec. text and recent critical editions which it would be impossible to decide unless the test can be employed in some other manner than is set forth above, and, as I fully believe that God has " not left himself without witness " in this matter, but that the HEPTAD TEST, when thoroughly investigated and rightly understood, is capable of restoring the entire text of the N.T. to its original state, some other means must be sought for accomplishing this object. With regard to most of these differences, if not quite all, these means are not far to seek.

"Even the very hairs of your head are all numbered." Is this hyperbole? It is the language of the Son of God himself. And if the very hairs of our head are all numbered, and if, as we have seen is undoubtedly the case, the occurrences of certain words and phrases in Scripture are numbered, need it excite any surprise to find that the words, nay, the very *letters*, in the continuous text of the sacred volume are numbered too?

In order to prove this I propose to deal with a longer passage ; but before going further, it will be necessary to say a few words on the subject of **Orthography.** A large number of the various readings in the N.T. are simply different modes of spelling certain words, and different dialectic and grammatical forms, involving no change whatever in signification. Though these matters are by no means unimportant, yet I have not thought it necessary to enter into them in this place, except where the number of letters in the two readings is different, when, of course, they cannot be passed over. The subject of the orthography of the original text of the N.T. is admittedly a difficult one, but its study has received a fresh impetus from the discovery and decipherment of many inscriptions and papyri of about the same date as the N.T. writings.

Westcott and Hort examined the subject with their usual care and thoroughness, and certainly did not overestimate its importance. They say : " The many points of orthography in which there is little hope of arriving at approximate certainty in the present state of knowledge throw some serious discouragement on the attempt to reproduce the autographs in this as well as in more important respects. . . . *We have acquiesced in the common orthography in two or three points*, not perhaps quite free from doubt, in which the better attested forms would by their prominence cause excessive strangeness in a popular text. . . . It is probable that the writers of the N.T. employed unclassical forms or spellings in many places where no trace of them now exists, and where therefore their present use could not be justified. . . . It would be unreasonable to assume that the same writer, even in the same book, always spells a word in the same way. Absolute uniformity belongs only to artificial times; and . . . the verdict of MSS is decisive against the supposition. . . . In early times scribes were much more prone to make changes which affected vowels only than to make any other changes; and every extant early document falls in this respect below its habitual standard of trustworthiness." [1]

" In Greek, in the time of the composition of the N.T., there was, as we know from manifold evidence of stone and papyrus, no one fixed orthography in existence, but writers fluctuated between the old historical spelling and a new phonetic manner of writing. . . . The weighing and recording of evidence in the case of individual words, e.g. words in -εια, -ια, is the most unprofitable of tasks that a man can undertake." [2]

" The orthographical problems of the N.T. writings are complicated in the extreme." [3]

" May not such MSS as א and B—and D still more—have conformed their orthography to the popular style, just as those of the ' Syrian ' revision conformed it in some respects to the literary standards ? . . . But there are some suggestive signs that the great uncials, in this respect as in others, are not far away from the autographs. . . . We must bear in mind throughout Hort's caution (*App.*, p. 141) that all our MSS have to a greater or less extent suffered from the effacement of unclassical forms of words." [4]

" Any attempt to determine the spelling adopted in the autographs of the LXX and the N.T. is beset with great difficulty, and in the present state of our knowledge finality is impossible, notwithstanding the assistance now afforded by the papyri. At the time when our oldest uncials were written (iv to vi cents. A.D.) and for centuries earlier there was no fixed orthography in existence. . . . The generalization suggested by the available data is that B is on the whole nearer to the originals in orthography as well as in text [than A or א]." [5]

The following are the principles upon which I have acted in the matter. (1) *Iota* subscript should be counted as a separate letter, as it, in fact, really is; (2) final *ν* should be added (*a*) when the next word

---

[1] WH., *Introd.*, pp. 303–309.
[2] Blass, *Gram. of N.T. Greek*, pp. 6, 7.
[3] Deismann, *Bib. Studies* (Eng. tr.), 181.
[4] J. H. Moulton, *Gram. of N.T. Greek*, i. 42, 43.
[5] Thackeray, *Gram. of the O.T. in Greek*, pp. 71–72.

begins with a vowel, and (*b*) at the end of an heptadic
section, whether the word which commences the
following section begins with a vowel or not, (3) so
also with ς in οὕτω-ς ; (4) such words as *suzēteō* must
be spelled *sunzēteō* ; (5) in other respects I have followed recent critical editions (especially WH, whose
debtor I am) or good MS authority.

We will now take for detailed examination the first
two chapters of St. Matthew's Gospel, which have been
chosen for these reasons : (1) they are the opening
chapters of the N.T., and contain many textual problems ; (2) they clearly teach the Virgin Birth of our
Lord, a doctrine which has been impugned in unex-
pected quarters of late years ; (3) In Matt. i. 16 the
recently discovered Sinaitic Syriac MS supports a
reading which seems at variance with this doctrine
(though it is not so when rightly interpreted) ; (4)
Some years ago a certain critic said that even though
he received the whole of the rest of the N.T. he could
never accept Matt. i., ii as genuine. It is proposed
to show that the chapters are clearly genuine, but that
a few unimportant emendations are required in the
text.

First, to take the chapters as a whole. Dr. Arthur
Wright points out that " the Gospel is formally divided
. . . into **7** parts. The number is doubtless chosen
(he proceeds) to symbolize completeness. Five of the
seven divisions are introduced by the formal phrase
" And it came to pass when Jesus had finished," etc.
The first division contains the Gospel of the Infancy,
chh. i. ii., the second reaches to the end of the Sermon
on the Mount, iii.–vii. 27, the third to the end of the
charge to the Twelve, vii. 28–x., the fourth to the end
of the eight Parables, xi.–xiii. 52, the fifth to the end
of a second charge to the Twelve, xiii. 53–xviii., the
sixth to the end of the Eschatological Discourses,
xix.–xxv., the seventh concludes the book xxvi.–
xxviii. Every one therefore of these divisions is clearly
marked, and the introductory note is a guide to the

memory. They are quite original, there being nothing corresponding to them in SS. Mark or Luke." [1]

We see then that the number 7 is stamped on St. Matthew's Gospel as a whole, the division into 7 Parts being, as Dr. Wright says, " clearly marked," though it does not obtrude itself upon our notice, but is only seen by the careful reader. Yet this division is quite natural and easy, and in no way forced or fanciful. We see further that chh. i., ii. constitute the first of these Parts. The closer examination which we are about to undertake will show that the two chh. must be taken together, each being incomplete without the other.

If we take each sentence commencing with "and " (χαὶ or δὲ in the Greek) as a " division " (sentences commencing otherwise being joined to the preceding sentence) there are in these chh. six "sections " or " heptads " containing 7 "divisions " each. In this arrangement the genealogy must be taken as a whole as constituting one division only, containing 42 (6 × 7) subdivisions. The appropriateness of the number 6 in both cases is at once apparent when we remember that it is "man's number " (see p. 39), and that these chapters contain the record of the human birth of the child Jesus, and his need during infancy of the care of human parents,[2] and also of his descent as a man from Abraham and David.

Otherwise it is the number 7 which engrosses our attention, and when the Greek text has been corrected, and brought back to its original state, the number of Words and Letters, even the number of Nouns, Verbs, etc., are all multiples of 7.

Unfortunately the text of these chh. as we now have it is not quite so pure as that of the *Magnificat* given in our first chapter, but that is the reason why they find a place in this chapter on Textual Criticism, for we have to show what alterations are needed for the

---

[1] *Synopsis of the Gospels in Greek*[3], pp. xxxii, lxvi.
[2] The word " parents " is used here as in Luke ii. 41.

restoration of the original text, and to justify these alterations.

In the early days of Christianity there was not quite the same reverence for the actual words of the scriptures of the N.T. as there is now, and scribes, when copying a MS, thought it quite permissible to change a grammatical form or to add a word or two, in order, as they thought, to make the meaning clearer. And as different scribes had different ideas, divergences arose and variant readings increased. Thus in Mat. i., ii. we are told three times of an angel appearing to Joseph. In both A.V. and R.V. the word "appear" is in the past tense in i. 20, and in the present in ii. 13, 19, the sense being the same in all three places. But in ii. 13, Cod. B differs from all other extant Greek MSS, and gives the past (aorist) tense, so that either the scribe of B has altered the word here to conform to i. 20, or other scribes have altered it to agree with ii. 19. Again in our A.V. we frequently find the verb "to be" and the objective pronoun in *italics*, signifying that they are not found in the original. Thus there is no verb in Mat. i. 17, and "are" is inserted as the English language requires. So in Mat. ii. 8 "him" is added after "found." Now in many similar cases the words have been added in the Greek by scribes, and where, as is frequently the case, the addition has got into all MSS, there is great difficulty in detecting it. In the three instances just given, and in many others, there is no change whatever in the meaning of the passages, but the number of words and letters is altered, and the heptadic symmetry destroyed.

In the Greek text about to be given the Revisers' text is taken as a basis. It has this advantage as compared with WH., that it leaves rec. unaltered in adding *v ephelkustikon* only when a vowel follows, though on the other hand it has the disadvantage that it also usually leaves rec. unaltered when the better attested reading would make no difference in the English translation.

In the two chh. the Greek text contains :—

	Words.	Letters.
According to the Revisers' text	896	4487
„ WH.	893	4552
„ „ True text	882	4459

The Revisers' numbers are both heptadic as it happens, but are not therefore necessarily correct. If we compare them with the true figures we find that

$$896 = 7 \times 4 \times 4 \times 4 \times 2$$

and

$$4487 = 7 \times 641$$

whereas the true figures yield the following remarkable result :

$$882 = 7 \times 7 \times 3 \times 6,$$

a combination of the double 7 with the divine number 3 and the human number 6, and

$$4459 = 7 \times 7 \times 7 \times 13,$$

the " trinal fraction " of 3.

There are then in the two chh. 42 divisions, 882 words and 4459 letters, and, as we saw in the case of the *Magnificat*, all these numbers are divisible by 7, *but by no other number.*

In each of the six sections or heptads the total number of words and letters is a multiple of 7, while if the words are divided according to the Parts of Speech we find there are :—

	Words.	Letters.
Verbs (excluding Participles)	133	1008
Proper Nouns	161	1008
Common Nouns (substantive and adjective)	126	798
Pronouns	56	252
Adverbs	28	112
Participles	49	401 } 798
Articles	145 } 210	397 } 798
Prepositions	65	179 } 483
Conjunctions	119	304 } 483
Total	882	4459

All the numbers, here and elsewhere, which are printed in **thick type,** are multiples of **7.**

It may be worth while to pause a moment to try and realize the significance of these remarkable figures.

In a short passage of **882** words, in which there is no apparent artificiality or stiltedness of construction —except it be the genealogy—we find there are **42** (7 × 6) " divisions " marked by a sentence beginning with " and " (καί or δέ), again excepting the genealogy, which itself contains **42** sentences. If these are divided into " sections " each containing **7** such divisions the number of words and letters in each section is each a multiple of **7.** The grand totals of the words and letters in the two chh. are of course also multiples of **7.** But they are more—the total of the Words is a multiple of double **7** combined with two other symbolical numbers (7 × 7 × 3 × 6), while the total of the Letters is a multiple of triple **7** (7 × 7 × 7 × 13). Then if all the words are divided according to the Parts of Speech (after the ancient Greek manner, not the modern English) we have **7** series of words—Verbs, Adverbs, Proper Nouns, Common Nouns, Pronouns, Participles, Conjunctions—each a multiple of **7,** while the Articles and Prepositions combined form an eighth multiple of **7.** If the letters in each group are counted we find again **7** series—Verbs, Adverbs, Proper Nouns, Common Nouns, Pronouns, Participles and Articles combined, Prepositions and Conjunctions combined— each a multiple of **7.**
All this in a plain, historical narrative of events, in which we cannot find one word other than we might expect to find in such a narrative.

What shall we say to these things ? Can they be matched in all literature outside the Bible ?

The following then is an heptadically corrected Greek text of Mat. i., ii., with a literal English rendering as nearly word for word as possible.

All differences from the Revisers' Greek text, and from WH except final *ν*, are specified at the foot of the page. More extended notes, when necessary, will be found at the end of ch. ii.

In the English column, (a) Words in parentheses ( ) are not in the Greek, but are needed to complete the sense, like the italics in A.V.; (b) three dots . . . indicate that one or more words have been deleted from the Revisers' text; (c) the Greek article is represented (1) by "the," (2) by other words printed in *italics;* or (3) by a small circle ° above the line; (d) words joined by a hyphen represent one word in Greek; AND in small capitals = *καὶ*, while and in ordinary type = *δέ*.

MATTHEW I

1 (*1*) Βίβλος γενέσεως 'Ιησοῦ Χριστοῦ, υἱοῦ Δαυείδ, υἱοῦ 'Αβραάμ.	Book of-generation of-Jesus Christ, son of-David, son of-Abraham.
2 ¹ 'Αβραὰμ ἐγέννησε τὸν 'Ισαάκ· ² 'Ισαὰκ δὲ ἐγέννησε τὸν 'Ιακώβ· ³ 'Ιακὼβ δὲ ἐγέννησε τὸν 'Ιούδαν καὶ τοὺς ἀδελφοὺς αὐτοῦ·	Abraham begat ° Isaac; and Isaac begat ° Jacob; and Jacob begat ° Judah AND his ° brethren;
3 ⁴ 'Ιούδας δὲ ἐγέννησε τὸν Φαρὲς καὶ τὸν Ζαρὰ ἐκ τῆς Θάμαρ· ⁵ Φαρὲς δὲ ἐγέννησε τὸν 'Εσρώμ· ⁶ 'Εσρὼμ δὲ ἐγέννησε τὸν 'Αράμ·	and Judah begat ° Pharez AND ° Zarah of ° Thamar; and Pharez begat ° Hezron; and Hezron begat ° Aram;
4 ⁷ 'Αρὰμ δὲ ἐγέννησε τὸν 'Αμιναδάβ· ⁸ 'Αμιναδὰβ δὲ ἐγέννησε τὸν Ναασσών· ⁹ Ναασσὼν δὲ ἐγέννησε τὸν Σαλμών.	and Aram begat ° Aminadab; and Aminadab begat ° Nahshon; and Nahshon begat ° Salmon;
5 ¹⁰ Σαλμὼν δὲ ἐγέννησε τὸν Βοὸζ ἐκ τῆς 'Ραχάβ. ¹¹ Βοὸζ δὲ ἐγέννησε τὸν 'Ιωβὴδ ἐκ τῆς 'Ρούθ· ¹² 'Ιωβὴδ δὲ ἐγέννησε τὸν 'Ιεσσαί·	and Salmon begat ° Boaz of ° Rahab; and Boaz begat ° Obed of ° Ruth; and Obed begat ° Jesse;

ver. I. *Δαυείδ*: So WH and most Edd., *Δαβίδ* R after rec., *Δαυίδ* Sod.; so vv. 6, 6, 17, 17, 20.

ver. 5, *'Ιωβὴδ* : so all Edd., *'Ωβὴδ* R after rec.

6 13 Ἰεσσαὶ δὲ ἐγέννησε τὸν Δαυεὶδ τὸν βασιλέα.
and Jesse begat °David the King.

14 Δαυεὶδ δὲ ἐγέννησε τὸν Σολομῶνα ἐκ τῆς τοῦ Οὐρείου.
And David begat °Solomon of *her of* Uriah ;

7 15 Σολομὼν δὲ ἐγέννησε τὸν Ῥοβοάμ·
and Solomon begat °Rehoboam ;

16 Ῥοβοὰμ δὲ ἐγέννησε τὸν Ἀβιά·
and Rehoboam begat °Abijah ;

17 Ἀβιὰ δὲ ἐγέννησε τὸν Ἀσάφ·
and Abijah begat °Asaph ;

8 18 Ἀσὰφ δὲ ἐγέννησε τὸν Ἰωσαφάτ·
and Asaph begat° Jehoshaphat :

19 Ἰωσαφὰτ δὲ ἐγέννησε τὸν Ἰωράμ·
and Jehoshaphat begat° Joram;

20 Ἰωρὰμ δὲ ἐγέννησε τὸν Ὀζείαν·
and Joram begat °Uzziah ;

9 21 Ὀζείας δὲ ἐγέννησε τὸν Ἰωάθαμ·
and Uzziah begat °Jotham ;

22 Ἰωάθαμ δὲ ἐγέννησε τὸν Ἄχαζ·
and Jotham begat °Ahaz ;

23 Ἄχαζ δὲ ἐγέννησε τὸν Ἐζεκίαν·
and Ahaz begat °Hezekiah ;

10 24 Ἐζεκίας δὲ ἐγέννησε τὸν Μανασσῆ·
and Hezekiah begat °Manasseh ;

25 Μανασσῆς δὲ ἐγέννησε τὸν Ἀμώς·
and Manasseh begat °Amon ;

26 Ἀμὼς δὲ ἐγέννησε τὸν Ἰωσείαν·
and Amon begat °Josiah ;

11 27 Ἰωσείας δὲ ἐγέννησε τὸν Ἰεχονίαν καὶ τοὺς ἀδελφοὺς αὐτοῦ ἐπὶ τῆς μετοικεσίας Βαβυλῶνος.
and Josiah begat °Jechoniah AND his °brethren at the Babylonian captivity.

12 28 Μετὰ δὲ τὴν μετοικεσίαν Βαβυλῶνος Ἰεχονίας ἐγέννησε τὸν Σαλαθιήλ·
and after the Babylonian captivity Jechoniah begat °Salathiel ;

29 Σαλαθιὴλ δὲ ἐγέννησε τὸν Ζοροβάβελ·
and Salathiel begat °Zerubbabel ;

13 30 Ζοροβάβελ δὲ ἐγέννησε τὸν Ἀβιούδ·
and Zerubbabel begat °Abiud ;

31 Ἀβιοὺδ δὲ ἐγέννησε τὸν Ἐλιακείμ·
and Abiud begat °Eliakim ;

32 Ἐλιακεὶμ δὲ ἐγέννησε τὸν Ἀζώρ·
and Eliakim begat °Azor ;

14 33 Ἀζὼρ δὲ ἐγέννησε τὸν Σαδώκ·
and Azor begat °Sadoc ;

34 Σαδὼκ δὲ ἐγέννησε τὸν Ἀχείμ·
and Sadoc begat °Achim ;

35 Ἀχεὶμ δὲ ἐγέννησε τὸν Ἐλιούδ·
and Achim begat °Eliud ;

15 36 Ἐλιοὺδ δε ἐγέννησε τὸν Ἐλεάζαρ·
and Eliud begat °Eleazar ;

37 Ἐλεάζαρ δὲ ἐγέννησε τὸν Ματθάν·
and Eleazar begat °Matthan ;

38 Ματθὰν δὲ ἐγέννησε τὸν Ἰακώβ·
and Matthan begat °Jacob ;

16 39 Ἰακὼβ δὲ ἐγέννησε τὸν Ἰωσήφ, τὸν ἄνδρα Μαρίας, ἐξ ἧς ἐγεννήθη Ἰησοῦς ὁ λεγόμενος Χριστός.
and Jacob begat °Joseph, the husband of Mary, of whom was-born Jesus, °called Christ.

---

ver. 6, Σολομῶνα: so WH and most Edd., -ῶντα R after rec. Οὐρείου: so Blass with B Pap¹, Οὐρίου R, WH ; see p. 85.

ver. 8, 9, Ὀζείαν, Ὀζείας : so WH and most Edd., Ὀζι- R after rec.

ver. 10, 11, Ἰωσείαν, Ἰωσείας : so WH and most Edd., Ἰωσί- R after rec.

ver. 16: see p. 90.

17 [40] Πᾶσαι οὖν αἱ γενεαὶ ἀπὸ
Ἀβραὰμ ἕως Δαυεὶδ
γενεαὶ δεκατέσσαρες·
[41] καὶ ἀπὸ Δαυεὶδ ἕως τῆς
μετοικεσίας Βαβυλῶνος
γενεαὶ δεκατέσσαρες·
[42] καὶ ἀπὸ τῆς μετοικεσίας
Βαβυλῶνος ἕως τοῦ Χριστοῦ
γενεαὶ δεκατέσσαρες.

So all the generations from
Abraham until David
(are) fourteen generations;
AND from David until the
Babylonian captivity
(are) fourteen generations;
AND from the Babylonian
captivity until the Christ
(are) fourteen generations.

18 (2) Τοῦ δὲ Ἰησοῦ Χριστοῦ ἡ γέννησις
οὕτω· μνηστευθείσης τῆς μητρὸς
αὐτοῦ Μαρίας τῷ Ἰωσήφ,

And the birth of Jesus Christ
(was) thus; his ° mother Mary
having-been-betrothed to
Joseph,

πρὶν ἢ συνελθεῖν αὐτούς,
εὑρέθη ἐν γαστρὶ ἔχουσα
ἐκ Πνεύματος Ἁγίου.

before that they came-together,
she-was-found having in womb
of (the) Holy Ghost.

19 (3) Ἰωσὴφ δὲ ὁ ἀνὴρ αὐτῆς
δίκαιος,
(4) καὶ μὴ θέλων αὐτὴν
δειγματίσαι, ἐβουλήθη
λάθρᾳ ἀπολῦσαι αὐτήν.

And Joseph her ° husband
(was) just,
AND not wishing to-expose
her, he-was-minded
to-dismiss her privily.

20 (5) ταῦτα δὲ αὐτοῦ ἐνθυμη-
θέντος, ἰδού, ἄγγελος
Κυρίου κατ' ὄναρ ἐφάνη
αὐτῷ λέγων, Ἰωσήφ,
υἱὸς Δαυείδ, μὴ φοβηθῇς
παραλαβεῖν Μαριὰμ τὴν γυναῖκά
σου· τὸ γὰρ ἐν αὐτῇ γεννηθὲν
ἐκ Πνεύματός ἐστιν Ἁγίου.

And (while) he was-thinking-on
these-things, behold, an-angel
of-(the)-Lord appeared to-him
in a-dream saying, Joseph
son of-David, fear not
to-take Mary thy ° wife;
for that which-is-conceived
in her is of (the) Holy Ghost.

21 (6) τέξεται δὲ υἱόν,
(7) καὶ καλέσεις τὸ ὄνομα αὐτοῦ
Ἰησοῦν, αὐτὸς γὰρ σώσει τὸν
λαὸν ἀπὸ τῶν ἁμαρτιῶν αὐτῶν.
864 words, 1827 letters.

And she-shall-bear a-son,
AND thou-shalt-call his ° name
Jesus, for he shall-save the
. . . people from their ° sins.

22 (1) Τοῦτο δὲ ὅλον γέγονεν,
ἵνα πληρωθῇ τὸ
ῥηθὲν ὑπὸ Κυρίου διὰ

And all this happened,
that it-might-be-fulfilled which
was-spoken by (the) Lord
through

---

ver. 18, γέννησις: so rec., Sod-mg., γενεσεις Codd. CW and
perhaps other MSS, γένεσις all other Edd.; see p. 85.
οὕτω: οὕτως ἦν all MSS and Edd.; see p. 85.
ver. 19, δίκαιος: add ὤν all MSS and Edd.; see p. 86.
δειγματίσαι so WH with most Edd., παραδειγ- R after rec.
λάθρᾳ: so La, WH, Sod., λάθρα R after rec. So ch. ii. 7.
ver. 21, λαόν: add αὐτοῦ all MSS and Edd.; see p. 86.
ver. 22, τοῦ Κυρίου R after rec., om. τοῦ WH and all Edd.

23 τοῦ προφήτου. λέγοντος, Ἰδού,   the prophet saying, Behold,
ἡ παρθένος ἐν γαστρὶ ἕξει,   the Virgin shall-have in womb,
(2) καὶ τέξεται υἱόν,   AND she-shall-bear a-son,
(3) καὶ καλέσουσι τὸ ὄνομα αὐτοῦ   AND they-shall-call his ° name
Ἐμμανουήλ· ὅ ἐστι μεθερμη-   Emmanuel, which is, being-
νευόμενον, Μεθ' ἡμῶν ὁ Θεός.   interpreted, ° God with us.
24 (4) ἐγερθεὶς δὲ ὁ Ἰωσὴφ ἀπὸ   And ° Joseph arising from
τοῦ ὕπνου ἐποίησεν ὡς   ° sleep, did as
προσέταξεν αὐτῷ ὁ ἄγγελος   the angel of-(the)-Lord
Κυρίου.   commanded him.
(5) καὶ παρέλαβε τὴν γυναῖκα αὐτοῦ.   AND he-took his ° wife.
25 (6) καὶ οὐκ ἐγίνωσκεν αὐτήν, ἕως   AND he-knew her not, until
οὗ ἔτεκε τὸν υἱόν.   that she-bare the son.
(7) καὶ ἐκάλεσε τὸ ὄνομα αὐτοῦ   AND he-called his ° name
ΙΗΣΟΥΝ.   JESUS.

70 words, 329 letters.

CHAPTER II

1 (1) Τοῦ δὲ Ἰησοῦ γεννηθέντος   And *when* Jesus was-born
ἐν Βηθλεὲμ τῆς Ἰουδαίας   in Bethlehem *of* Judæa
ἐν ἡμέραις Ἡρῴδου τοῦ βασιλέως,   in (the) days of-Herod the king,
ἰδού, μάγοι ἀπὸ ἀνατολῶν   behold, Magi from (the) east
παρεγένοντο εἰς Ἱεροσόλυμα   came to Jerusalem
2 λέγοντες, Ποῦ ἐστιν ὁ τεχθεὶς   saying, Where is the newborn
Βασιλεὺς τῶν Ἰουδαίων ;   King of-the Jews ?
εἴδομεν γὰρ αὐτοῦ τὸν ἀστέρα   for we-saw his ° star
ἐν τῇ ἀνατολῇ,   in the east,   [him.
(2) καὶ ἤλθομεν προσκυνῆσαι αὐτῷ.   AND we-have-come to-worship
3 (3) καὶ ἀκούσας ὁ βασιλεὺς Ἡρῴδης   AND Herod the king hearing
ἐταράχθη, καὶ πᾶσα Ἱεροσόλυμα   was-troubled, and all Jerusalem
μετ' αὐτοῦ.   with him.
4 (4) καὶ συναγαγὼν πάντας τοὺς   AND assembling all the
ἀρχιερεῖς καὶ γραμματεῖς   chief-priests AND scribes
τοῦ λαοῦ ἐπυνθάνετο παρ'   of-the people, he-enquired of
αὐτῶν ποῦ ὁ Χριστὸς γεννᾶται.   them where the Christ should-
   be-born,   [hem
5 (5) οἱ δὲ εἶπον, Ἐν Βηθλεὲμ   And *they* said . . . In Bethle-
τῆς Ιουδαίας· οὕτω γὰρ γέγραπται   of Judæa; for thus it-is-written

---

ver. 25, ἔτεκε τὸν υἱόν : ἔτεκεν υἱόν R, WH ; see p. 87.
   ch. ii, 1 Ἡρῴδου : so WH ; Ἡρώδου rec. R ; so vv. 3, 7, 12, 13, 15,
16, 19, 22.
   ver. 3 καὶ ἀκούσας : ἀκούσας δὲ all MSS and Edd. ; see p. 88.
   ver. 5, εἶπον : add αὐτῷ rec. R, WH, etc. ; see p. 88.
οὕτω : so R, not οὕτως as WH.

6 διὰ τοῦ προφήτου, Καὶ σύ, Βηθλεέμ, γῆ Ἰούδα, οὐδαμῶς ἐλαχίστη εἶ ἐν τοῖς ἡγεμόσιν Ἰούδα· ἐκ σοῦ γὰρ ἐξελεύσεται	by the prophet, AND thou, Bethlehem, land of-Judah, art nowise least among the princes of-Judah; for of thee shall-come-forth
ἡγούμενος, ὅστις ποιμανεῖ	a-governor, who shall-shepherd
7 τὸν λαόν μου τὸν Ἰσραήλ. τότε Ἡρῴδης, λάθρᾳ καλέσας τοὺς μάγους, ἠκρίβωσε παρ' αὐτῶν τὸν χρόνον τοῦ φαινομένου ἀστέρος.	my ° people ° Israel. Then Herod, having-called privily the Magi, ascertained from them the time of-the appearing star.
8 (6) καὶ πέμψας αὐτοὺς εἰς Βηθλεέμ εἶπε, πορευθέντες ἐξετάσατε ἀκριβῶς περὶ τοῦ παιδίου·	AND sending them to Bethlehem he-said, Going, search carefully concerning the child;
(7) ἐπὰν δὲ εὕρητε, ἀπαγγείλατέ μοι, ὅπως κἀγὼ ἐλθὼν προσκυνήσω αὐτῷ.	And when ye-have-found (him) report to-me, that I-also coming may-worship him.
140 words, 742 letters.	
9 (1) Οἱ δὲ ἀκούσαντες τοῦ βασιλέως ἐπορεύθησαν·	And *they* having-heard the king, departed.
(2) καὶ ἰδού, ὁ ἀστήρ, ὃν εἶδον	AND behold, the star which they-saw
ἐν τῇ ἀνατολῇ, προῆγεν αὐτοὺς ἕως ἐλθὼν ἐστάθη ἐπάνω τοῦ παιδίου.	in the east went-before them, until coming, it-stood over . . the child.
10 (3) ἰδόντες δὲ τὸν ἀστέρα ἐχάρησαν	And seeing the star, they-rejoiced
χαρὰν μεγάλην σφόδρα.	(with) exceeding great joy.
11 (4) καὶ ἐλθόντες εἰς τὴν οἰκίαν εἶδον τὸ παιδίον μετὰ Μαρίας τῆς μητρὸς αὐτοῦ.	AND coming into the house they-saw the child with Mary, his ° mother.
(5) καὶ πεσόντες προσεκύνησαν αὐτῷ.	AND falling-down they-worshipped him.
(6) καὶ ἀνοίξαντες τὰς πήρας αὐτῶν προσήνεγκαν αὐτῷ δῶρα, χρυσὸν καὶ λίβανον καὶ σμύρναν.	AND opening their ° wallets they-offered to-him gifts, gold AND frankincense AND myrrh.
12 (7) καὶ χρηματισθέντες κατ' ὄναρ μὴ ἀνακάμψαι πρὸς Ἡρῴδην δι' ἄλλης ὁδοῦ ἀνεχώρησαν εἰς τὴν χώραν αὐτῶν.	AND being-warned in a-dream not to-return to Herod they-departed into their own ° country by another way.
77 words, 899 letters.	

---

ver. 9, ἐστάθη : so WH and all Edd., ἔστη R after rec.
τοῦ παιδίου D ; οὖ ἦν τὸ παιδίον all Edd. ; see p. 88.
ver. 11, τὰς πήρας : τοὺς θησαυροὺς all Edd. ; see p. 88.

13 (1) Ἀναχωρησάντων δὲ αὐτῶν, ἰδού, ἄγγελος Κυρίου ἐφάνη

And they having-departed, behold, an-angel of-(the)-Lord appeared

κατ' ὄναρ τῷ Ἰωσὴφ λέγων, Ἐγερθεὶς παράλαβε τὸ παιδίον καὶ τὴν μητέρα αὐτοῦ.

in a-dream to Joseph saying, Arising, take the child AND his ° mother,

(2) καὶ φεῦγε εἰς Αἴγυπτον ἕως εἴπω σοί· μέλλει γὰρ Ἡρῴδης ζητεῖν τὸ παιδίον, τοῦ ἀπολέσαι αὐτό.

AND flee into Egypt . . . until I-tell thee; for Herod will seek the child, ° to-destroy him.

14 (3) ὁ δὲ ἐγερθεὶς παρέλαβε τὸ παιδίον καὶ τὴν μητέρα αὐτοῦ νυκτός,

AND ° arising, he-took the child AND his ° mother by-night,

(4) καὶ ἀνεχώρησεν εἰς Αἴγυπτον.

AND he-withdrew into Egypt.

15 (5) καὶ ἦν ἐκεῖ ἕως τῆς τελευτῆς

AND he-was there until the death

Ἡρῴδου· ἵνα πληρωθῇ

of-Herod; that it-might-be-fulfilled

τὸ ῥηθὲν ὑπὸ Κυρίου διὰ τοῦ προφήτου λέγοντος, Ἐξ

which was-spoken by (the) Lord through the prophet saying, Out-of

Αἰγύπτου ἐκάλεσα τὸν υἱόν μου.

Egypt I-called my ° son.

16   τότε Ἡρῴδης, ἰδὼν ὅτι ἐνεπαίχθη

Then Herod, seeing that he-was-mocked

ὑπὸ τῶν μάγων, ἐθυμώθη λείαν,

by the Magi, was-wroth exceedingly,

(6) καὶ ἀποστείλας ἀνεῖλε πάντας τοὺς παῖδας τοὺς ἐν Βηθλεὲμ

AND sending-forth he-slew all the male-children ° in Bethlehem

καὶ ἐν πᾶσι τοῖς ὁρίοις αὐτῆς, ἀπὸ διετοῦς καὶ κατωτέρω, κατὰ τὸν χρόνον ὃν ἠκρίβωσε παρὰ τῶν μάγων.

AND in all the borders thereof, from two-years-old AND under, according-to the time which he-ascertained from the Magi.

17   τότε ἐπληρώθη τὸ ῥηθὲν

Then was-fulfilled that which-was-spoken

διὰ Ἰερεμίου τοῦ προφήτου

by Jeremiah the prophet

18   λέγοντος, Φωνὴ ἐν Ῥαμᾶ ἠκούσθη,

saying, A-voice was-heard in Ramah,

κλαυθμὸς καὶ ὀδυρμὸς πολύς, Ῥαχὴλ κλαίουσα τὰ τέκνα αὐτῆς.

weeping AND great mourning, Rachel weeping-for her ° children.

---

ver. 13, ἐφάνη : so La, WH mg., with B, a cursive, some vss. and Irenæus ; φαίνεται "appeareth" rec. R, WH text, etc.
ἕως : καὶ ἴσθι ἐκεῖ ἕως ἄν all Edd. ; see p. 89.
ver. 15, Κυρίου so WH and all Edd., τοῦ Κυρίου R after rec.
ver. 16, λείαν : so the best MSS ℵ* B*D ; spelt λίαν by R, WH.

(7) καὶ οὐκ ἤθελε παρακληθῆναι,

AND she-would not be-comforted,

ὅτι οὐκ εἰσίν.

because they-are not.

140 words, 686 letters.

19 (1) Τελευτήσαντος δὲ τοῦ Ἡρῴδου, ἰδού, ἄγγελος Κυρίου φαίνεται κατ' ὄναρ τῷ Ἰωσὴφ ἐν

And ° Herod having-died, behold, an-angel of-(the)-Lord appeareth in a-dream *to* Joseph in

20 Αἰγύπτῳ λέγων, Ἐγερθεὶς παράλαβε

Egypt saying, Arising, take

τὸ παιδίον καὶ τὴν μητέρα αὐτοῦ,

the child AND his ° mother,

(2) καὶ πορεύου εἰς γῆν Ἰσραήλ· τεθνήκασι γὰρ οἱ ζητοῦντες τὴν ψυχὴν τοῦ παιδίου,

AND go into (the) land of-Israel for they-are-dead *that* sought the life of-the child.

21 (3) ὁ δὲ ἐγερθεὶς παρέλαβε τὸ παιδίον καὶ τὴν μητέρα αὐτοῦ,

And ° arising, he-took the child AND his ° mother,

(4) καὶ εἰσῆλθεν εἰς γῆν Ἰσραήλ.

AND he-came into (the) land of-Israel.

22 (5) ἀκούσας δὲ ὅτι Ἀρχέλαος βασιλεύει ἀντὶ Ἡρῴδου

And hearing that Archelaus reigneth . . . instead-of Herod

τοῦ πατρὸς αὐτοῦ ἐφοβήθη ἐκεῖ ἀπελθεῖν.

his ° father, he-feared to-go there.

(6) χρηματισθεὶς δὲ κατ' ὄναρ ἀνεχώρησεν εἰς τὰ μέρη τῆς Γαλειλαίας.

And being-warned in a-dream he-withdrew into the parts *of* Galilee.

23 (7) καὶ ἐλθὼν κατῴκησεν εἰς πόλιν λεγομένην Ναζαρέτ· ὅπως πληρωθῇ τὸ ῥηθὲν διὰ τῶν προφητῶν, ὅτι Ναζωραῖος κληθήσεται.

AND coming, he-dwelt in a-city called Nazareth ; that it-might-be-fulfilled *which* was-spoken by the prophets, that he-should-be-called a-Nazarene.

91 words, 476 letters.

The Greek text of the two chapters as given above contains :—

---

ver. 18, εἰσίν : so WH and all Edd., εἰσί R after rec., ν is added here because it is the end of a heptad.

ver. 21, εἰσῆλθεν : so WH and all Edd., ἦλθεν R after rec.

ver. 22, Βασιλεύει : add (ἐπὶ) τῆς Ἰουδαίας R, WH, etc. ; see p. 89. Γαλειλαίας so B, Γαλιλ- R, WH, etc. ; see p. 90.

		Words.	Letters.
Ch. i,	1–21	864	1827
	22–25	70	329
ii,	1–8	140	742
	9–12	77	399
	13–18	140	686
	19–23	91	476
Total		882	4459

All these numbers are multiples of 7.

The following notes include all words which differ from both R and WH.

Mat. i. 6 *Οὐρεῖον* (for *Οὐρίου*). Whereas WH have altered ι into ει in other Proper names, as in *Δαυείδ*, *'Οζείας*, *'Ιωσείας*, they hesitated here, as B was the only authority they had, and the scribe of B had a weakness for the diphthong ει. Had they known that a still older authority than B—a third-century papyrus—gave *Οὐρεῖον*, they would probably have adopted this spelling.

i. 18, *γέννησις* (for *γένεσις*). This is one of the most difficult words to deal with in the chapter, but as another letter was required to make the heptadic number, both in this heptad (i. 1–21) and in the Common Nouns, I have felt obliged to adopt the longer spelling. And yet there is good evidence for it : L, 33 (which has been called " the queen of cursives "), the perhaps equally good 892 (= ε 1016 Sod.) the mass of later MSS uncial and cursive, and the Bohairic version (perhaps also Syr-sin and -cu, but the Versions generally are not clear) ; while the Patristic support goes so far back as Irenaeus and Didymus. Tatian and Origen are quoted on both sides. *Γέννησις* would seem to suit the sense better. In ver. 1 *βίβλος γενέσεως* is taken from Gen. v. 1 (Sept) and means " genealogy " (RV marg.), but here the meaning is " birth," and as a different idea is to be conveyed we should expect a different word to be used, though both words may be translated " birth." Deissmann says : " A fluctuation in the orthography of those forms of *γεννάω* and *γίνομαι* which are identical except for the *ν(ν)* has often been remarked. . . . The uncertainty of the orthography is well indicated in a Fayyum papyrus (138–139 A.D.), where line 21 has *ἐπιγεννήσεως* and line 24 *ἐπιγενήσεως*."[1] But perhaps we should read *γένεσις* with Codd. C W and probably other MSS, for differences in spelling of this nature are not usually noted in published collations.

i. 18, *οὔτω* (for *οὔτως ἦν*). This is simply a question whether the verb " was " is to be expressed or understood. I have already

---

[1] *Bible Studies*, Eng. tr., p. 184.

pointed out that the verb " to be " is often left to be understood, and its omission here is required to make the words and letters in this heptad, and also in the Verbs, heptadic. It has been frequently inserted by scribes where it was not originally in the Greek, so as to make the meaning clearer,[1] so that it is difficult at present to make anything of the number of occurrences of ἦν. The heptadic proof here, therefore, must rest chiefly on what has just been stated. It may, however, be added that there are 7 words in the " division " without ἦν, but this may be accidental. The imperfect of εἰμί, all persons, occurs 39 times in Mat. (Geden)[2]; from which take xiv. 24 (so WH text R mg.), xii 40 (so D and other MSS), ii. 9 (see below) and here = 35. Οὕτω(ς), without a verb (i.e. requiring verb " to be " to be understood) occurs in N.T. 14 times, less Lu. xii. 21 [WH] and add here = same number 14. Οὕτω(ς) with verb " to be " expressed occurs in N.T., excluding this ver., 35 times, including 14 future 3rd sing., and in affirmative clauses 7 present 3rd sing. Of these 35, 14 have other words intervening, and in 21 οὕτως and the verb come together, except δέ in Mat. x. 43, which could not well be placed otherwise.

i. 19, δίκαιος (for δίκαιος ὤν). This is another instance of the insertion by scribes of the verb " to be," or rather of its participle. In the common text of this section there are only six " divisions," but to make a seventh we do not require to add words on, but we take one off, and so make one long sentence into two shorter ones, both beginning with " and." The sentence was originally " Joseph her husband just," without a verb, and this is proved by some ancient versions. A verb was needed to complete the sense, and Tatian, the Syriac-sin-cu-pesh, the Bohairic and the Ethiopic versions, six different authorities, all supply " was," while all extant Greek MSS whose readings have been published have inserted " being," and so carried the sentence on to the words following. Ὤν " being " occurs in N.T. 46 times (Geden)[3] from which we must deduct Jno. iii. 13 (WH[1], R[2]), Jno. vi. 71 (WH, R), Lu. xxiv. 44 (D Iren. Cypr. Hil.) and here = 42, of which 21 are in Jno. and Re., and 14 in Paul. The omission of ὤν makes both this section and the Participles heptadic.

i. 21, τὸν λαόν " the people " (for τὸν λαὸν αὐτοῦ " his people "). It was quite a common practice for scribes to insert pronouns where they were not in the original text. There are about 70 instances in the Gospels alone where αὐτοῦ is found in rec. text,

---

[1] The following are some texts in the Gospels where ἦν " was " is found in some MSS and omitted by others : Mat. ii. 9, xii. 10, 40, xxvii. 54 ; Mk. i. 45, xiv. 21, xv. 40 ; Lu. vii. 12 bis, xi. 14, xiii. 11, xv. 32, xvi. 20, xix. 2, xxiv. 10 ; Jno. xviii. 16, xix. 14.

[2] Bruder has 40, inc. xii. 10.

[3] Bruder has 48 inc. Mk. xiii. 16, xiv. 43.

but is omitted by recent editors, without counting other inflections of the word.[1] All MSS have it here, so we have to depend entirely on the HEPTAD TEST for proof that it should be omitted. There are in the two chapters in Revisers' text 58 pronouns containing 262 letters. By deleting two pronouns containing 10 letters, we should make both numbers heptadic, 56, 252. It does not seem feasible to take out any pronouns except here and in ch. ii. 5, and the number of words and letters in the two sections confirms this. Of the 56 pronouns, 49 refer to *persons*, of course excluding αὐτοῦ here and αὐτῷ in ii. 5. Αὐτός (masc. all forms) occurs 7 times in the sub-section i. 18–21 excluding αὐτοῦ here. "His people" (τ. λαοῦ-ῷ-ὸν αὐτοῦ) occurs 7 times in N.T. excluding here (Lu. i. 68, 77, vii. 16; Ro. xi. 1, 2, xv. 10; Heb. x. 30). Αὐτοῦ occurs in the two chh. 16 times, excluding here, of which 14 refer to Jews (Jesus, Judah, Jechoniah, Joseph) and 2 to Gentiles (Herod, Archelaus).[2]

In the earlier part of v. 21 αὐτοῦ is apparently omitted by ‏ℵ‎* ("thou shalt call the name Jesus"), but it is correct there, for καλέω "call" with τὸ ὄνομα αὐτοῦ is found 7 times in N.T. (Mat. i. 21, 23, 25; Lu. i. 31, 33, ii. 21; Re. xix. 13).

    i. 25 (1) τὸν υἱόν "the son," Bohairic and Syr-cu versions.
          (2)   ,,   ,,   αὐτῆς "her son," Sahidic version.
          (3)   ,,   ,,   ,,   τὸν πρωτότοκον, rec., Alford mg.
          (4)   ,,   ,,   τὸν πρωτότοκον, D[2] L d.
          (5) υἱόν "a son," R, WH and all Edd.

We have here no fewer than five variations, and if we ask which is the most likely to have given rise to the others (1) seems to suit best. (3) may be dismissed as having been copied from Lu. ii. 7, but this does not account for the article being found in (1) (2) (4). When a person is introduced for the first time, the art. need not be used, so in ver. 21 we read "she shall bear a son," but now it is said quite properly, "she bare the son," i.e. the son promised or previously spoken of. So also when the Magi are first mentioned (ii. 1) there is no art., but it is used when they are mentioned again. "She shall bear the son" apparently seemed a strange expression to early scribes, and while one tried to mend it by adding "her," and others went still further, others again took out the art., which seemed to them superfluous. Υἱός "son" occurs in the accus. in N.T. as follows: υἱόν (incg. Jno. i. 45) 21 times, υἱούς "sons" 7, total without art. 28; τὸν υἱόν "the son" incg. here 56 referring to our Lord, and 8 to others, τοὺς υἱούς "the sons" 6, total with art. 70;

---

[1] Cf. A.V. and R.V. and note the omission of "his" in Mat. viii. 13, 21, 25, etc.

[2] Αὐτοῦ and αὐτῷ occur 14 times in the two chh. meaning Jesus —7 masc. and 7 neut.—but this is scarcely permissible, as it leaves out αὐτός and αὐτό, which each occur once.

98 in all. The article occurs in this ch. **77** times including τὸν here.

ii. **3**, Καὶ ἀκούσας "and having heard " (for ἀκούσας δέ, same meaning). The reason for making this slight change is that there is one letter short in the heptad, and it can be made up in this way without disturbing the Parts of Speech. There are three places in the heptad where δέ might be changed to καί, vv. **1, 5** and **8**, and in ver. **1** there is some slight MS authority. But that ver. **3** is the proper place to make the change I think the following will show. It makes **7** occurrences of καί in this section. Ἀκούσας δὲ ὁ . . . occurs **7** times in N.T. (Mat. viii. **10**, xix. **22** ; Mk. vi. **16** ; Lu. xviii. **22** ; Jno. xi. **4** ; Ac. xxii. **26**, xxiii. **16** ; but excluding Mat. ii. **3** and Mat. xiv. **13**, where with rec. CWΔ, etc., we should read καὶ ἀκ.). Ἀκούσας δέ (without ὁ) **7** times (Mat. ii. **22**, iv. **12** ; Lu. vii. **3, 9,** xiv. **15,** xviii. **36** ; Ac. vii. **12**). With proper names ἀκούσας δὲ ὁ Mat. viii. **10** ; Mk. vi. **16** ; Lu. xviii. **22** ; Jno. xi. **4** ; ὁ δὲ . . . ἀκούσας Mat. xi. **2** ; Lu. viii. **50** ; ἀκούσας δέ Ac. vii. **12 = 7** ; this again excludes Mat. ii. **3**, xiv. **13**. Καὶ ἀκούσας occurs Mk. ii. **17,** vi. **20,** x. **47** ; Jno. xii. **29** + Mat. ii. **3**, xiv. **13** ; κἀγὼ ἀκούσας Eph. i. **15 = 7** in all. (In Mt. xxii. **7** ; Ac. xxiv. **22** rec. inserts ἀκούσας wrongly, R omits.) Again, καί followed immediately by a verb or participle occurs **21** times in the two chh. and δέ preceded by a verb or participle **7** times, with the corrected text.

ii. **5**, Omit αὐτῷ "to him," after εἶπον : So ℵ* **243** Tatian, Old Lat., Vulg-1-ms, Pesh, Chrysostom. See note on i. **21** above. In about **50** places αὐτῷ is found in rec. but omitted by recent Edd.[1] Αὐτός masc., all forms, occurs **7** times in this section (vv. **1–21**) excluding αὐτῷ here.

ii. **9**, τοῦ παιδίου "the child " (for οὗ ἦν τὸ παιδίον "where the child was "). So D and several MSS of old Lat., both African and European families. Οὗ with imperf. of εἰμί "to be " occurs **7** times in N.T. excluding this verse (οὗ ἦν Lu. iv. **16, 17**, xxiii. **53** ; οὗ ἦμεν Ac. xx. **8** ; οὗ ἦσαν Ac. i. **13**, ii. **2**, xii. **12 = 7**). Again τοῦ παιδίου occurs in N.T. **7** times incg. this passage (Mat. ii. **8, 9, 20** ; Mk. v. **40, 41**, ix. **24** ; Lu. ii. **17**). τὸ παιδίον occurs in nom. case **7** times excluding here (Mat. xviii. **4** ; Mk. v. **39, 40** ; Lu. i. **66, 80**, ii. **40** ; Jno. xvi. **21**). This is one of many instances where D has preserved the true reading against B, ℵ etc.

ii. **11**, τὰς πήρας "the wallets or travelling bags" (for τοὺς θησαυρούς "the treasures "). Although this reading is not now found in any MS or version, WH thought it worthy of notice in their Notes on Select Readings, and Souter also mentions it in his very limited *apparatus*, where many more important readings are passed over. It is found in the Apocryphal Gospel known as the

---

[1] Cp. A.V. and R.V. and note the omission of "unto him" in the latter in Mat. xvii. **26**, xviii. **34**, etc.

Protevangelion of James, dating from the beginning of cent. ii, which doubtless copied it from St. Matthew. It is also expressly given twice by Epiphanius, who was acquainted with both readings, and calls τοὺς θησαυροὺς a reading of "some copies." πήρα "wallet" occurs 7 times in N.T. incg. here, while θησαυρός "treasure" occurs in acc. sing. and pl. 7 times excluding here. As to the reason for the change, when tradition had elevated the Magi to the rank of kings, it was doubtless thought that the word "wallets" was not sufficiently impressive for the receptacles of the rich gifts of such exalted personages.

ii. 13, ἕως "until" (for καὶ ἴσθι ἐκεῖ ἕως ἄν " and be thou there until "). In the common text there are 8 divisions in this section : by taking these words out they are reduced to 7. Originally the passage ran : "Take the child and his mother, and flee into Egypt until I tell thee ; " a "pregnant construction," where St. Matthew shows what Dr. J. H. Moulton calls "his genius for compression."[1] The scribes' addition gives the right sense, but it was not what the evangelist wrote. It is a gloss adapted from ver. 15. The Word Test is rather complicated owing to scribal alterations elsewhere, the words being very common ones. Ἴσθι "be thou " and all other forms of the imperative including ἔστε in 1 Co. iii. 17[2] and excluding ἴσθι here, occur 21 times in N.T., of which 7 are in Lu. and Ac., and 7 in Paul. Ἐκεῖ "there," excluding here occurs 27 times in Mat., which is against us, but with its derivatives κἀκεῖ and ἐκεῖθεν 42, and with ἐκεῖνος and κἀκεῖνος also 98. Ἕως, ἕως ἄν and ἕως οὗ or ὅτου, all same meaning, are often interchanged by scribes. The following however may probably be relied upon. Ἕως occurs with verb 1 pers. sing. 14 times in N.T. including here, 7 alone and 7 with another particle : ἕως alone 7 (Mat. ii. 13, xxvi. 36 ; Mk. xiv. 32 ; Lu. xvii. 8 ; Jno. xxi. 22, 23 ; 1 Ti. iv. 13) ; ἕως ἄν 5 (all in same phrase Mat. xxii. 44 ; Mk. xii. 36 ; Lu. xx. 43 ; Ac. ii. 35 ; He. i. 13) ; ἕως οὗ Ac. xxv. 21 ; and ἕως ὅτου Lu. xiii. 8 ; total with another particle 7. Ἄν is therefore an interpolation here.

ii. 22, Βασιλεύει "is reigning" (for βασ. τῆς Ἰουδαίας WH, Βασ. ἐπὶ τ. Ἰουδ. R, "is reigning over Judea"). So Syr-sin rightly, against all Greek and other authorities.[3] Βασιλεύω governing the genitive is a very unusual construction. Blass, after giving a list of "verbs of ruling" which govern the genitive, says "but βασιλεύειν no longer governs the genitive, except in Mat. ii. 22."[4]

---

[1] *Gram.* v. 2, pt. i, p. 10.

[2] See p. 161.

[3] The Arabic "Gospel of the Infancy" may be cited in support ; it reads, "Hearing that Herod was dead, and that Archelaus his son reigned in his stead, he was afraid."

[4] *Gram.*, p. 104.

It is found once in the LXX, where this verb is used very frequently. It was doubtless on this account that the second interpolating scribe added ἐπί, which is now found in most MSS. Then it should be noticed that the verb here is in the present tense, not the past, as the A.V. and R.V. would imply. And it is not the "historic present," but we have the exact words of Joseph's informant (*oratio recta*) : "Archelaus is reigning in the room of his father Herod," and as the words were spoken in, or on the borders of, Judæa, there was no need to say "over Judæa." These words have been added as a gloss by a hypercritical scribe to show that Archelaus reigned over Judæa only, and to correct the inference which might be drawn that he succeeded to the whole of Herod's dominions, which included Galilee also. βασιλεύω occurs 21 times in N.T., 7 in Apoc. and 14 elsewhere ; 7 times it is followed by ἐπί or ἐν " to reign over *or* in," and 14 times including our present text, it stands alone, conveying the simple idea of reigning.

'Ιουδαία " Judæa " occurs 8 times in Mat. less here = 7, and 43 times in N.T. (incl. Lu. iv. 44[1], but excluding Mk. i. 5 and Jno. iii. 22, where the word is the fem. adj. from 'Ιουδαῖος[2]) less here = 42. The words 'Ιουδαία " Judæa," 'Ιουδαῖος " Jew " and 'Ιούδα " of Judah " occur in Mat. 15 times in all, less here = 14.

Τῆς tells both ways : it occurs 14 times in the two chh. incl. here, but of these 6 refer to women, and 8 to inanimate things, or 7 if taken out here.

ii. 22, Γαλειλαίας : so B ; Γαλιλαίας R, WH, etc. B is apparently the only authority for this spelling here, but it is found elsewhere in א 4 times and in D 7, also in C 3 times in Acts. As a rule differences of this nature are not shown in collations of MSS, but one of Scrivener's MSS (P) has Γαλλιλαίας. As it represents the Heb. גְּלִיל‎, גָּלִילָה‎. Galīl, Galīlah, with long ī. ει would appear to be the original spelling, altered in later times. The fact of א and C having this spelling in several places is especially striking.

One verse more remains to be examined, which we will deal with as briefly as possible.

Mat. i. 16, τὸν ἄνδρα Μαρίας, ἐξ ἧς ἐγεννήθη 'Ιησοῦς ὁ λεγόμενος Χριστός " the husband of Mary, of whom was born Jesus who is called Christ." So all Greek MSS except a small late group known as the Ferrar group, some MSS of which read ᾧ μνηστευθεῖσα παρθένος Μαριὰμ ἐγέννησεν 'Ιησοῦν τὸν λεγόμενον Χριστόν " to whom betrothed (the) Virgin Mary begat (*or* bare) Jesus who is called Christ." The Old Lat. and Old Syr. have similar readings

---

[1] St. Luke here and in some other places embraces the whole of Palestine, inclg. Galilee, in the term Judæa (Hastings' *D.B.* art. " Judæa ") so that there is no discrepancy between this ver. and Mk. i. 39. In Mk. i. 28, Lu. i. 26 א has Judæa for Galilee.

[2] Alford, marg. ref. on Jno. iii. 22.

with many variations, a common sign of spuriousness; thus, 7 MSS of the Old Lat. have five different readings, and the two Old Syr. MSS differ also. They all agree in giving an active verb instead of a passive, and so if we take the *text* of von Soden which is based on Syr-sin, we have 43 sentences in vv. 2–17 instead of 42, which at once condemns it, besides the fact that it would alter our other figures and destroy the heptadic symmetry of the whole passage.

An examination of some of the words leads to the same conclusion. ἐγεννήθη occurs 7 times in N.T. and ἐγέννησε(ν) 42 with present text; to change it would give 6 and 43. ὁ λεγόμενος with proper name before and after is found 7 times in N.T. (Mat. i. 16, x. 2; Jno. iv. 25, xi. 16, xx. 24, xxi. 2; Col. iv. 11); λεγόμενος alone (nom. masc.) 12 + λεγομένη (nom. fem.) 2 = 14, and λεγόμενον (acc. masc.) 10 + λεγομένην (acc. fem.) 4 = 14. These also would be altered by a change of text. ἐξ ἧς (fem.) "of whom" is found here only, but ἐξ οὗ (masc. and neut.) "of whom" etc., occurs 6 times (1 Cor. viii. 6; Eph. iii. 15, iv. 16; Ph. iii. 20; Col. ii. 19; He. xiii. 10), total 7. παρθένος "virgin" occurs 15 times, and its only derivative παρθενία "virginity" once. It is used once of males (Re. xiv. 4), but in the other 14 it has a female signification. It is found 7 times in Paul, 7 in nom. case, and 7 sing. with art. Counting pl. as = 2, it occurs in Mat. 3 pl. 1 sing. = 7, and in N.T. 6 pl. 9 sing. = 21. If we would bring παρθενία in we may add the 13 occurrences of παρθένος where it is used literally (all except 2 Cor. xi. 2; Re. xiv. 4), making 14. To adopt the Ferrar text would spoil most of these.

In Mat. i. alone ἐκ (ἐξ) occurs 7 times.

We may therefore unhesitatingly declare the common reading to be the true one. Why then was the alteration made? Not to get rid of the Virgin Birth; rather the contrary. As Mr. C. H. Turner says, "Doctrinal considerations may be safely put aside. . . . "The Virgin Birth is obviously of the essence of the narrative . . . the descent of Christ from David through Joseph would be meant to establish a legal rather than a natural descent and heirship."[1] The change was made in the second cent., the time when so many other textual alterations were made, probably to get rid of the word "husband" and to strengthen the orthodox belief by inserting the word "virgin."

The following is a list of all the words in the corrected Greek text of the two chh. showing the Parts of Speech according to the ancient Greek method, Noun including both Substantive and Adjective, while Verb and Participle are separate Parts of Speech. Proper Nouns

---

[1] *J.T.S.*, xi. 205.

are here separated from Common because of their exceptionally large number in these chh. The heptadic totals prove that Πνεῦμα Ἅγιον are rightly placed among the Proper Nouns, showing that Holy Spirit is the name of a Person, according to the orthodox Christian conception of the Third Person of the Trinity. Sometimes double names are treated as one Proper Noun, as Jesus Christ in Jno. xvii. 3, but they are not so here, showing that in doubtful cases the same rule is not followed everywhere. Sometimes (as in English) it is difficult to know whether to class a word as Adverb, Conjunction, or Preposition. The only word which needs mention here is ἕως,, which is an Adverb in ch. i. 17, and a Conjunction elsewhere.

GRAMMATICAL ANALYSIS OF MATTHEW i., ii.

	Verbs.	Nouns Proper.	Nouns Com. Subst. and Adj.	Pro-nouns.	Adverbs.	Participles.	Art.	Prep.	Conj.
i. 1–21	ἐγέννησε	Ἰησοῦ	βίβλος	αὐτοῦ	ἕως	λεγόμενος	τὸν	ἐκ	δὲ
	,,	Χριστοῦ	γενέσεως	,,	,,	μνηστευθείσης	,,	,,	,,
	,,	Δαυείδ	υἱοῦ	ἧς	,,	ἔχουσα	,,	,,	καὶ
	,,	Ἀβραάμ	,,	αὐτοῦ	οὕτω	θέλων	τοὺς	,,	δὲ
	,,	,,	ἀδελφοὺς	αὐτούς	μὴ	ἐνθυμηθέντος	τὸν	ἐπὶ	καὶ
	,,	Ἰσαάκ	βασιλέα	αὐτῆς	λάθρᾳ	λέγων	,,	μετὰ	δὲ
	,,	,,	ἀδελφοὺς	αὐτὴν	μὴ	γεννηθὲν	τῆς	ἐξ	,,
	,,	Ἰακώβ	μετοικεσίας	,,			τὸν	ἀπὸ	,,
	,,	,,	μετοικεσίαν	ταῦτα			,,	,,	,,
	,,	Ἰούδαν	ἄνδρα	αὐτοῦ			,,	,,	,,
	,,	Ἰούδας	πᾶσαι	αὐτῷ			,,	ἐν	,,
	,,	Φαρὲς	γενεαί	σου			,,	ἐκ	,,
	,,	Ζαρά	,,	αὐτῇ			,,	κατ'	,,
	,,	Θάμαρ	δεκατέσσαρες	αὐτοῦ			,,	ἐν	,,
	,,	Φαρὲς	μετοικεσίας	αὐτὸς			τὸν	ἐκ	,,
	,,	Ἐσρώμ	γενεαί	αὐτῶν			τῆς	ἀπὸ	,,
	,,	,,	δεκατέσσαρες				τὸν		,,
	,,	Ἀράμ	μετοικεσίας				,,		,,
	,,	Ἀμιναδάβ	γενεαί				,,		,,
	,,	,,	δεκατέσσαρες				,,		,,
	,,	Ναασσών	γέννησις				τῆς		,,
	,,	,,	μητρὸς				τοῦ		,,
	,,	Σαλμών	γαστρὶ				τὸν		,,
	,,	,,	ἀνὴρ				,,		,,
	,,	Βοόζ	δίκαιος				,,		,,
	,,	Ῥαχάβ	ἄγγελος				,,		,,
	,,	Βοόζ	ὄναρ				,,		,,
	,,	Ἰωβήδ	υἱὸς				,,		,,
	,,	Ῥούθ	γυναῖκα				,,		καὶ
	,,		υἱόν				,,		δὲ

GRAMMATICAL ANALYSIS OF MATTHEW i., ii.—*contd.*

	Verbs.	Nouns Proper.	Nouns Com. Subst. and Adj.	Pronouns.	Adverbs.	Participles.	Art.	Prep.	Conj.
i. 1 21	ἐγέννησε	Ἰωβὴδ	ὄνομα				τὸν		δὲ
	,,	Ἰεσσαί	λαὸν				,,		,,
	,,	,,	ἁμαρτιῶν				,,		,,
	,,	Δαυεὶδ					,,		,,
	,,	,,					,,		,,
	,,	Σολομῶνα					τοὺς		,,
	,,	Οὐρείου					τῆς		,,
	,,	Σολομὼν					τὴν		,,
	,,	Ῥοβοάμ					τὸν		,,
	ἐγεννήθη	,,					,,		,,
	συνελθεῖν	Ἀβιά					,,		οὖν
	εὑρέθη	,,					,,		καί
	δειγματίσαι	Ἀσάφ					,,		,,
	ἐβουλήθη	,,					,,		δὲ
	ἀπολῦσαι	Ἰωσαφὰτ					,,		πρὶν
	ἰδού	,,					,,		ἤ
	ἐφάνη	Ἰωράμ					,,		δὲ
	φοβηθῇς	,,					,,		καί
	παραλαβεῖν	Ὀζείαν					,,		δὲ
	ἐστιν	Ὀζείας					,,		γὰρ
	τέξεται	Ἰωάθαμ					ὁ		δὲ
	καλέσεις	,,					αἱ		καί
	σώσει	Ἀχάζ					τῆς		γὰρ
		,,					,,		
		Ἐζεκίαν					τοῦ		
		Ἐζεκίας							
		Μανασσῆ					ἡ,,		
		Μανασσῆς					τῆς		
		Ἀμώς					τῷ		
		,,					ὁ		
		Ἰωσείαν					τὴν		
		Ἰωσείας					τὸ		
		Ἰεχονίαν							
		Βαβυλῶνος					τὸν		
		,,					τῶν		
		Ἰεχονίας							
		Σαλαθιήλ							
		,,							
		Ζοροβάβελ							
		,,							
		Ἀβιούδ							
		,,							
		Ἐλιακείμ							
		,,							
		Ἀζώρ							
		,,							
		Σαδώκ							
		,,							
		Ἀχείμ							
		,,							
		Ἐλιούδ							
		,,							

GRAMMATICAL ANALYSIS OF MATTHEW i., ii.—*contd.*

	Verbs.	Nouns Proper.	Nouns Com. Subst. and Adj.	Pro-nouns.	Adverbs.	Participles.	Art.	Prep.	Conj.
		Ἐλεάζαρ ,, Ματθάν ,, Ἰακώβ ,, Ἰωσήφ Μαρίας Ἰησοῦς Χριστός Ἀβραὰμ Δαυείδ Βαβυλῶνος ,, Χριστοῦ ,, Ἰησοῦ Χριστοῦ Μαρίας Ἰωσήφ Πνεύματος Ἁγίου Ἰωσήφ Κυρίου Ἰωσήφ Δαυείδ Μαριὰμ Πνεύματος Ἁγίου Ἰησοῦν							
	53·414	112·673	33·233	16·76	7·23	7·58	66·191	16·40	54·119
		Total	364 words,	1827	letters				
i. 22-25	γέγονεν πληρωθῇ ἰδού ἕξει τέξεται καλέσουσι ἐστι ἐποίησεν προσέταξεν παρέλαβε ἐγίνωσκεν ἔτεκε ἐκάλεσε	Κυρίου Ἐμμανουήλ Θεός Ἰωσήφ Κυρίου Ἰησοῦν	ὅλον προφήτου παρθένος γαστρὶ υἱόν ὄνομα ὕπνου ἄγγελος γυναῖκα υἱόν ὄνομα	τοῦτο αὐτοῦ ὅ ἡμῶν αὐτῷ αὐτοῦ αὐτήν αὐτοῦ	ὡς οὐκ οὗ	ῥηθὲν λέγοντος μεθερμηνευό- μενον ἐγερθείς	τὸ τοῦ ἡ τὸ ὁ ,, τοῦ ὁ τὴν τὸν τὸ	ὑπὸ διὰ ἐν μεθ' ἀπὸ	δὲ ἵνα καὶ ,, δὲ καὶ ,, ἕως καὶ
	13·90	6·36	11·63	8·85	3·7	4·37	11·22	5·14	9·25
		Total	70 words,	329	letters				
ii. 1-8	ἰδού παρεγένοντο	Ἰησοῦ Βηθλεὲμ	ἡμέραις βασιλέως	αὐτοῦ αὐτῷ	τοῦ ,,	γεννηθέντος λέγοντες	τοῦ τῆς	ἐν ,,	δὲ γὰρ

GRAMMATICAL ANALYSIS OF MATTHEW i., ii.—*contd.*

Verbs.	Nouns Proper.	Nouns Com. Subst. and Adj.	Pronouns.	Adverbs.	Participles.	Art.	Prep.	Conj.
ἐστὶν	Ἰουδαίας	μάγοι	αὐτοῦ	οὕτω	τεχθεὶς	τοῦ	ἀπὸ	καὶ
εἴδομεν	Ἡρῴδου	ἀνατολῶν	αὐτῶν	οὐδαμῶς	ἀκούσας	ὁ	εἰς	"
ἤλθομεν	Ἱεροσόλυμα	βασιλεὺς	σύ	τότε	συναγαγὼν	τῶν	ἐν	"
προσκυνῆσαι	Ἰουδαίων	ἀστέρα	σοῦ	λάθρᾳ	καλέσας	τὸν	μετ᾽	"
ἐταράχθη	Ἡρῴδης	ἀνατολῇ	ὅστις	ἀκριβῶς	φαινομένου	τῇ	παρ᾽	"
ἐπυνθάνετο	Ἱεροσόλυμα	βασιλεὺς	μου		πέμψας	ὁ	ἐν	δὲ
γεννᾶται	Χριστὸς	πᾶσα	αὐτῶν		πορευθέντες	τοὺς	διὰ	γὰρ
εἶπον	Βηθλεὲμ	πάντας	αὐτούς		ἐλθὼν	τοῦ	ἐν	καὶ
γέγραπται	Ἰουδαίας	ἀρχιερεῖς	μοι			ὁ	ἐκ	γὰρ
εἰ	Βηθλεὲμ	γραμματεῖς	κἀγὼ			οἱ	παρ᾽	καὶ
ἐξελεύσεται	Ἰούδα	λαοῦ	αὐτῷ			τῆς	εἰς	ἐπὰν
ποιμανεῖ	"	προφήτου				τοῦ	περὶ	δὲ
ἠκρίβωσε	Ἰσραήλ	γῆ				τοῖς		ὅπως
εἶπε	Ἡρῴδης	ἐλαχίστη				τὸν		
ἐξετάσατε	Βηθλεὲμ	ἡγεμόσιν				"		
εὕρητε		ἡγούμενος				τοὺς		
ἀπαγγείλατε		λαόν				τὸν		
προσκυνήσω		μάγους				τοῦ		
		χρόνον				"		
		ἀστέρος						
		παιδίου						
20·154	**17·121**	**23·156**	**13·56**	**7·34**	**10·81**	**21·59**	**14·37**	**15·44**
		Total 140 words	742 letters					

ii. 9–12	Verbs.	Nouns Proper.	Nouns Com. Subst. and Adj.	Pronouns.	Adverbs.	Participles.	Art.	Prep.	Conj.
	ἐπορεύθησαν	Μαρίας	βασιλέως	ὃν	ἐπάνω	ἀκούσαντες	οἱ	ἐν	δὲ
	ἰδού	Ἡρῴδην	ἀστὴρ	αὐτούς	σφόδρα	ἐλθὼν	τοῦ	εἰς	καὶ
	εἶδον		ἀνατολῇ	αὐτοῦ	μὴ	ἰδόντες	ὁ	μετὰ	ἕως
	προῆγεν		παιδίου	αὐτῷ		ἐλθόντες	τῷ	κατ᾽	δὲ
	ἐστάθη		ἀστέρα	αὐτῶν		πεσόντες	τοῦ	πρὸς	καὶ
	ἐχάρησαν		χαρὰν	αὐτῷ		ἀνοίξαντες	τὸν	δι᾽	"
	εἶδον		μεγάλην	αὐτῶν		χρηματισθέντες	τὴν	εἰς	"
	προσεκύνησαν		οἰκίαν				τὸ		"
	προσήνεγκαν		παιδίον				τῆς		"
	ἀνακάμψαι		μητρὸς				τὰς		
	ἀνεχώρησαν		πήρας				τὴν		
			δῶρα						
			χρυσὸν						
			λίβανον						
			σμύρναν						
			ὄναρ						
			ἄλλης						
			ὁδοῦ						
			χώραν						
	11·88	**2·13**	**19·112**	**7·33**	**3·13**	**7·62**	**11·29**	**7·21**	**10·28**
			Total 77 words	399 letters					

ii. 13–18	Verbs.	Nouns Proper.	Nouns Com. Subst. and Adj.	Pronouns.	Adverbs.	Participles.	Art.	Prep.	Conj.
	ἰδού	Κυρίου	ἄγγελος	αὐτῶν	ἐκεῖ	ἀναχωρησάντων	τῷ	κατ᾽	δὲ
	ἐφάνη	Ἰωσὴφ	ὄναρ	αὐτοῦ	τότε	λέγων	τὸ	εἰς	καὶ
	παράλαβε	Αἴγυπτον	παιδίον	σοί	λελίαν	ἐγερθεὶς	τὴν	"	"
	φεῦγε	Ἡρῴδης	μητέρα	αὐτὸ	κατωτέρω	"	τὸ	ὑπὸ	ἕως
	εἶπω	Αἴγυπτον	παιδίον	αὐτοῦ	τότε	ῥηθὲν	τοῦ	διὰ	γὰρ

GRAMMATICAL ANALYSIS OF MATTHEW i., ii.—*contd.*

	Verbs.	Nouns Proper.	Nouns Com. Subst. and Adj.	Pro-nouns.	Adverbs.	Participles.	Art.	Prep.	Conj.
	μέλλει	Ἡρῴδου	παιδίον	μου	οὐκ	λέγοντος	ὁ	ἐξ	δὲ
	ζητεῖν	Κυρίου	μητέρα	αὐτῆς	,,	ἰδὼν	τὸ	ὑπὸ	καὶ
	ἀπολέσαι	Αἰγύπτου	νυκτός	ὃν		ἀποστείλας	τὴν	ἐν	,,
	παρέλαβε	Ἡρῴδης	τελευτῆς	αὐτῆς		ῥηθὲν	τῆς	,,	,,
	ἀνεχώρησεν	Βηθλεὲμ	προφήτου			λέγοντος	τὸ	ἀπὸ	ἕως
	ἦν	Ἱερεμίου,	υἱόν			κλαίουσα	τοῦ	κατὰ	ἵνα
	πληρωθῇ	Ῥαμὰ	μάγων				τὸν	παρὰ	ὅτι
	ἐκάλεσα	Ῥαχὴλ	πάντας				τῶν	διὰ	καὶ
	ἐνεπαίχθη		παῖδας				τοὺς	ἐν	,,
	ἐθυμώθη		πᾶσι				,,		,,
	ἀνεῖλε		ὁρίοις				τοῖς		,,
	ἠκρίβωσε		διετοῦς				τὸν		,,
	ἐπληρώθη		χρόνον				τῶν		ὅτι
	ἠκούσθη		μάγων				τὸ		
	ἤθελε		προφήτου				τοῦ		
	παρακληθῆναι		φωνὴ				τὰ		
	εἰσίν		κλαυθμὸς						
			ὀδυρμὸς						
			πολύς						
			τέκνα						
	22·148	13·86	25·152	9·37	7·31	11·82	21·58	14·40	18·52
		Total	140 words	686	letters				
ii.19–23	ἰδοὺ	Ἡρῴδου	ἄγγελος	αὐτοῦ	ἐκεῖ	τελευτήσαντος	τοῦ	κατ'	δὲ
	φαίνεται	Κυρίου	ὄναρ	,,		λέγων	τῷ	ἐν	καὶ
	παρέλαβε	Ἰωσὴφ	παιδίον	,,		ἐγερθείς	τὸ	εἰς	,,
	πορεύου	Αἰγύπτῳ	μητέρα			ζητοῦντες	τὴν	,,	γὰρ
	τεθνήκασι	Ἰσραὴλ	γῆν .			ἐγερθείς	οἱ	ἀντὶ	δὲ
	παρέλαβε	,,	ψυχὴν			ἀκούσας	τὴν	κατ'	καὶ
	εἰσῆλθεν	Ἀρχέλαος	παιδίον			χρηματισθεὶς	τοῦ	εἰς	,,
	βασιλεύει	Ἡρῴδου	παιδίον			ἐλθὼν	ὁ	,,	δὲ
	ἐφοβήθη	Γαλειλαίας	μητέρα			λεγομένην	τὸ	διὰ	ὅτι
	ἀπελθεῖν	Ναζαρὲτ	γῆν			ῥηθὲν	τὴν		δὲ
	ἀνεχώρησεν	Ναζωραῖος	πατρὸς				τοῦ		καὶ
	κατῴκησεν		ὄναρ				τὰ		ὅπως
	πληρωθῇ		μέρη				τῆς		ὅτι
	κληθήσεται		πόλιν				τὸ		
			προφητῶν				τῶν		
	14·114	11·79	15·82	3·15	1·4	10·81	15·38	9·27	13·30
		Total	91 words	476 l	etters				
Totals of ch. i. ii.	{ 133 w.	161 w.	126 w.	56 w.	28 w.	49 w.	145 w.	65 w	119 w.
	{ 1008 l.	1008 l.	798 l.	252 l.	112 l.	401 l.	397 l.	179 l.	304 l.
		Grand	total 882	word	s = 7 ×	7 × 3 × 6.			
			4459	letter	s = 7 ×	7 × 7 × 13			

A few Heptadic Notes on the two chh. may be added, though they may not all be deemed of equal import-ance.

The *Proper Names* make **98** words **588** letters in the genealogy i. 1–17, and **63** words **420** letters in the rest of the two chh. (including **14** words in i. 18–21). **49** persons (exclusive of Divine Persons) are mentioned by name—46 in the genealogy i. 1–17 (**42** men and **4** women) and 3 later, Herod, Archelaus and Jeremiah. Rachel is not counted, as the name does not stand for a real person, but is used figuratively.

The *Divine Names* occur (1) Of the Father : God **1**, Lord **6** = **7** ; (2) Of the Son : Jesus **6**, Christ **5**, Emmanuel **1** = **12** words **77** letters ; the 12 may be made into an heptadic number in two ways—by adding King of the Jews **1**, and Governor **1** = **14** words containing **105** letters, or by adding Παιδίον " young child " **9** = **21** words **140** letters. Or put in another way, Jesus Christ occurs 3 times, Jesus (alone) 3, Christ (alone) 2, Emmanuel **1** = **9**, the square of the Divine number 3. (3) The Holy Spirit is only named twice, both times in the form Πνεύματος Ἁγίου = **4** words, **28** letters.

Names of women occur **7** times : Mary **4**, Thamar, Rahab, Ruth, each **1** = **7** ; Uriah's wife is not mentioned by name, and Rachel is again excluded. Joseph occurs **7** times, and Herod (alone) **7**, besides " Herod the king," twice.

Common Nouns : Son **7** ; Father **1** and Mother **6** = **7** ; King **5**, Prince **1** and Governor **1** = **7**.

Of the **56** *Pronouns*, **49** refer to Persons ; **49** (but not the same) are Personal Pronouns and **7** other kinds ; 6 refer to Joseph, 6 to Mary, and 1 (pl.) to both = **7** to each ; 17 refer to Jesus : αὐτός **7**, αὐτό **9** and ὅστις **1**. Αὐτή (fem.) occurs **7** times in all (**35** letters), αὐτός (masc.) **7** in i. 18–21. There are **7** pronouns in the section ii. 9–12.

We have seen that παιδίον " young child " and its pronoun αὐτό, all referring to Jesus, each occur 9 times ; is this accidental, or is there in the double square of the Divine number 3 a reference to His Divine nature ?

The *Article* occurs **70** times in sing. accus. (all genders), and **21** in Neuter (all cases): τό **14**: nom. masc. **14**: gen. masc. sing. **14**: gen. fem. **14**; dative (all forms) **7**. There are **21** occurrences of the Article in the Sec. ii. 1–8, **21** in the Sec. ii. 13–18, and **56** in the genealogy i. 1–17, of which τόν = **42**, τῆς **7**, and other forms **7**.

Verbs are used **14** times in ii. 19–23, and *Participles* **7** in i. 1–21; **7** in ii. 9–12. Verbs and Participles together: ἔρχομαι and derr. 9 times in **7** forms; καλέω **7** times in **7** forms; act. part. of λέγω **7**; other words for " say," " spoken " are εἶπω etc. 3 and ῥηθέν 4 = **7**.

Adverbs occur **7** times in the sec. i. 1–21; **7** in ii. 1–8; **7** in ii. 13–18.

Conjunctions: In i. 1–21 καί occurs **7** and δέ **42** times; in i. 22–25 καί and δέ **7**; in ii. 1–8 καί **7**; in ii. 9–12 καί **7**; γάρ is used **7** times in all, and ἕως (as conj. and adv.) **7**.

Prepositions are used **14** times in ii. 1–8; **7** in ii. 9–12; **14** in ii. 13–18. 'Από occurs **7** times, κατά 6 + κατωτέρω 1 = **7**; ἐκ **7** besides ἐξ 2. There are **14** different prepositions used in the two chh. if we may count ἐκ and ἐξ separately.

Finally, the number of different words used by the Evangelist in the two chh. is **259** (7 × 37), or if we count each inflection separately the number of different forms is **357** (7 × 3 × 17). Now 37 is an important number according to Gematrists, being the " meta-cube " of 64, and a factor in a large number of Titles of our Lord.[1] 3 and 17 are also notable numbers.

Other Sevens may be found by the diligent searcher, but those which have been given are enough, and more than enough, for our purpose.

Until the whole of the N.T. has been heptadically examined, or at least the whole of St. Matthew's Gospel, it would be premature, perhaps, to speak

[1] Lea & Bond: *Apostolic Gnosis*, Pt. I, p. 26; Pt. II, p. 133; *Cabala*, p. 30.

positively ; but subject to this and to the spelling of one or two words, such as *Booζ* where I have simply followed R, I would pronounce the text just given to be in agreement with the autograph text of the Evangelist.

There are two other avenues which I have not explored where it is perhaps possible that further confirmation may be found. In the *Magnificat* we saw (see Ch. I) that counting the occurrences of each letter of the alphabet gave remarkable results ; perhaps the same would help us here to settle doubtful questions of orthography. The second avenue is Gematria, which has found advocates in Mr. Ivan Panin in America and Messrs. Lea & Bond in England. But I must leave these matters to younger eyes than mine.

It may be asked, Are there then some places in the N.T. where the true text has been lost from all existing documents ? On this point WH say, "We have never observed the slightest trace of undetected interpolations or corruptions *of any moment*,[1] and entirely disbelieve their existence. There are, however, some passages which one or both of us suspect to contain a primitive error of no great importance, and which [we have] accordingly indicated as open to question." [2] One of the few passages thus indicated by them I propose to examine. It is one of some little importance, on account of its possible bearing on the question of the length of our Lord's ministry, and it is a verse which not both, but only one of the co-editors, " suspects to contain a primitive error." The passage is John vi. 4, which reads in rec. text, and, indeed, in all others, " And *the passover*, the [3] feast of the Jews, was nigh." WH's joint note on the verse runs,

---

[1] I have italicized these words, for this reservation is necessary. Prof. A. Souter says, " A reading may be right, even if no single Greek MS contains it." (*Expositor*, February, 1922. p. 135.)

[2] *N.T. in Greek*, smaller ed. (1885), p. 564.

[3] So the Greek, and not *" a feast "* as A.V

"*Omit* ' the passover,' apparently, some Fathers and other ancient writers, though it stands in all extant Greek manuscripts and versions." Westcott's own opinion is given in his *Commentary :* "All direct documentary evidence whatever supports the disputed words. The ground for suspecting them is derived indirectly from patristic citations, and it is by no means clear that there is not in the passages quoted a confusion between vi. 4 and vii. 2."[1] He therefore holds the words to be genuine. But these patristic citations, as given by Mr. Henry Browne, in his Treatise on the Chronology of the Holy Scriptures,[2] hardly merit being dismissed so summarily. It is true the evidence is chiefly of a negative character, and Mr. Browne has an object in trying to get rid of the words, for, if genuine, they entirely overthrow his theory that " the Lord's ministry lasted little more than one year."[3] But he appears to show pretty conclusively (1) that Irenæus in the second century, Origen in the third, and (perhaps) Cyril of Alexandria in the early part of the fourth, all wrote as if they were ignorant of any such passover as that here mentioned ; and (2) that several early Fathers " concur in assigning to the ministry of our Lord after His baptism a term of little more than one year,"[4] which they could hardly have done had their copies of St. John's Gospel spoken distinctly of three passovers, as do ours. Other evidence may be seen in the long note of Dr. Hort, who, in opposition to his colleague, gave it as his opinion that " it is difficult, if not impossible, to account for the large body of indirect evidence which points to the neglect of [" the passover "] here, except on the supposition that these words (or the whole verse) were absent from various texts of Cent. II. and III."[5]

Let us now apply the HEPTAD TEST.

The heptad in which the words stand consists of

[1] *Speaker's Comm.*, St. John's Gospel, introd. note to ch. vi.
[2] *Ordo Sæclorum*, pp. 86–89.   [3] Idem, p. 92.   [4] Idem, p. 81.
[5] Appendix to *N.T. in Greek*, p. 80.

John vi. 1-5, and contains in rec. text 74 words, 353 letters. The following corrections are supported by nearly all editors : In ver. 2, for *kai ēkolouthei*, "and followed," read *ēkolouthei de* (same meaning) ; in ver. 3 omit the article before " Jesus ; " and, again, in ver. 5, before " Philip." The Greek word for " saw," ver. 2, stands in several forms in the ancient MSS, all having practically the same meaning : (1) rec. א, etc., read *heōrōn ;* (2) B, D, etc., *etheōroun ;* (3) A, Θ, have *etheōrōn*, which is also found in some good cursives 13–346. No. (2) has the best support, and is adopted by Rev. and most Editors ; but I believe (3) to be the original, for it is the most difficult, being an unusual, if not quite unique, grammatical form, and it best accounts for the other two variants.[1]

None of these four alterations affect the English translation in the slightest degree. But there is another word which requires examination, viz. *autou*, " his," in ver. 2. It is omitted by all the most ancient manuscripts, א, A, B, D, W (C is defective in this chapter), and by all the ancient versions : but is found in Δ, E (two good manuscripts of the eighth or ninth century), and in the mass of later authorities ; Chrysostom (fourth century) is also cited in its favour. It is not surprising, therefore, that, while rec. contains the word, it is omitted by Rev. and all recent editors ; yet it is genuine. *Autou* is too common a word, and is dealt with too loosely by scribes to apply the test by counting its occurrences in the whole of the New Testament, or even in the whole of St. John's Gospel, until the other places where doubt exists have been carefully examined ; but we need not go so far afield. The sixth chapter of St. John forms a complete section : the word *autou* occurs in it in rec. 19 times, but must be struck out once in ver. 22 (so all editors), leaving 18 : of these it is joined to "disciples " 11 times, and 7 times (including ver. 2) to other words. If the distinction between αὐτοῦ, " his," and αὐτοῦ, strictly " his own," can be

[1] So Abbott: *Johannine Vocabulary*, 1605*.

maintained, as I believe from the following that it can (and I am happy to find that WH, though to a limited extent, take the same view [1]), the proof is much clearer: αὐτοῦ occurs (less ver. 22, as before noted) **14** times in the chapter, **7** times connected with " disciples," and **7** not. Again, αὐτός occurs with *theōreō*, " to see," in N.T. **7** times in masc. gender, though I am not sure whether this can be insisted upon. We must acknowledge, then, the correctness of rec. in reading *autou* in ver. 2 ; it has been omitted at a very early date on account of its apparent redundancy, as it also is in ch. ii. 23, in several authorities.

We now come to the words *to pascha*, " the passover." *Pascha* occurs in N.T. in rec. 29 times ; omit here, and we have **28** : the art. occurs in the heptad **10** times in sing., but we have already deleted it in two places ; omit here also, and we have **7** : the words, therefore, are spurious ; they are a very early " gloss."

Thus we have taken out from rec. 4 words, 10 letters, leaving **70** words, **848** letters, in the heptad—a proof that our alterations are rightly made. In Rev., which has 73 words 350 letters, the following corrections are required : ver. 2 for ἐθεώρουν read ἐθεώρων αὐτοῦ ; and take out ver. 3 ὁ, ver. 4 τὸ πάσχα, ver. 5 τὸν.

It may be well to give the heptad in full, in order to show the divisions.

JOHN VI.

1   (*1*) After these things Jesus went over the sea of Galilee,
2 which is (the sea) of Tiberias. (*2*) *And* a great multitude
   followed him, (*3*) because they *saw* his miracles which he did on
3 them that were diseased. (*4*) And . . . Jesus went up into a
4 mountain, (*5*) AND there he sat with his disciples. (*6*) And . . .
5 the feast of the Jews was nigh. (*7*) When Jesus then lifted up
   (his) eyes, AND saw a great company come unto him, he saith
   unto . . . Philip, Whence shall we buy bread, that these may
   eat ?

   Italics signify an alteration from rec., and three dots an omission.

---

[1] Appendix to *N.T. in Greek*, p. 144. So also Winer, Moulton & Robertson.

It will be remembered that in St. John's Gospel each grammatical sentence forms an heptadic division, without reference to its commencing with " and." [1]

THE inquiry now suggests itself, What is the state of the text of the New Testament ? I would answer this by referring to the case of Job. Of him we are told that he was " perfect and upright, and one that feared God and eschewed evil." [2] Yet the man upon whom the word of God pronounces such a high eulogium was afflicted as few men have been. But only so far as God permitted it. " The LORD said unto Satan, Behold, he is in thine hand ; only *spare his life*." [3] Even so " the word of the LORD is tried," [4] but its LIFE is untouched. And in nothing is the providence of God more clearly manifested than in this, that amid all the corruptions which succeeding centuries have laid upon Scripture, it has always been, and still is, " *living* and active, and sharper than any two-edged sword." [5] It has always been, and still is, " able to make . . . wise unto salvation through faith which is in Christ Jesus." [6] And many as are the errors which the received text of the New Testament undoubtedly contains, none of them are of very great moment ; and I have no hesitation in saying that it is a far truer representation of the word of God than is either the Vatican MS (B) or the Sinaitic (ℵ). Not that I would underrate the value of those excellent manuscripts. They are probably the two best *helps* we possess for the study of the text of the New Testament, but they must be used *as* helps, and not

---

[1] It by no means necessarily follows from the omission of " the passover " here, that our Lord's ministry lasted only one year. An insuperable difficulty in the way of that theory has, however, been removed ; and it is rendered more probable still if Mr. Browne is right (as he appears to be, see Dr. Ginsburg in *Kitto's Cyclopædia*, Alexander's ed., iii. 927) in stating that the phrase *the feast*, standing by itself, always denotes the feast of Tabernacles (*Ordo Sæclorum*, p. 87). So Hastings' *D.C.G.*, art. " Dates," i. 412[a].

[2] Job i. 1.   [3] Job ii. 6, R.V.   [4] Ps. xviii. 30.

[5] Heb. iv. 12, R.V.   [6] 2 Tim. iii. 15.

allowed to dominate over all other authorities. Modern criticism has, on the whole, run in the right direction, but the principles it has laid down must only be acted upon *generally*, and not be deemed to be of universal application. As to the respective merits of the Authorized Version and the Revised, as representatives of the true Greek text, while the latter contains but few errors in comparison with the former, those few are of a far more serious nature. Let Englishmen, therefore, for the present, hold fast by their Authorized Version; on no account must the Revised Version, as it now stands, be allowed to be substituted for it. The Authorized Version unquestionably needs revision, and it is to the glory of the Church of England that she has, by virtue of her position as the leading representative in this land of the catholic Church, which is " a witness and a keeper of holy writ," [1] attempted the work. But it was not the act of the whole Church, but of a *Committee* appointed by a *section* of the Church. The Revision of the Authorized Version, it must be remembered, was undertaken by the Convocation of the Province of Canterbury only, in conjunction with other scholars, British and American. The Convocation of the Northern Province distinctly refused both to join in the work beforehand, and to express approval of it when completed. When the time is ripe for re-revision, doubtless it will be otherwise ; and when the whole Church unites in the work of preparing for her children a more faithful translation of the word of God than they now possess, no doubt a book worthy to succeed the present Authorized Version will be produced. Until then, we can well afford to wait. At the same time, the Revisers were indeed worthy of the most " sincere thanks " for their " arduous and conscientious labours."

Meanwhile, the way must be prepared—as in the past so now—by the labours of individual scholars. But it should be done in the spirit which animated, that noble and faithful servant of God, Dr. Tregelles

[1] Article XX.

when he wrote " I cannot, however, cease to state, that it is only a Christian scholar who can use these things rightly in the fullest sense ; for he alone knows the full value of Holy Scripture as the record of the Holy Ghost, given to make wise unto salvation, through faith which is in Christ Jesus : and he only can rightly apprehend what that spirit of prayer is, in which all Biblical studies should be carried on." [1]

OLD TESTAMENT.

We now come to the study of the text of the Old Testament, to which we must apply the same principles as to that of the New, due allowance being made for difference in language, etc.   But here we meet with an initial difficulty.   " The Textual Criticism of the Old Testament," says the American scholar Dr. C. A. Briggs, " is at least half a century behind the New Testament.   And the reason of it is, that scholars have hesitated to go back of the Massoretic text." [2]   But this is not the only reason.   For it is a very difficult matter to " go back of the Massoretic text."   Unlike the New Testament, " the Received, or, as it is commonly called, the Massoretic Text of the Old Testament Scriptures," say the Revisers in their preface, " has come down to us in manuscripts which are of no very great antiquity, and which all belong to the same family or recension.[3]   That other recensions were at one time in existence is probable from the variations in the Ancient Versions, the oldest of which, namely the Greek or Septuagint, was made, at least in part, some two centuries before the Christian era."

The chief authorities at present [4] available for the

---

[1] Tregelles' *Greek Testament*, Introductory Notice to Part I, p. vii.   [2] *Biblical Study*, p. 150.

[3] " The earliest MS of which the age is certainly known bears date A.D. 916 " (*Revisers' Note*). Ginsburg describes a MS which he assigns to *c.* A.D. 830, *Intr. Heb. Bib.* 475.   Driver's *Samuel*[2], xxxiv. n. 3.

[4] I say "at present," for recent discoveries tend to keep alive the hope that still more valuable documents may some day be unearthed,

revision of the text of the Old Testament may be thus briefly described :—

(1) HEBREW MANUSCRIPTS. These, as we have seen, are almost all of comparatively recent date. A large number were examined and collated (i.e. compared with the received text, and their differences therefrom noted down) by Kennicott and De Rossi towards the close of the eighteenth century, and more recently Ginsburg and others have laboured in the same field. The variations which have been discovered are for the most part of comparatively slight importance. The common printed Heb. text can be shown to be practically the same as that current among the Jews as far back as the second cent. A.D., except the vowel points.

(2) SAMARITAN MANUSCRIPTS (Pentateuch only), presenting the Hebrew text in Samaritan characters. The origin of the Samaritan Pentateuch is not known, but most scholars are of opinion that it existed at least as early as the fifth century B.C.,[1] so that it is an important witness, all the more so from the fact that "the Jews have no dealings with the Samaritans."[2] Where it differs from the Heb. it is often supported by the Sept.

(3) The chief VERSIONS used in the criticism of the text of the Old Testament are the Greek, Aramaic, Syriac, and Latin.

Greek. (a) First in importance is the LXX, or *Septuagint*, which modern scholars suppose to have been made at different times, part in the third and the remainder in the second century B.C. or later. MSS of this version, written in the fourth and fifth centuries A.D., still exist ; for the four best extant manuscripts

[1] Prof. J. E. H. Thomson makes out a strong case, based largely on the ancient Heb. script and the pronunciation of the gutturals, for dating it many centuries earlier, but admits a drastic revision of it (*Samaritans*, p. 325). He holds that the Heb. and Sam. recensions parted company about the time of Solomon or the division of the kingdom in the succeeding reign (*id.*, p. 385. *Jrnl. of Victoria Institute* lii. 154).

[2] John iv. 9,

of the Greek N.T. originally formed part of complete Bibles, and although most of the O.T. portions of א and C have been lost, yet A and B remain almost entire. As in the N.T. so here, the text of B is generally, but not always, the best, and it forms the basis of the editions of the Septuagint in common use. Dr. Swete's edition contains a collation of the above four MSS and some others. At the beginning of the last century, a splendid edition of the Septuagint, in five volumes, folio, was published at the Oxford University Press. It was prepared by Holmes and Parsons, and gives the various readings of a large number of MSS, also of certain versions and Fathers. The cost of its preparation, like that of Kennicott's edition of the Hebrew Bible, was defrayed by public subscription. A new critical edition, brought up to date, is now in course of publication by the Cambridge Univ. Press.

At least three other Greek translations of the O.T. were made in the second century A.D., but none of them now exist in anything approaching to a complete state. (b) That of *Aquila*, a Jewish proselyte, is exceedingly literal, at times indeed ridiculously so, but this makes it all the more valuable in the criticism of the Hebrew text. (c) That of *Theodotion* appears to have been based upon the Sept. (d) That of *Symmachus* is freer than either of the others, and is therefore less useful for critical purposes. The whole of these three translations, as complete works, have perished, the only considerable portion of any of them remaining being Theodotion's version of the Book of Daniel, which was substituted for that of the Sept. by the early Christians, as being more correct. With this exception, our knowledge of these versions is derived chiefly from notices in the writings of the Fathers, on the margin of manuscripts of the Sept., etc. The fragments (for such they literally are, consisting of sometimes a single word, sometimes a phrase, occasionally a few verses) which have been thus preserved have been carefully collected by several scholars, and are given in Field's edition of the *Hexapla* of Origen, published in 1875 at the Oxford University Press. Since then some further portions have been discovered and published.

The *Aramaic* Versions of the Old Testament are known as *Targums*. The most ancient and most literal is that on the Pentateuch, ascribed to *Onkelos ;* next to which in value is that on the Prophets and most of the historical books, by *Jonathan ben Uzziel*. These appear to have been made early in the Christian era, but the exact dates are not known.

The *Syriac* Version, called the *Peshitta*, was probably made in the second century A.D. or earlier, directly from the Hebrew for the most part.

Latin. (*a*) The *Old Latin* Version of the O.T. was not made from the Hebrew (a language of which but few of the early Christians had any knowledge) but from the Sept., and therefore is of more use in the criticism of that version than of the Heb. ; it exists, however, only in fragments. (*b*) Jerome translated the whole of the O.T. direct from the Heb., finishing the work A.D. 405 ; and this (with the exception of the Psalter) became the accepted version of the Roman Church, under the name of the *Vulgate*.

(4) QUOTATIONS by ancient writers, Jewish and Christian, in some instances afford a little help.

A real critical edition of the Hebrew Scriptures does not exist. Much has been done, however, in this direction, as in Kittel's *Biblia Hebraica*, the *Sacred Books of the O.T.* series, and other works.

But the want of a critical edition, giving at one glance various readings of MSS, versions, and other authorities, and selected conjectural emendations, is but one of the difficulties which meet us in attempting to apply to the Old Test. the principles we have laid down with regard to the New. Another is the want of a Concordance giving the various readings ; such as we have to the N.T.[1]

---

[1] The *Oxf. Heb. Lex.* gives valuable help here.

To apply, then, as well as we can, the HEPTAD TEST to a few passages where doubt exists as to the true text.

(1) Gen. xi. 12–15 (*according to the Hebrew*) : " And Arphaxad lived 35 years, and begat Salah : and Arphaxad lived after he begat Salah 403 years, and begat sons and daughters. And Salah lived 30 years, and begat Eber : and Salah lived after he begat Eber 403 years, and begat sons and daughters."

(*According to the Septuagint*) : " And Arphaxad lived 135 years, and begat *Cainan :* and Arphaxad lived after he begat *Cainan* 330 years,[1] and begat sons and daughters ; and he died. *And Cainan lived 130 years, and begat* Salah : *and Cainan lived after he begat* Salah 330 *years, and begat sons and daughters ; and he died.* And Salah lived 130 years and begat Eber : and Salah lived after he begat Eber 330 years, and begat sons and daughters ; and he died."

There are several differences here : (1) the clause " and he died " is evidently an interpolation prompted by ch. v. ; the Samaritan goes still further in the same direction : (2) the differences in the figures I do not propose to deal with here ; but in the chapter on Chronology I shall endeavour to show that those of the Sept. are the correct ones : (3) there remains the question of the existence of Cainan, which is one of considerable importance, from its bearing both on the subject of the early chronology of the world, and on that of the credibility of the sacred writers. For as they stand there is a palpable contradiction between Gen. xi. 12 and Luke iii. 36. Now St. Luke's genealogy of our Lord contains 77 names, which at once stamps that of Cainan as genuine. Nor must it be thought that, by adding the name of GOD, St. Luke has resorted to artificial or questionable means of arriving at this number : he has simply followed his exemplar, the fifth chapter of Genesis, which, in giving the genealogy

---

[1] So most MSS ; a few have 430, and so both Targums. The reading of the common Greek text, 400 years, rests on very slight authority, Cod. B being defective here.

of the early patriarchs, commences with the statement that God created Adam in his own likeness ; and then goes on to say that Adam begat Seth in *his* own likeness, and so on.

But unless the existence of this Cainan can be proved from the Heb. text itself, the contradiction still remains. The section in which the passage stands extends from ver. 10 to ver. 26 inclusive, and that this forms a complete section is shown by the fact that vv. 10 and 27 both begin with the words, " These are the generations of . . ." The following is a transcription of the entire section, with all the *con. waws* marked, and joined to the verbs with which they are connected in the Heb. The paragraph concerning Cainan is included in order to show that it is necessary to complete the heptadic arrangement. The number of years is also taken in each case from the Sept.

GENESIS XI.

10   (*1*) These are the generations of Shem : Shem was an hundred years old, (*2*) AND-he-begat Arphaxad two years after the
11 flood : (*3*) AND-lived Shem after he begat Arphaxad five hundred years, (*4*) AND-he-begat sons and daughters.

12   (*5*) And-Arphaxad lived an hundred thirty and five years,
13 AND-he-begat *Cainan :* (*6*) AND-lived Arphaxad after he begat *Cainan* three hundred and thirty years, (*7*) AND-he-begat sons and daughters.

   (8) And-Cainan lived an hundred and thirty years, AND-he-begat Salah, (*9*) AND-*lived Cainan after he begat* Salah *three hundred and thirty years,* (*10*) AND-*he-begat sons and daughters.*

14   (*11*) And-Salah lived an hundred and thirty years, AND-he-
15 begat Eber : (*12*) AND-lived Salah after he begat Eber three hundred and thirty years, (*13*) AND-he-begat sons and daughters.

16   (*14*) AND-lived Eber an hundred thirty and four years, (*15*)
17 AND-he-begat Peleg : (*16*) AND-lived Eber after he begat Peleg two hundred and seventy years, (*17*) AND-he-begat sons and daughters.

18   (*18*) AND-lived Peleg an hundred and thirty years, (*19*)
19 AND-he-begat Reu : (*20*) AND-lived Peleg after he begat Reu two hundred and nine years, (*21*) AND-he-begat sons and daughters.

20   (*22*) AND-lived Reu an hundred thirty and two years, (*23*)

21 AND-he-begat Serug, (24) AND-lived Reu after he begat Serug
   two hundred and seven years, (25) AND-he-begat sons and
   daughters.
22   (26) AND-lived Serug a hundred and thirty years, (27) AND-
23 he-begat Nahor : (28) AND-lived Serug after he begat Nahor two
   hundred years, (29) AND-he-begat sons and daughters.
24   (30) AND-lived Nahor nine and seventy years,[1] (31) AND-he-
25 begat Terah : (32) AND-lived Nahor after he begat Terah an
   hundred twenty and nine[1] years, (33) AND-he-begat sons and
   daughters.
26   (34) AND-lived Terah seventy years, (35) AND-he-begat
   Abram, Nahor, and Haran.

The first thing that strikes us here is, that though the
word " lived " is used 18 times (including the Cainan
paragraph), and always in precisely the same connection,
it is joined to *waw con.* 15 times only, and stands alone
in the other three places. Why is this ? Why do
we not find " AND-lived Arphaxad," " AND-lived Salah,"
as well as " AND-lived Terah," etc. ? Why are Arphaxad and Salah [and Cainan], the only proper names to
which " and " is joined ? To these questions only one
answer can be given : *the heptadic structure of the section
would have been spoiled had waw con. been used uniformly
throughout.* Had " and " never been joined to a proper
name, but always to the verb, we should have had 34
divisions without the Cainan paragraph, and 38 with it,
neither of them heptadic numbers ; but the simple yet
ingenious arrangement which the Hebrew text pre-
serves to us gives 32 divisions without the Cainan
paragraph, *and* 35 *with it.* I submit, therefore, that
the Hebrew text originally contained the disputed
words, and that this Cainan had a real existence. In
consequence of the discrepancy which exists between
the different authorities as to the numbers in the
passage, it is difficult to arrive at the exact words of the
original Hebrew, so that I will not attempt to go far
into the verbal test. If the form " AND-lived " occurs
14 times in the *present* Hebrew text, on the other hand
" begat " occurs 28 times in the text as emended above,

[1] So nearly all MSS.

the same number as in ch. v., and *eth*, the accusative particle, **21** times.

The phrase " sons and daughters " in the O.T. will repay examination. Including the Cainan paragraph it occurs as follows :—

I. Without pronominal suffix :

" And he begat sons and daughters " without intervening words (except in two cases the *number* of sons and daughters)   **21**

Others with ילד " to beget " in imperfect tense **7**

Others, miscellaneous [1] . . . **14**

— **42**

Of the above **42**, **28** are mentioned in connection with their father.

II. With pronominal suffixes :

Without intervening words except particles **49**

With not more than two intervening words **7**

—

98

Without the Cainan paragraph, the above numbers **21, 42, 28, 98** would all be one less; so that by the common text four heptads are destroyed. Again the word בת, *bath*, " daughter " occurs in O.T. 587 times,[2] but adding this paragraph $588 = 7 \times 7 \times 12$.

It will be noticed that I have given the Cainan paragraph the same form, as regards *waw con.*, as the paragraphs on either side of it.

If the Heb. text, then, or some copies of it, contained this paragraph in the third century before Christ, when the Septuagint was translated, can any reason be given for its subsequent omission ? A glance at the text as given above at once suggests an answer to this question.

[1] In Ex. xxi. 4 או " or " should be ו " and : " so Sept.-A and many other MSS, and three other Versions.

[2] *Oxf. Heb. Lex.*

The similarity in the numbers relating to Arphaxad, Cainan, and Salah forms a trap into which some unwary scribe may have fallen.   He may have passed from the words "thirty years and three hundred years,[1] and begat sons and daughters," in the Arphaxad paragraph, to *the same words* in the Cainan paragraph, unwittingly leaving out the intervening matter.   The confusion in the names which would result would afterwards be set right by some one ignorant of the true reading, and so the text would be brought to its present state.[2]

The inclusion of Cainan receives powerful support from the *Book of Jubilees*, a Jewish document of ii/B.C., which purports to give the history of Genesis with supplementary matter.   It states that the wife of Arphaxad bare Kainam [so the name is spelt] who left home and found carved on a rock the teaching of the fallen angels [the "sons of God" of Gen. vi. 2] and he transcribed it and sinned owing to it.   This is the more remarkable as the ages in *Jubilees* are not taken from the Sept. but are nearer to the Heb.   Its testimony therefore is quite independent of the Sept.   Is it possible that the Jews struck Cainan's name out of the Heb. text because they would not recognize him as their ancestor, owing to his unnatural sin ?

There are some who believe the omission to have been made in order to reduce the number of generations from Shem to Abraham to *ten*, the same number as those from Adam to Noah.   But here, again, the

---

[1] Such is doubtless the true reading : "thirty" is found in all good MSS of the Sept., and also in the Targums of Onkelos and pseudo-Jonathan.   The termination has been lost in the Heb., making it read "three."   For the hundreds, the Heb. takes one hundred years off the earlier part of Arphaxad's life, and adds it on to the later, as in many other cases ; Codex A of the Sept. has here been conformed to the Heb., probably owing to the confusion introduced by the Hexaplarian text of Origen, but a still older MS, the Codex Cottonianus, of the fourth century, with nearly all others, has *three* hundred.

[2] From the same cause—homœoteleuton—has doubtless arisen the omission in the common Heb. text of two other verses, Josh. xxi. 36, 37, where see the Revisers' marginal note.

H

symbolic use of numbers helps us. For as God waited until ten generations were completed (for ten is the number which symbolizes completeness) before bringing destruction upon the world, leaving the new world to be peopled by the men of a new decad—Shem and his brothers being the eleventh generation from Adam, —so he waited *ten* generations after the flood, to show that, even with this terrible warning before his eyes, man must relapse, without a special revelation from Him, into ignorance and idolatry. Abraham, then, is not the end of the second but the beginning of the *third* decad, the 21st from Adam, even as Enoch, another man who " walked with God," was the " 7th from Adam."

Another reason, if the omission were designedly made, might be that the Jews would not care to number among their ancestors a man bearing a name so similar (in sound, though in Hebrew the spelling would probably be very different) to that of a man who had previously been pronounced " cursed " by God, viz. Caanan the son of Ham. To the first Cainan (Gen. v. 10, R.V. " Kenan ") who lived at an earlier period, this would not apply.[1]

(2) Leviticus xiii. 30 : " (It is) leprosy of the head or [leprosy] of the beard." The word in brackets is in the Sept., but not in the Heb. צרע, *tsara*, " a leper," and צרעת, *tsaraath*, " leprosy," occur together 55 times in the O.T., but with this addition 56, of which 35 occur in Leviticus (including this passage), 7 in 2 Kings v. (the history of Naaman), and 14 elsewhere. The Sept. is therefore correct.

On the other hand, the Sept. is wrong in ver. 29, where it reads, " If a man or woman have a plague *of leprosy* upon the head or the beard ; " for not only would this make the word " leprosy " occur once above

---

[1] It is rather singular that Codex A spells the name Kaina*m* in Gen. x. 24 (twice), which is also the reading of B, ℵ, and other MSS, in Luke iii. 36, but *not* of A.

the heptadic number, but it would also give 15 occurrences of the phrase " plague of leprosy," 14 being the correct number, as in the present Hebrew text.

(3) 2 Kings iv. 16 : " And she said, Nay, my lord, [(thou) man of God]." The words in brackets are omitted by Codex B of the Sept., but are found in A, which supports the Heb. The phrase " man of God " occurs 8 times in the history of the Shunammite, and is applied to Elisha 29 times in all. It must, therefore, be struck out here, which will reduce these numbers to 7 and 28.

(4) Ezra i. 8 : " Even those did Cyrus king of Persia bring forth [and he delivered them] into the hand of Mithredath the treasurer." The words in brackets are not in the Hebrew, but three manuscripts of the Septuagint have them, and they are also found in the Apocryphal book of 1 Esdras, ch. ii. ver. 11 (10). They would be represented in Hebrew by the one word ויתנם, from נתן, *nathan*, " to give, deliver," etc. Now, this word occurs in the Book of Ezra in Kal perfect 7 times, and in Kal imperfect 6 times, but if it be added here, 7. Two of Kennicott's MSS have the word in this verse, but not in this place. The heptadic structure of the chapter also requires the insertion of the word, for with it we can make either 7 or 14 divisions in the chapter, according to the principle adopted, but without it only 6 and 13 respectively. The Apocryphal book of 1 Esdras is therefore rightly regarded by scholars as being a valuable help in the criticism of the Heb. text of Ezra, of portions of which it gives a translation rather freer than, but quite independent of, the Sept.

(5) Cant. viii. 6, 7 :—

6 Set me as a seal upon thine heart,
   As a seal upon thine arm :
   For love is strong as death ;
   Jealousy is cruel (*Heb.* hard) as the grave :
   The flashes thereof are flashes of fire,
   A flame of JAH.

7 Many waters cannot quench love,
  Neither can the floods drown it :
  If a man would give all the substance of his house
      for love,
  He would utterly be contemned.

So practically both the A.V. and R.V. The name of God does not occur elsewhere in the Song of Solomon, and there seems no reason why it should be introduced here. It is not a question of whether the Heb. text is corrupt or not, but simply of whether the letters שלהבתיה are meant to form one word or two, some MSS having them the one way and some the other.[1] They are now almost universally regarded as two, meaning literally " a flame of JAH," but the Sept. treats them as one, and renders " her flames ; " and so, nearly, the Vulgate. JAH, an abbreviation of JEHOVAH, occurs in Exodus 2, Psalms 43, and Isaiah 4 times, or 49 times in all, excluding this passage. I consider, therefore, that these letters form one word only, which the Sept. rightly renders " her flames." Still, the passage is a difficult one, and I see no way out of the difficulty but by striking out the word קנאה, qinah, " jealousy." This word occurs in the O.T. 43 times, including 15 times in the singular absolute ; by omitting it here, these numbers are reduced to 42 and 14. A careful examination of the root leads to the same result. קנא, qana, " to be jealous," occurs 34 times (including Ezek viii. 3, which some Concordances give under קנה) ; קנא, qanna, " jealous," 6 ; קנוא, qanno, " jealous," 2 ; קנאה, qinah, " jealousy," 43 ; total, 85 ; but if the word be omitted here, 84.

The translation of the passage would then run thus :—

(1) Set me as a seal upon thine heart,
    As a seal upon thine arm :

[1] In ancient times no division was made between one word and another, the letters following on without any break. This has been a frequent source of error.

(2) For strong as death is love,
(3) Unyielding [1] as the grave are her burnings,
(4) Burnings of fire are her flames.
(5) Many waters cannot quench this love, [2]
(6) Neither can the floods drown it :
(7) If a man would give all the substance of his
house for love,
He would utterly be contemned.

If the word be an interpolation, we must suppose
that some early scribe did not understand how love
could be said to be "*hard* as the grave," and thought
the sentiment more applicable to jealousy, which word
he accordingly inserted. But the passage reads much
better without it, for why should the writer introduce
jealousy between two references to love? nay, why
should jealousy be brought in at all? Modern critics
are beginning to see this, and some would render *qinah*,
"ardent, zealous love," instead of "jealousy." The
natural climax of the passage, too, is lost unless the
whole be understood of love: "burnings of fire are
her flames (flames which even) many waters cannot
quench."

With this word omitted, the Heb. text of the heptad
contains 38 words, **140** letters.

(6) Isai. lxv. 16: "He who blesseth himself in the
earth shall bless himself in the God of *truth ;* and he
that sweareth in the earth shall swear by the God of
truth." For "truth" the Heb. is literally "Amen,"
אָמֵן (see R.V., marg.); the Heb. word meaning
"truth" being אֹמֶן, *omen*. The difference, it will be
seen, is simply in the vowel points, which are generally
supposed to be not older than the sixth or seventh
century after Christ (though the Vulgate here has
Amen, while the Sept. has *truth*, or rather *true*, "the
true God"). Leaving out this passage, the word

---

[1] "*Unyielding, hard*, as the grave will not let go those whom it
once holds" (Fausset, *Comm., in loco*).

[2] Heb, "the love," i.e. the love just described.

" Amen " occurs **28** times in the Old Testament, viz. **14** times in the Pentateuch, **7** in the Psalms, and **7** elsewhere, being always so translated, or rather left untranslated, in the A.V., except in Jer. xi. 5, where it is rendered " So be it," with " Amen " in the margin.   The Heb. pointing and the Vulgate rendering are therefore wrong, the Sept. and A.V. right.   On the other hand, these figures show that the Heb. is correct in reading " Amen, Hallelujah," at the end of Ps. cvi., where the Sept. erroneously has " Amen, Amen."

(7) Isa. lxvi. 11 : " The *abundance* of her glory." For זיז, *ziz*, " abundance," some MSS have זיו, *ziv*, " brightness," and so A.V., margin.   *Ziz* occurs **3** times in the O.T., and מזוזה, *m'zuzah*, " doorpost," from same root, **19** : total from root, **22**.   *Ziv* (Aram.) occurs **6** times, there being no other appellatives from the same root. If the marginal reading be adopted, these figures will become **21** and **7** ; " brightness " would, therefore, seem to be correct.   It will be seen from the similarity of the letters, how easily the mistake may have arisen.

(8) Jer. x. 11.   The whole of the book of Jeremiah is in Hebrew in the original except this verse, which is in Aramaic.   Some modern critics, therefore, being unable to account for this, pronounce it an interpolation.   One of the words in it is עבד, *abad*, " to make," which occurs in all **28** times ; the other Aramaic words from the same root are עבד, *abad*, " servant," **7** ; עבידא, *abida*, " work," **6** ; and מעבד, *mabad*, " work," **1** ; total from root, **42**.   Another word occurring here is אבד, *abad*, " to perish," which occurs **7** times.   Another is אלה, *elleh*, " these," which occurs twice ; the occurrences of other words from the same root being אילן, *illen*, **5** ; and אלך, *illek*, **14,** both words likewise meaning " these ; " total from root, **21**.   The verse is, therefore, undoubtedly genuine.

(9) Ezek. xliii. 11 : " Show them (1) the form of the house, (2) and the fashion thereof, (3) and the goings out thereof, (4) and the comings in thereof, (5) and all the forms thereof, (6) and all the ordinances thereof, (7) *and*

all the forms thereof, (8) and all the laws thereof." The words in italics are omitted by several MSS and by the Sept., thus restoring the heptad. The word צורה, *tsurah,* "form," occurs 4 times (all in this verse) ; its root, צור, *tsūr,* occurs with the sense of " to form *or* to fashion," 3 times (Exod. xxxii. 4 ; 1 Kings vii. 15 ; Cant. viii. 9) ; and the noun צור, *tsūr,* with the sense of " form," once, Ps. xlix. 15 : total from root, 8. Strike out the words numbered (7) above, and again a heptad is made. They are, therefore, an interpolation.

(10) Zech. i. 16, 17 : And a line shall be stretched forth upon Jerusalem [yet. And the angel that communed with me said unto me], Yet cry thou, saying," etc. The words in brackets are in the Sept., but not in the Heb. Vv. 12–17 of this chapter are a heptad, but only 6 divisions can be made out from the Heb. ; these words supply the seventh. They have evidently been omitted from homœoteleuton, the scribe having unwarily passed from the first " yet " to the second, omitting the intervening words.

A few further examples of the application of the WORD AND LETTER TEST must next be given, and I propose to begin with the first two of the " Songs of Degrees." These Pilgrim Psalms, as they are sometimes called (Pss. cxx.–cxxxiv.), are aptly styled by Perowne " a Psalter within a Psalter," for, though forming a portion of the Book of Psalms, they have a certain completeness of their own. They are 15 in number, and, says Dr. John Forbes, " are arranged with much precision, the central psalm (cxxvii.) being Solomon's with 7 psalms on either side of it." [1] And in two other ways can this 15 be reduced to the heptadic number 14. It might be supposed, from the A.V. and R.V., that the title was the same in the Hebrew in every case ; but it is not so, for Ps. cxxi. is styled *Shir lammaaloth,* " A Song *for* the Goings-up " (or " Ascents," as R.V.), the other 14 being each entitled *Shir hamma-*

[1] *Symmetrical Structure of Scripture,* p. 136.

aloth, "A Song of the Goings-up." Then **14** of them are exceptionally short psalms, only one (Ps. cxxxii.) having more than nine verses, and that has eighteen. There are many words and groups of words which occur in these psalms **7**, or a multiple of **7**, times. Thus *bayith*, "house;" *banim*, "children;" *hinneh*, "behold;" *yashab*, "to dwell," etc.; *kol*, "all;" *einayim*, "eyes;" *shalom*, "peace;" each occur **7** times, as does also "Zion;" the only other proper names mentioned—David, Jacob, Israel, and Jerusalem—occurring together **21** times. עלם, *olam*, and עד, *ad*, both meaning "for ever," occur together **7** times; אל, *al*, and לא, *lo*, both meaning "not," **21** times; *tōb*, "good," with its verb and noun, **7** times; *ashrei*, "blessed," *barak*, "to bless," and *b'rakah*, "blessing," **14** times; while *shamar*, "to keep," is used **7** times of the LORD keeping His people, and **5** times otherwise. *Erets*, "earth," and *shamayim*, "heaven," occur **7** times, as do also *shem*, "name," and *sham*, "there,"— two words of quite different meaning, but spelled (in Heb.) with the same letters. This list might easily be extended, but I have said enough to show what a valuable critical help we have here.

The hundred and twentieth psalm contains in the Heb. (excluding the title) **49** words, **176** letters. But, in the last verse, *waw*, "but," is omitted by two MSS. the Targum, Sept., Symmachus, Vulgate, and perhaps Aquila and Theodotion. This letter, therefore, must be struck out, which will leave **49** words **175** letters.

But the Heb. language supplies an additional check which the Greek does not admit of. One of the peculiarities of Hebrew is the facility with which, by a system of prefixes and suffixes, it admits of a word being expanded so as to represent two, three, or even four words in Greek or English. Thus, take the word וּבְדָרְכּוֹ, *u-b'dar-ko*, which occurs in Ezek. xlvi. 8. The foundation word of this is דרך, *dereh*, "a way;" to which are prefixed [1] בְ, *b'*, a preposition signifying "in"

[1] It must be remembered that Hebrew is read from right to left,

or " by ; " and ו, *waw* (here pronounced *ū*), the conjunction " and ; " and there is affixed ו, *ō*, " its : " so that the whole word stands for " and by its way," or, as in the A.V., " and by the way thereof." This, therefore, though only one word, is really compounded of *four* words ; and as some distinguishing terms are required, I shall call such a word as this *one* COMPOUND WORD, or *four* SIMPLE WORDS.

Now, the psalm just dealt with contains in the received text **49** compound words, or 64 simple words, but if *waw* be omitted in the last verse (as above), then the psalm contains **49** compound words, **63** simple words, and **175** letters, all heptadic numbers.

The text of Ps. cxxi., the Traveller's psalm, is not quite so pure. It contains, indeed, if the title be included, **56** compound words, **84** simple words (counting Isra-el as *two*), and **203** letters, all heptadic numbers. This, however, is only one of those coincidences which are sometimes met with, and must not lead us on a false scent, for it can hardly be right to include the title in one psalm and exclude it in another. Leaving the title out, then, the figures are 54, 81 (counting Isra-el as two), and 194 respectively, vv. 2 and 6 containing 6 words each, and all the others **7**. The first clause of the second verse is without a verb, which is supplied in the Authorized and Revised Versions by " cometh," printed in *italics* to denote that it is not in the original. But though it is not in the original now, I believe it was there once. The word בוא, *bo*, " to come," occurs in the Psalms of Degrees 6 times, but if added here, **7** ; the particular form of the word required here, יבוא, *yabo*, occurs 6 times in the whole Book of Psalms (sometimes spelled יבא), but if added here **7**.

We still require another word, and ver. 6 naturally attracts our attention, as it is now the only verse in the psalm which does not contain **7** words, and as its second clause has no verb. It stands in the Hebrew, " By

day the sun shall not smite thee, and [1] the moon in the
night," on which Dimock remarks that, " as the *smiting*,
or *burning*,[2] *of the moon* seems to be an improper expression, perhaps יאיר has been accidentally omitted,
' and the moon *shall give light* by night.' "[3] And
though Dimock is wrong in speaking of " being smitten
by the moon " as an improper expression, as a good
Commentary will show, yet the danger is such a comparatively slight one, and one so easily guarded against,
that the promise of protection from it seems hardly
necessary, unless, indeed, we take the verse to mean
that the LORD is a defence from all dangers, both great
and small.   Dimock's suggestion, therefore, is a very
good one, as the following will testify.   The verb אור,
ōr, " to give light," occurs in the Hiphil conjugation 34
times, of which 7 are in the Infinitive, 7 Imperative, 7
Preterite and Participle, and 13 Future ; if we add
here יאיר, *yaïr* " shall give light," this last becomes 14,
and the total 35.   This verb occurs in the Psalms 16
times, 10 times figuratively and 6 with its literal meaning of " giving light ; " the addition proposed will
increase this last to 7.   Still there seems something
wanting ; for to say that " the moon shall give light
by night " seems rather weak.   I would therefore add
to יאיר the pronominal suffix, ך " thee," and read יאירך,
yaïrka, " shall give thee light," for which there is
heptadic support, there being 13 words in the psalm
which have suffixes, but, with this, 14.

With these two additions, the psalm contains 56
compound words, 84 simple words, and 203 letters ;
and each verse contains 7 words.

The heptadic division of the psalm also requires the
addition of a verb in ver. 6 :—

[1] Is it correct to translate *waw* by " nor," standing in the connection in which it does here ? Compare vv. 3 and 4.

[2] " Burn," the reading of the Sept., is wrong ; נכה, *nakah*, " to
smite," occurs 14 times in the Pss., and the particular form used here
is found 7 times in the O.T. The Heb. is therefore correct.

[3] *Notes, Critical and Explanatory, on the Books of Psalms and
Proverbs*. Gloucester, 1791.

PSALM CXXI.

1 (1) Shall I lift up mine eyes unto the mountains?
  (2) From whence shall my help come?
2 (3) My help cometh from the LORD,
      The maker of heaven and earth.
3 (4) Let him not suffer thy foot to be moved:
  (5) Let him not slumber that keepeth thee.
4 (6) Behold, he will not slumber;
  (7) And he that keepeth Israel will not sleep.
5 (1) The LORD is thy keeper:
  (2) The LORD is thy shade upon thy right hand.
6 (3) By day the sun shall not smite thee:
  (4) And in the night the moon shall give thee light.
7 (5) The LORD will keep thee from all evil;
  (6) He will keep thy soul.
8 (7) The LORD will keep thy going out and thy coming in,
      From this time forth and for evermore.

The figure in ver. 6, thus restored, is a most beautiful
one, being taken from the pillar of cloud and pillar of
fire which guided, protected, and enlightened the Israelites in their journey through the wilderness; as it is
written:

"He spread a cloud for a covering,
 And fire to give light in the night" (Ps. cv. 39).

And here the same blessings are promised to the child
of God, in his journeys through the wilderness of this
world, which the children of Israel miraculously enjoyed
in the desert.   As the pillar of cloud was a shade from
the fierce rays of an almost tropical sun to them, so to
him the promise still comes, " By day the sun shall not
smite thee; " and as the pillar of fire gave light by
night to them, so is it still said, " The moon in the night
shall give thee light."

The Sept. adds " the LORD " in the second clause
of the seventh verse of this psalm; but that the Heb.
is right is easily proved. " JEHOVAH " (alone) occurs
49 times in the Psalms of Degrees; and other names of
God 7 times, viz. *Adonai*, " Lord," (in small type), 3;
Jah, " LORD," (in capitals), 2; and " JEHOVAH our
God," 2. It will be seen that, in this last, two names

of God are combined as one, so that, in counting the occurrences in a concordance, care must be taken not to count them as two separate names.

The hundred and seventeenth psalm is so short that some have supposed it to be a part of the preceding psalm, and others of the following one. But both it and the preceding one end with " Hallelujah," a word which, as is shown on p. 324, occurs in **7** psalms *once*, either at the beginning or end, and in **7** others *twice*, at both beginning and end. Either of the above changes would destroy this arrangement ; the psalm is therefore complete as it stands. It contains, according to the present Heb. text, 17 compound words, 23 simple words, and 62 letters. But I believe one letter to be wanting, which the Sept. and two Heb. MSS enable us to supply. These authorities insert the article before " nations," which then corresponds with " the peoples " (so Heb.) in the next clause. The psalm then contains 17 compound words, 24 simple words, and **63** letters. Only the last of these numbers is heptadic, but 17 (= 10 + 7) has a certain mystical meaning of its own, and 24 is **7** more, there being now **7** words in the psalm which have either a prefix or suffix.

This psalm is so short that it only contains five sentences, yet (as in Ps. cxxxiv.) a certain septenary arrangement can be perceived, thus :—

(*1*) Praise the LORD, (*2*) all the nations ;
(*3*) Laud him, (*4*) all the peoples.
(*5*) For great is his mercy toward us ;
(*6*) And the truth of the LORD (endureth) for ever.
(*7*) Hallelujah.

Before going further, brief reference must be made to Hebrew Script and Orthography. " The O.T.—except possibly the latest portions—was not written originally in the characters with which we are familiar." (Driver, *Samuel*, *Int.* p. i.) Whether the Pentateuch was originally written in Heb., or in Babylonian cuneiform, as Col. Conder, Prof. Naville and others assert, and how many stages the sacred script has passed through from the earliest times to the date of extant Heb. MSS, we need not discuss. But each change, whether one or more, involved the danger of errors in transcription. The non-division, or indistinct division, of words was another source of error.

Then the different modes of spelling which are found in manuscripts must be taken into account before satisfactory results can be arrived at. Thus the word *m'ōrōth*, "lights," in Gen. i. 14, is spelt in different manuscripts in no fewer than four different ways— מארת, מארת, מארות, and מאורות, all of which have precisely the same pronunciation and meaning. The explanation of this is, that the long sound of the vowel *o* may be represented either by ו with a point over it, or by a point over the previous letter *without* ו. And so with some of the other vowels. It has been maintained,[1] not only that in ancient Heb. writing these "vowel-letters" were never used in such instances as the above, but that the present system of affixes to mark the distinction between singular and plural, masculine and feminine, etc., are the production of an age posterior to the introduction of Christianity.

This has been contested, but Dr. Ginsburg says, "Without going the full length of those who maintain that the Heb. codex from which the Sept. was made had no *matres lectiones* at all, it is now established beyond a doubt that the letters אהוי commonly called quiescent or feeble letters have been gradually introduced into the Heb. text. It is, moreover, perfectly certain that the presence or absence of these letters in our text in many instances is entirely due to the idiosyncrasy of the Scribes."[2]

If to these we add errors arising from the similarity

---

[1] *Proofs of the Interpolation of the Vowel Letters in the Text of the Hebrew Bible,* by C. W. Wall, D.D. London, 1857.

[2] *Introd. to Heb. Bible,* p. 137. See also Driver, *Samuel*[2] xxx.

of some of the letters, both in the old and the later
Heb. characters, the occasional interchange of letters,
the blunders of scribes, etc., we cannot expect that
the text has come down to us in its original purity.

Let us now take the record of the Creation of the
world in Gen. i. 3–ii. 3, a most interesting and instructive passage, not only because it shows us that the
heptadic arrangement begins almost with the first
words of Scripture, but also from the fact that it contains two variations from that arrangement, both of
them, as I believe, full of meaning.

As might be expected in the opening page of Scripture, all the heptads in this chapter are of the most
perfect kind, i.e., every division commences with *waw
con.* with the imperfect or future tense ; and as the
sections themselves are plainly marked by the different
days' work, the passage is an exceptionally easy one to
divide.

Passing by vv. 1, 2, which will be dealt with in the
chapter on Interpretation, and premising that words
in square brackets [ ] are not in the Heb., words in
italics denote an alteration in the Heb., and three dots
. . . an omission from the Heb., we go on with

Genesis I. 3–5.—The First Day.

3 (*1*) And-said God, Let there be light : (*2*) and-there-was
4 light. (*3*) And-saw God the light, that it was good : (*4*) and-
divided God between the light and the darkness. (*5*) And-called
5 God the light Day, and-the-darkness he called Night. (*6*)
And-there-was evening, (*7*) and-there-was morning : one day.

Vv. 6–8—The Second Day.

6 (*1*) And-said God, Let there be a firmament in the midst of
the waters, and-let-it divide the waters from the waters. (*2*)
7 And-made God the firmament, (*3*) and-divided [God][1] between
the waters which were under the firmament, and the waters
8 which were above the firmament : (*4*) and-it-was so. (*5*)
And-called God the firmament Heaven. (*6*) And-there-was
evening, (*7*) and-there-was morning : second day.

---

[1] So the Sept.

Vv. 9–13—The Third Day.

9 (*1*) And-said God, Let the waters under the heaven be gathered together unto one place, and let the dry land appear:
10 (*2*) And-it-was so. (*3*) And-called God the dry land Earth; and the gathering together of the waters called he Seas: (*4*)
11 And-saw God that it was good. (*5*) And-said God, Let the earth bring forth grass, the herb yielding seed [after his kind],[1] the fruit tree yielding fruit after his kind, whose seed is in itself,
12 upon the earth: (*6*) And-it-was so. (*7*) And-brought-forth the earth grass, herb yielding seed after his kind, and the tree yielding fruit, whose seed was in itself, after his kind: (*8*) And-
13 saw God that it was good. (*9*) And-there-was evening, (*10*) And-there-was morning: third day.

Vv. 14–19—The Fourth Day.

14 (*1*) And-said God, Let there be lights in the firmament of the heaven, to divide between the day and the night, and let them
15 be for signs, and for seasons, and for days, and years: and let them be for lights in the firmament of the heaven to give
16 light upon the earth: (*2*) And-it-was so. (*3*) And-made God two great lights; the greater light to rule the day, and the lesser
17 light to rule the night. . . . (*4*) And-set God them in the
18 firmament of the heaven to give light upon the earth, and to rule over the day and over the night, and to divide between the light
19 and the darkness: (*5*) And-saw God that it was good. (*6*) And-there-was evening, (*7*) And-there-was morning: fourth day.

Vv. 20–23—The Fifth Day.

20 (*1*) And-said God, Let the waters bring forth abundantly the moving creature that hath life, and fowl that may fly above the earth in the open firmament of heaven: [(*2*) And-it-was
21 so].[2] (*3*) And-created God great whales, and every living creature that moveth, which the waters brought forth abundantly after their kind, and every winged fowl after his kind: (*4*)
22 And-saw God that it was good. (*5*) And-blessed them God, saying, Be fruitful, and multiply, and fill the waters in the seas,
23 and let fowl multiply in the earth. (*6*) And-there-was evening, (*7*) And-there-was morning: fifth day.

Vv. 24–27—The Sixth Day, I.

24 (*1*) And-said God, Let the earth bring forth the living creature after his kind, cattle, and creeping thing, and beast of the earth
25 after his kind: (*2*) And-it-was so. (*3*) And-made God the beast of the earth after his kind, and cattle after their kind, and every

---

[1] So the Sept.   [2] So the Sept.

thing that creepeth upon the earth after his kind: [(*4*) AND-blessed them God, saying, Be fruitful and multiply.] (*5*)
26 AND-saw God that it was good. (*6*) AND-said God, Let us make man in our image, after our likeness: and-let-them-have-dominion over the fish of the sea, and over the fowl of the air, and over the cattle, and over all the earth, and over every
27 creeping thing that creepeth upon the earth. (*7*) AND-created God man in his own image, in the image of God created he him; male and female created he them.

Vv. 28–31—The Sixth Day, II.

28 (*1*) AND-blessed them God, (*2*) AND-said God unto them, Be fruitful, and multiply, and replenish the earth, and subdue it; and have dominion over the fish of the sea, and over the fowl of the air, and over every living thing that moveth upon the earth.
29 (*3*) AND-said God, Behold I have given you every herb bearing seed, which is upon the face of all the earth, and every tree, in the
30 which is the fruit of a tree yielding seed; to you it shall be for meat. And to every beast of the earth, and to every fowl of the air, and to every thing that creepeth upon the earth, wherein there is life, I have given every green herb for meat: (*4*) AND-
31 it-was so. (*5*) AND-saw God every thing that he had made, and, behold, it was very good. (*6*) AND-there-was evening, (*7*) AND-there-was morning: the sixth day.

Ch. ii. 1–3.

1 (*1*) AND-were-finished the heaven and the earth, and all the
2 host of them. (*2*) AND-ended God on the *sixth*[1] day his work which he had made; (*3*) AND-he-rested on the seventh day
3 from all his work which he had made. (*4*) AND-blessed God the seventh day, (*5*) AND-he-sanctified it: because that in it he had rested from all his work which God created to make.

Vv. 20–23 contain in the present Heb. text only six divisions, but as the words "and it was so" are found in the Sept. in ver. 20, and are plainly required by the analogy of the rest of the chapter, it is tolerably certain that they were once in the Heb., and the fact that they complete the heptad confirms this. Vv. 24–27 also contain six divisions only; this we will deal with presently.

The record of the third day's work, it will be noticed, contains not seven divisions, but *ten*, and it is worth

[1] So Sam., Sept., Syr.

inquiry why the septenary arrangement is here departed from. All writers on the symbolism of numbers agree that Ten signifies " completeness," [1] and by the use of that number here we are doubtless to understand that on the third day the earth itself was completed, made ready for the reception of its future inhabitants. So some have understood the words of Gen. ii. 1 to refer to the two triads of days in the creative week : " Thus the heaven and the earth were finished," to the first three ; and the words following, " and all the host of them," to the last. And in confirmation of this we find the phrase " And God saw that it was good " used twice in the accounts of the third and sixth days' work, but of no other.

Another variation occurs in ch. ii. 1–3, where we find *five* divisions only, though *waw*, " and," occurs **7** times. As ten is the symbol of completeness, so five, its half, signifies incompleteness, and such, doubtless, is its meaning here. For God's rest was soon to be broken in upon by sin, and His work of creation would need to be supplemented by another work, that of redemption. So that the very words which tell us that " God *ended* his work which he had made," tell us also that the work, though "ended" for the time, was still incomplete.

The recital of the sixth day's work, it will be seen, occupies two heptads.

It is worthy of note that the sayings of God in this chapter, are none of them divided, but that each one, whether long or short, forms only one division of a heptad or other section.[2] The longer sayings, however —namely, those in vv. 14, 26, 28 and 29–30—form minor heptads under Remark IV. (p. 55).

In the fifth verse we have an illustration showing how the *waws* are arranged so that the right number of con-

---

[1] See Appendix C.

[2] I use the term *section* to denote either a heptad, decad, or pentad, and *division* for a seventh, tenth or fifth part respectively of such section.

versive *waws* shall not be exceeded. In the first clause of the verse the *waw* is conversive and joined of course to the verb, but in the second it is prefixed to the noun. Had the verse read "AND-called God the light Day, AND-he-called the darkness Night," the heptad would have been spoiled.

The following is a list of all the heptadic occurrences of words, etc., which I have noticed in the common text of Gen. i. 3–ii. 3, as it stands, except where noted, the first and second verses of ch. i. being outside the limits of our present inquiry, while the first three verses of ch. ii. really form part of the first chapter, and should not have been separated from it : [1]—

וירא, *vaiyar*, "and saw," 7 ; כי, *ki*, "that," 7 ; , טוב, *tŏb*, "good," 7 ; יום, *yŏm*, "day," 14 ; ואת, *v'eth*, "and" (with accusative particle), 7 ; עוף, *ŭph*, "to fly," and עוף, *ŏph*, "fowl," 7 ; רמש, *ramas*, "to creep," and רמש, *remes*, "creeping thing," 7 ; חשך, *choshek*, "darkness," and לילה, *lailah*, "night," 7 ; ים, *yam*, "sea," and מים, *mayim*, "waters," 14 ; בדל, *badal*, "to divide," and בין, *beyn*, "between," 14 ; דשא, *dasha*, "to put forth grass," דשא, *deshe*, "grass," and עשב, *eseb*, "herb," 7 ; ויהי, *vaihi*, "and it was," or (differently pointed) *vihi*, "and let it be," 7 in vv. 3–8 (days one and two), 7 in vv. 9–19 (days three and four) ; and 7 in vv. 20–31 (days five and six) ; [2] כן, *ken*, "so," 7 ; [3] "God," 7 in vv. 26–31 (creation of man) ; and "after its [*or* their] kind," 7 in reference to living creatures, vv. 20–25 ; upon the earth 7 ; There are seven words used, occurring 21 times, for living creatures : חי living creature, חיה beast, עוף fowl, בהמה cattle, רמש creeping thing, דגה fish, תנין sea-monster. It will be noticed that Man is not classed with the animals.

Of the inseparable particles : ל, *l*, prefixed to verbs in the infinitive 7, and as denoting an object 7 ; ב, *b*, "in," etc., prefixed to *words* (not including the pro-

[1] See the first Lessons for Septuagesima Sunday in the Prayer-Book Table of Lessons.

[2] Including "and it was so," v. 20.

nominal suffix ‎וֹ), **21** ; ‎ו, *w*, " and," **7** in ch. ii. 1–3 (day seven) ; ‎ה, *h*, " the," **7** in vv. 3–8 (days one and two), and **7** in vv. 9–13 (day three).   There are **14** prefixes of all kinds in vv. 3–5 (day one), **28** in vv. 9–13 (day three) and **42** in the heptad vv. 28–31.

Of the pronominal suffixes : ‎ם and ‎הם " them," **7** ; ‎ו, " it," **7** in vv. 9–13 (day three).   There are **7** suffixes of all persons in the heptad vv. 28–31.

There are **7** occurrences of verbs in the third person plural, and **7** of verbs in the infinitive ; **7** verbs are used in the preterite (or perfect) of Kal, and **4** verbs in **7** forms as participles.

Lastly, of the **22** letters of the Hebrew alphabet, ‎ס, *samech*, is not used, but all the other **21** occur more or less frequently.[1]

This is a tolerably extensive list, and shows, I think, that the chapter cannot be very greatly corrupted.

There are two words—or, rather, one word (‎אלהים, *Elohim*, " God ") and one particle (‎ו *waw*, " and ")— which would appear to have originally occurred, not only an heptadic number of times in the total, but to have been used with some degree of regularity throughout the chapter, though neither of these is the case now.

Occurrences of ‎אלהים, *Elohim*, " God : "

	vv. 3–5	6–8	9–13	14–19	20–23	24–27	28–31	ch. ii. 1–3	Total.
Present text	4	3	5	4	4	6	4	•3	= 33
Should be	4	4	5	4	4	7	4	3	= 85

i.e. **4** times each in five heptads, **5** times in the decad, **3** times in the pentad, and **7** times in the heptad which records the creation of man.   The word is therefore missing from the present text in two places.   One of these is pointed out by the Sept., which reads, in ver. 7, " And *God* divided the waters," etc., where " God " is absent from all Heb. MSS.   The other is not so easily found, but we have a clue, I think, in the fact that, while God blessed man after He had created

[1] So in the Ten Commandments the letter ‎ט *teth*, does not occur, but all the other **21** are found.

him, and while He blessed birds and fishes, He is not said to have blessed animals. I know of no good reason why animals should have been denied that blessing which was given to birds and fishes, and as the section vv. 24–27 contains only *six* divisions instead of *seven*, I suggest that there has been lost from the original text, at the end of ver. 25, some such clause as "And God blessed them, saying, Be fruitful and multiply." Let us examine the word "blessed." (1) *Barak*, "to bless," occurs in the Hebrew Scriptures 330 times, and in the Aramaic 5, giving a total one short of the heptadic number, **336**. (2) Together with its noun, *b'rakah*, "blessing," it occurs in the Pentateuch 167 times, one short of the heptadic number, **168**. (3) In the Piel and Pual conjugations (which are spelled alike, but differently pointed), the verb occurs 244 times, one short of the heptadic number, **245**. (4) It occurs in the Piel future 41 times in Genesis, one short of the heptadic number, **42**. (5) Lastly, it is found in the Piel future, third person sing. masc., with *waw* prefixed—which is the form that would be required here—48 times, or one short of **49**. All these numbers, therefore, would be made heptadic by inserting the clause suggested above. The next word is "them." The particle *eth* occurs in this chapter with a suffix 6 times, but if *otham*, "them," be added here, **7**. The next word suggested is "be-fruitful." This already occurs twice in this chapter, and its noun, "fruit," 4 times; total, 6: but if read here, **7**. The word used for "and-multiply," in vv. 22, 28, occurs altogether in the O.T. 6 times, but if added here, **7**. The clause I have proposed is of course only suggestive, but the foregoing gives it some appearance of probability.

Let us now take the particle *waw*, and its occurrences throughout the chapter.

	vv, 3–8	9–13	14–19	20–23	24–27	28–31	ch. ii. 1–3	Total.
Present text	18	13	19	12	16	18	7	= 103
Should be	18	13	18	13	18	18	7	= 105
			49		49			

If this be correct, *waw*, " and," occurs once too often in vv. 14–19. But I do not see that any one of the 19 occurrences can be spared, except that at the end of ver. 16. The whole verse reads in the Heb. thus: " And God made the two great lights ; the great light for the ruling of the day, and the small light for the ruling of the night ; and the stars." It is very unlikely that this verse left the hand of the original writer as it stands here. He would never have added the words " and the stars " in this manner ; if he had wanted to speak of them he would have said, " And God made the stars." But there is no reason why the stars should be introduced in this chapter. The mention of them here is altogether out of place. For this chapter (I am not now speaking of vv. 1 and 2, which are outside the portion at present under consideration) does not profess to give a particular account of the creation of the universe, but only of the preparation of the earth for the use of its intended inhabitant, Man. It is not said that the sun and moon were *created* on the fourth day. They had been in existence for ages before ; but such arrangements were then made as *fitted* them to be lights (the Heb. word means " luminaries," or " light-bearers "), for the newly formed earth. But, however useful the stars may be to man, the feeble light they give hardly entitles them (*looking at the matter from a terrestrial standpoint solely*) to be called " luminaries." I have, therefore, no hesitation in saying that the words " and the stars " are an unauthorized addition to the original text of this chapter.[1] This is confirmed by the absence of all reference to the stars in Ps. civ.—a psalm which " is, as it were," says Bp. Wordsworth, " the first chapter of Genesis set to music." It may be said, however, that the words are supported by Ps. cxxxvi. 9—

" The sun for ruling in the day . . .
The moon *and stars* for ruling in the night."

---

[1] So Dean Payne Smith in Ellicott's *Comm.*; Skinner, *I.C.C.*

They are : and the words " and stars " must be struck out there too. The word *kokab*, " star," occurs 37 times in the O.T., but if omitted in these two places, **35.** The sun, moon, and stars are spoken of together in the *New* Test. 7 times (Matt. xxiv. 49; Mark xiii. 24; Luke xxi. 25; 1 Cor. xv. 41; Rev. vi. 12; viii. 12; xii. 1). In the O.T., they are mentioned together twice with " stars " first (Isa. xiii. 10; Ezek. xxxii. 7); and **7** times (*if we exclude the passage in Psalms*) in the regular order, sun first, moon second, and stars last (Gen. xxxvii. 9; Deut. iv. 19; Ps. cxlviii. 3; Eccles xii. 2; Jer. xxxi. 35; Joel ii. 10; iii. 15). To introduce the words in the hundred and thirty-sixth psalm, therefore, would spoil the heptad. Both there and in the passage before us they have been added, in very early times, by some one who thought the absence of reference to the stars was a blot upon the sacred narrative. So man is always trying to mend God's work. Possibly from the same hand came the word " great " before "lights," in Gen. i. 16, though I can offer no support for this suggestion.

In vv. 20–23, if the above is right, " and " occurs once too seldom. This is accounted for by the clause which we have already seen must be added, on the authority of the Sept., at the end of ver. 20, " and it was so." This clause is required to complete the heptad. ויהי, " and it was " or " and let it be," and כן, *ken*, " so," will then each occur an heptadic number of times in the chapter.

In vv. 24–27 " and " should occur twice oftener than it does, which in some measure confirms the clause I have suggested should be added after ver. 25, " *And* God blessed them, saying, Be fruitful *and* multiply."

In ch. ii. 2 the Heb. reads, " And on the *seventh* day God ended his work which he had made ; " but for " seventh " the Samaritan, Sept., and Syriac, more in accordance with fact, read " sixth," and so, too, Josephus. שביעי, *sh'bii*, " seventh," occurs **98,** and ששי, *shisshi*, " sixth," **28** times in the O.T., which would appear to stamp the Heb. as correct. But closer examination proves that it is not. "Seventh" occurs in the Pentateuch 57 times, but if deducted here, **56**; "on the seventh day" and "and on the seventh day" occur respectively 27 and 17 times in the O.T., total **44**, of which 36 are in the Pentateuch, and 8 elsewhere. But in Judg. xiv. 15 the Heb. is wrong again, for in place of "on the seventh day" (ביום השביעי), the Sept., Syriac, and Arabic read "on the fourth day" (ביום הרביעי), thus removing a difficulty from the narrative. The difference, it will be seen, is only in one letter, and the error might easily be made by a Jewish scribe. With this alteration, and that proposed in the text before us, the phrase is found **35** times in the Pentateuch, and 7 elsewhere ; total **42**. In confirmation of the emendation in Judges, it may be added that "the fourth day" occurs 6 times in the O.T., but with this passage, **7**. With regard to the word "sixth" which—as we have seen already, occurs **28** times in the O.T.—in Ezek. viii. 1, for ששי *shisshi*, "sixth (month)," the Sept. reads חמשי, *chamishi*, "fifth," which balances the addition proposed in our text ; and the form הששי, *hasshisshi*, "the sixth," occurs 6 times in the Pentateuch, always in connection with "day," but with our correction, **7** ; "the sixth day" occurs nowhere else but in these six (now **7**) places. The true reading, therefore, is, "And on the *sixth* day God ended his work which he had made ; " and it is significant that the older critics supported this reading *because it removed a difficulty from the sacred text*, whilst later ones stood by the Hebrew *because it caused one.* Some more recent critics, however, adopt "sixth" as the correct reading.[1]

A few more slight alterations must be made. There are **14** prefixes in the 1st day's record and **28** in the 3rd, but only **20** in the 2nd. This may be made into **21** by altering בין into מבין. The form בין occurs 15 times in Gen. and 64 in Pent., while מבין is

[1] e.g. C. J. Ball, in *S.B.O.T.*

found 13 times in O.T. The proposed alteration will make all these numbers heptadic—**14, 63, 14,** with no practical difference in the meaning.

Vv. 3–8 are still short of two letters, but after what has been said about Heb. orthography, this will occasion no surprise. Probably we should spell ויבדיל instead of the shortened form ויבדל twice, vv. 4, 7.

In ver. 11 the Sept. adds "after its kind," למינהו. מין "kind" occurs 31, and its only derivative תמונה "likeness" 10 times in O.T. Adding the word here makes a total of **42.** The same word is found in the Heb. in the same verse spelt למינו, but everywhere else in the chapter it is spelt למינהו, and should be so here.

In ch. ii. 1–3 there are two letters over. Probably the word שביעי "seventh," which occurs twice, should be spelt שבעי, as it is in about a dozen other places.

We are now in a position to count the words and letters in the records of the 1st, 2nd, 3rd, and 7th days.

	Compd. words.	Simple words.	Letters.
In vv. 3–8 there are in the common Heb. text	69	103	265
Add אלהים, ver. 7	1	1	5
For בין read מבין , ver. 6. . . .	—	1	1
For ויבדל read ויבדיל , vv. 4, 7 . . .	—	—	2
	70	105	273
In vv. 9–13 there are.	69	102	259
Add למינהו, ver. 11.	1	3	6
Read ,, for למינו, ver. 11 . . .	—	—	1
	70	105	266
In ii. 1–3 there are	35	60	144
For השביעי (1°) read הַשִּׁשִּׁי			
For ,, ,, חשבעי, vv. 2, 3 } .	—	—	4
	35	60	140

(Note that בְ is reckoned as two simple words = בה)

Two only of these last are multiples of 7, but they are all multiples of 5, and as there are only 5 divisions in this section, this is doubtless the reason.

This is as far as I propose to go at present. In the other verses (14–31) there are a few differences between the Heb. and Gk., but none of any moment. Considering that over 2000 years elapsed (or even on the modern critical theory 1500) between the time when the chapter was written and the date of the earliest extant Heb. MS, the few critical aids we possess, and other matters such as the differences arising from changes of script and orthography to which we have referred, our examination demonstrates that the text has come down to us in a state of remarkable purity.

Before parting from the subject of Textual Criticism, a word of caution is necessary. SEVEN *does not invariably point out the true text*, though it usually does. Gen. ii. 2 is a proof of this, for though we have two heptadic numbers, **98 and 28,** in support of the received reading, it is nevertheless wrong. So in David's lamentation over Saul and Jonathan (2 Sam. i. 19–27), ו, " and," occurs **7** times (as do also the other prefixes, ה, " the," and ב, " in "), and though there is no doubt that " and " *should* occur **7** times, yet it is probable the seven now found in the Hebrew text are not all in the right places. So the words " come (and) see " are found **7** times in the N.T. according to the A.V. (see Mimpriss's *Harmony*, note on John i. 39) ; yet it does not follow that they are all correct. Neither must we, because " Israel " occurs in rec. text **28** times in Luke and Acts, and **42** times in the rest of the N.T.— **70** in all—refuse to question the authenticity of the word in Acts iv. 8, and Rom. x. 1. And I have already shown that " Verily " is spurious in Mark vi. 11, and Luke xiii. 35, although the word occurs in the received text **14** times in the one Gospel, and **7** in the other.

Examples of these *False Heptads*, as they may be termed, might be multiplied ; but the above are sufficient. Where there is the least doubt, therefore, confirmation should be sought by trying to find additional heptads in other directions, not relying simply upon one. It is true that in many of the illustrations given in this chapter the conclusion arrived at is only supported by one application of the TEST, and therefore it is just possible that, in a few instances, it *may* be wrong ; but on the one hand I have chosen the illustrations with due care, and, on the other to have pursued every example to its fullest possible limits would have far exceeded the space at my disposal, and would have made the subject tedious and uninteresting to the reader, besides being in most cases wholly unnecessary.

CHAPTER III

THE CANON OF SCRIPTURE

THE questions to be dealt with in this chapter are (1) Have all of the books now commonly received as Scripture a right to be so considered? and (2) Are any books which ought to form part of the Bible *lost* or excluded therefrom? In other words, Does the Bible of the Reformed Churches contain the *whole* word of God, and *no more* than the word of God? These questions have to be treated here simply by the light thrown upon them by the number 7.

First, as regards the number of the main divisions of Scripture.

The Old Testament is divided by the Jews into 3 portions: (1) the Law, (2) the Prophets, (3) the Hagiographa, or Sacred Writings. This triple division can be traced as far back as the second century B.C., for Jesus the son of Sirach, who wrote about that time, speaks expressly of "the law and the prophecies and the remainder of the books." [1] Our Lord is thought to allude to the same division when He speaks of "the law of Moses, and the prophets, and the psalms;" [2] and it is also found in Philo and Josephus, Jewish writers of the first century, and in the Talmud.

Of the New Testament no similar *official* division is now recognized, but anciently it was divided into 4 portions or volumes, containing (1) the Gospels, (2) the

---

[1] Prologue to Ecclesiasticus (in the Apocrypha).
[2] Luke xxiv. 44.

Acts and Catholic (or General) Epistles, (3) the Pauline Epistles, (4) the Apocalypse.[1]

According, therefore, to the usage of ancient times, the Bible consists of **7** main sections, divided, as 7 so frequently is, into a 3 and a 4. Perhaps a more appropriate division of the New Testament than the above would be (1) the Gospels, (2) the Acts, (3) the Epistles, (4) the Revelation ; but this does not affect the total number.

Another division of the Bible frequently found is the following :—*Old Testament :* (1) the Pentateuch, (2) the Historical Books, (3) the Poetical Books, (4) the Prophetical Books. *New Testament :* (5) the Historical Books, (6) the Doctrinal Books, or Epistles, (7) the Prophetical Book (Revelation). Still, however, we reach the same total **7,** and still we have the same subdivisions 3 and 4.

Secondly, as regards the number of the books of Scripture. This, according to the modern mode of counting, is 39 in the Old Testament and **27** in the New, total 66. It is, indeed, so near to **70** as at once to suggest either that four inspired books have been lost, or that some books now called uncanonical or " deutero-canonical " ought to find a place in the sacred volume.

But the question is not, What is considered to be the total number of books in the Bible *now* ? but, How were they counted when the Canon of Scripture was closed ? The latest book of the N.T. was written before the end of the first century,[2] and the number of the books in this portion of the Bible cannot be made either less or more than 27. Now, of how many books

---

[1] Manuscripts of the N.T. are still classified according to this grouping, and in the critical editions of the Greek Testament of Westcott & Hort, Lachmann, Tischendorf, Tregelles and von Soden, the same order is followed, the Catholic Epistles being placed *before* those of St. Paul, and not after, as in the common editions.

[2] To say *second* century here would not affect the argument, and would perhaps avoid any appearance of " begging the question." I adhere, however, to the statement in the text.

was the O.T. said to consist in the first century?
History supplies the answer. Josephus says distinctly, " We [i.e. the Jews] have not an innumerable
multitude of books among us, disagreeing from, and
contradicting one another, but only *twenty-two* books,
which contain the records of all the past times ; which
are justly believed to be divine. And of them *five*
belong to Moses, which contain his laws, and the
traditions of the origin of mankind till his death. . . .
But as to the time from the death of Moses till the
reign of Artaxerxes, king of Persia, who reigned after
Xerxes, the prophets, who were after Moses, wrote down
what was done in their times in *thirteen* books. The
remaining *four* books contain hymns to God, and precepts for the conduct of human life." [1] That this (22)
was the number generally received is evident from the
writings of the early Christians which have come down
to us, that being the number given by Origen (*Comm.
on Ps. i.*), Cyril of Jerusalem (*Catech.* iv. c. 33, *seq.*),
Athanasius, John Damascene, Gregory of Nazianzus,
Epiphanius, etc.,[2] though the same unanimity is not
shown with regard to the number of books in each of
the three divisions. The number 22 is arrived at in the
following manner :—

1. Genesis.	12. Ezekiel.
2. Exodus.	13. The Twelve Minor Prophets.
3. Leviticus.	14. Daniel.
4. Numbers.	15. Chronicles, 1 and 2.
5. Deuteronomy.	16. Ezra (with Nehemiah).
6. Joshua.	17. Esther.
7. Judges (with Ruth).	18. Job.
8. Samuel, 1 and 2.	19. Psalms.
9. Kings, 1 and 2.	20. Proverbs.
10. Isaiah.	21. Ecclesiastes.
11. Jeremiah (with Lamentations).	22. Song of Solomon.[3]

[1] *Against Apion*, bk. i. § 8. (This work was written towards the
close of the first century, say between A.D. 93 and 100.)

[2] Gaussen's *Canon of the Holy Scriptures*, Eng. transl., p. 441 ;
Ryle's *Canon of O.T.*, *Excursus C.*

[3] *See* Swete's *Introd. to O.T. in Greek*, p. 220.

Josephus's three divisions doubtless included respectively numbers 1–5, 6–18, and 19–22, in the above list. Jerome, in the fourth century, gives a catalogue specifying the 22 books as above, but including numbers 1–5 in the Law, 6–13 in the Prophets, and 14–22 in the Hagiographia. He states also that some counted Ruth and Lamentations as separate books, placing them in the Hagiographa, and so making the total number of books 24,[1] and this is the way in which these books are now placed in the Hebrew Bible.

We see, therefore, that up to the [third or] fourth century of the Christian era, the books of the Old Testament were so counted as to make a total of 22, that being, as Jerome remarks, the number of letters in the Hebrew alphabet.[2] Now, if to this we add the 27 books of the N.T., we have **49,** or *seven* times *seven*, as the number of books of which Scripture is composed, according to the mode of counting current when the latest books were written, and for some time after.

Nor can it be said that there has been any straining to get at this eminently heptadic number, that certain books have been added or left out so as to make exactly **49.** I am not aware that any previous writer, ancient or modern, has called attention to this being the number of the books of Scripture. Indeed, the Bible, as a collected whole, has never been considered to contain exactly **49** books. For although the 27 books of the N.T. were all written in the first century, yet 7 of them —Hebrews, James, 2 Peter, 2 John, 3 John, Jude, and Revelation—were not *universally* received as Scripture until about three centuries later. " Even the most reluctant," says Archdeacon Lee, " are forced to admit that the reception of the different parts of the N.T.,

[1] *Prologue Galeatus*; Ryle, *Canon of O.T.*, 231.

[2] He further notices that, as there are five double letters in Hebrew, so there are five double books—Samuel, Kings, Chronicles, Ezra, Jeremiah. He might perhaps have added a sixth double letter—*shin, sin*; and a sixth double book—Judges. If to these we add the Minor Prophets, we have **7** books of the 22 which are now subdivided.

as Scripture, took place without external concert,—
from an inward impulse, as it were,—at the same time
and in the most different places ; and that, with scarcely
an exception, each writing which it contains was all
at once, and without a word of doubt, placed on a level
with the O.T., which had hitherto been regarded as
exclusively divine.   In short, the authority conceded
to this new component of the Scriptures, seems to have
grown up without any one being able to place his finger
upon the place or moment when adhesion to it was first
yielded."[1]   An approximate date, however, may be
arrived at.   "By the end of the fourth century" the
doubtful books   "seem   to   have   been   universally
received ; " and " from the beginning of the fifth century the Canon of the New Testament was fixed in the
Churches ; and any divergencies from the standard
thus exhibited, made either by Churches or individuals
in later times, are to be viewed as mere utterances of
opinion, and carry with them no evidential authority."[2]
But by this date the Books of Ruth and Lamentations,
hitherto regarded as parts of Judges and Jeremiah
respectively, had taken their places as separate books ;
thus raising the total number in the Old Testament to
24, and making the Old and New Testaments together
to contain 51.
     But has the number 66 no significance ?   Unques-
tionably it has, for Six is " man's number," as we saw in
Ch. I.
     We find then, that the Bible, according to the
Protestant Canon, and also that of the Orthodox
Eastern Church,[3] contains 49 books, if we take the

[1] *Inspiration of Holy Scripture*, 4th ed., p. 48.
[2] Kitto's *Bib. Lit.*, i. 437.
[3] "We accept the Canon of Scripture as it is defined by St.
Athanasius [A.D. 367] and as it has been received by the whole
Catholic Church—namely, the 22 books of the Old Testament which
are contained in the Hebrew Canon, and the 27 books of the
New Testament."—Abp. of Canterbury's Eastern Churches Committee : *Suggested terms of intercommunion* (S.P.C.K.), *Guardian*,
15th April, 1921, p. 285.

reckoning current when the last portion of it was written, or 66 books if each one be counted separately. The latter number, in which 6 is plainly and emphatically seen, denotes that outwardly it is a human book, written by human hands, and coming to us in human dress; the former number, in which 7 is also emphatically contained but not *seen*, denotes that, for those who have eyes to see and hearts to receive it, it is nothing less than the Word of the Living God.

But so far we have only proved that our present Bible contains the right *number* of books, and not that they are really the right books. It was to prove this that, in *Seven the Sacred Number*, a chapter was given from each one of the 66 books, rather than a selection here and there, showing that each book contains the heptad mark, and as we have seen that the total number is right, we are justified in saying that *each book of the 66 is inspired*, and that *no inspired book is lost*.

This result—the safe preservation of all the books of Scripture, and the exclusion of all merely human productions from the Canon—has not been brought about by man's agency alone. As in the writing so in the preservation of the Scriptures, man has been but an instrument in the hand of God. " The collection of sacred books," says Archdeacon Lee, speaking of the Old Testament, " was defined under the divine guidance, and closed at the divine command."[1] And so with regard to the New Testament : " while the Church of Rome has put forth such pretensions with respect to the Old Testament, neither this sect, powerful as it is, nor any of the other Christian sects, has been able *to add a single apocryphal book to the New Testament ;* God has not permitted it, and will not permit it. He will not permit it, because all Christian Churches, good or bad, faithful or unfaithful, have been entrusted with this sacred deposit, and because all must preserve it

[1] *On Inspiration*, p. 51.

inviolate, as the Jews have preserved the Old, God having constituted Himself the guarantee of their fidelity." [1]   So Bp. Westcott, at the close of his able work on the subject, remarks that the " whole history [of the Canon] is itself a striking lesson in the character and conduct of the Providential government of the Church." [2]

As an instance of the jealous care of God over His Holy Word, the Psalter may be referred to.   The number of separate psalms, as is shown in Part II, [3] was originally 147. - Man, however, would insist upon making this into the " even number," 150.   God suffered this to be done, but only by dividing three genuine psalms into two portions each, and that was done so clumsily as to leave evident traces of the hand of man in the work of God.   An additional psalm, purporting to be written by David, is indeed found in the Septuagint, Syriac, and other versions, but it has never been received as canonical, either by Jews or Christians.

This, perhaps, is the most appropriate place to deal with the question of the **Authorship** of the books of Scripture.

One example will suffice.   Some modern writers say that the **Second Ep. of St. Peter** is not from the same hand as the First, though there are many defenders of the traditional belief.   The following is a list (but not a complete one) of words, etc., occurring **7** or a multiple of 7 times in the two Epp. together.   The figures show the number of occurrences in each Epistle.

[1] Gaussen on *The Canon of the Holy Scriptures*, Eng. trans., p. 474.
[2] *History of the Canon of the New Testament*, p. 496.
[3] p. 324.

	1 Pe.	2 Pe.	Total:
1. *Angelos* " an angel " (in a good sense and excluding " the angels that sinned," 2 P. ii. 4) 2, 1 ; *exangello* 1, 0 ; *epangellomai* 0, 1 ; *epangelia* 0, 2 ; *epangelma* 0, 2 ; *euangelizo* 3, 0 ; *euangelion* 1, 0 ; *anangello*, 1, 0 ; total from Root	8	6	14
2. *Hagios* [1] " holy " (incg. 2 P. i. 21 with Treg. Sod.)	8	6	14
3. *Hagios* [1] " holy," referring to men and women	5	2	7
4. *Aiōn* " ever " (omg. aiōnōn 1 P. v. 11 WH) 4, 1 ; *aiōnios* 1, 1 total	5	2	7
5. *Hamartia* " sin " (omg. 2 P. i. 9, Ti. Tr. WH[1])	6	1	7
6. *Apo* [1] " from " (excg. 2 P. i. 21)	5	2	7
7. *Autois* " (to) them "	1	6	7
8. *Autou* " of him "	10	4	14
9. *Ginōskō* " to know," spoken of man 0, 2 ; *epiginōskŏ* 0, 2 ; *proginōsko* 0, 1 ; *gnōrizo* 0, 1 ; *gnōsis* 1, 3 ; *epignōsis* 0, 4 ; total (*proginōskŏ* and *prognōsis* are each used once of God)	1	13	14
10. *En* " in," governing a pronoun	11	10	21
11. *Ergon* " work " 2, 2 ; *argos* 0, 1 ; *argeo* 0, 1 ; *katergazomai* 1, 0 ; total	3	4	7
12. *Hina* " that " (besides *hina mē* once)	13	1	14
13. *Kaleo* " to call "	6	1	7
14. *Kata* " according to," etc.	10	4	14
15. *Kosmos* " world " (besides once " adorning ")	2	5	7
16. *Kurios* " Lord " (besides once used of Abraham)	7	14	21
17. " Lord . . . Jesus Christ ".	1	6	7
18. *Meno* " to abide " 2, 0 ; *diameno* 0, 1 ; *hupomeno* 2, 0 ; *hupomone* 0, 2 ; total	4	3	7
19. *Nous* " the mind " : *agnoeo* 0, 1 ; *agnoia* 1, 0 ; *agnōsia* 1, 0 ; *dianoia*|1, 1 ; *ennoia* 1, 0 ; *metanoia* 0, 1 ; total	4	3	7
20. *Houn* " therefore "	6	1	7
21. *Peri* " of," " for "	5	2	7
22. *Pistis* " faith "	5	2	7
23. *Strepho* " to turn " : *anastrepho* 1, 1 ; *anastrophe* 6, 2 ; *epistrepho* 1, 1 ; *katastrophe* 0, 1 ; *hupostrepho* 0, 1 ; total	8	6	14
Anastrepho and *anastrophe* used of a good " manner of life "	6	1	7
24. *Sozo* " to save " 2, 0 ; *Sotēr* 0, 5 ; *sotēria* 4, 1 ; *asōtia* 1, 0 ; *diasozo* 1, 0 ; total	8	6	14
25. *Timē* meaning " preciousness " (R.V.) 1, 0 ; *timios* 1, 1 ; *entimos* 2, 0 ; *isotimos* 0, 1 ; *polutimos* 1, 0 ; all translated " precious " " preciousness " R.V. (besides *timē*, *timao*, " honour " 4, 1) ; total	5	2	7
26. *Humas* " you "	14	7	21
27. *Hupo* " by," " under "	2	5	7
28. Names and titles of God—the three persons of the Trinity —occur.	73	25	98

There are 7 names and titles of God (the Father) and 14 of our Lord in the two Epp.

Where several words are given together, they are the whole of the occurrences from the Root which occur in the two epistles.

---

[1] Both ἅγιος and ἀπό favour the rec. rdg., " holy men of God spake," agst. R, WH, " Men spake from God " (2 P. i. 21). It is easy to see how *ΑΓΙΟΙ* (espec. if at the end of a line the last letter was crowded out) was read as *ΑΠΟ*. And " holy " agrees best with the author's style (1 P. iii. 5 ; 2 P. iii. 2, etc.) ; he is fond of calling persons and things holy.

This list might be enlarged, but it is sufficient, I think, to show that the two epistles are by the same author.

What then, in conclusion, may we learn in connection with the Canon of Scripture by studying it in the light thrown upon it by the number *Seven* ? Hitherto something has been wanting to make the chain of proof complete in regard to this subject. " To the last," says Westcott, " it will be impossible to close up every avenue of doubt, and the Canon, like all else that has a moral value, can be determined only with practical and not with demonstrative certainty." [1] It is always unsafe to prophesy, and what was perhaps " impossible " when those words were written is so no longer. The application of the number *Seven*, both to the Bible as a whole, and to each separate book in detail, enables us to determine the question " with demonstrative certainty," and to affirm that " the books specified as canonical in the sixth Article of the Church of England, and the first of the Confession of the Church of Scotland, [and] received as such by the majority of Protestants," [2] constitute the whole Word of God, neither less nor more, and the only rule of faith binding upon mankind.

[1] *Canon of the N.T.*, 498.
[2] Kitto's *Cyc. Bib. Lit.* i. 431.

CHAPTER IV

TRANSLATION

IN the preceding chapters many instances have been given showing the influence of the Septenary Structure of Scripture upon its translation into our own language, so that it will not be necessary to deal with the subject here at any great length. In Gal. ii. 20 the common translation is substantially correct, " I am crucified with Christ, nevertheless I live ; yet not I, but Christ liveth in me," for the rendering (as in the marg. of the R.V., which is supported by the American company), " I am crucified with Christ, and it is no longer I that live, but Christ liveth in me," would only give six divisions in vv. 20, 21 where *seven* are required.

In Acts vi. 1, instead of " there arose a murmuring of the Grecians against the Hebrews, *because* their widows were neglected in the daily ministration," which makes two sentences, we must render "*that* their widows," etc., one sentence. The difference is that the former admits the charge to be true, while the latter does not. The Greek may mean either. We have then **7** sentences (divisions) in vv. 1–6.

1 Cor. x. 17 is another place where the heptadic division obliges us to depart from the common translation, the *marg.* of the R.V. being here substantially correct : " For (there is) one bread ; we the many are one body." This gives us **7** divisions in vv. 16–18.

2 Tim. iii. 16, 17, is, perhaps, a more important passage. Here the A.V. reads (and so substantially the *marg.* of the R.V.), (1) " All scripture (is) given by inspiration of God, (2) and (is) profitable for doctrine,

(3) for reproof, (4) for correction, (5) for instruction in righteousness : (6) that the man of God may be perfect, (7) throughly furnished unto all good works." The first two divisions here the R.V. text joins into one, thus : "Every scripture inspired of God (is) also profitable," etc. It will be seen that it is simply a question whether the verb *to be* is to be introduced once or twice, and on this point the R.V. text is wrong and the A.V. right.[1]

The Heb. word *saris*, "eunuch," etc., occurs in the O.T. 45 times, but in three places (2 Ki. xviii. 17 ; Jer. xxxix. 3, 17) it is translated, in the A.V., as part of a proper name (Rab-saris). This would leave 42 occurrences of the word as an appellative, therefore the A.V. is probably right. There are two other words beginning with Rab which are translated as proper names in the A.V.—Rab-mag, which occurs twice, and Rab-shakeh, 16 times. This gives a total of 21 (3 + 2 + 16), which would seem to confirm the A.V. Other authorities translate the first two "chief eunuch" and "chief magian," leaving Rabshakeh as a proper name. It would be difficult, perhaps, to say which side the R.V. takes.

Deut. i. 7 : "(1) In the Arabah, (2) in the hill country, (3) and in the lowland, (4) and in the South, (5) and by the sea shore, (6) the land of the Canaanites, (7) and Lebanon." So the R.V., correctly ; the A.V., by rendering "*to* the land of the Canaanites, and *unto* Lebanon," obscures the sense.

Exod. xxv.[1]: "37 (1) AND thou shalt make the seven lamps thereof ; (2) AND they shall light the lamps thereof, (3) AND it shall give light over against it. 38 (4) And (thou shalt make) the tongs thereof, (5) and

---

[1] There are 6 other passages, making 7 in all, with the same construction in the Greek, viz., a subject, two or more adjectives joined by και as predicates, and no verb, all translated in R.V. on the principle first named. (Ro. vii. 12; 1 Co. xi. 30; 2 Co. x. 10; 1 Ti. ii. 3, iv. 4; He. iv. 13. See also 1 Ti. i. 15, iv. 9.) Bullinger, *Figures of Speech, Companion Bible, in loc.*

(thou shalt make) the snuffdishes thereof, of pure gold. 39 Of a talent of pure gold shall it be made, with all these vessels. 40 (6) And see, (7) and make (them) after their pattern which thou (wert) shown in the mount." So the thirty-eighth verse should be rendered, not as in the A.V. and R.V.

Exod. xxxvi. 1 : "Then wrought Bezaleel and Aholiab," etc. So the A.V.; but the R.V. joins the whole verse to the preceding chapter, treating it as a continuation of Moses' speech, and renders, "And Bezalel and Oholiab shall work," etc. An examination of the heptadic structure of the passage shows the R.V. to be correct.

A careful study of the Heb. word בצר, *batsar*, " to cut off," etc., enables us to decide the following points : (1) The rendering of the A.V. and R.V. in Mic. ii. 12, " I will put them together as the sheep *of Bozrah*," is wrong; for the proper names derived from this root occur in all **14** times without this passage, while the appellatives occur **91** times with it. It is strange that the parallelism did not save the Revisers from error here :—

> " I will put them together as sheep *into a fold*,
> As a flock in the midst of their pasture."

So most critics : see the *Variorum Bible*. The Sept. takes the word to be derived from another root, and renders " as sheep *in trouble*," which is altogether wrong. (2) The Bozrah mentioned in Jer. xlviii. 24 is not the Bozrah in the land of Edom, as Gesenius and Robinson supposed, for this city is spoken of **7** times elsewhere in Scripture; it was probably in the land of Moab. (3) The A.V. text in Zech. xi. 2, " The forest *of the vintage* is come down," is wrong, though the translators are, perhaps, not to blame, for they simply followed the marginal or corrected reading of the Heb. The Heb. text, however, is correct, " the strong [*or* defenced] forest is come down," and so the R.V. and the A.V. marg. *Batsir*, " vintage," occurs **7** times without this passage. (4) In Ps. ix. 9 ; x. 1, the rendering " in times of *trouble*," though practically right, is not strictly correct ; it should be " in seasons of *drought*." The Hebrew word is not derived from צרר, but from בצר. Including these two passages, the word בצר, *batsar*, and its derivatives occur together **91** times ; without them, only 89.

Isa. ix. 6 : " His name shall be called Wonderful, Counsellor." The marg. of the R.V. reduces these two titles to one, " Wonderful counsellor," and that this is correct the following, I think, will show. The whole reads thus :—

> (*1*) Unto us a child is born,
> (*2*) Unto us a son is given,
> (*3*) And the government shall be upon his shoulder ;
> (*4*) And his name shall be called
> Wonderful counsellor,
> (*5*) Mighty God,
> (*6*) Father of Eternity,[1]
> (*7*) Prince of Peace.

Dr. Kay, whose opinion is entitled to respect, says, indeed, that the Hebrew will not bear this rendering ; but the testimony of most moderns is on the other side. The title then agrees with Isa. xxviii. 29, " the LORD of hosts . . . is *wonderful in counsel*." The parallelism of the passage also requires this rendering.

Luke iv. 18 :—

> (*1*) The Spirit of the Lord (is) upon me,
> (*2*) Because he hath anointed me to preach the gospel to the poor ;
> (*3*) He hath sent me *to heal the brokenhearted*,
> (*4*) To preach deliverance to the captives,
> (*5*) And recovering of sight to the blind,
> (*6*) To set at liberty them that are bruised,
> (*7*) To preach the acceptable year of the Lord.

So the A.V. But the R.V. omits the words " to heal

[1] See R.V., marg..

the brokenhearted," and thus gives us only *six* lines instead of seven. Is the R.V. wrong in omitting these words, or does the septenary arrangement not apply here? There is a third course. By simply altering the position of the semicolon, we may read—

(*1*) The Spirit of the Lord is upon me,
(*2*) Because he hath anointed me ;
(*3*) To preach good tidings to the poor he hath sent me,
(*4*) To proclaim release to the captives,
(*5*) And recovering of sight to the blind,
(*6*) To set at liberty them that are bruised,
(*7*) To proclaim the acceptable year of the Lord.

It is simply a matter of punctuation ; and the Hebrew text of Isa. lxi. 1 is thus translated by Bps. Lowth and Horsley and others, while many editions of the Sept. punctuate in this manner, and some editions of the Greek Testament in the passage before us. The difference is of some importance, however. The " anointing " of our Lord was not simply " to preach the gospel to the poor," however important a part of His work that might be ; but it referred to His whole mission. So that when our Lord declared in the synagogue of Nazareth, " He hath anointed me " (for there could be no ambiguity in the words as *spoken*), and then told the astonished Nazarenes, " This day is this scripture fulfilled in your ears," it was equivalent to His saying, " I am the Messiah, the Christ, the *Anointed* One."

Matt. vi. 13 : " But deliver us from evil." On no point, perhaps, were the N.T. Revisers more fiercely assailed than for the change they made in the last petition of the Lord's Prayer, " But deliver us from *the evil* (*one*)." Does the HEPTAD TEST enable us to decide between the two? The Greek words *tou ponērou* may be either masculine or neuter (for in the genitive case the two genders are alike), may be either spoken of a person, " the evil *one*," or of a thing, " the evil *thing*," or simply " evil " in the abstract. We have, therefore, to find out whether they are here masculine or neuter. Taking the text adopted by the Revisers, with which all recent critics agree,[1] a careful study of the prayer yields the following results. It contains 57 words (the " trinal fraction " of 7), of which 15 are duplicates, leaving 42 different words, counting each grammatical form as a separate word. It contains 259 letters (7 × 37, a number which possesses some significance) which, if counted separately, present this peculiarity, that 4 letters (a, η, λ, ν) occur 7 times or a multiple of 7, and 7 letters (a, γ, θ, μ, ϱ, σ, φ,) occur 4 times or multiple ; while 3 letters (μ, ϱ, σ) occur 8 times or multiple, and 8 letters (η, $\varkappa$, ν, o, π, σ, τ, ν) occur 3 times or multiple. If we take the parts of speech separately we find that the article occurs in 7 different forms ; that the pronoun occurs 7 times in the genitive case, and also that its total occurrences are 3 singular and 9 plural, equal, if the plurals be counted as two, to 21 ; and that 7 different verbs are used, 8 times in all, of which 7 occurrences are in the aorist tense and singular number and one is in the plural. Is it not reasonable, then, to expect that the noun can also be connected in some way with the number 7 ? But I can find no other way than this, that, if we exclude *ponērou*, the noun (a term which according to ancient Greek includes adjectives) occurs 7 times in the masculine gender. *Ponērou* is therefore neuter, and " deliver us from evil " is correct.

Heb. xii. 18: "For ye are not come unto (1) the mount that might be touched, (2) and that burned with fire, (3) nor unto blackness, (4) and darkness, (5) and tempest, (6) and the sound of a trumpet, (7) and the voice of words." So the A.V., and so practically the text of the R.V; but the R.V. marg. (omitting "mount") joins (1) and (2) together, rendering " a palpable and kindled fire." This would reduce the whole to six, and is therefore incorrect.

[1] With the slight exception that for ἐλθέτω some read ἐλθάτω.

The **Precious Stones** of Scripture form an interesting heptadic study. Not only is there considerable difference of opinion as to what stones are meant by certain Hebrew words, but also, as to some words, whether they designate precious stones or not. It is with this latter point that I propose to deal now. Precious stones are frequently mentioned in the O.T. The names of the twelve which were set in the high priest's breastplate occur in the Hebrew text 55 times. In Isa. liv. 11, for בפוך, *bappūk*, "with fair colours," the Sept. have evidently read נפך, *nophek*, the name of the fourth stone in the breastplate, for they have *anthrax*, which they use in Exodus as the translation of *nophek*. נ might easily be mistaken for ב by a copyist, and the ו added afterwards for vocalization. The parallelism favours this reading :—

> "Behold, I will lay thy stones with *emeralds*,
> And thy foundations with sapphires,
> And I will make thy pinnacles of rubies,
> And thy gates of carbuncles,
> And all thy border of pleasant stones."

This gives us **56** occurrences of the names of the twelve stones of the breastplate. Besides these twelve the only precious stones mentioned in the O.T. are probably the כדכד, *kadkod* ("agate," A.V.; "ruby," R.V.), which occurs in Isa. liv. 12; Ezek. xxvii. 16; and the אקדח, *eqdach*, "carbuncle," Isa. liv. 12. This gives a total of **14** stones and 59 occurrences in the O.T.

In the N.T., precious stones are nowhere mentioned but in the book of Revelation, where the names of 12 stones (probably the same as those in the breastplate) occur 18 times. This would give a total for the whole Bible of **14** stones, mentioned **77** times.

These stones can be further connected with the number **7** as follows : *tarshish*, "beryl,"[1] occurs **7**

[1] It is difficult to understand on what principle the Revisers have dealt with this word. In their text, it is true, they everywhere follow the A.V., and translate "beryl," but in their margin there is no such uniformity. In Exod. xxviii. 20 (to which may be added

times in the O.T. Presuming the *yash'pheh* of the
O.T. to be identical with the *iaspis*, "jasper," of the
New, the former occurs 3 times and the latter 4:
total 7. *Shoham*, "onyx" ("beryl," R.V. marg.),
occurs 7 times in Exodus, and it is 7 times in the O.T.
joined to "stone" or "stones." The other words are
connected with "stone" in the following places:
sappir, "sapphire," Ezek. i. 26; x. i.: *tarshish*,
"beryl," Ezek. x. 9: *eqdach*, "carbuncle," Isa. liv. 12:
iaspis, "jasper," Rev. iv. 3; xxi. 11;—only six in the
two Testaments combined. This should doubtless
be 7, and perhaps the missing one is Sol. Song v.
14, where the Heb. reads, according to our Authorized
translation, "His belly (is as) bright ivory *overlaid
(with) sapphires.*" But, for "overlaid (with) sapphires,"
the LXX. have "upon a sapphire stone." They
appear to have read מעל אבן, *meal eben*, "upon a
stone," not מעלפת, *m'ullepheth*, "overlaid."

Of the whole 77 occurrences, 49 are found in Gen.,
Ex., and Rev.; 21 in the historical and prophetical
books, Chron., Isa., Ezek., and Dan.; and 7 in the more
strictly poetical books, Job, Song of Sol., and Lam.

Thus far we have dealt more with the Text than the
Translation, except that we have seen that in Ezek. x. 9
the R.V. marginal rendering, "stone of Tarshish," is
incorrect; for not only would it destroy three of the
heptads already given, but "Tarshish" occurs as an
undoubted proper name 28 times without this passage,
of which 14 refer to Tarshish the place, 10 speak of
"ships of Tarshish," and 4 are names of individuals
(*see* Young's *Analytical Concordance*).

We are now, however, in a position to deal with the
doubtful words. (1) *P'ninim* is translated "rubies" in
Exod. xxxix. 13), the margin gives "chalcedony," though not in
what may be called the parallel passage, Ezek. xxviii. 13. Neither
is there any alternative rendering in Ezek. i. 16; Dan. x. 6. In
Cant. v. 14, however, the margin gives "topaz," while in Ezek.
x. 9 it is treated as a proper name, "stone of Tarshish" being given
in place of the "beryl stone" of the text! This last is certainly
wrong.

both the A.V. and the R.V., though the latter gives
two alternatives in the margin, "*or* red corals, *or*
pearls," Job xxviii. 18. One of these, probably the
former, is doubtless the correct rendering. The word
occurs six times. (2) *Shamir*, which occurs three times,
is translated "diamond" once, and "adamant"
twice, alike in the A.V. and the R.V. The true rendering is perhaps "emery stone," as maintained by some;
the Oxford *Heb. Lex.* gives adamant *or* flint. (3)
B'dolach is translated *anthrax* by the Sept. in Gen. ii.
12, and *krustallos* in Num. xi. 7, while some have taken
it to mean "beryl." "Bdellium," however, is doubtless correct. To take any of these three words to mean
precious stones would destroy the heptadic symmetry
of the undoubted precious stones.

The influence of the Heptadic Occurrence of Words
from the Same Root upon the subject of **Etymology**
will doubtless have been already perceived. Leaving
its full development to those more competent to deal
with it, I will just give two or three instances of doubtful etymology where it appears to afford some help.

פסח, *pasach*, has two meanings, "to pass over" and
"to limp," and some suggest two roots. The total
occurrences of root(s) and derivatives are (1) *pasach*, to
pass over, 4, *pesach*, "passover," **49** = 53; (2) *pasach*,
"to limp," 3, *pisseach*, "lame," **14** = **17**. But if,
with most authorities, we recognize only one root, the
figures are: *pasach* **7**, *pesach* **49**, *pisseach* **14**, total **70**.

Isa. lxi. 6: "In their glory shall ye boast yourselves." So the A.V. and the text of the R.V., with
the Targum, Syriac, and Vulgate, taking the word
translated "boast yourselves" to be derived from
אמר, *amar*, "to say;" but most modern critics translate "of their glory shall ye receive in exchange,"
or, as the margin of the R.V. has it, "to their glory
shall ye succeed," deriving it from ימר, *yamar*, "to
exchange." The word מור, *mūr*, "to change, exchange," occurs **14** times, and its derivative, תמורה,

t'murah, " exchange," etc., 6 : total 20. The cognate root יָמַר, *yamar*, occurs only in Jer. ii. 11, giving a total of **21** without the passage before us. The A.V. is therefore probably right, though this proof is only of a negative character, and I am not sure whether any stress should be laid on the fact that *amar*, " to say," occurs 6 times in the oblique conjugations without this text, or **7** with it.

It is not certainly known what is the primary meaning of the Greek word *arōma*, " spice." It has been suggested, however, that its roots are *aroō*, " to plough," and *ozō*, " to smell," and that it means " the smell of a ploughed field." That this is probably correct will appear from the following : *arotriaō*, " to plough," and *arotron*, " a plough " (from *aroō*), occur three times, to which, if the four occurrences of *aroma* be added, we have **7**. Again, *ozō*, " to smell," with its derivatives *osmē*, " odour," and *euōdia*, " sweet smell," occur 10 times, or with *arōma*, **14**. (*Osphrēsis*, " smelling," is by some derived from *ozō*, but others differ.)

Halōn, " a threshing floor," and *aloaō*, " to thresh," are usually considered to be separate roots ; but as, with the two derivatives of the latter, *patralōas*, " a murderer of his father," and *metralōas*, " a murderer of his mother," they occur together **7** times, they are doubtless etymologically allied.

Manteuomai, " to divine," is derived from *mantis*, " a soothsayer," which, in turn, is said by some authorities to be derived from *mainomai*, " to be mad." But *mainomai*, with its derivatives *mania*, " madness," and *emmainomai*, " to be mad against," already occurs 7 times. *Mantis* is, therefore, doubtless a root itself. Other words of similar import are *magos*, " a wise man, sorcerer," which with its derivatives occurs 8 times ; and *pharmakeus*, " a sorcerer," which with its derivatives occurs 5 times ; making a total, with the single occurrence of *manteuomai*, of **14**.

CHAPTER V

INTERPRETATION

IT is impossible to draw a hard and fast line between Translation and Interpretation; the translator must be to some extent an interpreter, though he should be careful not to exercise this function more than is necessary. Much, therefore, that has been already said bears upon the subject of this chapter, still there are many things which could not conveniently be spoken of under any other heading.

The fact that the first two verses of Genesis are not heptadic is surely one of deep significance. Why are they thus cut off from the rest of the chapter? Is it not because they refer to a subject entirely distinct? I will not refer to the old quarrel between Genesis and Geology, for now " science and theology have learned to dwell together." [1] Rightly understood, there *can be* no contradiction between what are equally works of God.

I have said that the two verses are not heptadic. Not in the same sense as is the rest of the chapter; yet the number 7 is found in them. The first verse contains 7 words, 28 letters; the second verse 14 words, but (if the common orthography is correct) 52 letters. So that they are distinct in form, not only from the following verses, but from each other. Two intervals of time may, therefore, be allowed (and this is all that geology requires): first, between vv. 1 and 2; and, again, between vv. 2 and 3. The chapter may be epitomized in the following words, which are from a far

[1] Hugh Chisholm in *Enc. Brit.* i. p. xxi.

abler pen than my own : " First, there is a creation
of God announced—then a partial ruin—then a restoration. ' In the beginning God created the heavens and
the earth.' Of these first ' heavens ' nothing further
is here revealed to us : but of the ' earth ' we read that
it was [or rather " became "] ' without form and void,'
language used by the prophets to describe a state of
judgment and utter ruin.[1] In some way, not revealed,
God's work had been destroyed. God then, in the
six days, restores that earth, not made dark by Him,
yet now in darkness ; and on this ruined earth His
work proceeds, till His image is seen, and He can
rest there. Thus a creation utterly wrecked is the
ground for the six days' work. On this dark and
ruined mass appears what God can do." [2]

Psalm xxiii. We dealt with the text and translation
of·this psalm in Ch. I. The chief difference between
interpreters of the psalm is as to whether the figure
of shepherd and sheep is carried through to the end,
or is changed in the latter portion. Does the number
7 help us here ? The heptadic structure of the psalm
shows that it is divided in the middle of ver. 4, and as
the figure of the shepherd is certainly found in the
second section (" thy rod and thy staff ") we should
expect to find it carried right through. We have seen
that the derivation from *shoob*, " return," in the last
verse gives us three heptads of words, which are all
spoiled if we adopt *yashab*, " dwell." And on this word
the interpretation largely hinges ; thus Dr. Briggs, who
thinks the figure of shepherd and sheep does not extend
to the last verse, says, " *dwell*, which is given in Sept.

---

[1] " Jer. iv. 23. The same original words occur in Isa. xxxiv. 11,
there translated *confusion* and *emptiness*. Cf. Isa, xlv. 18."

[2] *The Types of Genesis*, by Andrew Jukes, p. 5. I cannot mention Mr. Jukes's name without acknowledging my indebtedness to
his writings. It was from them that I received my first ideas respecting the symbolism of numbers, and it is to be regretted that he
should have been deterred by a fear of the charge of mysticism from
entering more fully into the subject.

and Jerome, is more suited to the context than the Heb. *return.*" [1] To justify the translation "return," therefore, we must see that it makes good sense. The psalm is not strictly a parable, but it may be likened to a parable and explanation combined. Several of the Heb. words have a double meaning, or rather have both a primary and a derived meaning. Thus (1) the word " soul " (which by the way occurs **756** times in O.T.) may mean simply " life," " self " (cf. Ps. cv. 18, " the iron entered into *his soul*," P.B.V., but simply " *he* was laid in iron " A.V.). So (2) " righteousness " is primarily " what is right." (3) " Paths of righteousness " = " right tracks " (E. G. King, Briggs). (4) " Spread a table " is a common formula for furnishing a meal (Perowne), cf. Ps. lxxviii. 19, " Can God prepare a table in the wilderness ? " (5) " Mercy " = " kindness," and is so frequently translated. (6) " Restore " = " refresh " (*Oxf. Heb. Lex.*). (7) The word translated " house " is used " as shelter or abode of animals " (*Oxf. Heb. Lex.*) and is translated " home " (of cattle) Ex. ix. 19 ; 1 S. vi. 7, 10 ; " web " of spider, Job viii. 14. The wilderness is the " house " of the wild ass, Job xxxix. 6, and the rocks the " houses " of the conies, Pr. xxx. 26. And so the word here means " fold."

The psalm may be read, then, from the sheep's standpoint :

1. The LORD is my shepherd,
2. I shall lack nothing,
3. He maketh me to lie down in green pastures,
4. He leadeth me beside the still waters,
5. He refresheth my life,
6. He guideth me in right tracks for his name's sake.
7. Yea, though I walk through the valley of the shadow of death I will fear no evil.

1. For thou art with me,
2. Thy rod and thy staff, they comfort me.

---

[1] *I.C.C., in loc.*

3. Thou preparest a table (i.e. a meal) before me in the presence of mine enemies.

4. Thou hast anointed my head with oil,

5. My cup is overflowing.

6. Only [1] goodness and kindness will follow me all the days of my life,

7. And I shall return into the house of the LORD (i.e. the fold of my Shepherd, ver. 1) for length of days.[1]

But as "return" is followed by the prep. "in," not "to," it is doubtless a "pregnant construction," as many have pointed out, for "return and dwell in," and the line may be paraphrased, from the believer's point of view : "And I shall return and dwell in the house of the LORD" (i.e. not the Temple, but "my Father's house" of the "many mansions," Jno. xiv. 2), "for length of days (i.e. for ever, as Ps. xxi. 4)."

1 Cor. iii. 17. "The temple of God is holy, οἵτινες ἐστε ὑμεῖς which (temple) ye are," A.V. and R.V. text ; "and such are ye," R.V. marg., but there is no "and" in the Gk. Two questions arise here : (1) does "which (such)" refer to "temple" or "holy"? (2) is ἐστε indicative "ye are," or imperative "be ye"? Take the latter first. Ἐστε occurs 92 times in N.T. (incg. Gal. iv. 28 with most edd., making 7 in Gal.) and is everywhere considered as indic., whereas here it may be imperat., leaving **91** indic. Ὑμεῖς with ἐστε occurs 34 times in N.T., incg. John Gosp. and Ep. **7**, and Paul 15, so if our text be considered imperat. it leaves **14** indic. Ἴσθι, etc. (all forms of imperat.), occur **21** times in critical texts (Mt. xx. 26, 27 rec. being omd.) incg. **7** Lu. and Ac. and 6 Paul, but if ἐστε be added here it makes **7,** and as we have seen that ἴσθι "be thou" must be omd. in Mt. ii. 13 [2] there are still **21** in N.T. There are 10 commands to be holy addressed to God's people generally, **7** in O.T., 3 in N.T. incg. this text :—"Ye shall be holy," (3) Num. xv, 40 ; Ex. xxii. 31 ; 1 Cor. iii. 17 (which, i.e. holy, be ye) ; "Ye shall be holy, for I (the Lord) am holy,"

---

1 R.V. marg.   2 Ch. II, p. 89.

(7) Lev. xi. 44, 45, xix. 2, xx. 7,[1] 26 ; 1 Pe. i. 15, 16. Our text, therefore, is an exhortation to be holy, coupled with a warning : " If any man defile (*or* destroy) the temple of God, him shall God destroy ; for the temple of God is holy, which be ye."

The **Apostles of Our Lord** were 12, a number which there can be no doubt was chosen because that was the number of the tribes of Israel. The only way apparently in which **the 12 tribes** can be connected with the number 7 (further than that, as has often been pointed out, $12 = 4 \times 3$, as $7 = 4 + 3$) is this : Jacob had 12 sons, but Joseph's 2 sons, Ephraim and Manasseh, were counted as Jacob's (Gen. xlviii. 5), making 13 ; for though Jacob still reserved a place for Joseph in addition (ver. 6), he had no other children to claim it. But in the division of the land the tribe of Manasseh was divided in *two*, one part taking territory east of Jordan, the other west. And though, in order to preserve the number 12, Levi had no tract of territory assigned to it, yet the Levites had 48 [2] cities assigned to them out of the other tribes ; so that the land was really divided into **14** parts. If we take, however, the whole of the children of Jacob, we find that (*a*) they were born in, as it were, **7** groups : (1) Leah bare Reuben, Simeon, Levi, and Judah ; (2) then Bilhah bare Dan and Naphtali ; (3) then Zilpah bare Gad and Asher ; (4) then Leah bare Issachar and Zebulun ; (5) " and *afterwards* she bare a daughter . . . Dinah ; " (6) next, Rachel bare Joseph ; (7) last of all, Rachel bare Benjamin. Again, (*b*) Leah, Jacob's first wife, had **7** children, 6 sons and a daughter. (*c*) Jacob, in giving to Joseph " one portion above his

---

[1] This ver. should read " Ye shall be holy : for I the LORD your God (am) holy." The second " holy " has dropped out of the Heb. text but is found in 4 Heb. MSS, the Sam., Sept. and Arab.

[2] If to this number be added Jerusalem, which in later times became practically a Levitical city, we have **49**. Of these **35** belonged to the Levites proper, and **14** (including Jerusalem) to the priests (Josh. xxi. 13-40).

brethren," [1] declared to him, " Thy two sons, Ephraim and Manasseh . . . are mine ; as Reuben and Simeon, they shall be mine " ; [2] so that, counting them *instead* of Joseph, we have 14 children of Jacob, or counting them *in addition* to Joseph (according to Jacob's apparent intention), 14 sons.

Though, however, we cannot connect the 12 tribes with the number 7 (further than as above stated), there is no such difficulty in the case of the 12 Apostles. (*a*) 7 of them were specially called, before the 12 as a whole were appointed : (1) Andrew, John i. 40 ; (2) John, John i. 35–39 ; (3) Simon Peter, John i. 41, 42 ; (4) Philip, John i. 43 ; (5) Nathanael, John i. 47–51 ; (6) James the son of Zebedee, Matt. iv. 21 ; (7) Matthew, Matt. ix. 9. (*b*) The Twelve were called at 7 different times : (1) Andrew and John, John i. 35–39 ; (2) Peter, John i. 41 ; (3) Philip, John i. 43 ; (4) Nathanael, John i. 47–51 ; (5) James the son of Zebedee, Matt. iv. 21 ; (6) Matthew, Matt. ix. 9 ; (7) the remaining five, Luke vi. 13–16. (*c*) May we go a step further, and say that the twelve Apostles belonged to 7 different families ? (1) Andrew and Peter were brothers, Matt. iv. 18 ; (2) James and John were brothers, Matt. iv. 21 ; (3) James the less, Jude, and Matthew were probably brothers ; for James is called the son of Alphæus, Matt. x. 3, Mark iii. 18, and so is Matthew, Mark ii. 14, while Jude was certainly a relative of James, brother according to the common opinion, son according to the Revisers, Luke vi. 16 ; Acts i. 13. It is no objection to this that the relationship of Matthew to the others is not distinctly stated, for neither Matthew nor Mark mentions that James and Jude were related. (4) Simon Zelotes and Judas Iscariot were probably father and son : in John vi. 71, xiii. 26 (R.V.), Judas is called the son of Simon Iscariot, and Matthew, who gives the names of the Twelve in couples (ch. x. 2–4), doubtless coupling those who were sent forth by Jesus " two and two " (Mark

[1] Gen. xlviii. 22. [2] Gen. xlviii. 5.

vi. 7), joins Simon Zelotes with Judas Iscariot. If such relationship existed, it is easy to understand why the three earlier Evangelists should omit any notice of it, out of regard for the feelings of the survivor. When John wrote his Gospel, Simon was doubtless dead. (5) Thomas ; (6) Philip ; (7) Bartholomew, or Nathanael. These last three were probably without any relative in the apostolic band, though some have thought differently, but without Scriptural authority.[1]   (d) The number 12 was an appropriate one for the Apostles so long as their mission was to " the lost sheep of the house of Israel," but afterwards, the sphere of their labours having been extended to " all the world," it was fitting that the number 12 should be increased to **14** by the addition of Paul and Barnabas.[2] That Barnabas was an Apostle, in the highest sense of the word, is clear from such texts as Acts xiii. 2 (his name, both here and in ver. 7, being mentioned before that of Paul ; and Acts xiv. 14, where again we read, " The apostles, Barnabas and Paul ; " while the bestowal of the name Jupiter on Barnabas, ver. 12, Paul being called after the inferior deity, Mercury, seems to show that Paul, rather than Barnabas, occupied the subordinate position.   So, at the council of Jerusalem, Barnabas seems to have spoken before Paul (Acts xv. 12), and he is named first in the apostolic letter, ver. 25.   See, also, 1 Cor. ix. 5, 6.   But those who accept the Church as an interpreter of Scripture will be satisfied with the fact that she dedicates a special day to the memory of " Saint Barnabas the Apostle."

---

[1] *See* Farrar's *Life of Christ*, ch. xviii. (vol. i. pp. 251, 254 note, in Library edition).

[2] The same truth, that the gospel, after being offered to the Jews, was also to be preached to the Gentiles, was shadowed forth in the sending out by our Lord of the **70** disciples, Luke x.   In the instructions given to them we find no such command as that laid upon the Twelve, " Go not into the way of the Gentiles, and into any city of the Samaritans enter ye not " (Matt. x. 5).

John xxi. 11 : " Simon Peter went up, and drew the
net to land full of great fishes, *an hundred and fifty and
three.*" Has this number any special meaning, or is it
recorded simply to show the magnitude of the miracle
which had been wrought ? That the miracle itself is
eminently symbolical is admitted by most expositors,
and it would be strange if this were the only thing connected with it which is not so. " Our Lord's words to
St. Peter," says Bishop How, " on the occasion of the
other Miraculous Draught of fishes [Luke v. 1–11]—
' Fear not ; from henceforth thou shalt catch men '—
teach us to turn these two miracles into parables.
They both plainly speak of truths very like those
taught by the Parable of the Draw-net (Matt. xiii.
47–50). But there are differences between the two
miracles which (as St. Augustine pointed out) lead to
our seeing in the earlier miracle [wrought at the beginning of our Lord's ministry] a picture of the visible
Church, with its gathering of ' all sorts,' and in the
later [wrought *after the Resurrection*] a picture of the
invisible Church, and the eternal salvation of the
saints. Thus [in the first, Christ is on the water ; here
He is on the land, for in heaven there shall be " no
more sea " ;] in the first the disciples are not bidden
to cast the net on one side more than the other ; while
in the second they are bidden to cast on the ' right
side,' the side of the redeemed in the picture of the
judgment-day given by our Lord (Matt. xxv. 33, 34) :
in the first, the nets were broken, for many once
caught in the net of the Gospel break away and are
lost ; in the second, ' for all there were so many yet
was not the net broken,' for this is the final gathering
of the redeemed, of whom not one shall be lost : in
the first ' the fish are brought into the boats still
tossing on the unquiet sea [and which seem on the
point of sinking with their load], as men, who are
taken for Christ, are brought into the Church, still
itself exposed to the world's tempests ; ' in the second
[the boat is not laden, but] ' the nets are drawn to

land, to the safe and quiet shore of eternity : ' in the first, we are told only of a great multitude of fishes being caught, in which doubtless were great and small, good and bad ; in the second, none are taken but the good, and of these a distinct and definite number, even as the number of God's elect is known and fore-ordained by Him." [1]

So far good ; but does the symbolism stop here ? Does this definite number, 153, signify no more than that "the number of the elect is fixed and pre-ordained " ? [2] It is, perhaps, not to be wondered at that most modern expositors should hold this opinion when we consider the explanations which have been given by some of those who have thought differently.[3] Augustine and Gregory the Great have probably come nearest to the truth : both start with the number 17, as the sum of 10 and 7 ; and while Augustine points out that the sum of all the numbers from 1 to 17 inclusive is 153, Gregory multiplies 17 by 3=51, and by 3 again = 153.[4] Here, then, there are three numbers brought into play, and those the three sacred numbers, 10, 7, and 3,[5] and the number 153 is arrived at in two different ways :—

(1) $1 + 2 + 3 + 4 + 5$, etc. $+ 17 = 153$.
(2) $(10 + 7) \times 3 \times 3 = 153$.

---

[1] S.P.C.K. Commentary, note on John xxi. 12.

[2] So Trench, Notes on the Miracles, p. 194 ; and Mr. Malcolm White, who devotes a whole chapter, in his Symbolical Numbers of Scripture, to this subject, arrives at the same conclusion. Westcott will not even go so far as this, but thinks that "the record of the exact number probably marks nothing more than the care with which the disciples reckoned their wonderful draught " (Speaker's Commentary).

[3] See Westcott's "Additional Note " for the chief of these ; and Wordsworth's Commentary for others.

[4] Fuller details are given by Westcott.

[5] The product of the same three numbers—which above all others are entitled to be called sacred numbers—multiplied by "man's number," 6, gives us the great Apocalyptic number 1260 $(10 \times 7 \times 3 \times 6 = 1260)$ Rev. xi. 3 ; xii. 6.

In (1) the number 3 finds no (special) place, and the attention is wholly drawn to 17, the sum of 10 and 7. In (2) 17 again occupies the first place, but it must be multiplied twice by 3. The numbers, therefore, are treated differently: 10 and 7 are *added*, but 3 is *multiplied*. The double multiplication by 3 may signify nothing; the square of a number often means no more than the number itself, and the double multiplication must be made in order to obtain the number 153, which was arrived at in (1) quite independently of 3; besides, a draught of 51 fishes would not have made the miracle seem such a great one.[1] Augustine and Gregory, however, have not attached the right meaning to the number 17. They appear to agree practically in regarding 10 as representing the Old Testament saints (10 being the number of the commandments), and 7 the New (that number denoting the Holy Spirit, Isa. xi. 2; Rev. i. 4). But we are not left in doubt as to what 7 and 10, when contrasted together, respectively denote. In the later chapters of Exodus God's commands to Moses respecting the tabernacle and its furniture are couched in heptads, but the account of Moses carrying out these commands is mostly in decads. Ten, therefore, clearly occupies the higher place: it denotes the completion of what was commanded or foreshadowed in connection with 7. So in Ps. lxxxiii. 6–11, where we read that 7 enemies of Israel had been destroyed: (1) the Midianites, (2) Sisera, (3) Jabin, (4) Oreb, (5) Zeeb, (6) Zebah, (7) Zalmunna, vv. 9–11; but now 10 others had risen up against her: (1) Edom, (2) the Ishmaelites, (3) Moab, (4) the Hagarenes, (5) Gebal, (6) Ammon, (7) Amalek, (8) the Philistines, (9) Tyre, (10) Assur. And, again, in Rom. viii. 35, St. Paul asks, " Who shall separate us from the love of Christ? shall (1) tribulation, or (2) distress, or (3) persecution, or (4)

---

[1] It is doubtful whether the number 9 possesses any special symbolical meaning; yet "the fruit of the Spirit" comprises 9 graces, Gal. v. 22, 23; and the gifts of the Spirit are also 9 in number, 1 Cor. xii. 8–10.

famine, or (5) nakedness, or (6) peril, or (7) sword ? "
And he replies, " Nay, . . . for I am persuaded that
neither (1) death, nor (2) life, nor (3) angels, nor (4)
principalities, nor (5) things present, nor (6) things to
come, nor (7) powers, nor (8) height, nor (9) depth,
nor (10) any other creature, shall be able to separate
us from the love of God, which is in Christ Jesus our
Lord." [1] I.e. shall *seven* things separate us from the
love of Christ ? No, not even *ten* things can do so.
These passages sufficiently prove that 10, symbolically
as well as numerically, stands higher than 7 when
the two are used together.[2] But there is another
passage more apposite still to our present purpose,
Heb. xii. 18–24, where the Law and the Gospel are
contrasted in the following terms : " Ye are not come
unto (1) the mount that might be touched, (2) and that
burned with fire, (3) nor unto blackness, (4) and darkness, (5) and tempest, (6) and the sound of a trumpet,
(7) and the voice of words ; . . . but ye are come unto
(1) mount Sion, (2) and unto the city of the living God,
(3) the heavenly Jerusalem, (4) and to an innumerable
company of angels, (5) to the general assembly, (6)
and to the church of the firstborn, which are written
in heaven, (7) and to GOD the Judge of all, (8) and to
the spirits of just men made perfect, (9) and to Jesus
the mediator of the new covenant, (10) and to the
blood of sprinkling, that speaketh better things than
(that of) Abel."

Here, then, we have the key to the number 17, as
composed of 7 and 10, in connection with the text under
consideration ; 7 signifies the Old Testament saints,[3]

---

[1] See Forbes's *Symmetrical Structure of Scripture*, p. 318.

[2] Compare, also, 2 Chron. ii. 7, 14.

[3] Not those saved under the Law only, but under the Patriarchal
dispensation also, for " the ' first testament ' (Heb. ix. 15) includes
the whole period from Adam to Christ, and not merely that of the
covenant with Israel, which was a concentrated representation of
the covenant made with mankind by sacrifice, down from the fall to
redemption " (Brown and Fausset's *Commentary*, note on Heb. ix.
15).

and 10 the New ;[1] the *sum* of the two numbers, therefore, and not their product, denotes the whole number of the saved after the general resurrection. Seventeen itself might well, indeed, have been used instead of 153, but for the following reasons : (1) it was too small a number for the draught to appear miraculous ; (2) it required to be concealed, for "it is the glory of God to conceal a thing ; "[2] (3) it did not show by whose power they were saved. One hundred and fifty-three fulfils all these conditions : (1) it is a number sufficiently large to prove the draught of fishes miraculous ; (2) its connection with 17 is by no means apparent at first sight; (3) being the product of 17 by 3 twice, it signifies emphatically that the salvation accomplished, like the miracle itself, is by Divine power, three being universally regarded as the number symbolical of the Godhead.[3]

One hundred and fifty-three denotes, then, the whole number of the redeemed, as saved by the power of the Triune God.[4]

[1] The following are too doubtful to be adduced in support of thiis but are, perhaps, worthy of mention : (1) The Heb. word for Almighty, *Shaddai*, occurs in the O.T. 48 times, which should doubtless be 49 (7 × 7) ; the Greek word *Pantokratōr* (same meaning) occurs in the N.T. 10 times. (2) *Diathēkē*, "covenant or testament," occurs in the Ep. to the Hebrews, where the two covenants are contrasted, 17 times—6 with clear reference to the Old Covenant, and 9 to the New; the other two are general, but, if divided, it will give 7 O.T. and 10 New. From its frequent occurrence in Scripture, 17 would appear to have a meaning of its own as a whole number, but what that meaning is it is not easy to see.

[2] Prov. xxv. 2.

[3] So Bähr, Stuart, Forbes, White, Lee, etc. (See Appendix B.)

[4] Wordsworth arrives at the same conclusion, but in a less satisfactory manner : the square of 12 (the number of the Church) added to the square of 3 (the number of the Godhead), he points out, = 153 (*Commentary, in loc.*). The following notes may be added here : (a) 17 is the 7th prime or indivisible number. (b) If the figures of 153 are taken separately, their cubes ($1^3 + 5^3 + 3^3$) = 153 (*Biblia Cabalistica*, 117). This is probably unique. (c) Gematrists point out that the Heb. *Beni-ha-Elohim* "Sons of God" = 153, and the Greek *ichthues*, "fishes," and *to diktuon*, "the net,"

There are two other points of contact between this miracle and the number **7** which deserve notice, the number being in both cases concealed. (1) This was the *third* appearance of our Lord to the *Apostles*, but a careful comparison of the four Gospels shows it to have been the *seventh in all* after His resurrection, out of a total of *ten*.[1] The Apostles present were "Simon Peter, and Thomas called Didymus, and Nathanael of Cana in Galilee, and the sons of Zebedee, and two other of his disciples."[2] How many are here? Had we St. John's Gospel only, we should not know. Again we need to compare with the other Gospels, from which we learn that "the sons of Zebedee" were two in number (James and John), and that consequently there were *seven* disciples in the ship when the miracle was wrought —fit number to represent the Church through which the salvation of souls is effected. "Here were *seven* of the disciples, so fitly representative, whether as individuals or as a company, of the general church of God."[3] As individuals, for, says Mr. White, "every name is here significant."[4] "The three chief," writes Mr. Jukes, "Peter, James, and John, respectively reveal

both = 1224, i.e., 153 × the resurrection number 8. (*d*) 153, as being the sum of the numbers 1 to 17 is in Pythagorean language a "triangular number" and was held to have the symbolic value of 17. (*e*) There were 17 nations and peoples represented at Pentecost, Acts ii. 9–11.

[1] So the best harmonists: see Robinson's *Harmony of the Gospels*, introd. note to Part IX; J. B. McClellan, *The Four Gospels*, ii. 615–620; S. D. Waddy, *Harmony*; Abp. W. Thomson: art. "Jesus Christ" in *S.D.B.* Dr. Swete, from whom I differ with regret, says, "Notwithstanding the manifest differences between the details of this story [of the appearance to the women] and those of the appearance to Mary [Magdalene] it may reasonably be doubted whether the two narratives do not relate to the same incident!" Yet he adds that these differences "cast no shadow of suspicion on the general truth of the narrative." (*Appearances of our Lord*, 11, 12.) He thus unwarrantably reduces the figures 7 and 10 to 6 and 9, and so misses the symbolism.

[2] John xxi. 2.

[3] *Symbolical Numbers of Scripture*, p. 220.

[4] Idem, p. 219.

faith, hope, and charity."[1]   Then we have Thomas,
type of the desponding, doubting Christian,[2] and
Nathanael, the pure in heart.   But who were the other
two ? and why are they not named ?   John certainly
knew who they were, for he was one of the party.
The omissions of Scripture, it has been well said, are
often as full of meaning as its plain statements.[3]   And
is it going too far to consider the unnamed disciples as
representing the Old Testament Church, two in number, even as there were two Dispensations prior to the
Christian—the Patriarchal and the Jewish ?

But, after all, is 153 the right number to work upon ?
There can be little doubt that it is, and yet it should
not be forgotten that " as soon as [the disciples] were
come to land they saw a fire of coals there, and *a fish*[4]
laid thereon, and bread."[5]   Must we add this one to the
153, as symbolical of those who, like the thief on the
cross, are saved directly by Christ without the agency
of the Church, and so obtain the heptadic number 154
(7 × 22) ?   We cannot separate Christ from His
Church ; they are one : nor is there any proof that this
fish was caught in the lake whence the others were
taken.   The scene probably means simply that, when
we reach the heavenly shore, " then comes the feast
with Christ—communion with Him in what He has
prepared, the fish and the bread [being] both well-
known figures of Him."[6]

[1] *The New Man and the Eternal Life*, p. 262 ; see also p. 260.
[2] But not the sceptic, in the modern sense of the word, for such
Thomas was not.
[3] See Jukes's *Types of Genesis*, p. 45 and *note*.
[4] So the R.V. marg., and so Trench and Westcott.
[5] John xxi. 9.
[6] *The New Man and the Eternal Life*, p. 261.

CHAPTER VI

CHRONOLOGY

IT was evidently the intention of the writers of Scripture, or rather of their Divine Inspirer, to furnish data from which an exact system of chronology could be constructed from the Creation onwards, and the date, relative and actual, of every important event ascertained. But in this, as in so many other things, the wise purpose of God has been temporarily frustrated by the carelessness or perversity of man ; so that, now, such is the confusion that exists, that hardly any two chronologers arrive at the same result in attempting to trace out the relative dates of the Creation of Adam and the Birth of Christ.[1] But if the number *seven* occupies the paramount position in relation to Scripture which is claimed for it in these pages, may we not hope to derive some help from it in connection with this matter also ? This idea is no new one, but the schemes of "scientific chronology" hitherto presented to the world have not met with the assent of those who should be competent to form a correct judgment in such a matter. Whether, however, the scheme I am about to propose be the true one or no, of this I feel certain, that it is to the symbolic use of numbers, and especially to the number *seven*, we must look for aid to enable us to unravel the tangled web of sacred chronology.

The first artificial division of time we meet with in

---

[1] It has been stated that over three hundred different computations have been made as to the length of the period which separates these two events.

Scripture is in connection with **7.** The year is a natural division, so is the day, and so also, originally, was the month, but there is nothing in nature corresponding to the *week* of **7** days. Either God ordained this septenary division of time *because* His work and rest in the creation of the world occupied so long, or, more probably He so arranged His work that, with the day of rest, it *should* occupy just so long. But it is essential to note that from the very beginning **7** is stamped upon time. And when God appointed a system of ritual for His people Israel, not only was the sabbatic character of the **7**th day maintained and enforced but the number **7** constantly meets us in connection with times and seasons. To give a few examples, the period of **7** days is constantly met with in the ceremonies of the Levitical law ; the second great feast was **7** weeks after the first, as our Whitsunday is **7** weeks after Easter ; the **7** festivals of the Mosaic calendar all took place during the first **7** months of the year ; the **7**th month was specially sacred on account of the number of festivals it contained ; the **7**th, or sabbatic, year was a year of rest for the land and of release for Israel ; while after **7** times **7** years the trumpet of the jubilee proclaimed " liberty throughout the land unto all the inhabitants thereof." These **sabbatic and jubilee years** would have been of the greatest use in the matter of chronology had they been observed by the Jews, and a record of even a few of them kept. But as it is, not only is there no clear notice of a single jubilee year from the very beginning, but it is matter of dispute *how often* and *when* they recurred. This must be settled before we go further ; for if man forgot these years, God did not, and I believe that the careful study of this question will yield valuable results. There are at least three theories on the point : (1) That the jubilee year recurred every **49** years, and was identical with the **7**th sabbatic year ; (2) That it recurred every **49** years, but was always the year following the **7**th sabbatic year ; (3) That it recurred every **50** years, but was still always the year following the 7th sabbatic year. This last is the opinion of the modern Jews,[1] and has been held by Mr. Browne and many other scholars. The great, and as I conceive insuperable, objection to it is, that, as regards both the sabbatic and jubilee years, it destroys the *septenary* character of them. For by this theory the sabbatic year is sometimes the seventh year, and sometimes (i.e. twice in a century, immediately after each jubilee) the eighth. But there is no hint of this change in the commands relative to this year ; and if the number 7 occupies the prominent position we have assigned to it, such a break in the septennial sequence cannot be allowed.[2] And if regard be had to the nature and typical character of the year of jubilee, it will be seen at once that it is quite out of the question to attempt to connect the number 50 with it. For 50, i.e. 5 times 10, the half of a century, bears upon it the stamp of incompleteness, while if anything characterizes the law concerning the year of jubilee, it is the complete and sweeping nature of its provisions. It was the climax of all of the Mosaic festivals ; [3] and while it prefigured in some sense the advent of the Messiah,[4] its complete fulfilment, as a type, is still in the distant future.[5] Seven times seven is undoubtedly the number of years which separated one jubilee from another. Nor is there anything in Scripture which contradicts this. The law concerning the jubilee is contained in the twenty-fifth chapter of Leviticus, and was delivered, it must be carefully

---

[1] But it was not that of the ancient Jews, for in *The Book of Jubilees*, a Jewish production of (probably) ii/B.C., time from the creation is distinctly divided into Jubilee-periods of 49 years.

[2] It is true there is often a peculiar and almost indefinable connection between the numbers 7 and 8 (see appendix E) but never, so far as I am aware, one of this character.

[3] Ginsburg, in Kitto's *Bib. Cycl.*, ii. 667.

[4] Luke iv. 18–21.

[5] See Jukes's *Restitution of All things*, pp. 50, 51 ; Smith's *Student's O.T. Hist.*, p. 214.

borne in mind, while the children of Israel were still in the wilderness. The command is, "When ye come into the land which I give you, . . . six years thou shalt sow thy field, . . . but in the seventh year shall be a sabbath of rest. . . . And thou shalt number seven sabbaths of years unto thee, seven times seven years ; and the space of the seven sabbaths of years shall be unto thee forty and nine years. Then shalt thou cause the trumpet of the jubilee to sound. . . . And ye shall hallow the fiftieth year . . . a jubilee shall that fiftieth year be unto you." [1] That is, the seventh year after the conquest of the land was to be a sabbatic year, and so on each succeeding seventh year. After seven sabbatic years had passed, then, in the year following, i.e. the *fiftieth year from the conquest of the land*, the trumpet of jubilee was to be sounded, and that too, be it noted, " throughout all the land," for no half measures characterized the year of jubilee. There is no difficulty here ; on the contrary, to have said " the forty-ninth year " would, in relation to the *first* jubilee, to which, of course, the command in the first instance applied, have been positively incorrect ; while as regards succeeding jubilees, each one was the fiftieth from the preceding one, both inclusive, a method of counting quite common in Scripture, as, to give a notable example, in the case of our Lord's resurrection, which is invariably spoken of as having taken place on " the third day " from the crucifixion, though only one day intervened.[2] Unquestionably, therefore, the jubilee recurred every 49 years, and it

---

[1] Lev. xxv. 2–11.

[2] A case more in point, indeed exactly parallel to the jubilee, is found in Lev. xxiii. 15, 16, where we read, "And ye shall count unto you from the morrow after the sabbath, from the day that ye brought the sheaf of the wave offering ; seven sabbaths shall be complete : even unto the morrow after the seventh sabbath shall ye number *fifty days*." Now, from the morrow after one sabbath to the morrow after the seventh succeeding one is only 49 days, *unless both the first and last days of the series be counted.*

would appear to have always immediately followed a sabbatic year.[1]

When we come to inquire what aid is afforded by the sabbatic and jubilee systems in the construction of a scheme of chronology, we are met by the difficulty that " there is no positive record of any *jubilee year*, having been kept at any time. The dates of three *sabbatic years* have, however, been preserved. These were current B.C. 163, 135, and 37, and therefore commenced in each case about three months earlier than the beginning of these Julian years (Jos., *Ant.* xii. 9, 5 ; xiii. 8, 1 ; xiv. 16, 2 ; xv. 1, 2 ; *B.J.*, i. 2, 4 ; and 1 Mac. vi. 49, 53). "[2]

---

[1] Mr. R. S. Poole comes to the same conclusion, and says, " That such was the case is rendered most probable by the analogy of the weekly sabbath, and the custom of the Jews in the first and second centuries before Christ " (Smith's *Dic. Bib.*, i. 316 ; iii. 1807). Mr. Samuel Clark, however, the writer of the article " Jubilee " in the same work, takes the opposite view.

[2] R. S. Poole, in Smith's *Dict. Bib.*, art. " Chronology," vol. i. p. 317 ; and so Wieseler, *Chronological Synopsis of the Four Gospels*, Eng. trans., p. 186, and Hastings' *D.B.* iv. 326. Mr. Browne, however, states that " it is on record that a sabbatical year began in the autumn of B.C. 163 " (*Ordo Sæclorum*, p. 287). Without pretending to be able to decide between these conflicting authorities as to the matter of fact, I have followed Wieseler and others rather than Browne. This difference of a year illustrates the difficulty there is in arriving at *exact* dates in ancient chronology. Other instances of this difficulty are—(1) the Destruction of Solomon's Temple, for which, although the date is apparently so clearly stated, the best chronologers range between B.C. 588, 587, and 586, others giving 589 and 585 ; (2) the Foundation of Rome, for which Varro's date, B.C. 753, is adopted by chronologists, although some ancient authorities give 752 ; (3) the Birth of Christ, about which there is the greatest disagreement, the common reckoning, A.D. 1, being four or five years wrong ; (4) Wieseler states (p. 186) that a sabbatical year happened, " according to Rabbinical tradition, in the year *before* the destruction of Jerusalem ; " but Browne asserts that " there is a well-attested tradition that the year *in which* Jerusalem was taken was a sabbatical year " (p. 291) ; agreement might surely have been looked for here. Doubtless much of this confusion arose (1) from the many different *Eras* in use, and (2) from the different periods adopted for the commencement of the year, which was

We are not left, however, entirely without guidance in the matter. The first words of our Lord recorded by St. Mark, after the commencement of His ministry, are, "*The time is fulfilled*, and the kingdom of God is at hand : repent ye, and believe the gospel,"[1] where the word for " time " in the Greek is not *chronos*, the ordinary word for " time," but *kairos*, which often signifies " a set *or* appointed time." These words, " the appointed time is fulfilled," the words with which, according to St. Mark, our Lord commenced His ministry, are surely not without meaning. The first words of our Lord's ministry recorded by St. Luke are those which were uttered in the synagogue of Nazareth, where He said, quoting the prophecy of Isaiah,—

(*1*) The Spirit of the Lord is upon me,
(*2*) Because he hath anointed me ;
(*3*) To preach good tidings to the poor he hath sent me,
(*4*) To proclaim release to the captives,
(*5*) And recovering of sight to the blind,
(*6*) To set at liberty them that are bruised,
(*7*) To proclaim the acceptable year of the Lord.

Then, after a pause, He declared, " To-day hath this Scripture been fulfilled in your ears."[2] That there is a reference here to the year of jubilee is admitted by all, but most expositors consider the reference to be only figurative or typical. The word of God, however, has often a fuller, a deeper meaning than is suspected, and I therefore agree with those who hold that at the time when our Lord spoke these words a jubilee year was actually current. We know that a sabbatic year com-

sometimes in January, sometimes in March, April, October, etc., and sometimes the year was reckoned from the commencement of the reign of an emperor or king. Then a part of a year was sometimes reckoned as a whole year, so that a period of even less than two years might be called three years, as containing one whole year and parts of two others. In this chapter, therefore, I shall not concern myself about arriving at *exact* dates, except where absolutely necessary.

[1] Mark i. 15.   [2] Luke iv. 18–21.

menced in the autumn of A.D. 26, about which time John the Baptist began his call to repentance, and it has been considered that the peculiar sanctity of this year, and the comparative leisure enjoyed by the Jews, owing to the cessation of all agricultural labour, had a very great deal to do (humanly speaking) with the success of John's ministry.[1] The Baptism of Jesus took place in this sabbatical year, and His proclamation in the synagogue of Nazareth of " the acceptable year of the Lord," *the year of jubilee*, in the year following.

We have here, then, an important starting-point. The year current from Autumn, A.D. 27, to Autumn, A.D. 28, was not only a *jubilee year*, but it was one which was in some way the " fulfilment " of some "appointed time."

Let us now endeavour to ascertain the date of the first jubilee.

The Exodus from Egypt took place, according to the received chronology given in the margin of our Bibles (which I shall for the present assume to be correct), in Spring,[2] B.C. 1491. The Return of the Spies was a year and a half later, Autumn, B.C. 1490.[3] The Jordan was crossed in Spring, B.C. 1451, exactly forty years after leaving Egypt. Canaan was virtually conquered after six and a half years' fighting,[4] which brings us to Autumn, B.C. 1445. This date is pretty certain, being 45 years from the Return of the Spies (see Josh. xiv. 7–10), and whether the survey of the land and its division among the tribes took six months or twelve [5]

---

[1] Wieseler, *Chron. Synopsis*, Eng. trans., p. 186.

[2] I use the term Spring as a sufficiently near equivalent for the Jewish month Abib or Nisan, and Autumn for Tisri. The former was the first and the latter the seventh month of the Jewish sacred year.

[3] Smith's *Student's O.T. Hist.*, p. 123.

[4] This does not include the wars against Sihon and Og on the other side Jordan. These would probably bring up the period to 7 years.

[5] Mr. Browne appears to allow only six months, for he says " the tribes were settled in the Promised Land at the end of seven years from the Eisode " (*Ordo Sæclorum*, p. 278).

does not matter for our present purpose, as the sabbatic year certainly began in Autumn. By Autumn, B.C. 1444, therefore, the land had been divided, and the people were settled in their allotments, and *from this date the sabbatic and jubilean cycles commence.* During the next six years the Israelites sowed and reaped, and at the end of these six years, Autumn, B.C. 1438, *the first sabbatic year commenced.*[1] The seventh sabbatic year began Autumn, B.C. 1396, and *the first jubilee year Autumn,* B.C. 1395. Now, from Autumn, B.C. 1444, to Autumn, A.D. 27, which saw the commencement of the jubilee year in which our Lord's ministry began, is **1470 years,**[2] ($3 \times 10 \times 7 \times 7$) or *exactly thirty jubilees.*

This combination of the three sacred numbers, 3, 7, and 10—7 being doubled because of its special importance as a Scripture number, and also because this is necessary on account of the jubilee—is certainly not accidental. It is a number which may well denote that " fulness of the time " when " God sent forth his son,"[3] proclaiming, " The appointed time is fulfilled, and the kingdom of God is at hand : repent ye, and believe the gospel."

The received or Ussherian date of **the Exodus,** B.C. 1491, is therefore correct. Other chronologers, disregarding the note of time given in 1 Kings vi. 1, give much higher dates, as 1531 (Petavius), 1586 (Browne), 1593 (Jackson), 1625 (Clinton), 1639 (Cuninghame and Wallace), 1648 (Hales), 1652 (R. S. Poole), while Petrie, endeavouring to harmonize Heb. and Egyptian chronology, dates it about 1220, but no one of these, nor yet that of the modern Jews (1314) gives anything like the

[1] So R. S. Poole, Smith's *Dict. Bib.*, i. 316 : " The first sabbatical year to be kept after the Israelites had entered Canaan would be about the fourteenth."

[2] Will the reader pardon me pointing out that, in order to arrive at the number of years from any year B.C. to any year A.D. he must add the two numbers together, *and deduct* 1

[3] Gal. iv. 4.

remarkable result which follows from accepting as correct the period of 480 years in the passage just named.[1]

Nor is further jubilean confirmation of this date wanting. One of the most important events in the religious history of the children of Israel was the **Dedication of Solomon's Temple,** of which, however, Scripture does not give the exact date. The foundation of the Temple was laid, according to Ussher, on Monday, May 21, B.C. 1012, and from this date the best authorities do not differ by more than a year or two. The building occupied seven and a half years,[2] and was completed in " the eighth month " (November) B.C. 1005. This date is obtained from the last verse of the sixth chapter of 1 Kings, a chapter which records with some minuteness the building of the house, but not the making of the furniture and vessels, with the exception of the huge cherubim, which possibly it was necessary, on account of their size, to place in position before the partition wall was put up. Then, in ch. vii., is given an account of the making of the two pillars, Jachin and Boaz, the molten sea with its twelve oxen, the ten bases and lavers, the golden altar, the table of shewbread, the ten golden candlesticks, and all the multitudinous pots, shovels, and other vessels of one kind or another which would be required for the due performance of Divine service. And considering the scale of magnificence upon which everything about the

---

[1] In the *Speaker's Commentary*, though it professes to give the A.V. unaltered at the head of its pages, the words "in the four hundred and eightieth year after the children of Israel were come out of the land of Egypt," are printed within brackets, implying that they are of doubtful authority. This is the more remarkable, as, notwithstanding Prof. Rawlinson's opinion, the editor of the work believes the words to be genuine. See Canon Cook's note on Exod. xii. 40. The phrase "children of Israel " occurs 21 times in 1 Kings, and " out of the land of Egypt " (*meērets Mitsrayim*) 7 times in 1 and 2 Kings, including this passage. It is not necessary to pursue the textual argument further.

[2] 1 Kings vi. 38, compared with ver. 1.

Temple was made, one year seems hardly sufficient to allow for all these things to be got ready for use. The Temple was dedicated at the Feast of Tabernacles in the seventh month, the year not being stated, and must, therefore, have taken place at least eleven months, but, as I suppose, one year and eleven months, after the building of the house itself was completed. This brings us to Autumn, B.C. 1003, *a jubilee year*, the ninth (3 × 3) from the Division of the Land, and the 21st (7 × 3) (or 1029 years = 7 × 7 × 7 × 3) before the commencement of Christ's ministry.

The Dedication of the **Second Temple** also, there can be little doubt, took place in a jubilee year, viz. that commencing Autumn, B.C. 513. Ussher's date is 515, and Browne's 513 ; but, as the dedication took place in the early part of the year, the true date is probably Spring, B.C. 512. The Building of this Temple was commenced in B.C. 535, a sabbatical year.

The Repairing of the Temple, after the great reformation under Joash, also fell in a jubilee year, B.C. 856–5.[1]

B.C. 954–3, the date of the reformation under Asa, was also a jubilee year.[2]

In B.C. 458, Ezra arrived at Jerusalem and in December of that year assembled the people.[3] This was the third month of a sabbatical year.

In B.C. 444,[4] in the sixth month (September), the wall of Jerusalem was rebuilt, and in the month following there was a solemn reading and expounding of the Law, by Ezra and his assistants, all the people being gathered together to hear it.[5] This is exactly what was commanded to be done every sabbatic year,[6] and the year commencing Autumn, B.C. 444, was a year of this description.

We may therefore accept as correct the received date of the Exodus—Spring, B.C. 1491.

---

[1] Smith's *Student's O.T. Hist.*, p. 589.
[2] Idem, p. 588.   [3] Idem, p. 542.
[4] Idem, p. 545.
[5] Neh. viii. 1–3.   [6] Deut. xxxi. 10–13.

Our next inquiry must be as to the true date of the **Birth of Christ.**

We have seen that our Lord began His ministry in the year commencing Autumn, A.D. 27. He was then over thirty years of age,[1] consequently he must have been born previous to Autumn, B.C. 4. Without going into the matter fully, it is sufficient here to state that in the opinion of many scholars our Lord's Birth took place somewhere between September in the year of Rome **749** = B.C. 5 and April, A.U.C. 750 = B.C. 4.[2] Can we for a moment hesitate which of these two years to accept ? **749** is a number so eminently heptadic as to force us to the conclusion that it represents the date we seek. Nor is it any objection that this was a heathen Era, based upon an event with which Scripture has nothing whatever to do. " Is God the God of the Jews only ? is he not also of the Gentiles ? Yes, of the Gentiles also." [3] Who moved the Emperor Augustus to issue a decree that " all the world should be taxed," just at the time when Mary was about to be delivered of her Divine Son ? The O.T. supplies many instances, in the histories of Cyrus, Nebuchadnezzar, and others, of heathens being the instruments of carrying out the Divine Will. There is therefore no difficulty whatever in believing that the building of Rome —the *seven*-hilled city,—the founding of an Empire destined to play such an important part in the history of Christ and Christianity, was ordered by Divine Providence. We may set down the date of our Lord's Birth, then, as sometime during the last four months of the year B.C. 5 = A.U.C. 749. This is a sufficiently near approximation for the present.[4]

[1] Luke iii. 23, R.V.

[2] The argument will be found briefly stated in Farrar's *Life of Christ*, Excursus i. (vol. ii., p. 450, library edition) ; and more fully in Browne and Wieseler.

[3] Rom. iii. 29.

[4] Ussher adopts December 25, B.C. 5, as the date ; Browne, December 7 or 8, B.C. 5 ; Wieseler does not attempt to fix the exact day, but says, " While we consider it not impossible that Jesus was

We have next to ask, At what *period of the year* was Adam created ? Ussher is very exact on this point. He says, the "beginning of time, according to our Chronology, fell upon the entrance of the night preceding the twenty-third day of October." [1] Browne shows, from the dates given in connection with the Flood, that " the ancient Hebrew year began before the Exode with the month afterwards numbered 7th, and called Ethanim and Tisri, agreeably with the usage of the other nations of Western Asia from time immemorial, which continued among the Jews themselves in civil matters, and *in the regulation of the sabbatical and jubilean cycle.* . . . That is to say," he further remarks, " the series of the mundane Era bears date from the 1st day of Tisri, . . . I do not mean to say that the very day of the creation of Adam is hereby determined, but only that the years of Adam and of our race are dated from that point of time." [2] At the Exodus the beginning of the year was changed,[3] and so were hidden, as students of God's Word and works know that He is wont to hide,[4] two remarkable coincidences, which cannot be regarded as accidental, and which may be here mentioned as showing that in endeavouring to establish a scheme of Mystical Chronology (as Mr. Browne calls it), we are in pursuit of no mere myth. Scripture carefully informs us that " the ark rested in the seventh month, on the seventeenth day of the

born towards the end of 749 A.U.C., 5 B.C., yet we must hold it to be far more probable that He was born in one of the early months of 750 A.U.C. = 4 B.C. (*Chron. Synops.*, p. 114). And again, "The *day* cannot now be determined at all ; while, as regards the months, our choice lies between the close of December, January, and February, of which, however, December is the least probable, January more so, and February decidedly the most probable of all " (*Id.*, p. 129). Hastings' *D.C.G.*, art. "Dates," gives B.C. 5, Dec. (25) [or June].

[1] *Annals of the World*, p. 1.
[2] *Ordo Sæclorum*, p. 322, 323.   [3] Exod. xii. 2.
[4] Prov. xxv. 2. See some interesting remarks in Jukes's *Restitution of All Things*, pp. 9–14.

month, upon the mountains of Ararat ; " [1] " the self-same day," remarks Mr. Browne, " on which, in the fulness of time, God led His people safe through the waters of the [Red] sea "; [2] while Mr. Jukes, rightly regarding the ark of Noah as a type of Christ, points out that on that very day He rose from the dead. [3]

We have established, then, that in the Autumn Adam was created ; and in the Autumn, or, at any rate, towards the close of the year, Christ was born. We have now to ascertain the period of time which separates these two events.

It will be most convenient if I first set down in outline the scheme which I propose, and then endeavour to support it briefly by such proofs, scriptural and otherwise, as are available.

		Years.
I. From the Creation [4] to the Commencement of the Flood . . .		2261½
II. From the Commencement of the Flood to the Birth of Terah . . .		1003
III. From the Birth of Terah to the Birth of Abraham		130
IV. From the Birth of Abraham to his Call .		75
V. From the Call of Abraham to God's Covenant with him (Gen. xv. 18) . .		4
VI. From God's Covenant with Abraham to the Exodus		430
VII. From the Exodus to the Birth of Christ		1486½
Total number of years from the Creation to the Birth of Christ . . .		5390

For every one of these seven periods, except V., there

---

[1] Gen. viii. 4. [2] *Ordo Sæclorum*, p. 322.

[3] *The Law of the Offerings*, p. 22. In quoting these words, I express no opinion as to the exact date of the Crucifixion, whether the 14th or 15th Nisan.

[4] By the word Creation here and elsewhere is meant the Creation of Adam.

is direct proof. Let us now examine each of them separately.

I. *From the Creation to the Commencement of the Flood.* The length of this period is arrived at by adding together the ages of the patriarchs at the birth of the son who succeeds them in the genealogy. Here we have three sets of figures to decide between, the Hebrew, Septuagint, and Samaritan all differing from one another. Of these the Samaritan may be at once set aside; it has been too obviously manipulated to entitle it to any credit. The following table exhibits the variations between the three texts :—

TABLE I.

(The two dots indicate that the figures are the same as those of the Septuagint.

	Age of Each when the Next was born.			Years of Each after the Next was born.			Total Length of the Life of Each.		
	Sept.	Heb.	Sam.	Sept.	Heb.	Sam.	Sept.	Heb.	Sam.
Adam	230	130	130	700	800	800	930	..	..
Seth	205	105	105	707	807	807	912	..	..
Enos	190	90	90	715	815	815	905	..	..
Cainan . . .	170	70	70	740	840	840	910	..	..
Mahalaleel . .	165	65	65	730	830	830	895	..	..
Jared	162	162	62	800	..	785	962	..	847
Enoch . . .	165	65	65	200	300	300	365	..	..
Methuselah . .	187[1]	187	67	782	..	653	969	..	720
Lamech . . .	188	182	53	565	595	600	753	777	653
Noah	502	502	502	448	..	..	950	..	..
Shem (*to the Flood*)	98	98	98	500	..	..	600	..	..
A.M.	2262	1656	1307	Year of the Flood.					

[1] The Sixtine text of the Sept. has 167 here, but it must be remembered that the great Vatican manuscript (B), on which this text is founded, does not now contain the first forty-five chapters of Genesis; 187 is the true reading, and is the one given both in Swete's text and in that of the larger Cambridge edition.

There is thus a difference between the Hebrew and the Septuagint of 606 years, which arises (except the odd six years) from the fact that in six cases 100 years have been either added to or taken from the true age at the son's birth, and adjusted in the years after this event, leaving the total length of life exactly the same. That this has been done designedly there can be no question, and various reasons have been assigned, both for the addition and the deduction. Into these reasons I do not propose to enter : to impute motives is rarely a wise thing, and the imputations made by some writers in regard to this question are far more likely to hinder than to help the settlement of it. One remark only I would make : the alterations must *in either case* have been made by Jews, not by Christians, for from the Jews both the Heb. text and the Sept. Version have been received.

(1) I have said that the Samaritan bears obvious traces of alteration. On looking at the third division of the table, " we perceive that the *whole lives* of these patriarchs, with the exception of that of Lamech, are exactly the same in the Heb. and the Sept. ; but that in the Samaritan three of them are very considerably different, namely, those of Jared, Methuselah, and Lamech. It is plain, therefore, that we must prefer the testimony of the two former [texts] to that of the latter. Moreover, it is evident that the lives of the three patriarchs in question have been shortened in the Samaritan, in order that their deaths should be represented as all occurring *in the year of the Flood ;* for had their lives been preserved as entire in this text as in the other two, they would, contrary to the express words of Scripture, have *survived the Flood* by 115, 249, and 100 years respectively ! " [1]

(2) Now, it is remarkable that the three patriarchs whose ages have been thus audaciously altered in the Samaritan text, are the *only ones* among those who died before the Flood *in regard to whom the Heb. and Sept.*

[1] Prof. Wallace's *True Age of the World*, p. 17.

agree. I do not see how we can avoid the conclusion that the Heb. figures have been altered; that it was seen that to reduce all the generations by 100 years would make these three patriarchs appear to survive the Flood; and that, rather than falsify their total ages as the Samaritan has done, their generative ages were left untouched.[1]

(3) The three sons of Noah were all apparently about 100 years old at the Flood, yet *none of them had any children.* Now, according to the Heb. generations, sixty years was about the usual age of marriage before the Flood, and it is certainly singular that *all three* should have lived forty years past this time without having children. According to the Sept. generations they would be but youths, capable of marriage, but much under the usual age, and we must suppose that Noah took wives for them just before entering into the ark, in order to preserve the race. No argument to the contrary can be founded on Gen. vi. 18, which, indeed, is commonly supposed to have been spoken just after his sons' birth; it is doubtless only another illustration of the truth that God sometimes " calleth those things which be not as though they were." [2] I do not, however, press this argument.

(4) It is difficult, if the Heb. numbers are correct, to account for the paraphrase of Gen. iv. 25, still found in the Targum of Palestine (pseudo-Jonathan), which reads: " And Adam knew his wife again at the end of 130 years after Abel had been slain; and she bare a son, and called his name Seth." But this agrees well enough with the Sept., supposing Abel to have been born soon after the Fall, and to have been about 100 years old when murdered by Cain.

---

[1] Jared's generative age, however, might have been safely altered so long as the other two were left untouched, but those who made the alterations do not seem to have been clever enough to see this; or it may have been left in order to give an appearance of greater consistency to the whole.

[2] Rom. iv. 17.

(5) And though all Heb. MSS now extant agree with the printed text, yet Kennicott shows, "from Eusebius, that some Heb. copies, having the *larger* numbers, existed in the fourth century ; and others, on the authority of Jacobus Edessenus, as late as the year 700 ; whilst others, much later, are mentioned in the Chronicle of Ecchellensis." [1]

The other arguments in favour of the Sept. numbers must be given very briefly.[2]

(6) The shorter generations are repugnant to the course of nature. "The idea of persons whose life is 830 years marrying and having children at sixty-five, as Mahalaleel is represented to have done, is just as absurd as to suppose that persons who live to the age of seventy should marry and have children before they are six years old." [3]

(7) According to the Heb., there were at one time nine and at another time (after the Flood) ten genera-tions all alive at the same time, but according to the Sept. never more than six (and that only twice) which seems more natural.

(8) The argument derived from the records of **heathen nations** is also an important element in the case. Greece, Crete, India, even China seem to go a long way back if the records are rightly understood and can be relied upon. But the only countries which need con-cern us here are Babylonia and Egypt, respecting which it was the fashion not very long ago to name very extravagant figures, running back to seven, eight and nine millenniums B.C. But now more moderate estim-ates are accepted. As regards Babylonia the state-ment of Nabonidus, who reigned in the middle of the sixth cent. B.C., was at one time taken as correct, but it is now known to be 1,000, or more probably 1,500 years wrong, and about 3000 B.C. is named as "the

[1] *Remarks on Select Passages in the O.T.*, p. 17.
[2] They may be seen more fully in the works of Hales, Jackson, Russell, and Wallace. It is to the last I am chiefly indebted.
[3] Rouse's *Dissertation on Sacred Chronology*, p. 16.

very commencement of cuneiform sources,"[1] while Dr. Leonard King says that "the Biblical chronology is more accurate than has hitherto been supposed." So with Egypt. The *Encyclopedia Britannica* gives a table showing the date of the commencement of the First Dynasty according to noted Egyptologists, as follows : Meyer B.C. 3315, Sethe 3360, Breasted 3400, Petrie 5510.[2] Sir Gardner Wilkinson's date was 2691. These figures show us the unwisdom of dogmatizing. In dealing with ancient lists of kings, who admittedly reigned at different capitals, there is always the danger of making dynasties successive instead of contemporaneous.[3] While then our Sept. figures for the Creation (B.C. 5395) leave ample margin, the Heb. (B.C. 4004) scarcely allow sufficient time.

(9) **Geology** deserves a passing notice, but need not detain us long. I have already pointed out [4] that the structure of Gen. i. 1, 2 separates them from the rest of the chapter, and it is with the creation of Adam only that we are now interested. "The difficulties in accepting our date do not seem to be geological, especially in the light of the new views on the Glacial Age put forward by Profs. Hull and Upham."[5] There is no proof that man existed previous to the Great Ice Age, which took place within comparatively recent times. Again, Niagara Falls is calculated by some geologists to be anything over 35,000 years old ; others say the river would have eroded the whole gorge in 7000 years from the present time.[6] Then the estimates of antiquity from droppings in caves and fossil remains are "probably ill-founded."[7] Thus an estimate of 300,000 years was reduced by Prof. Boyd Dawkins to a possible 250 years.[8] The subject has been examined

[1] H. Zimmern in *Enc. Rel. Eth.*, art. "Babylonians," ii. 309.
[2] Art. "Egypt," ix. 79.
[3] F. Hommel in Hastings' *D.B.*, i. 223.
[4] See p. 158.
[5] So Girdlestone, *Bib. Chron.*, 60.
[6] S. Bramley-Moore, *Fable or Fact* (a useful little book).
[7] *Enc. Brit.* **xxv.** 767b.   [8] *Cave Hunting*, 40.

carefully by (among others) the Rev. Martin Anstey, to whose work I refer the reader for fuller details.[1] We may well say then with Dr. Gore, that " on such subjects as the origin of the human race, its exact relation to animal ancestry, and the right interpretation of the fact of sin, before science can make demands on theology, there must be more agreement in her own camp." [2]

Some of these arguments will receive additional strength when we come to examine the period after the Flood ; they appear to me to prove incontestably that the Sept. has preserved the numbers which were originally in the Heb. text.

This gives the date of the commencement of the Flood as the seventeenth day of the second month, A.M. 2262, or a little over **2261** years [3] from the Creation ; for the Flood commenced " in the six-hundredth year of Noah's life ; " [4] i.e. when he was 599 years old, Shem being then in his **98**th year.

II. *From the Commencement of the Flood to the Birth of Terah.* The table on the following page exhibits the variations of the three texts.

The Sixtine text of the Septuagint gives 179 years as the generative age of Nahor, but this rests on no good authority ; all the best MSS have seventy-nine, and so the larger and smaller Cambridge editions. The manuscript variations in the second division of the table it is not necessary to take any notice of. The totals in the third division are arrived at, in the case of the Sept. and Heb., by adding together the figures in the other two divisions ; the Samaritan text, true

---

[1] *Romance of Bib. Chron.*, 89*f*. See also F. A. Jones, *Dates of Genesis*, 69*f*; *Earliest Days of Man*, 33*f*.

[2] Some would solve geological and other difficulties by supposing that a pre-Adamite race of men existed and perished in the age between the first and second verses of Genesis.

[3] I have called this period 2,261½ years, as it is not necessary to go into smaller fractions of a year ; the other four months must be accounted for somewhere before the Exodus.

[4] Gen. vii. 11.

TABLE II.

	Age of Each when the Next was born.			Years of Each after the Next was born.			Total Length of the Life of Each.		
	Sept.	Heb.	Sam.	Sept.	Heb.	Sam.	Sept.	Heb.	Sam.
Shem	3[1]	3[1]	3[1]						
Arphaxad. . .	135	35	135	330	403	303	465	438	438
Cainan . . .	130			330			460		
Salah	130	30	130	330	403	303	460	433	433
Eber	134	34	134	270	430	270	404	464	404
Peleg	130	30	130	209	209	109	339	239	239
Reu	132	32	132	207	207	107	339	239	239
Serug	130	30	130	200	200	100	330	230	230
Nahor . . .	79	29	79	129	119	69	208	148	148
	1003	223	873						

to its character for making alterations, gives the figures in full, and agrees generally with the Heb., though, in the generative ages, which are the most important, it agrees exactly (except as regards Cainan) with the Sept., which is the more remarkable as these figures are altogether out of harmony with those it gives for the patriarchs before the Flood. If the Sept. figures before the Flood be accepted, then we are bound to follow it here, too, but a few further arguments in its favour may be briefly stated.

(1) I have already proved [2] that the " second Cainan " had a real existence between Arphaxad and Salah; his name may have fallen out of the Heb. text through carelessness in copying.

(2) According to the Heb., the age of marriage

---

[1] Arphaxad was born "two years after the Flood" (Gen. xi. 10), which lasted exactly a year. (Compare Gen. vii. 11; viii. 13, 14.)

[2] Chap. II., page 109 seq.

after the Flood was about thirty years. Terah, however, had no son until he was seventy ; still, that might be exceptional. Neither can we argue anything rom the case of Abraham ; [1] but let us look at his descendants. He had a great dread of his son marrying a wife " of the daughters of the Canaanites among whom he dwelt ; " he would therefore, especially as he was himself " old and well stricken in age," [2] take care that Isaac married *young*, before he had time to form any connection among his neighbours. Yet what do we find ? That when Isaac· married Rebekah he was forty years old, an age which well agrees with the Septuagint figures, when we take into account the increasing shortness of human life, but not with the Hebrew. Let us go a generation lower. Esau was a wild youth, evidently fond of female society, for he had three if not five wives, and he married before his parents dreamt of looking out a wife for him. Yet he was then forty years of age. His brother Jacob did not marry until he was at least sixty-four, if not eighty-four years old. I will take the lower number as being more probable in itself and as suiting the history better.

There are no ages given in the family of Laban, but a little study yields results here, also, which exactly agree with the preceding. Taking the Birth of Terah as a starting-point, and assuming for the present that he was 70 years old at the birth of Haran, and 130 at the birth of Abraham, then we find that Rebekah was married to her grand-uncle Isaac 270 years after the Birth of Terah, and Leah was married to Jacob 354 years after the same event. The following table will then show the hypothetical ages of Terah's descendants at the birth of their children :—

[1] It should not, however, be overlooked that Sarah was " very fair," so much so as to excite general admiration, when over 65 years of age (Gen. xii. 11, 14).

[2] Gen. xxiv. 1.

			Age.	Years from Birth of Terah.
1. Terah at birth of Haran			70	70
2. Haran „ Milcah			60?	130?
3. Milcah „ Bethuel			60?	190?
4. Bethuel „ Laban			50?	240?
5. „ „ Rebekah			55 or 50?	245 or 240?
6. Laban „ Leah			64 or 60?	304 or 300?
7. Rebekah at her marriage			25 or 30?	270
8. Leah „ „			50 or 54?	354

Milcah evidently married young, for she married her uncle Nahor; she had eight children, of whom Bethuel is mentioned last,[1] not necessarily because he was the youngest (though probably so, from the mention of Huz his [i.e. Nahor's] firstborn), but possibly because the historian wished to record the birth of his daughter Rebekah, who afterwards married into the chosen family. I have put Rebekah's age at her marriage as low as twenty-five or thirty, as she is called a "damsel," a term only applied to a young woman. Leah's age, about fifty, is perhaps not too high when we consider that her father appears to have thought that her chance of getting a husband by fair means was past. To reduce this age would mean to raise that of one of her ancestors.

The Hebrew text, then, calls upon us to believe that, from the Flood to Nahor, the Father of Terah, the usual age of marriage was from thirty to thirty-five years, but from Terah for several generations onwards, *when the duration of human life was very much shorter*, it rose to from forty to sixty or seventy. I submit that this is utterly incredible, and that we must seek refuge from such inconsistencies by adopting the figures of the Septuagint Version.

Other arguments will be found in the works I have named, but the above are sufficient to show that the figures of the Sept. must be accepted, and the birth of Terah placed 1,003 years after the Commencement of the Flood, or in A.M. 3265.

[1] Gen. xxii. 22.

N

III. *From the Birth of Terah to the Birth of Abraham.* We have now reached the end of our textual difficulties, and shall not have further need to disagree with the Hebrew figures ; still, it is not all plain sailing yet.

"The days of Terah were 205 years : and Terah died in Haran."[1] So both the Heb. and Sept. "And Abram was 75 years old when he departed out of Haran."[2] As this departure took place after his father's death,[3] it follows that Terah was 130 years old when Abraham was born. But some stumble at Gen. xi. 26, where it is said that "Terah lived 70 years and he begat Abram, Nahor, and Haran." But they were not all born together, and Abram is mentioned first, not because he was the eldest, but the greatest. Isaac, the second generation from Terah, through Abraham, married Rebekah (who was doubtless, as we have seen, his junior), the *fourth* generation from Terah through Haran, and the third through Nahor. Abraham therefore must have been born long after Haran. So it is said, "Noah was 500 years old ; and Noah begat Shem, Ham, and Japheth."[4] But Shem was not the eldest, for Noah was over 502 years old when he was born.[5] The Samaritan text, true to its character, attempts to solve the difficulty by making Terah's age at death 145 years ; but it is really surprising that any critics should have deemed this worthy of credence. It has been altered to reconcile an apparent contradiction ; but no reason whatever can be given for altering 145, supposing that to have been the original reading, to 205, which is found in the Heb. and Sept.

But it is further objected that, if Abraham was born when his father was 130 years old, he would not have manifested surprise when told that he himself should have a son at 100. But the wonder was, not his

---

[1] Gen. xi. 32.   [2] Gen. xii. 4.

[3] Acts vii. 2. It is noteworthy how often a gap in the O.T. history is filled by an incidental statement in the New.

[4] Gen. v. 32.

[5] Compare Gen. viii. 13 ; xi. 10.

having a child at 100, but his wife having one at 90, especially as she had hitherto been barren. For Abraham had children by Keturah after Sarah was dead. And the two passages in the N.T. which are brought forward in support of this objection are, I believe, misunderstood. Thus Heb. xi. 11, 12, may be translated as follows : " By faith also Sarah herself received power for the founding of a seed [*i.e.* family] when she was past age, since she counted him faithful who had promised ; wherefore there sprang [1] even from one thing,[2] [i.e. the body of Sarah], and that [3] deadened, as the stars of heaven in multitude, and as the sand which is by the sea shore innumerable." The passage in the Greek is a little obscure, and, as usual, meddlesome scribes have made it more so by trying to improve it ; first, by inserting the word translated in the A.V. " was delivered of a child," and next, by altering the word rendered " sprang " so as to make it apply to a male (Abraham) instead of to a female (Sarah). For it is not of the birth of one child that the writer is

---

[1] The common reading here, *egennēthēsan*, is right, and is followed by the best critics ; Lachmann, Alford and von Soden read *egenēthēsan*, Alford apparently for subjective reasons, for he says, " The reading is doubtful, but *ἐγεν. ἀπό* seems to suit better the *father*, whereas *ἐγενν. ἀπό*, ' there were born from,' would almost necessarily be said of the *mother*." It is strange he could not see that it was the *mother* who is spoken of, and that therefore the latter reading is correct, especially as on the previous verse, he says with reference to *καὶ αὐτή* (" also [Sarah] herself "). " The words merely indicate transition from one personal subject to another, the new subject being thus thrown out into prominence." Yet, in spite of these his own words, he goes back to the old subject in ver. 12, when there is no call for it.

[2] The Greek *ἑνός* may be either masculine or neuter, the context must determine ; here it agrees with *ταῦτα*, " that," which is neuter, showing that we must translate, not " one (man)," but " one (thing)," i.e. the body [*σῶμα*, a neuter noun] of Sarah.

[3] Literally, " these things," *ταῦτα*, " following the usage by which *ταῦτα* is so often put where one thing only is intended " (Alford on 3 John 4). And again here : " *ταῦτα* in such sentences is perpetually the collective plural = *τοῦτο*." But the common interpretation of the verse twists a *plural neuter* into a *singular masculine !*

thinking. Through Sarah's faith far mightier results than that were accomplished. The miracle before his mind is, that from *one dead thing*, that dead thing having been quickened by the power of God, there sprang an innumerable multitude of living beings. For this reason, the rendering " for the founding of a seed " is to be preferred to that of the English Versions, " to conceive seed," as being more agreeable to the context.

The other passage, Rom. iv 19, is more difficult, but here, again, the corrupting hand of the scribe has been at work, though expositors extract the same meaning from the verse whether they read " he considered his own body already deadened," or " he considered *not* his own body already deadened." [1]

However, the question is surely settled by the fact, which some appear to have overlooked, that two generations later, when human life was still further contracted, Jacob had a son (Benjamin) when he was certainly not less than ninety-eight years of age. [2]

We may therefore, without hesitation, accept the plain words of Scripture, that Abraham was born when Terah his father was 130 years old, or in A.M. 3395.

IV. *From the Birth of Abraham to his Call*, or rather to his Departure from Haran. About this period there is no dispute ; for we read that " Abram was seventy-five years old when he departed out of Haran." [3] This event took place, therefore, in A.M. 3470.

V. *From the Call of Abraham to the Covenant*, Gen. xv. The record in the Book of Genesis does not furnish us with any chronological data respecting the

[1] Still, even if the common interpretation be correct, it must be remembered that Terah lived to be thirty years older than Abraham was.

[2] The common chronology makes him about 108. Levi also, a generation lower still, could hardly have been less than 100 years old at the birth of his daughter Jochebed, the mother of Moses.

[3] Gen. xii. 4.

events of Abraham's life between the Call and the Birth of Ishmael, eleven years later. I assume, for the present, that the remarkable revelation made to Abraham while the " deep sleep " was upon him, and the covenant made with him " in the same day," must be dated four years after the Call, or in A.M. 3474.[1]

VI. *From the Covenant with Abraham to the Exodus.* In Exod. xii. 40, 41, we read, " Now the sojourning of the children of Israel, *who dwelt in Egypt,*[2] was four hundred and thirty years : and it came to pass at the end of the four hundred and thirty years, even the self-same day it came to pass, that all the hosts of the LORD went out from the land of Egypt." From what date must these 430 years be reckoned ? Many modern expositors say from the descent of Jacob and his family into Egypt. But this is to set Moses at variance with himself ; for it is utterly impossible that Moses could be the grandson of Levi, as he is plainly averred to be,[3] if the Israelites dwelt in Egypt 430 years. The other genealogies all agree with this, as Mr. Browne, who argues the question most ably, has well shown.[4] It was the unanimous opinion of ancient times, and, indeed, the reading of the Septuagint and Samaritan in this verse plainly states, that these 430 years included the sojourning of their fathers in the land of Canaan. And most modern chronologers of note, however much they may differ on other points, agree in this, that the period named must be dated back from the time of Abraham. Here a slight difference manifests itself : for while most reckon from the Call, and others from Abraham's going down into Egypt in (apparently) the

---

[1] " This is the only conjectural element in the scheme here proposed." I borrow these words from Mr. Browne (*Ordo Sæclorum,* p. 12) for they are true of my scheme as well as his.

[2] So the A.V., which the R.V. quite unnecessarily alters to " which they sojourned in Egypt," for either suits the Hebrew.

[3] Exod. vi. 16–20 ; Num. xxvi. 59.

[4] See, on the whole subject of this period, *Ordo Sæclorum,* pp. 295–308. The arguments are well and briefly stated in Wordsworth's *Commentary* on Exod. xii. 40.

year following, Mr. Browne dates it from the Promise and Covenant in Gen. xv. And that this is a very ancient opinion is shown by the following extract from the Targum of Palestine (pseudo-Jonathan) on Exod. xii. 40 : " And the days of the dwelling of the children of Israel in Egypt were 30 weeks of years (30 times 7 years), which is the sum of 210 years. But the number of 430 years (had passed away since) the Lord spake to Abraham, in the hour that He spake with him on the 15th of Nisan, between the divided parts (Gen. xv. 10), until the day that they went out of Egypt." But we have a higher authority than this ; one, indeed, which settles the matter beyond dispute. St. Paul writes, " Now to Abraham and his seed were the promises made. He saith not, And to seeds, as of many ; but as of one, And to thy seed, which is Christ. And this I say, that the *covenant*, that was confirmed before of God in Christ, the law, *which was four hundred and thirty years after*, cannot disannul, that it should make the promise of none effect." [1] Now, the Law was given within two months (probably 49 days) after the Exodus, therefore in the same year ; and as this took place 430 years after the *covenant* with Abraham (which covenant is mentioned for the first time in Gen. xv. 18), then, if we are right in dating the Covenant four years after the Call, it follows that the Exodus from Egypt took place in Spring, A.M. 3904.

VII. *From the Exodus to the Birth of Christ.* The date of the Exodus we have already fixed at Spring, B.C. 1491, and we have also seen that the Birth of Christ must be placed towards the end of B.C. 5. This gives the length of the period as 1,486½ years, or a month or two longer, and fixes the date of the Birth of Christ as the extreme end of A.M. 5390, or, more probably, one of the early months of A.M. 5391.

The following table exhibits the dates A.M. and B.C. of certain events from the Creation to the Birth of Christ.

[1] Gal. iii. 16, 17.

A.M.[1]			B.C.[1]
1, Tisri (1st mo.)	The Creation of Adam	.	5395, Autumn.
2142 . . .	" Yet his days shall be 120 years " . . .	.	3254
2262, 2nd mo. .	Commencement of the Flood .		3134, end.
2263, 2nd mo. .	End of the Flood .	.	3133, end.
2793, end . .	The Earth divided .	.	2602, Autumn.
2794, beginning .	Birth of Peleg .	.	2602, end.
3395 . . .	Birth of Abraham .	.	2000
3470 . . .	Call of Abraham .	.	1925
3474, Nisan .	The Covenant with Abraham		1921, Spring.
3480 . . .	Abraham marries Hagar .		1915
3504 . . .	Isaac weaned, and Hagar cast out		1891
3555 . . .	Jacob born . . .		1840
3612 . . .	Jacob goes to Padan-Aram		1783
3652 . . .	„ returns to Canaan .		1743
3685 . . .	„ goes down into Egypt		1710
3904, Nisan .	The Exodus . .	.	1491, Spring.
3906, Tisri .	Return of the Spies .	.	1490, Autumn.
3944, Nisan.	Entrance into Canaan .	.	1451, Spring.
3951 . .	Canaan conquered .		1445
3952 . .	Canaan divided by lot .		1444
3958, Tisri .	Commencement of 1st Sabbatic year . .	.	1438, Autumn.
4001, Tisri .	Commencement of 1st Jubilee year . . .	.	1395, Autumn.
4353 . . .	The Ark removed to Jerusalem		1042
4383, 8th mo. .	Solomon's Temple founded		1012, May.
4393, Tisri . .	„ „ dedicated .		1003, Autumn.
4642 . . .	Foundation of Rome . .		753, April.
4807, end .	Solomon's Temple destroyed .		588, Aug.
	(some say 1, others 2 years later)		
5391, beginning .	Birth of Christ . .	.	5, end.

We have now to see what confirmation of this scheme can be found in the " mystical " use of numbers. But, first, a word as to the numbers to be used, which must not, of course, be too many. *Seven* must necessarily occupy the chief place, as being the number specially employed in matters relating to God's dealings

[1] The years A.M. begin in Tisri (Sept.–Oct.), those B.C. in January. So that to turn A.M. years to B.C., the rule is : if between 1 Jan. and 1 Tisri, deduct A.M. year from 5395 ; if between 1 Tisri and 1 Jan. deduct A.M. year from 5396.

with the world and with man. *Ten*, as being the symbol of completeness, we may expect to find connected with any complete and important period. *Three* is the remaining sacred number, and this we may look for, and that in places where *ten* would not be applicable. *Six* is "man's number," and will accordingly be used but sparingly in the Divine times and seasons. *Seventeen* is found occasionally; I have already remarked [1] that this number appears to possess some mystical significance, though I can offer no opinion as to what it is. *Nineteen*, the number of years in the Metonic Cycle (the *Golden Number* of the Prayer-Book), may also not improperly, perhaps, find a place among mystical numbers when time is the subject.[2] This cycle is called after an ancient Athenian philosopher named Meton, who noticed that the changes of the moon regularly fell on the same days of the solar year as they did nineteen years before, as explained more fully in Ch. I.

There is also a series of numbers called *trinal fractions*, which should, perhaps, be mentioned here. I am loth to ascribe any significance to them, but they appear to be met with sometimes.[3]

(1) The number on which most stress must be laid is that which represents the period between the Creation and the Birth of Christ, the Creation of the *first* Adam

---

[1] p. 169, note.

[2] So "to the number 19 great importance is attached by the Bābīs, and so far as possible, it is made the basis of all divisions of time, money and the like." *Enc. Rel. Eth.* ii. 206.

[3] "Trinal fractions" were discovered, or should we say invented, by Mr. William Cuninghame, and are described in his works, *The Season of the End*, pp. 6-18, and *Dissertation on the Apocalypse*, pp. 518-524; also in Professor Wallace's *True Age of the World*, pp. 116-118. The formula is $\dfrac{n + n^2 + n^3}{n}$. Thus the "trinal fraction" of 2 is $\dfrac{2 + 2^2 + 2^3}{2} = 7$. The result is obtained more easily by multiplying the number by the number next above it, and adding 1. Thus $2 \times 3 + 1 = 7$. So the "trinal fraction" of 3 is 13; of 4, 21; of 5, 31; of 6, 43; of 7, 57; of 8, 73, etc.

and the Birth of the *second*. This period, according to the scheme sketched above, is **5390** complete years. Now 5390 = 77 × 7 × 10. Seventy-seven is a number not only eminently heptadic in itself, but it is the number of generations from God through Adam to Christ, according to St. Luke's genealogy, and therefore may well find a place here. Seven we should also expect to find, even independently of the 77 ; whilst no number professing to set forth " the *fulness* of the times " could be considered right if 10 were not represented in it.

(2) But when God made the world He made *two* " lights," and said of them that they were to be " for signs and for seasons, and for days and years." [1] Now, the word rendered " seasons " answers to the Greek *kairos*, and is frequently translated " appointed time," [2] and in order that it may not be thought that the word refers only to the sun, as do the words " for days and years," the Psalmist tells us that " He appointed the moon for *seasons*." [3] We are therefore justified in asking whether the period between the Creation and the Birth of Christ is marked in lunar time as well as in solar. Now, 5390 solar years are equal (within one day) to 66,665 lunar months ! That is to say, 66,666 lunar months expired 5390 years and (about) 31 days from the Creation. [4] Six is " man's number," as seven

[1] Gen. i. 14.
[2] See, especially, Dan. viii. 19 ; xi. 27, 29, 35.   [3] Ps. civ. 19.
[4] Authorities differ as to the precise mean length both of the solar year and the lunar month, though not so much as to make any practical difference in the figures given above. Mr. Browne appears to have studied the subject very carefully, and as his scheme of chronology differs very widely from mine, I cannot be charged with favouring my own case in taking the figures he gives (*Ordo Sæclorum*, p. 455). The average length of the tropical year he puts at 365·24224 days, or 365^d 5^h 48^m 48^s. As to the lunar month, he says, "The moon's motion is . . . in a state of acceleration. The following formula will give the mean length of a lunation at any time, which we will call t centuries before or after the year 1700 ; viz.— 29^d 12^h $44'$ $2·854788'' \pm t$. $0·028434'' \pm t^2$. $0·0000885''$, the sign being + when the time lies before, and — when after, the year 1700."

is God's. As Adam was the first man, so Christ is " the second man." [1] When the moon had completed 66,666 revolutions round the earth, then " the second man " was born into the world, at the end of **5890** years (77 × 70 Ps. xc. 10) and one month from the Creation. So both sun and moon bear testimony to the fact that " God, having of old time spoken unto the fathers in the prophets, . . . hath *at the end of these days* spoken unto us in his Son ; " [2] that " when *the fulness of the time* came, God sent forth his Son, born of a woman, born under the law, that he might redeem them which were under the law ; [3] that " now once *at the end of the ages* hath he been manifested to put away sin by the sacrifice of himself ; " [4] that Christ " was foreknown indeed before the foundation of the world, but was manifested *at the end of the times.*" [5] " His [man's] days are determined, the number of his months is with thee, thou hast appointed his bounds that he cannot pass." [6]

And there is a noteworthy difference in the way in which the numbers 7 and 6 are used here. We saw the same difference in the number of the books in Scripture, which, according to the Divine count, is 49, a number strongly heptadic, but wherein, nevertheless, 7 lies concealed ; but which, according to man's reckoning, is 66, in which 6 is palpably present. So here : in the solar reckoning there is no outward trace of the number 7 ; it must be searched for : but in the lunar number 6 stares us in the face.

I regard, therefore, this extraordinary concurrence of the two numbers 6 and 7, the latter in conjunction with 10, as furnishing indubitable proof that the scheme of chronology here proposed, resting as it does

---

[1] I Cor. xv. 47. See also Rom. v. 14, where Adam is called " the figure [Gr. *type*] of him that was to come."

[2] Heb. i. 1, 2. R.V.   [3] Gal. iv. 4, R.V.

[4] Heb. ix. 26, R.V.   [5] I Pet. i. 20, R.V.

[6] Job xiv. 5. For other texts of a similar character, see *Ordo Sæclorum*, pp. 433–435.

upon a sound Scripture basis, is in its main features correct.

As to whether the figures just given furnish any clue to the exact day of Christ's birth, I hesitate to express an opinion. As 5390 years is not an exact measure, but allows one month over,[1] so possibly 66,666 months may allow some days over. Knowing nothing of the use of astronomical tables, I cannot tell when the 1st Tisri, B.C. 5395, must be dated in the Julian year, but taking Ussher's date for the Creation (23rd October), then 5390 years and 31 days would bring us to the 23rd of November, B.C. 5, or only fifteen days earlier than the date arrived at by Mr. Browne for the Nativity.

The date here proposed for the Creation does not differ very widely from that given by some of the best chronologers ; thus Hales gives B.C. 5411 ; Jackson, B.C. 5426 ; and R. S. Poole, B C. 5421 or 5361.

We will now see what corroboration can be found for the dates of other events, and will take first that period for which Scripture furnishes no clue, viz. the interval between the Call of Abraham and God's Covenant with him.

(3) From the Call to the Exodus, which was also a call from God,[2] is (430 + 4 =) 484 years = 7 × 62, which is twice 31, the trinal fraction of 5.

(4) From the Covenant with Noah (immediately after the Flood, Gen. ix. 8–17) to the Covenant with Abraham, is 1211 years = 7 × 173.

(5) From the end of the Flood to the Exodus is 1641 years, which number is the trinal fraction of 40, a number intimately associated with both events.

(6) From the Creation to the commencement of the Flood is 2261 complete years = 7 × 17 × 19.

(7) The date of the Flood is given in Scripture with great exactitude : " And Noah went in, and his sons, and his wife, and his sons' wives with him into the ark,

---

[1] There is a similar difference of about a month with respect to the date of the Flood.

[2] Hosea xi. 1 : " When Israel was a child, then I loved him, and called my son out of Egypt."

because of the waters of the flood.   Of beasts, etc., . . .
there went in two and two unto Noah into the ark. . . .
And it came to pass after seven days, that the waters of
the flood were upon the earth.   In the six hundredth
year of Noah's life; in the second month, the seventeenth day of the month, the same day were all the
foundations of the great deep broken up, and the win-
dows of heaven were opened." [1]   Noah, therefore,
entered the ark on the tenth day of the second month,
A.M. 2262, or about 2261 years and 40 days from the
Creation.   Now, this period is exactly equal to 27,966
lunar months $= 6 \times 4661$.   There is not, perhaps, any
significance in this, but if we add six months more we
get a notable number, for $27,972 = 666 \times 6 \times 7$.
Six months, however, carry us forward to the tenth
day of the eighth month, or about twenty-two days
after the ark rested upon the mountains of Ararat.
But we have proceeded upon an assumption for which
there is no proof, which is, indeed, almost certainly
false, viz. that the first day of the first month of this
year began *exactly* 2261 solar years from the Creation.
For " that the form of year intended in these dates was
lunar," says Mr. Browne, " does not admit of a doubt.
The Jews, and Semitic nations generally, knew no
other ; certainly their year was of this form at the
time when the Book of Genesis was written and
delivered to them, and of course they would refer these
day-names to their own calendar." [2]   So that a year of
twelve lunar months, or 354 days, would be 11 days in
advance of the true solar time : in two years 22 days
would be gained ; but in the third year some approach
to accuracy would be made by adding a thirteenth
month, just as we, for a similar purpose, add a 366th
day to our calendar every fourth year.   Now, 2261
solar years = 27,964 lunar months and 19 days, and
it would make the calendar correspond more nearly
with the seasons if ten days more were added to the
year before the Flood, and that year made to contain

[1] Gen. vii. 7–11.   [2] *Ordo Sæclorum*, p. 322.

thirteen months, rather than that the year A.M. 2262 should commence nineteen days before the proper time. In this case the month in which the ark rested—the seventh month of the year—would be 22,972 lunar months from the Creation, and this number, as before remarked $= 666 \times 6 \times 7$.

(8) Peleg was born at the beginning (counting complete years from the Flood) of the year 2794 A.M. His name signifies Division, " for in his days was the earth divided." [1] Now, it is surely most natural to suppose that the Division of the Earth took place just before, or about the time of, Peleg's birth, for there is no hint that the name was given prophetically in advance of the event, but rather the contrary is implied.[2] I would therefore put down the Division of the Earth at the end of A.M. 2793, or possibly just after the close of that year. Now $2793 = 49 \times 3 \times 19$; or $7 \times 7 \times 57$, the trinal fraction of 7.

(9) The date of the first jubilee year is A.M. 4001, or exactly 4000 years from the Creation. This may, however, be a mere accident.

(10) From the End of the Flood to the Call of Abraham is 1207 years $= 17 \times 71$.

(11) I have put down the date of Hagar being cast out from Abraham's house [3] as A.M. 3504, or nine years after the birth of Isaac, when Ishmael, therefore, was twenty-three years old. Isaac's age is usually set down as about three years when he was " weaned," whatever the word so rendered may mean here, for it has a variety of meanings ; but I have dated the incident six years later, for the following reason. When God made the covenant with Abraham, He told him that his seed should be afflicted 400 years,[4] " which began," says

---

[1] Gen. x. 25.

[2] So R. S. Poole : "The event, whatever it was, must have happened at Peleg's birth, rather than, as some have supposed, at a late period in his life, for the Easterns have always given names to children at birth, as may be noticed in the cases of Jacob and his sons " (Smith's *Dict. Bib.*, i. 321).

[3] Gen. xxi. 14.　　　　[4] Gen. xv. 13.

Ainsworth, in his note on the passage, " when Ishmael, son of Hagar *the Egyptian*, mocked and *persecuted* Isaac (Gen. xxi. 9 ; Gal. iv. 29), which fell out thirty years after the promise [*rather*, the covenant, Gen. xv. 18] which [covenant] was 430 years before the Law (Gal. iii. 17), and 430 years after that [covenant] came Israel out of bondage (Exod. xii. 41)." [1]   For the words do not mean, as some moderns would make them do, that the Israelites were in bondage for 400 years, but, by a usage not unknown to Scripture,[2] that from the time when *first* the seed of Abraham was " persecuted " by Egyptians (for Hagar doubtless sided with her son) till the final deliverance from Egyptian bondage should be 400 years. I therefore date the mocking, or " persection," as St. Paul calls it, and the consequent casting out of Hagar and her son from Abraham's house, thirty years after the Covenant and 400 years before the Exodus, or in A.M. 3504.   Now, Hagar became Abraham's wife (she is so called, Gen. xvi. 3) ten years after the Call, or in A.M. 3480, from which date until she was cast out is *twenty-four years*.   We must turn now to the typical meaning of this history, which is given by St. Paul in Gal. iv. 22–31, where he tells us that " these (women) are two covenants ; one from Mount Sinai, bearing children unto bondage, which is Hagar.   Now this Hagar is Mount Sinai in Arabia, and answereth to the Jerusalem that now is : for she is in bondage with her children.   But the Jerusalem that is above is free, which is our mother." [3]   Now, Jerusalem attained its eminence as " the city which the LORD did choose out of all the tribes of Israel to put his name there," [4] in the year B.C. 1042, when David with great ceremony removed the ark of God thither.   From this date until A.D. 135, when Jerusalem was finally de-

---

[1] Adam Clarke quotes this note of Ainsworth's, but, by omitting the words " the Egyptian," misses the point of the whole.

[2] See the very able note on the " Chronology of the Period of the Judges," in Smith's *Student's O.T. Hist.*, p. 285.

[3] Gal. iv. 24–26, R.V.   [4] I Kings xiv. 21.

stroyed by the Romans, is **1176** years $= 24 \times 7 \times 7$. That is to say, from Hagar's marriage with Abraham until she was cast out of his house was 24 years : from the time when Jerusalem was, as it were, married to God,[1] until Hadrian "obliterated the existence of Jerusalem as a city," when "the ruins which Titus had left were razed to the ground, and the plough passed over the foundations of the Temple,"[2] was **49** times 24 years.[3]

(12) From the Exodus to the Destruction of Solomon's Temple (B.C. 588), i.e. from the commencement to the close of the history of the Israelites as an independent nationality, is **903** years, $= 7 \times 3 \times 43$, the trinal fraction of 6.

(13) As already stated, from the Division of the land of Canaan under Joshua to the commencement of Christ's ministry is **1470** years, $= 7 \times 7 \times 3 \times 10$, or thirty jubilees.

(14) There can be no doubt that the death, resurrection, and ascension of Christ all took place at preappointed times. "When the days were being fulfilled that he should be received up."[4] "Jesus knowing that his hour was come that he should depart out of this world unto the Father."[5] "Father, the hour is come."[6] "My appointed time (*kairos*) is at hand."[7] "When we were yet without strength, at the appointed time (*kairos*) Christ died for the ungodly."[8] These

[1] Compare Rev. xxi. 2, "I saw the holy city, new Jerusalem, coming down from God out of heaven, prepared as a bride adorned for her husband."

[2] Smith's *Student's N.T. Hist.*, p. 110.

[3] Ishmael, therefore, the son "born after the flesh," is a type of the Jewish dispensation. He lived 137 years, the same age as Levi, who, above all the sons of Jacob, typified the same thing. The only other one of the sons of Jacob whose age at death is given is Joseph, who lived 110 years, to which age his great descendant Joshua also attained, both of them being eminent types of Christ, who was born 110 jubilee-periods of 49 years each from the Creation of Adam.

[4] Luke ix. 51, R.V. marg.

[5] John xiii. 1.

[6] John xvii. 1.

[7] Matt. xxvi. 18.

[8] Rom. v. 6.

texts clearly teach that, as there was an appointed time for the birth of Christ, as there was an appointed time for the commencement of His ministry, so there was also for His death. But here we enter upon the vexed question of the duration of our Lord's ministry, one which I confess I am loth to touch. I have been too long accustomed to the common opinion that it lasted about three and a half years to part readily from it, yet I can find no *figures* in support of it. And one of the chief objections to the one-year theory—which has been revived and set forth with much ability by Mr. Browne—is disposed of by the fact, which is proved in a former chapter,[1] that the words " the passover," in John vi. 4, are an interpolation. Now, the great type of our Lord's death in the Old Testament is the Passover, which was instituted at the time of the Exodus, and from this event (B.C. 1491) to A.D. 29, the year of the Crucifixion, is **1519** years $= 7 \times 7 \times 31$, the trinal fraction of 5.

(15) If we take Mr. Browne's dates for the birth and crucifixion of our Lord, the 8th of December, B.C. 5, and 18th of March, A.D. 29,[2] we find they are separated by a period of 32 years and 100 days, or 399 lunar months and 5 days. Now, **399** $= 7 \times 57$, the trinal fraction of 7 ; or $7 \times 3 \times 19$.

(16) The Offering of Isaac is a striking type of the death and resurrection of Christ, but, unfortunately, we do not know the date of it. It probably occurred, however, **1911** years before the Crucifixion, $= 7 \times 7 \times 3 \times 13$, the trinal fraction of 3.

(17) The taking of Joseph out of prison and his exaltation by King Pharaoh are also typical of the resurrection of Christ and His ascension into heaven. Now, the date of Joseph's being made governor of Egypt is A.M. 3676, and from then to Spring, A.D. 29 = A.M. 5423 is 1747 years, which are = 21,607 lunar months and (about) 11 days. If, therefore, we place

[1] p. 99 *seq.*
[2] This date is accepted by most recent authorities.

Joseph's accession in, say, the month of February, we have an interval of **21,609** lunar months from that event to the Resurrection, and $21,609 = 7 \times 7 \times 7 \times 7 \times 3 \times 3$. If we take the number of *years* to work upon instead of months, then 1750 years $= 7 \times 5 \times 5 \times 10$, but not only has 5 too prominent a place here, but this interval would carry us too far, making our Lord's ministry last over four years, which is out of the question. The figures point plainly to A.D. 29 as the date of the Crucifixion, which will allow a period of not more than eighteen months as the duration of the ministry.

We have here, therefore, the outlines of a scheme of Sacred Chronology from the Creation to the Crucifixion, which it is suggested is the true one, founded as it is upon Scripture, and supported by such remarkable combinations of mystical numbers, but especially by the number SEVEN.

CHAPTER VII

THE NUMBERS SEVEN AND FOUR IN NATURE

"THE type of all that is in Scripture is in God's older book of nature, that book having been created for no other purpose than to be itself a word of God." [1] Nor may these be set aside as the words of a mystic; they are but one way of putting a truth which has been present to the minds of men since the days of Bishop Butler, and, indeed, for ages before that time. "The whole face of nature," says Dr. Hugh Macmillan, "to him who can read it aright, is covered with celestial types and hieroglyphics, marked, like the dial-plate of a watch, with significant intimations of the objects and processes of the world unseen. The Bible discloses all this to us. It not only gives us the knowledge of salvation, but reveals to us the spiritual source of the physical world; shows to us that the supernatural is not antagonistic to the constitution of nature, but is the eternal source of it. . . . Every natural fact," he proceeds, "is a symbol of some spiritual fact; every object of creation is the shadow of some important moral truth." [2]

Professor Henry Drummond, in a work which deservedly attracted considerable attention some years ago, goes a step further. "The position we have been led to take up," he says, "is not that the Spiritual Laws are analogous to the Natural Laws, but that *they are the same Laws*. It is not a question of analogy, but of *Identity*." [3]

[1] A. Jukes, *New Man*, p. 104.
[2] *Bible Teachings in Nature*, preface, pp. vi., ix.
[3] *Natural Law in the Spiritual World*, p. 11.

If, then, there are in Nature and in Revelation so many points of resemblance as to force him who has rightly studied both to declare, in the words of an eminent geologist, that "it was He who created the worlds that dictated the Scriptures,"[1] if the Natural world and the Spiritual world—that is, the world which is revealed to us in and through the Scriptures—are governed by the same laws, and so betray an identity of origin, may we not expect to find that if numbers play an important part in one they will also in the other? Undoubtedly, And this question of the use of numbers in nature is one which has not escaped notice, though it has not received the attention it deserves. The Rev. Charles Girdlestone endeavours to show that it tends " to make evident the existence and the unity of God, and man's likeness to the most High as of a child to a parent."[2] Dr. Balfour adduces very strong grounds for asserting that " the doctrine of the Trinity is not one which is peculiar to Scripture, but which is inwoven in the very constitution of man, and to which all Nature bears its willing testimony."[3] In McCosh and Dickie's *Typical Forms and Special Ends in Creation*, a special chapter is devoted to the " Typical Systems of Nature and Revelation," one section of which treats of " Typical Numbers." Mr. Edward White, in an admirable popular lecture on the subject, argues that " Number pervades Nature ; and that whether seen in weight, motion, time, force, mass, distance, structure, or vibration, everywhere the idea is suggested of a Mind which counts, measures, weighs, regulates, with minute and eternal purpose ; "[4] and Mr. H. L. Hastings, of Boston, in a companion paper, declares that " the recurrence of special numbers in the varied departments of nature indicates the pre-

---

[1] Hugh Miller, in *The Witness* newspaper, August, 1851.
[2] *Number : a Link between Divine Intelligence and Human*, p. 33.
[3] *The Typical Character of Nature : or, All Nature a Divine Symbol*, by T. A. G. Balfour, M.D., p. 26.
[4] *Number in Nature an Evidence of Creative Intelligence*, p. 21.

sence of a Mind which works according to well-established principles and familiar laws, dealing mainly with the simpler forms of number, . . . and going through higher ranges of mathematical thought, until the wisest are baffled and astonished." [1]

But none of these writers attribute to the number *Seven* that special prominence in nature which it has in Scripture. It may be that they are right in not doing so. In two different works by the same author, while we look for a certain similarity of style and harmony of sentiment, we do not expect to find the same thoughts repeated, unless, indeed, the two works treat of the same subject. While, therefore, we may expect to find numbers used symbolically in nature as they are in Scripture, it depends upon the ideas we attach to the number *seven*, upon what we consider was God's intention in creating the world—whether it was allied to or distinct from His purpose in dictating the Scriptures,—and perhaps upon other considerations, whether we deem we have a right to look for *seven* occupying a position of pre-eminence or not.

With the presence of other numbers in nature we are not now specially concerned, but mainly with the number *seven* ; and it will be my object in this chapter to endeavour to show that this number is found in the world around us much more extensively than is commonly supposed. But another number—FOUR—is also found so frequently and in such important positions as to show that it stands there by no mere accident, and this number must also find a place in our study.

"How we are amazed," says Mr. Malcolm White, " when we look forth on the rainbow, that world-wide sign of God's covenant of grace, to discern there 7 colours ! and when we listen to the trilling of the human voice, to catch the same strange number 7 ! More : science tells us it is no mere chance that there should be 7 colours in the sunlight and 7 notes in music. It is because of essential relations between light and sound.

[1] *Atheism and Arithmetic*, p. 60.

The very simplicity with which these can be stated is striking. A tenor voice produces 400 vibrations per second; a soprano voice 800. We have merely to multiply by a million million, and we come to numbers that have to be dealt with in the case of light; 400 million million vibrations per second corresponding to red light, 700 million million to violet, and so forth. But this is suggestive of a much wider range of harmonies. For the same prism which breaks up the ray of light into its 7 constituent colours performs other wonders as well. Apply a thermometer to one side of the solar spectrum, and carry it along through the different zones of colour till the red be reached, and you will observe that the mercury gradually rises. Continue to carry the thermometer further along, and the mercury still rises. You find, in fact, that you are getting into a scale of heat, similar to the scale of light visible to the eye, and apparently very similar to the scale of music audible to the ear. Once more: let the photographer carry his prepared plate in the exactly opposite direction, and he observes that, as he approaches the last lavender tints of the spectrum, the silvery surface of his sheet is being perceptibly darkened. He advances still, and blacker, by degrees, does the sheet become. There is a scale of chemical effects being exhibited, strikingly like the scale of light, of sound, of heat. Then can it be that there is not merely a diatonic scale in music, but one that sweeps throughout the circle of the sciences? Is the number 7 not merely involved in the rays which strike the eye, and in the eye on which they fall,—in the notes which affect the ear, and the ear which is formed to receive them, but is the number 7 also mysteriously involved in the modifications of heat, that have such an influence on our frames, and in the ten thousand nerves that transmit these impressions? Is it associated with those chemico-electrical processes that are unceasingly at play within and around us? . . . Stranger still, however, than the mere fact that 7 seems to run throughout the universe, is it to observe that the numbers 3 and 4 are found combining in order to its formation. There are 3 primary colours, red, yellow and blue, from which the others are formed. In like manner, there are 3 notes in the scale of music that the ear can more readily dwell on than others—the first, third, and fifth. The *do, me, sol*, as every one knows, are those a precentor invariably chooses to run over. And if analogy can be any guide, the fact of the 3 and the 4 being marked out in light and in sound seems to indicate how prevalent may be their existence throughout the whole bounds of nature." [1]

Mr. White then calls attention to the fact, which is one we have already had occasion to notice, that 7, *as made up of 3 and 4*, has as distinct a place among the typical numbers of Revelation as of creation.

Professor Moses Stuart has some remarks which are worth quoting here. " There are *sevens* in the world of nature," he says, " which, to the mind of the ancients, were striking and significant. For example, the well-known and familiar appellation of the world in Greek is *Kosmos ;* which means, in its primitive sense, *ornament, arrangement, order* according to fixed laws, a *harmony* in all the parts of anything, and the like. The Pythagoreans found in the 7 musical tones a striking emblem of this harmony, especially as viewed in connection with the 7 planets, the only ones known to them. All these, as is well known, move in perfect order, and preserve an entire harmony. Hence they imagined a resemblance between them and the 7 musical tones, which, taken together, make up the circle of harmony in music. Hence *Pan*, the personification of the Universe, was represented as having a flute of 7 reeds, emitting 7 different notes when breathed upon by its owner ; and his music-moving breath was compared to the igneous æther which the ancients regarded as diffused through the universe, and occasioning all the revolutions of the planets in what might

[1] *The Symbolical Numbers of Scripture*, pp. 141–146.

be named a musical order. From this came, in an obvious way, the idea of the *music of the spheres.* The God who created the universe, created it, as the *anthropomorphitic* heathen supposed, so as to regale Himself with the music which it was continually sending forth while the evolutions of the planets were performed. The latter, of course, were considered as performing in their movements a *choros,* or *circling dance,* which usually accompanied music." [1]

Whilst speaking of **Music,** which itself is one of " the 7 liberal arts," the species of melody called a *chant* may be referred to. " A single chant," says Dr. Stephen Elvey, " consists of 7 portions or bars, divided into two parts : the first part, to which is sung the first part of each verse as far as the colon, consists of *three* bars ; and the second part, to which is sung the remainder of the verse, consists of *four* bars." [2] Nor may it be out of place to note that what is called " *Common* Measure," as being " the measure commonly used in psalms and hymns," consists of lines containing alternately *four* and *three* " feet," or 7 feet in every two lines : anciently, however, two lines in compositions of this kind were written as one, each line therefore containing 7 feet or 14 syllables. [3]

Musicians divide the compass of the human voice into 7 ranges, and singers are classed accordingly : four male, (1) Bass, (2) Baritone, (3) Tenor, (4) Counter tenor or Alto ; and three female : (5) Contralto, (6) Mezzo-soprano, (7) Soprano. [4]

In Vocal Music the usual number of parts is *four :* Soprano (or treble), Alto, Tenor, Bass.

The terms usually employed to denote the volume of sound are 7 : *ff, f, mf, m, mp, p, pp.*

There are in Music 7 time-notes : (1) Breve, (2)

[1] *Commentary on the Apocalypse.* Excursus II.
[2] *The Psalter Pointed,* p. xxi.
[3] The key-board of a pianoforte, it may here be remarked, is usually about 7 octaves in length.
Chambers' Ency.

Semibreve, (3) Minim, (4) Crotchet, (5) Quaver, (6) Semiquaver, (7) Demi-semiquaver.

By far the most important of the fundamental discords are those founded upon the dominant (hence the reason for the name given to the 5th of the scale), and of these the most common and the most useful is the chord of the dominant 7th. This chord consists of *four* notes, and is the least pungent of all discords.[1]

A diminished 7th can be made to belong to *four* keys . . . every diminished 7th can be enharmonically varied *four* times.[2]

The difference in pitch between any two musical tones is called an interval, and in the diatonic scale, which is the one universally employed by civilized nations, 14 intervals are usually recognized.[3]

In **Arithmetic** certain peculiarities attach to the number 7. If the vulgar fractions having 7 for a denominator are brought to decimals, we have in each case a recurring decimal consisting of the *same* figures and in the *same* order, but beginning at a different part of the period : thus—

$$\tfrac{1}{7} = \cdot\dot{1}4285\dot{7}.$$
$$\tfrac{3}{7} = \cdot\dot{4}2857\dot{1}.$$
$$\tfrac{2}{7} = \cdot\dot{2}8571\dot{4}.$$
$$\tfrac{6}{7} = \cdot\dot{8}5714\dot{2}.$$
$$\tfrac{4}{7} = \cdot\dot{5}7142\dot{8}.$$
$$\tfrac{5}{7} = \cdot\dot{7}1428\dot{5}.$$

No other number possesses this peculiarity until we come to 17, which is the 7th prime or indivisible number, the series running 2, 3, 5, 7, 11, 13, 17.[4] It follows from the above that if 142857 be multiplied by 2, 3, 4, 5, 6, we get for the product the same figures in the same order, beginning at a different point.

[1] Mansfield's *Student's Harmony*[11], pp. 58, 60.
[2] *Id.*, p. 157.
[3] *Chambers' Ency.*, art. " Diatonic."
[4] It is remarkable that in the decimals for $\tfrac{1}{7}$, etc., the only digits which do not occur are 3, 6, 9 ; while in the decimals for $\tfrac{1}{17}$, etc., these three digits, together with 0, are each met with *once*, and the other six (viz. those which occur in the $\tfrac{1}{7}$ series) each *twice*,

But multiplied by **7** the result is entirely different, for we get nothing but nines. 8 and 9 give similar results to the lower numbers. Thus :

142,857 × 1 = 142,857
  „   × 2 = 285,714
  „   × 3 = 428,571
  „   × 4 = 571,428
  „   × 5 = 714,285
  „   × 6 = 857,142
  „   × 7 = 999,999
  „   × 8 = 1,142,856 } add first and { = 142,857 the original number.
  „   × 9   1,285,713 } last figures { = 285,714

and so on.

The *circle* is divided into 360 degrees, which number is divisible without a remainder by all the nine digits except **7**. The lowest number exactly divisible by *all* the digits is 2520.

To find the *area of a circle*, the rule as usually given is to multiply the square of the diameter by ·7854. It is a curious fact that this number is equal to

$$
\begin{array}{rcr}
7 \times 1000 = & 7000 \\
7 \times 100 \ = & 700 \\
\text{twice } 7 \times 10 \ = & 140 \\
\text{twice } 7 \qquad = & 14 \\
\hline
& 7854
\end{array}
$$

But this number is only an approximation, though sufficiently near for ordinary purposes.

"There cannot be *seven Prime Numbers* in arithmetical progression, unless their common difference be divisible by **210**; except the first of those prime numbers be **7**, in which case there may be seven prime numbers in arithmetical progression, of which the common difference is not divisible by **210**, but there cannot be more than seven,"[1] e.g. :

7, 157, 307, 457, 607, 757, 907 (com. diff. 150).
47, 257, 467, 677, 887, 1097, 1307 (com. diff. 210).
1619, 2039, 2459, 2879, 3299, 3719, 4139 (com. diff. 420).

---

[1] Barlow's *Theory of Numbers*. p. 67.

There cannot be more than three *Square Numbers* in arithmetical progression. The number of series of three is infinite, but the lowest consists of the squares of 1, 5, 7 ; thus :

					Squares.		Common difference.
1	5	7	=	1	25	49	24
2	10	14	=	4	100	196	96
3	15	21	=	9	225	441	216
4	20	28	=	16	400	784	384
5	25	35	=	25	625	1225	600
6	30	42	=	36	900	1764	864
7	35	49	=	49	1225	2401	1176
	etc.				etc.		

It will be noticed that in the **7th** row **49** appears both as a root number and a square.

A few other series of threes are :—

					Squares.		Common difference.
1	29	41	=	1	841	1681	840
7	13	17	=	49	169	289	120
7	17	23	=	49	289	529	240
17	25	31	=	289	625	961	336

the common difference being always a multiple of 24, and so of 4. But I do not attempt to deal with the number 4 in these arithmetical notes.

The term *Partition of Numbers* is given to the number of ways in which a number may be divided. 4 may be divided in 4 ways and **7** in **14.** These are the only two numbers below 10 where the number of divisions bears any relation to the number itself. 8 has often a subtle connection with **7,** and it may be noted that 8 is capable of **21** divisions. The divisions of the three numbers are as follows :—

4 = 31, 22, 211, 1111. = 4.
7 = 61, 52, 511, 43, 421, 4111, 331, 322, 3211, 31111, 2221, 22111, 211111, 1111111. = **14.**
8 = 71, 62, 611, 53, 521, 5111, 44, 431, 422, 4211, 41111, 332, 3311, 3221, 32111, 311111, 2222, 22211, 221111, 2111111, 11111111. = **21.**

A pound weight avoirdupois contains exactly **7000** grains, the grain being the smallest unit of weight in this country.

In any geometrical series beginning with unity, the 7th term is at once a square and a cube ; thus :—

1	2	3	4	5	6	7
1	2	4	8	16	32	64
1	3	9	27	81	243	729
1	4	16	64	256	1024	4096
1	5	25	125	625	3125	15625

the numbers in the 7th column being each both a square and a cube.

7 was called by the Pythagoreans "virgin" and "Athene" (Minerva, the goddess of wisdom) because within the decade it has neither factors nor product.[1]

In none of the natural sciences does Number play a more important part than in **Chemistry.** Everything is governed by laws, and these laws are chiefly numerical. They have been discovered and formulated by man, but were not made by him, for they are inherent in the nature of things. Thus, the lightest substance known is hydrogen, which was therefore taken as the standard of comparison, its atomic or combining weight being considered as 1.[2] Oxygen is approximately 16 times as heavy, so its atomic weight is 16, and in like manner every element has its own atomic or combining weight, and when any two or more elements combine to form a compound, they do so in the precise ratio or proportion of their com-

[1] *Enc. Brit.* xxii. 699[b].

[2] As it is not necessary here to go into minute fractions or decimals, this statement may stand, though it is not now strictly correct, for a few years ago oxygen for greater convenience was made the standard with an atomic weight of 16 exactly, hydrogen being now called 1·008. More recently it has been found that "if oxygen is taken as 16, the atomic weights of the elements, with the exception of hydrogen, are represented by whole numbers." *Enc. Brit.*[11], xxxi. 196[d].

bining weights or an exact multiple thereof, *and in no other*. This is known as the Law of Multiple Proportions, or the Law of Combining Weights, and so important is it that it has been said that " the study of chemical composition would be unmanageable but for this law." [1] Then we have the Law of Definite Proportions, the Law of Reciprocal Proportions, and the Law of Volumes of Gases. " These *four* laws are the foundations upon which the whole superstructure of modern chemistry rests." [2] In addition we have the Law of Compressibility of Gases, the Law of Expansion of Gases by heat, the Law of Avogadro (which was not recognized by the chemical world until 50 years after it was first published), the Law of Diffusion of Gases, the Law of Specific Heats, and so on, all based more or less upon Number.

It would be difficult to say whether Four or Seven occupies the more important place in Chemistry. In any ordinary group of numbers it may, of course, be expected that the smaller figures and their multiples will be found more frequently than the larger ones, but it is not only the frequency of their occurrence but the importance of the positions they occupy, to which we must look.

The number of Elements now known is about 84 $(4 \times 7 \times 3)$, [3] of which the earth's crust (taking the term in its widest sense to include the sea and the atmosphere) is built up in very varying proportions. Sixteen elements (4×4) make up about $99\frac{1}{2}$ per cent. of it—9 metals and 7 non-metals, or as others reckon them, 8 metals and 8 " metalloids " (4×2). These range from oxygen, over 49 per cent. down to manganese 0.07. [4] Indeed these 16 may be further reduced to 8 (4×2)—oxygen, silicon, aluminium, iron, calcium, magnesium, sodium and potassium—for of these 8

[1] Friend, *Inorg. Chem.*, i. 14.
[2] G. S. Newth, *Text-book of Inorg. Chem.*, 9th ed., p. 26.
[3] But see p. 228.
[4] Friend, *Inorg. Chem.*, i. 8.

about 99 per cent. by weight of the earth's solid crust is composed. All the elements are found in the solid crust except *four*—argon, neon, krypton and xenon, which are found only in the atmosphere.

Matter is generally said to be capable of assuming three different states or conditions—the solid, the liquid, and the gaseous, but " it appears that ordinary matter is capable of subsisting in a *fourth* state, differing as much from the solid, liquid and gaseous states as these do from one another." [1]

Substances as they are found in nature may be divided into four groups : I. (1) Heterogeneous Substances or Mixtures (as granite, which possesses different properties in different parts) ; II. Homogeneous substances : (2) Solutions (3) Elementary substances, (4) Compounds.[2]

The Elements are usually divided into two classes, metals and non-metals. It is difficult, perhaps impossible, to draw a rigid line between the two, but the elements usually classed as non-metals are 21 (7 × 3) in number, leaving about 63 as metals. All the non-metallic elements except the inert gases (helium, neon, argon, krypton, xenon and niton) form volatile compounds with hydrogen, and if these be compared it is found that they fall into *four* classes [3] :—

1. Fluorine	Chlorine	Bromine	Iodine	= 4	Univalent.
2. Oxygen	Sulphur	Selenium	Tellurium	= 4	bivalent.
3. Nitrogen	Phosphorus	Arsenic	Boron	= 4	tervalent.
4. Carbon	Silicon			= 2	quadrivalent.
			Total	14	

These with hydrogen and the six inert gases make up the 21 non-metals. Eleven of these are gases at common temperatures, which may be divided into two groups of 4 and 7 : *four* being the common gases

[1] Tilden, *Intr. to Chem. Philosophy*[11], p. 28. *Enc. Brit.*, vii. 501[d], xxx. 622[a].

[2] Friend, *Inorg. Chem.*, i. 6.

[3] Roscoe & S., *Treatise on Chemistry*, i. 145.

oxygen, hydrogen, nitrogen and chlorine, and **7** being the rarer ones fluorine and the six inert gases.

Plants and the soft parts of animals consist chiefly of *four* elements—carbon, hydrogen, oxygen, and nitrogen, and the bones and shells of animals of *four* more.

The term *halogen* is applied to the *four* elements, fluorine, chlorine, bromine, and iodine, whose maximum valency is **7**. There are three other elements which have the termination -gen—oxygen, hydrogen, nitrogen—making **7** " -gens " in all.

There is another natural group of *four* elements— oxygen, sulphur, selenium and tellurium—which when united with hydrogen possess analogous properties, and like the *four* halogens are electro-negative towards the remaining elements, which are more or less positive. But it is impossible to draw a hard and fast line here.[1]

It will be seen that the numbers *four* and *seven* are so interwoven together that it is practically impossible to deal with them separately ; with no other two numbers is this the case. This will be further evident as we proceed.

One of the most remarkable discoveries in connection with Chemistry is what is termed the Periodic Law of the elements, it being now fully established that " the properties of the elements stand in a definite relation to their atomic weights,"[2] a proposition which at first " appeared to some chemists to be almost as absurd as the proposal of an alphabetical arrangement of the elements as a natural one would be."[3] If we examine any table showing this arrangement we shall find that the horizontal lines (Series) give the names of the elements in the numerical order of their atomic numbers (and weights with one or two trifling exceptions), whilst in the vertical columns (Groups)

[1] *Enc. Brit.*, vi. 39.
[2] Tilden, *C.P.* 231. Rather, "atomic numbers," according to recent research.
[3] Roscoe.

they are grouped according to their chemical properties.   In the first column we have half a dozen elements,
the first of which was only discovered so recently as
1894, and as it would not combine with any of the
other elements it was called Argon (inert), a name
which is characteristic of the other members of the
Group, for they also refuse to combine with the other
elements, and so are known as Group 0 (zero) signifying that they are devoid of " valency " or combining
power.   Turning to the other end of the table we find
another anomalous cluster of elements, for whereas
in Groups I to VII each space in the table is occupied
by not more than one element, and the elements are
fairly distributed through the different Series, the nine
members of Group VIII occur in three series only,
three elements in each, the spaces in the other Series
being blank, each group of three "being the connecting link between the elements of the even series
which precedes and those of the odd series which
follows." [1]   But the most recent arrangement does
away with Group VIII, and includes its members
in Group VII.   This arrangement is confirmed by
" Soddy's Law," according to which the loss of an α-
particle causes an element to move its place in the
periodic table two groups backward. [2]

The Periodic Scheme therefore divides the elements
into 7 regular Groups of combinable elements, with an
8th (4×2) non-combinable Group. [3]

The arrangement, however, as commonly shown, is
not quite free from difficulty, and an alternative method
of tabulation has been suggested showing 7 " Periods,"
2 of them short or typical and 5 long or double, *four*
of the latter each including two Series. [4]   So that again
we have 7 and 4 combined.

[1] Roscoe & S., ii. 1160.
[2] Caven and Lander's *Systematic Inorg. Chemistry* (1922 edn.) pp.
426, 430.   *Enc. Brit.*[12], xxxii. 221[a].
[3] This connection between 7 and 8 is analogous to what is frequently found in Scripture, see Appendix E.
[4] Friend, *Inorg. Chem.*, frontispiece.   Roscoe & S., ii. 52.

This will appear further if we consider the numbers at the head of the groups, which stand for something more than merely to show their numerical order, for they are also an index to the valency or combining capacity. Thus an element in Group I may combine with 1 atom of oxygen, in Group II with 2 atoms, in III with 3, in IV with 4, in V with 5, in VI with 6, in VII with 7, to form oxides; while the hydrogen valencies gradually rise from 1 to 4 only, in Group IV, and then as gradually fall back to 1 in Group VII thus: 1 2 3 4 3 2 1.

The following table will illustrate this, and also the succeeding paragraph :—

Valency	0	1	2	3	4	5 or 3	6 or 2	7 or 1
	He 4	Li 7	Be 9	B 11	C 12	N 14	O 16	F 19
	Ne 20	Na 23	Mg 24	Al 27	Si 28	P 31	S 32	Cl 35
	Ar 40	K 39	Ca 40	Sc 44	Ti 48	V 51	Cr 52	Mn 55

(The letters stand for the names of the elements and the figures for their atomic weights, omitting decimals.)

On this Prof. Sir Wm. A. Tilden remarks : " In passing from series to series in the periodic table the difference in the atomic weights of the common elements is approximately a multiple of *four*. Take the first three rows of elements after hydrogen [as above], the difference between the first and second row of the elements is uniformly very close to 16. The differences between the second and third rows vary somewhat, inasmuch as three are very near to 16, while in four cases they are very near to 20. Both these numbers are multiples of *four*, which is the atomic weight of helium." [1]

The two commonest things in the world are air and water. Air is composed almost entirely, in the proportions roughly of 1 to 4, of oxygen and nitrogen, the atomic weights of which are 16 (4 × 4) and 14 (7 × 2) respectively. Water is composed, in the proportions of 8 (4 × 2) to 1, of oxygen and hydrogen. Now

[1] *Chemical Discovery and Invention in the Twentieth Cent.* 140, 165.

oxygen is the 7th element in its series (see table above), or the 8th (4×2) in the list of all the elements, hydrogen being first. The velocity of diffusion of hydrogen is *four* times as great as that of oxygen. While, as we have seen, hydrogen combines with **14** elements to form volatile compounds, all the elements except **7** (fluorine and the inert gases) i.e. about **77**, are found to unite with oxygen to form an important class of compounds termed oxides.[1] Oxygen, therefore, by far the most important and widely diffused substance in nature, composing as it does about one-fifth of the atmosphere, eight-ninths (by weight) of water, and nearly one-half of the earth's crust, is connected with both *four* and **7**. Next to oxygen, silicon is the largest constituent of the earth's crust, of which it comprises more than one-fourth ; its atomic weight is **28** (4×7). Only about one-fourteenth of the earth's crust is composed of aluminium, the next in order ; its atomic weight is nearly the same, 27. The atomic weight of iron, the next in order, and the most useful of the metals, is **56** ($4 \times 7 \times 2$) and that of gold, "the king of metals," **196** ($4 \times 7 \times 7$).

The composition of sulphuric acid, "perhaps the most important of all chemicals, both on account of the large quantities made in all industrial countries and of the multifarious uses to which it is put,"[2] is H_2SO_4 ; i.e. a molecule contains **7** atoms, and its molecular weight is **98** ($7 \times 7 \times 2$). Its electro-chemical equivalent is **49**.[3]

"The *metals* as a class are distinguished by certain physical properties. They are (1) opaque in bulk, (2) possess a characteristic lustre, and are (3) more or less malleable, (4) and ductile ; they are (5) good conductors of heat, (6) and electricity. (7) The formation of alloys should also be mentioned [which includes

[1] Roscoe & S., i. 260.   [2] *Enc. Brit.*, xxvi. 65.
[3] Tilden, *Chem. Disc. & Inv.*, 186.

their fusibility]. Each of the metals, however, does not exhibit all these properties in a high degree."[1]

There are some elements which, though they resemble metals in most characteristics, yet lack some one or more of the features which typical metals generally present, and are sometimes called *metalloids*. Fifteen elements are included in the metalloids, of which one (hydrogen) is a gas, and the other 14 are solids.[2]

Chemical changes are of the following 7 types: (1) Combination; (2) decomposition; (3) dissolution or reversible decomposition; (4) displacement of one element in a compound by the action of another element; (5) double decomposition or metathesis; (6) substitution, in which the displaced element combines with the displacing element; (7) internal rearrangement, in which one substance is quantitatively transformed into another without either the addition or subtraction of any material substance [e.g. yellow into red phosphorus; oxygen into ozone].[3]

If we examine the atomic weights of the elements we find that many are more or less exactly multiples of 4 and 7, and many of both, (H = 1):[4]

[1] Friend, *Inorg. Chem.*, i. 8.
[2] *Id.* i. 9; Tilden, *C.P.*, 182.
[3] *Id.* i. 159.
[4] These figures are based on the old standard (hydrogen = 1) and are therefore a little less than the present official weights, especially in the higher numbers. But "it ought to be understood (says Sir Wm. A. Tilden) that the atomic weights given in the list are not equally trustworthy. Some, for various reasons, will probably suffer some slight revision in future years" (*Chem. Disc. & Inv.*, 125).

Later research has established the fact that an element may be a mixture of "isotopes"—substances of the same chemical attributes but of varying atomic weight. Many elements, therefore, have two or more atomic weights. Lead should doubtless have a place in this table at $206\frac{1}{2}$ ($3\frac{1}{2} \times 59$), 208, or perhaps 204 on the hydrogen standard.

Multiples of 4.		*Multiples of both 4 and 7 (28).*		*Multiples of 7.*	
Helium . . .	4	Silicon . . .	28	Lithium . .	7
Carbon . . .	12				
Oxygen . . .	16	Iron	56	Nitrogen . .	14
Neon . . .	20				
Magnesium . .	24	Rubidium . .	84	Chlorine . .	35
Sulphur . . .	32				
Argon . . .	40	(Krypton . . 84)		Copper . . .	63
Calcium . . .	40				
Scandium . .	44	Cadmium . .	112	Gallium . 69 or 70	
Titanium . .	48				
Chromium . .	52	Cerium . 139 or 140		(Zirconium . . 90)	
Germanium .	72				
Bromine. . .	80				
Yttrium . . .	88	Praseodymium . 140		Palladium . .	105
Columbium 92 or 93					
Molybdenum 95 or 96		Thulium 167 or 168		(Tin . . .	118)
Ruthenium . .	100				
Caesium. . .	132	Gold . . .	196	Antimony . .	119
Barium . . .	136				
Neodymium .	144	Radium . . .	224	Tellurium . .	126
Gadolinium . .	156			Iodine . . .	126
Ytterbium . .	172	Actinium . .	224	Dysprosium. .	161
Tantalum . .	180			Tungsten . .	182
Iridium . . .	192			Osmium . .	189
Mercury. . .	200			Thallium . .	203
Niton . . .	220			Thorium . .	231
Uranium . .	236				

The middle column should of course be added to each of the others.

These are long lists, the middle column being especially remarkable for the very large number of elements whose atomic weights are multiples of **28**, i.e. of both 4 and **7**. It is further noteworthy that the lightest of all the elements, after hydrogen, are helium, whose atomic weight is 4, and lithium **7**. These two numbers, 4 and **7**, therefore, head the list in the Periodic table.

About **70** of the elements are solids.

It is unsafe however to lay any stress upon **84** as the total number of the elements, for on the one hand there may be others in existence at present unknown, and on the other the possibility is recognized that some of the substances now considered elements may " by the application of more powerful means than are at present known " turn out to be compounds. Indeed " the discovery of the radio-elements has made it difficult to define precisely what is to be understood by an element. . . . There is therefore no logical reason for denying the title òf element to each of the other radio-elements." [1]

Since the foregoing was prepared for the press, new discoveries have been made in Chemistry, and a new term introduced, " atomic numbers." It is now believed that there are 92 elements, or " species of elements," of which a few still remain to be discovered. But they do not all answer to the old definition of an element, for a few of them, such as Radium, are members of what has been called a " Suicide Club," undergoing spontaneous decomposition and changing into another " element." [2]

Some liquids, like mercury, oil, and water, are quite incapable of mixing together under any circumstances ; whilst others, such as water and solution of hydrochloric acid, mingle rapidly. If two such miscible liquids be placed together in the same vessel, however carefully, and left undisturbed, this process of spontaneous intermixture or " diffusion " will go on. The rapidity with which diffusion of this kind takes place, however, and the limit of its action, depend very much upon the nature of the liquids employed. Hydrochloric acid is one of the most diffusive substances known, and may therefore be taken as a standard : it diffuses $2\frac{1}{3}$ times ($= \frac{1}{3}$ of **7**) as rapidly as chloride of sodium (common salt), **7** times as rapidly as sugar or sulphate of magnesium, **49** times as rapidly as albumen, and **98** times as rapidly as caramel.[3]

---

[1] Friend, *Inorg. Chem.*, i. 279.
[2] *Enc. Brit.*[12], xxx. 622[b].
[3] Tilden, *C.P.*, pp. 341, 342. The above are all the illustrations Tilden gives.

It is, perhaps, a matter of historical interest merely that " the ancients were acquainted with only 7 metals, viz. gold, silver, copper, tin, iron, lead, and mercury," which were " originally supposed to be in some way connected with the 7 heavenly bodies then known to belong to our system." [1]

Our last illustration is from **Organic Chemistry—** the chemistry of the Carbon compounds. These form a " mighty host of compounds numbering thousands upon thousands," [2] a host " far exceeding all the compounds of the other elements taken together," and their importance may be judged accordingly. The simplest hydride that carbon forms, " the first parent of this mighty host," is methane or marsh gas, whose composition is CH_4, i.e. 1 atom of carbon combined with 4 of hydrogen. Now as the atomic weight of carbon is 12, and that of hydrogen 1, the molecular weight of this important compound—important not so much in itself as in being the starting point of so many other compounds—is 16 (4×4). A single atom of carbon combines with four of hydrogen, but if a second atom of carbon be added, two more atoms of hydrogen are sufficient, and so on, for every additional atom of carbon, two more of hydrogen, giving an additional molecular weight of ($12 + 2$) 14. Now a remarkable feature of the carbon compounds is the very large number of *homologous series*, as they are termed, i.e. series of compounds each containing many members, the molecular weight of each member differing by 14 (CH_2) from that of the member next to it. These homologous series include such important substances as the Paraffins, the Olefines, the Acetylenes, the Benzenes, the Alcohols, the Ethers, the Glycerines, the Acetic, Lactic and Oxalic Acid series, the Aldehydes, the Anilines, and a large number of others, all characterized by the same feature,

[1] Roscoe.
[2] *Enc. Brit.*, xxvii. 847.

that each member of a series differs from the next one by a molecular weight of 14 (CH_2). So that again we have the multiples of 4 and 7, the starting point of the whole group being 16 (4 × 4)—and of the oxygen compounds (which form more than half of the whole) 32 (CH_4O)—while the constant difference between the members of each series is 14 (7 × 2). "It is more than remarkable that it should have been possible to erect so vast and complex a system upon so simple a foundation."[1]

To turn now to the world around us. Nature is divided into **Three Kingdoms**[2]**—Animal, Vegetable, and Mineral,** a number in which some have seen reflected the Tripersonality of God. Each of these Three Kingdoms has been further divided and subdivided; but, unfortunately, there is no system of classification which can be considered as final, for with the advance of knowledge, the opinions of naturalists change, and new or modified systems spring up. But however much they may differ as to the true sys ems of classification in the Animal and Vegetable worlds —the two kingdoms in which *Life* exists,—they mostly concur in this, that the classification must consist of 7 degrees. "The animal kingdom," says Prof. Alex. Macalister, "is a vast assemblage of individuals, and we require to arrange these in larger categories for purposes of study. Those individuals which are so far identical in structure as to lead us to believe that they are descended from common parents, we speak of as belonging to the one species. (1) *Species* is thus our unit in systematic zoology. . . . A group of allied species embodying the same structural ideas is called (2) a *genus*. An assemblage of allied genera is (3) a *family*; a group of related families make up (4) an *order*; while related orders make up (5) a *class*, and

---

[1] *Enc. Brit.*[12], xxx. 625[b].
[2] The term Kingdom is now not used by some naturalists.

the several classes included in the animal kingdom are united in certain primary categories called (6) *sub-kingdoms.*" [1] The 7th and highest term, of course, is *kingdom.* And in the Vegetable world precisely the same terms are used. Thus the dog is called by zoologists *Canis familiaris*, the latter being (1) the specific name, the former (2) the generic. It belongs to (3) the family Canidæ, (4) order Carnivora, (5) class Mammalia, (6) sub-kingdom Vertebrata, and (7) the Animal Kingdom. So the exact place in creation of the Damask Rose is thus defined by botanists : (1) kingdom Vegetabilia, (2) sub-kingdom 'Phanerogamia, (3) class Angiospermæ, (4) order Rosifloræ, (5) family Rosaceæ, (6) genus Rosa, (7) species Damascena.

Why, then, may we not go a step further, and ask whether the numbers 7 and 4 will not assist us to arrive at systems of classification in the Animal and Vegetable worlds respectively, which may make some claim to be considered the true ones ? " No department of knowledge," says Professor Drummond, " ever contributes to another without receiving its own again with usury." [2] If, therefore, the Bible is indebted to Science, as—notwithstanding the fact that some of the fiercest assaults upon Scripture have been made in the name of Science —undoubtedly it is indebted, both illustratively and apologetically, then the time will come—nay, may we not say has come ?—for the Bible to pay back the debt.

Let us take first the **Animal world,** starting with Bohn's English edition of Cuvier's great work, *The Animal Kingdom.*[3]

This edition contains, according to the preface, **7** departments : (1) Mammalia, (2) Birds. (3) Reptiles, (4) Fishes, (5) Radiata, (6) Molluscous Animals, (7)

[1] *Zoology of the Invertebrate Animals*, p. 11. So Lankester, *Enc. Brit.*, xxviii. 1032 substituting Phylum for Sub-Kingdom.

[2] *Natural Law in the Spiritual World*, p. 31.

[3] *The Animal Kingdom*, translated and adapted to the present state of science ; new edition. London, 1863. In Huxley's opinion " Cuvier was beyond all comparison the greatest anatomist who had ever lived."

Articulated Animals. Cuvier divided the Animal Kingdom into *four* great divisions, or sub-kingdoms :—

(1) Vertebrate Animals (*Vertebrata*).
(2) Molluscous Animals (*Mollusca*).
(3) Articulate Animals (*Articulata*).
(4) Radiate Animals (*Radiata*).

Of these, the sub-kingdom *Vertebrata* is of over-whelming importance, as compared even with all the others put together, and it strikes the non-scientific mind at first as somewhat singular that quadrupeds, birds, reptiles, and fishes are all included in one great sub-kingdom, while such insignificant creatures as shell-fish, worms, insects, star-fishes, zoophytes, and the like, are thought of sufficient importance, or are marked by such different characteristics, as to claim division into *three* sub-kingdoms. Thus the elephant and the humming-bird, the serpent and the herring, all belong to the one sub-kingdom *Vertebrata ;* while the oyster, the star-fish, and the butterfly are repre-sentatives of three different sub-kingdoms. According to Cuvier's classification, therefore, the Animal King-dom may be divided into *four* sub-kingdoms or **7** groups, a striking illustration of the association of four and seven :—

I. INVERTEBRATE ANIMALS—
    Sub-kingdom 1. Mollusca.
              2. Articulata.
              3. Radiata.
II. VERTEBRATE ANIMALS (Sub-kingdom 4)—
    Class 1. Mammalia.
          2. Birds.
          3. Reptiles.
          4. Fishes.

" The names Vertebrate and Invertebrate, and the dichotomy they imply, have persisted from their con-venience, although zoological science has come to recognize that the groups are not morphologically equivalent, and that the division is not logical."[1]

Let us now turn to the classification given in Prof. A. Macalister's books.[2] We find there the Invertebrate Animals divided into 7 sub-kingdoms, but still the Vertebrates form only one. In place of four classes, however, the sub-kingdom *Vertebrata* is made to consist of six. But this arrangement makes the mistake, common to all modern systems, of including the whale, seal, and manatee along with land mammals. Now, the first chapter of Genesis states that, on the fifth day of the creative week, " God created great sea-monsters, [R.V.], and every living creature that moveth, which the waters brought forth abundantly, after their kind," and that land animals (except birds) were not made until the sixth day. To class, therefore, the whale, seal, manatee, and their congeners with land animals does violence to the order of creation, as revealed to us in Scripture. So that, instead of all the Mammalia being placed in one great class, they should be divided into two classes, (1) Land Mammalia ; (2) Aquatic Mammalia. This will increase the number of classes of vertebrate animals to 7.[3]

With this single modification, the subdivisions of the Animal Kingdom, according to the classification given by Macalister, stand thus :—

I. INVERTEBRATE ANIMALS :—

Sub-kingdom 1. Protozoa (Animalcules, etc.).
2. Polystomata (Sponges).
3. Cœlenterata (Jelly-fishes, etc.).
4. Echinodermata (Star-fishes, etc.)
5. Vermes (Worms).
6. Mollusca (Oysters, etc.).
7. Arthropoda (Crabs, Insects, etc.).

[1] P. Chalmers Mitchell : *Enc. Brit.*, xxvii. 1047ᵈ.
[2] *Zoology of the Vert.*, and *of the Invert. Anims.*, 4th ed., 1885.
[3] Of course, a similar alteration would need to be made in Cuvier's arrangement, but as in that arrangement a single class includes both reptiles and amphibia, so the aquatic mammalia may be placed in the same class with fishes proper, under a name which would include both. This would not disturb the total number of classes.

II. VERTEBRATE ANIMALS (Sub-kingdom 8) :—

    Class 1. Acrania, *or* Leptocardia.
        2. Land Mammalia.
        3. Aquatic Mammalia.
        4. Fishes.
        5. Amphibia.
        6. Reptiles.
        7. Birds.

The class *Mammalia* is divided by Cuvier into nine orders. By taking away the Aquatic Mammalia (as above) these are reduced to eight, and if we again follow Scripture rather than science, a further reduction must be made. Cuvier's first order, *Bimana*, contains but one species, Man. Now, the Bible reveals to us that though man was formed on the same day as the land animals, it was not at the same time, but by a separate and distinct creation. To man was given lordship over all the lower animals, and he must, therefore, not be classed *with* them.[1] Excluding, therefore, Cuvier's first and last orders—*Bimana* and *Cetacea*— (and, of course, the aquatic *Carnivora*), we have left **7** orders of Land Mammals :—

		Example.
1. *Quadrumana*	Monkey.
2. *Carnaria*	Lion.
3. *Marsupiata*	Kangaroo.
4. *Rodentia*	Rabbit.
5. *Edentata*	Anteater.
6. *Pachydermata* . . .	Horse.
7. *Ruminantia*	Ox.

Cuvier divided *Birds* into six orders, but later naturalists found fault with him for including *Grallatores* and *Cursores* in the same order, and, by separating them, increased the number to **7**. The following are the names, as given by Professor Huxley in his *Manual*

[1] So Abp. Thomson in *Modern Scepticism*. Prof. J. Arthur Thomson divides the observed world into the domain of the inorganic, the realm of organisms, and the Kingdom of Man. (*System of Animate Nature*, 1920.)

of the Anatomy of Vertebrated Animals, under the title
of " the old orders of Birds " :—

Example.

1. *Accipitres*, or *Raptores*   . Eagle.
2. *Scansores*   .   .   .   . Parrot.
3. *Passeres*, or *Insessores*   . Sparrow.
4. *Gallinæ* (with *Columbæ*)   . Common Hen.
5. *Cursores*   .   .   .   . Ostrich.
6. *Grallæ*   .   .   .   . Crane.
7. *Palimpedes*   .   .   . Duck.

The two remaining classes in Cuvier's system must
be taken together.   He divides *Reptiles* into four orders
and *Fishes* into eight, giving a total of twelve.   But to
these must be added the *Aquatic Mammalia*, which,
according to Cuvier's classification, would constitute
two orders : 1. *Cetacea* (whale, manatee) ; 2. *Pinni-
grada*, or *Aquatic Carnivora* [1] (seal, walrus).   This gives
a total of **14** orders in the two classes.

To recapitulate : with very slight, and as we have
seen necessary modifications, Cuvier's classification of
the Vertebrate Animals stands thus :—

Class I. Land Mammals   .   .   .   **7** Orders.
    II. Birds **7**
   III. Reptiles   .   .   .   ⎫
   IV. Fishes and Aquatic Mam-⎬ **14**
      malia   .   .   .   ⎭

Total   .   **28** (4 × 7)

Cuvier's system, however, is now considered to be
antiquated, the increase of knowledge and the advance
of science having caused several schemes differing
widely from it and from one another, to be propounded.
It will be necessary, therefore, to inquire whether the
number **7** can be connected with any of the later
systems.

To take again the sub-kingdom *Vertebrata*, which we
have seen may be divided into **7** classes.   The class

[1] Cuvier's name for this group is *Amphibia*.

Mammalia, according to the system set forth in Prof. Macalister's *Manual*, contains sixteen orders. From these must be deducted the Aquatic Mammalia, which are here divided into three orders : 1. *Sirenia* (manatee) ; 2. *Cetacea* (whale) ; 3. *Pinnipedia* (seal). *Man*, of course, must also be taken away, but this makes no difference in the number of orders, for science has advanced since Cuvier's day, or rather, we should say, retrograded—doubly retrograded, in fact,—for whereas Cuvier placed Man in a separate order, distinct (at least to this extent) from all other " animals," modern science has gone back to the system of his great predecessor, Linnæus, who classed Man and monkeys together, under the name *Primates*. But surely science can learn from other things besides skeletons ? Because it cannot explain what LIFE is, or whence it comes, will it refuse to seek knowledge from the study of the living creature ? will it learn nothing except from dry bones ? However like the skeleton of a man may be to that of an ape, the spirit which is in man has no affinity with that which animates even the highest representative of the monkey tribe. It needs no revelation from God to teach this.

Everything in nature points upwards—the plant to the "zoophyte," the zoophyte to the more highly organized invertebrate, the invertebrate to the vertebrate, the lower forms of vertebrates to the higher, the most highly organized vertebrate to Man, and, finally, Man to GOD, in whose image he was created.[1] It is in this truth—that every living thing is a type of something higher, that God has made all things in a regular progression from the lowest form of vegetable life to Man, the image of Himself, Who is *the* LIFE, and from Whom all life flows,—and not in the doctrine of Evolution, as taught by Haeckel and his followers,

---

[1] " No organ appears for the first time in animals in a state of complexity, but, on the contrary, there is always in lower forms a *prophetic foreshadowing of it* in the modification of some part already existing " (Macalister, *Invertebrata*, p. 15).

that we must seek the explanation of the fact that man in some things resembles an ape.

We have, then, in Macalister's classification, thirteen orders of Land Mammals, Man being excluded. If we compare these with the 7 orders of Cuvier,[1] we find that each one of Cuvier's orders forms one or more complete orders in the later scheme, with (besides Man) the one exception that *Ruminantia* is made to form part of the order *Ungulata*. In place, therefore, of the Ruminants—that is, animals which chew the cud—forming a separate order, later zoologists reduced them even below the rank of a sub-order, classing them along with the pig and the hippopotamus.

It is not necessary to dwell upon the mention of animals which chew the cud in Scripture. The fact that so great a naturalist as Cuvier placed them in a separate order is sufficient justification for suggesting that they be again restored to that position.[2] This would give a total of 14 orders of Land Mammals.

[1] The following is a rough comparison of the orders of *Mammalia*, according to the two systems, the Aquatic orders being printed in *italics :*

CUVIER.			MACALISTER.	
No. Order.	Family or Tribe.		No. Order.	Example.
1. BIMANA			16. Primates	MAN. / Monkey.
2. Quadrumana	(1) Apes and Monkeys			
	(2) Lemurs		13. Prosimii	Lemur.
3. Carnaria	(1) Cheiroptera		15. Cheiroptera	Bat.
	(2) Insectivora		14. Insectivora	Hedgehog.
	(3) Carni-vora.	(1) Plantigrada / (2) Digitigrada	9. Carnivora	Dog.
		(3) *Amphibia*	8. *Pinnipedia*	*Seal.*
4. Marsupiata			2. Marsupialia	Kangaroo.
5. Rodentia			11. Rodentia	Rabbit.
6. Edentata	(1) Tardigrada		4. Bradypoda	Sloth.
	(2) Ordinary Edentata		3. Edentata	Anteater.
	(3) Monotremata		1. Monotremata	Platypus.
7. Pachydermata	(1) Proboscidea		12. Proboscidea	Elephant.
	(2) Ordinary Pachydermata		10. Hyracoidea	Coney.
				Pig, Tapir.
	(3) Solidungula		6. Ungulata	Horse.
8. Ruminantia				Ox.
9. *Cetacea*	(1) *Herbivora*		5. *Sirenia*	*Manatee.*
	(2) *Ordinary Cetacea*		7. *Cetacea*	*Whale.*

[2] Some may prefer the authority of Sir Richard Owen to that of Cuvier. Owen placed the *Ruminants* and the *Bunodonts* (Pig, Hippopotamus) in one order, under the title *Artiodactyla*, or even-

To turn now to the present day.

The names given in Macalister's list are still retained, but " there are," says Sir Ray Lankester, " and probably always will be, differences of opinion as to the exact way in which the various kinds of animals may be divided into groups and those groups arranged in such an order as will best exhibit their probable genetic relationships." [1] Some of the old Orders are now called Sub-orders, and to get a fair grasp of the present position we must take the latter into account also.

The following is the classification adopted by Lankester and other experts in the *Encyclopedia Britannica*, 11th ed., 1910–11 (variations therefrom being shown in *italics*) omitting as before Aquatic Mammalia and Extinct Animals. It agrees on the whole with that given in the *Cambridge Natural History* (1902).

LAND MAMMALIA

Order.	Sub-Order.	Example.
	I. Sub-Class PROTOTHERIA.	
1. Monotremata		Platypus.
	II. Sub-Class METATHERIA.	
2. Marsupialia	Polyprotodonta	Opossum.
	Diprotodonta	Kangaroo.
	Paucituberculata *or Epanorthidæ*	Cænolestes.
	III. *Sub-Class* PARATHERIA.	
3. Edentata	Xenarthra	Anteater, Sloth, Armadillo.
	Pholidota *or Manidæ*	Pangolin.
	Tubulidentata	Aard-vark.
	IV. Sub-Class EUTHERIA.	
4. Ungulata	Proboscidea	Elephant.
	Hyracoidea	Hyrax *or* Coney.
	Perissodactyla	Horse, Tapir.
	Artiodactyla : *Bunodontia*	Pig, Hippopotamus.
	Ruminantia or *Selenodontia*	} Ox, Camel

toed ; and the remaining *Ungulata* (Horse, Rhinoceros, Tapir) in another, *Perissodactyla*, or odd-toed. This will give the same total number of orders, 14. Huxley appeared inclined to favour this view, and would probably have adopted it had he been able to keep fossil forms out of sight. These, however, should not be allowed to interfere with the classification of existing animals. (See *Manual Anat. Vert. Animals*, pp. 341, 342.)

[1] *Enc. Brit.*, xxviii. 1032ᵈ.

5. Carnivora	Fissipedia	Dog
6. Rodentia	Simplicidentata	Rat.
	Duplicidentata	Hare.
7. Insectivora		Hedgehog.
8. Dermoptera		Flying Lemur.
9. Chiroptera	Megachiroptera	Flying Fox.
	Microchiroptera	Bat.
10. Primates	Prosimiæ	Lemur.
	Anthropoidea	Ape, Monkey.

By most authorities the Sub-class Paratheria is not recognized, largely owing to the influence of fossil forms, but there are good grounds for placing Edentata in a Sub-class by itself, instead of under Eutheria.

Ten Orders are shown above, but the *Cambridge Nat. Hist.* says of the four divisions of Ungulata that " each division has quite the value of an Order." [1] Then if we restore the Lemurs to the rank of an Order, which they formerly occupied, we have **14** Orders of Land Mammals.

There are **21** Sub-Orders (including of course the three Orders which are not divided) if we count Ruminantia. Or some might think it preferable to divide Xenarthra into two Sub-Orders : the Sloths formerly ranked as a full Order, but again fossil forms have intervened. Either they or the Armadillos might rank as a Sub-order.

We have then *four* Sub-classes, **14** Orders and **21** Sub-orders of Land Mammals, without any departure from the principles which govern these titles.

The number of systems of classification of **Birds** is almost endless. The old division, as stated above, was into **7** Orders.

Huxley proposed an entirely different system, and W. K. Parker in the 9th ed. of the *Enc. Brit.*, art. "Birds," adopted it with a few modifications which gave **7** large groups and **28** Orders (omitting an extinct Order) :—

Ratitæ	2 groups	5 Orders.
Carinatæ	5 ,,	23 ,,
	7	28

---

[1] *Mammalia*, 195.

In 1888 another notable classification was published by Fürbringer, who divided Birds into **7** large Orders and **22** Sub-orders (again excluding fossils).[1] But if, following Gadow,[2] we include his Halcyoniformes with the Coraciiformes, we have **21** Sub-orders.

It is difficult to describe the Classification of **Fishes** without giving a list of the Orders and Sub-orders. The following is practically that given by Boulenger,[3] variations therefrom being shown in *italics*, and the Lancelet and Aquatic Mammalia being added :—

FISHES AND AQUATIC MAMMALIA

Main Divisions.	Order.	Sub-order.	Example.
I. 1. Acrania			Lancelet.
II. 2. Cyclostoma	Myxinoides		Hag-fish.
	Petromyzontes		Lamprey.
III. Pisces (True Fishes)			
(Sub-class 3 Elasmobranchii	Plagiostomi	Selachii	Shark.
		Batoidei	Ray.
	Holocephali		Chimæra.
4. Teleostomi	Crossopterygii	Cladistia	Polypterus.
	Chondrostei [4]		Sturgeon.
	Holostei [4]		Bowfin.
	Teleostei	Maalacopterygii	Herring.
		Ostariophysi	Carp.
		Symbranchii	Cuchia.
		Apodes	Eel.
		Haplomi	Pike
		Heteromi	Fierasfer.
		Selenichthyes	Opah.
		Thoracostei	Sea-horse.
		Percesoces	Grey Mullet.
		Anacanthini	Cod.
		Acanthopterygii	Perch.
		Opisthomi	Mastacembelus.
		Pediculati	Angler.
		Plectognathi	Globe-fish.
(Sub-class) 5 *Dipneusti*			Lepidosiren.
or *Dipnoi* [4]			
IV. Aquatic Mammalia			
6. Herbivorous	Sirenia		Manatee.
7. Carnivorous	Cetacea	Mystacoceti	Whale.
		Odontoceti	Porpoise.
	Pinnipedia		Seal.

[1] *Enc. Brit.*, art. " Ornithology," xx. 325.
[2] *Id.*, art. " Bird," iii. 977.
[3] *Id.*, xiv. 248 and refs.
[4] So *Cambridge Nat. Hist.*

There are thus *four* Main Divisions, **7** Subdivisions, **13** Orders and **28** Sub-orders. The **13** should doubtless be **14.** To the unscientific mind it seems strange that fishes so unlike in many respects as the shark and the ray should be in the same Order. If the two Sub-orders were raised to the rank of Order we should have the numbers 4, **7, 14, 28,** which seem eminently suitable.

There are **14** Sub-orders in *Teleostei.*

With regard to the Geographical Distribution of modern Fishes, they may be roughly divided into the following categories :—

I. Marine fishes: 1. shore fishes.
                 2. pelagic fishes.
                 3. deep-sea fishes.
II. 4. Brackish-water fishes.
III. 5. Fresh-water fishes.
IV. Migratory fishes : 6. anadromous (ascending fresh waters to spawn).
                     7. catadromous (descending to the sea to spawn).[1]

Again 4 large divisions, **7** smaller ones.

The two remaining classes of *Vertebrata* (which were included in one by Cuvier) present no difficulty. The later classifications are as follows :—

REPTILIA (Four Orders).

Order (old).	Example.	Order (new)	Example.
1. Lacertilia	Lizard	Squamata	Lizard, Snake.
2. Ophidia	Snake	Rhyncocephalia	Sphenodon
3. Chelonia			Tortoise.
4. Crocodilia			Crocodile.

AMPHIBIA or BATRACHIA (Three Orders).

Order 1. Gymnophiona *or* Apoda   Cæcilia.
       2. Urodela   Newt.
       3. Anura   Frog.

There are, therefore, **7** orders in the two classes combined.

[1] *Enc. Brit.,* xiv. 268.

Before leaving the Animal Kingdom [1] one more analogy between Nature and Scripture may be pointed out. We have seen that Animals are divided into 8 sub-kingdoms. It is also shown (Part II., Ch. I., Class VII.) that in Scripture the number 8 often includes two different series of *sevens*, which, however, cannot exist together. Now, of the 8 sub-kingdoms into which the Animal Kingdom is divided, if we take away the last (*Vertebrata*), the other **7** are collectively called *Invertebrata ;* if we take away the first (*Protozoa*), the other **7** are collectively called *Metazoa*.[2] Further, as we have seen that the *Vertebrata*, the most highly organized animals, may be divided into **7** classes, so Professor Huxley shows that the *Protozoa*, the simplest animals, also consist of **7** " series." [3]

Vegetable Kingdom. " The man above all others," said M. Figuier in 1867 " to whom modern science is most indebted for perfecting the botanical arrangement of plants is the late Dr. Lindley." [4]

Dr. Lindley's classification was as follows :—

Asexual or Flowerless Plants.
Class I. Thallogens.   II. Acrogens.

Sexual or Flowering Plants.
Class III. Rhizogens.   IV. Endogens.
      V. Dictyogens.   VI. Gymnogens.
      VII. Exogens.

Other classifications have since been put forward, and the following *four* groups or Sub-kingdoms are now generally recognized :— [5]

---

[1] In the edition of Cuvier's *Animal Kingdom* already referred to in this chapter, there is, on p. 640, a foot-note by the English editor, in which mention is made of " the *septenary* system developed in Mr. Newman's *Introduction to the History of Insects and System of Nature*," a work which I have not seen.

[2] Macalister, *Invertebrata*, p. 14 ; Huxley, *Man. Anat. Invert. Anims.*, p. 47.

[3] *Invert. Anims.*, p. 677. A later classification makes 4 phyla, **14** classes.

[4] *The Vegetable World :* Eng. trans.   [5] *Enc. Brit.*, xxi. 728.

I	Thallophyta	{	1. Algæ.
		{	2. Fungi.
II	Bryophyta		3. Mosses.
III	Pteridophyta		4. Ferns.
IV	Spermatophyta	{	5. Gymnosperms.
	or	{	6. Monocotyledons.
	Phanerogamia	{	7. Dicotyledons.

The differences between botanists as to classification and as to the use of the terms Class, Order, etc., make it difficult to carry the subject further. But on another plan " the vegetable kingdom may be divided into the **7** following classes : 1. Woody plants ; 2. Succulent plants, such as the cacti ; 3. Climbing plants (lianes) ; 4. Parasites or epiphytes, like the mistletoe ; 5. Herbaceous plants ; 6. Grasses ; 7. Cellular plants." [1]

Botany may be divided into **7** departments : (1) Morphology, (2) Anatomy, (3) Cytology, (4) Physiology, (5) Classification, (6) Distribution, (7) Ecology. [2]

There are **7** stages in the life of a fruit-bearing plant : (1) root, (2) stem, (3) leaves, (4) peduncle or flower-stalk, (5) flower, (6) fruit, (7) seed.

A complete flower has *four* distinct whorls of leaves, which may be divided into **7** parts :—

1.	The Calyx		of sepals 1.
2.	Corolla		of petals 2.
3.	Andrœcium	{	anthers 3.
	or stamens	{	pollen 4.
4.	Gynœcium	{	ovary 5.
	or pistil	{	style 6.
		{	stigma 7.

There are *four* different kinds of leaves : radical, cauline, floral, and seed leaves. [3]

The most useful plants to man are the *Cereals*, which are **7** in number, and are found in all parts of the world. They are (1) wheat, (2) oats, (3) barley, (4) maize, (5) rice, (6) rye, (7) millet.

[1] Thomé : *Structural and Physiological Botany*, Eng. tr., 434.

[2] *Enc. Brit.*, iv. 302. We omit Palæobotany as being outside our limits. [3] *Enc. Brit.*, xvi. 327ª.

"The righteous. shall flourish like the *palm tree.*" It is impossible to over-estimate the utility of palms, and they have been termed the princes of the vegetable kingdom. The order *Palmaceæ* contains 132 genera (4 × 33) ranged under **7** tribes.[1] The words translated palm tree occur in the O.T. 33 times (see above) and **35** in the whole Bible, 4 words in all.

Mineral Kingdom. The third great division of Nature does not lend itself to classification so readily as the other two ; still a little study will yield fruitful results. The subject may be divided into the follow-ing *four* heads : Geology, Mineralogy, Crystallography and Chemistry. In the first two of these the lines of demarcation are not so clearly marked as in the two last, in which, especially in Chemistry, which we have already dealt with, numbers play a very important part.

Geology. That the earth was in existence, and that life existed upon it, for long ages before the time assigned to the creation of Adam, does not admit of question. From the study of fossil remains found under the present surface of our planet, geologists formerly divided the past history of the earth into **7** epochs or ages.

"Each epoch," says Mr. Ralph Tate, "has had its peculiar species and forms of life, the groups of forms which at first existed being replaced by others, and these by fresh forms, till those which now live made their appearance. The progress of life is, therefore, taken as the basis of the subdivision of the stratified rocks into groups representing geological epochs or ages, which are as follows :—

"1. Azoic epoch, containing no traces of animal life.
2. Silurian epoch, or age of Crustaceans.
3. Devonian epoch, or age of Fishes.
4. Carboniferous epoch, or age of Acrogens—characterized by coal plants, which are chiefly Acrogens.

---

[1] *Enc. Brit.,* art. " Palm."

5. Reptilian age.
6. Mammalian age.
7. The Age of Man." [1]

Later research, however, has made the stratified rocks to yield more minute divisions of past time than these. "I must request the student," says the eminent geologist, Mr. J. Beete Jukes, "now to fix his attention chiefly upon *time*, and to suppose that all geological time is divided into three great portions or successions of periods, which we may call Primary, Secondary, and Tertiary." These three include **14** shorter periods, systems, or eras, as they are called indifferently. "Geological time, then," proceeds Mr. Jukes, "may be thus arranged :—

"III. TERTIARY OR CAINOZOIC PERIODS.

1. Human, Historical or Recent era.
2. Pleistocene era. [Post Pliocene, *Tate.*]
3. Pliocene era.
4. Miocene era.
5. Eocene era.

II. SECONDARY OR MESOZOIC PERIODS.

6. Cretaceous era.
7. Jurassic era.
8. Triassic era.

I. PRIMARY OR PALÆOZOIC PERIODS.

9. Permian era.
10. Carboniferous era.
11. Devonian and Old Red Sandstone era.
12. Silurian era.
13. Cambrian era.
14. Laurentian or Pre-Cambrian era." [2]

---

[1] *Historical Geology* (1875), p. 1.
[2] J. B. Jukes's *Student's Manual of Geology*, third ed., edited by A. Geikie, pp. 518, 519 ; Tate's *Historical Geology*, pp. 3, 4. Later, Sir A. Geikie (*Enc. Brit.*, xi. 670) divided the Miocene into two— Miocene and Oligocene ; the Cretaceous into two—Upper and Lower ; and exalted the Pre-Cambrian into a separate division with six subdivisions ; thus making 21 subdivisions in all, still an heptadic number.

More recently, Mr. A. J. Jukes-Brown, stating that since the above terms were proposed a series of stratified rocks has been discovered below those which were called 'Primary, divides geological time into *four* " Eras," but still retains the same number of **14** systems.

ERAS.	SYSTEMS.
I. Tertiary or Cænozoic	{ 1. Neogene. { 2. Palæogene.
II. Secondary or Mesozoic	{ 3. Cretaceous. { 4. Jurassic. { 5. Triassic.
III. Primary or Palæozoic	{ 6. Permian. { 7. Carboniferous. { 8. Devonian. { 9. Silurian. { 10. Ordovician. { 11. Cambrian.
IV. Archæan or Eozoic	{ 12. Eparchæan. { 13. Mesarchæan. { 14. Protarchæan.[1]

It is somewhat remarkable that in the system proposed by De la Beche, which, though now obsolete, was superior to any that had preceded it, the same number **14** appears as the total of the groups of rocks, including, however, both stratified and unstratified. The following are the names of his groups, commencing at the earth's surface :—

Stratified Rocks : (1) Alluvial, (2) Diluvial, (3) Supercretaceous, (4) Cretaceous, (5) Oolitic, (6) Red Sandstone, (7) Carboniferous, (8) Greywacke, (9) Lowest Fossiliferous, (10) Non-fossiliferous stratified.

Unstratified Rocks : (1) Volcanic, (2) Trappean, (3) Serpentine, (4) Granitic.

Crystallography. " Crystallization may be defined as the spontaneous assumption of well-defined geometrical forms by bodies in passing from the fluid or aëriform state to the solid condition." Crystals have been classified according to their shape, and divided

[1] *Stratigraphical Geology*, 2nd ed. (1912), p. 5.

into 7 systems, of which the following are the names and characteristics :—

Triaxial Forms.

I. Orthic Systems.
1. Monometric, Cubic or Regular. The axes equal.
2. Dimetric or Tetragonal. Two equal, and the third greater or less.
3. Trimetric or Rhombic. The three axes unequal.

II. Clinic Systems.
4. Monoclinic. One of the axes inclined to a second, but at right angles to the third.
5. Diclinic. One axis at right angles to a second, but all the other angles made by three axes with each other oblique.
6. Triclinic or Anorthic. All the angles made by the intersection of the crystallographic axes oblique.

Tetraxial Forms.

7. Hexagonal. Three axes in the same plane, and the fourth perpendicular to them.[1]

" It was proved by J. F. C. Hessel in 1830 that 32 types of symmetry (4 × 4 × 2) are possible in crystals. Hessel's work remained overlooked for 60 years, but the same important result was independently arrived at by the same method by A. Gadolin in 1867. At the present day, crystals are considered as belonging to one or other of 32 classes, corresponding with these 32 types of symmetry." [2]

The following is the arrangement as now given by Roscoe and Schorlemmer in their *Treatise on Chemistry*.[3] It agrees exactly with the above, but different names are given to some of the systems :—

System.					No. of Axes.	No. of Symmetry Classes.
1. Triclinic	.	.	.	.	3	2
2. Monoclinic	.	.	.	.	3	3
3. Rhombic [Trimetric]	.	.	.	3	3
4. Tetragonal [Dimetric]	.	.	.	3	7
5. Trigonal [Diclinic]	.	.	.	3	7
6. Hexagonal	.	.	.	.	4	5
7. Cubic or Regular [Monometric]	.	3	5
						32

---

[1] J. B. Jukes's *Manual of Geology*, third ed., pp. 29, 30.
[2] *Enc. Brit.*, vii. 571.
[3] 5th ed., ii. 186. So Friend, *Inorg. Chem.*; Lewis, *Crystallography.*

In many of the classes there are **7** kinds of simple forms.

The various " space-lattices " in crystals were studied thoroughly in 1850 by Bravais, who showed that **14** types are distinguishable, falling under the 7 crystalline systems.[1]

Out of the 40 known crystalline forms of elements, **20** (4 × 5) crystallize in the cubic, and **14** (7 × 2) in the hexagonal systems.[2]

There are *four* Types of Forms of Crystals : Pinacoids, prisms, domes, pyramids.

Mineralogy. The following scheme of classification of *Mineral Deposits* shows *four* classes and **14** types :—

    I. Of IGNEOUS ORIGIN.
        1. Eruptive masses of non-metalliferous rock.
        2. Basic segregations from fused and cooling magmas.
        3. Deposits produced in contact metamorphism.
        4. Pegmatites.
    II. PRECIPITATED FROM SOLUTION.
        5. Surface deposits.
        6. Impregnations in naturally open-textured rocks.
        7. Impregnations and replacements of naturally soluble rocks.
        8. Deposits along anticlinal summits and in synclinal troughs.
        9. Deposits in shear zones.
        10. Deposits in faults.
        11. Deposits in volcanic necks.
    III. DEPOSITED FROM SUSPENSION.
        12. Placers.
        13. Residual deposits.
    IV.   14. CARBONACEOUS DEPOSITS FROM VEGETATION.[3]

" In Rocks the least number of components that can be regarded as essential is 7 (SiO_2, Al_2O_3, Fe_2O_3, CaO, MgO, K_2O and Na_2O)." [4]

[1] Roscoe & Schorlemmer, ii. 206. *Enc. Brit.*, vii. 584. Miers, *Mineralogy*, 284.
[2] *Id.*, ii. 222.
[3] *Enc. Brit.*, xviii. 506[*].   [4] *Id.*, xxxii. 86[*].

The following classification of minerals is put forth on authority. "Except in a few details it is the classification of Dana's *System of Mineralogy* (1892)."[1] I Native Elements, II Sulphides, Arsenides, Tellurides, etc., III Sulpho-salts, IV Haloids, V Oxides, VI Oxygen salts, VII Hydrocarbon compounds.

Minerals which are soluble in water have characteristic *Tastes*, which have been classified thus :—

1. Saline,	the taste of	common salt.
2. Alkaline,	„	potash and soda.
3. Cooling,	„	nitre, chlorate of potash, etc.
4. Astringent	„	green vitriol.
5. Sweetish Astringent	„	alum.
6. Bitter	„	Epsom salts.
7. Sour	„	sulphuric acid.[2]

The *Lustre* of minerals is of **7** kinds, in *four* degrees of intensity :—

Kinds :	1. Metallic,	the lustre of metals.	
	2. Adamantine,	„	the diamond.
	3. Vitreous,	„	broken glass.
	4. Resinous,	„	the yellow resins.
	5. Greasy (Dana) or Waxy (Miers).		
	6. Pearly, like pearl.		
	7. Silky, like silk.		

The degrees of Intensity are (1) Splendent, (2) shining, (3) glistening, (4) glimmering. When there is a total absence of lustre a mineral is characterised as dull.[3]

Precious Stones. "Strictly speaking, the only *precious* stones are (1) the diamond, (2) ruby, (3) sapphire, and (4) emerald, though the term is often extended to others."[4]

The Colours of Precious Stones are said to be : (1) Colourless, (2) Blue, (3) Red, (4) Pink, (5) Purple, (6) Yellow, (7) Green.[5]

[1] *Enc. Brit.*, xviii. 515, 516.
[2] Rutley and Read, *Elements of Mineralogy* (1916), p. 35.
[3] Dana, *Mineralogy* (1892), p. xxxiv. Miers, *Mineralogy*, 258.
[4] G. F. Kunz, quoted in *Enc. Brit.*, xxii. 275[b].
[5] *Harmsworth's Self-Educator*, col. 5853.

From this brief examination of the kingdoms of Nature we see the important position occupied by the number **Four.**   Thus :—

1. The Animal Kingdom contains *four* great divisions : Vertebrata, Mollusca, Articulata, Radiata.[1]

2. The Vegetable Kingdom is also divided into *four* sub-kingdoms : Thallophyta, Bryophyta, Pteridophyta, Phanerogamia.

3. The Mineral Kingdom shows *four* classes of Mineral Deposits : Of Igneous origin, Precipitated from solution, Deposited from suspension, Carbonaceous deposits.

4. There are *four* " Spheres " in and around the Earth : the Atmosphere, Hydrosphere (the Ocean), Lithosphere (the Earth's crust), Centrosphere (the interior mass).

5. There are *four* states of Matter : Solid, Liquid, Gaseous and " Radiant Matter."[2]

6. May we not say then that there are four Kingdoms of Nature, Animal, Vegetable, Mineral, and the Kingdom of Man ?

7. And if the Kingdom of Man ought to be capable, like the other three, of a four-fold division, man may be grouped "round *four* leading types, which may be named the black, yellow, red and white, or the Ethiopic, Mongolian, American and Caucasic."[3]

We will now give some miscellaneous examples of the number **7** without any attempt to exhaust the subject.

Winds have been classified under the following designations according to their velocity : (1) Calm, (2) Light breeze, (3) Moderate wind, (4) Strong wind, (5) Gale, (6) Storm, (7) Hurricane.[4]

---

[1] Cuvier.   Cf. 1 Kings iv. 33, Jas. iii. 7.

[2] *Enc. Brit.* ix. 192°.

[3] Prof. A. H. Keane, *International Geography*, 108, quoted in *Enc. Brit.*, xi. 635°.   See also *id.*, art " Hair," xii. 823.

[4] *Enc. Brit.*, iii. 587°.

Halos, etc. The optical phenomena of this nature include (1) Halos, (2) Coronæ, (3) Rainbows, (4) Fog-bows, (5) Mist-halos, (6) Anthelia, (7) Mountain-spectres.[1]

" *Classification of* Clouds.—Clouds are grouped into 7 classes—*three* primary, and *four* secondary or compound forms, viz. :—

" Primary : (1) *Cirrus*, or Curl Cloud ; (2) *Cumulus*, or Summer Cloud ; (3) *Stratus*, or Fall Cloud.

" Compound : (4) *Cirro-cumulus ;* (5) *Cirro-stratus ;* (6) *Cumulo-stratus ;* and (7) *Nimbus*, or Rain Cloud." [2]

This system remains as the broad basis of those in use to-day. The International Classification (1896) gives three further subdivisions or ten classes in all, but it does not give universal satisfaction, and in 1905 another classification was put forward which goes back to 7 classes or genera with many species.[3]

To return to **the Earth,** its *Land surface* may be divided into 7 continents, viz. (1) Europe, (2) Asia, (3) Africa, (4) North America, (5) South America, (6) Oceania, and (7) the Antarctic Continent, of which only the first *six* (" man's number ") are inhabited ; and its *Waters* into 7 oceans, viz. (1) Arctic, (2) Antarctic, (3) North Atlantic, (4) South Atlantic, (5) North Pacific, (6) South Pacific, and (7) the Indian Ocean.[4] These divisions, however, are perhaps to some extent artificial, as some also may consider the two following. The eastern shore of the *Pacific Ocean* " presents the most extended line of unbroken coast in the world, having no considerable opening save (1) the Gulf of California and (2) the Bay of Panama. On the Asiatic shore, however, it is distinguished by five large land-locked seas, shut in by peninsulas and island chains : viz. (3) the Sea of Kamtschatka, (4) the Sea of Okhotsk,

[1] *Enc. Brit.*, xii. 864*.
[2] Macturk's *Physical Geography,* p. 99.
[3] *Enc. Brit.*, vi. 559.
[4] " The seven seas " is a common expression for all the oceans of the world.

(5) the Sea of Japan, (6) the Yellow Sea, and (7) the Chinese Sea." [1] The *Atlantic Ocean* " is the ocean of inland seas—having two on the east, (1) the Baltic and (2) the Mediterranean, . . . and two on the west, (3) Hudson's Bay and (4) the Gulf of Mexico. It has also the land-locked seas of (5) the North Sea, (6) the Caribbean, and (7) the Gulf of St. Lawrence." [2]

The classification of the land surface of the globe into areas inhabited by distinctive groups of plants has been attempted by many, but no general agreement has been reached. According to climatic zones we may count :—

(1) The Arctic-Alpine zone.

(2) The Boreal zone, including the temperate lands of N. America, Europe and Asia, all of which are substantially alike in botanical character.

(3) The Tropical zone, New World ⎰ the forms of which
(4)   Do.   Old World ⎱ differ in a significant degree.

(5) The Austral zone, Southern S. ⎰ the floras of which
                America ⎱ are strikingly
(6)   Do.   South Africa ⎱ distinct.
(7)   Do.   Australia ⎱

The Oceanic islands contain no distinctive flora. [3]

Another method of division, based on vegetational activity, is as follows :—

(1) The ice-deserts of the arctic and antarctic, and the highest mountain regions.

(2) The tundra, or region of intensely cold winters.

(3) The moor, bog and heath of warmer climates.

(4) The temperate forests of evergreen or deciduous trees.

(5) The grassy steppes or prairies.

(6) The arid desert.

(7) The tropical forest. [4]

---

[1] Macturk, p. 50.   [2] *Idem*, p. 51.
[3] Slightly altered from Drude, *Enc. Brit.*, xi. 635ᵃ.
[4] Slightly altered from *Enc. Brit.*, xi. 635ᵃ.

Animal life affords another method of division, and some naturalists suggest the following faunal regions :—

(1) Holarctic—northern Europe and Asia, and N. America north of Mexico.

(2) Mediterranean—Southern Europe and northern Africa.

(3) Sonoran—between N. and S. America.

(4) Ethiopian—Africa south of the Atlas range.

(5) Oriental—India, Indo-China and Malaya.

(6) Australian—including Australia, New Zealand, New Guinea and Polynesia.

(7) Neotropical—South America.[1]

In the **Human Body** there is not much outwardly to remind us of the number seven. It has *four* limbs, to which if we add the head, neck and trunk, we have **7** parts in all. Then "there are **7** holes in a man's head, two at the ears, two at the eyes, two at the nose, and one at the mouth." There are also **14** bones and **14** joints in the fingers of each hand, and in the toes of each foot. But closer examination will show that these are by no means the only occurrences of heptadic numbers in the human frame. "The spine consists in an adult of **26** bones [or vertebræ], in a young child of **33** [i.e. **7** more], certain of the bones in the spine of the child becoming ankylosed or blended with each other in the adult."[2] There are **7** vertebræ in the neck (*cervical*), **12** in the back (*dorsal* or *thoracic*), and **7** (or **14** in the infant) below these, which are further subdivided. The 7th cervical vertebra is distinguished by its long prominent spine. "Each vertebra consists of a body and **7** processes."[3] "Each lateral border of the [breast-] bone is marked by **7** depressed surfaces for articulation with the **7** upper ribs. . . . The upper **7** ribs are connected by their costal cartilages to the side of the sternum [or breast-bone], and are called *sternal*

---

[1] *Enc. Brit.*, xi. 635ᵇ, slightly altered.

[2] *Enc. Brit.*, xxv. 169.

[3] Beeton's *Dict. of Universal Information*, art. "Anatomy."

or *true* ribs ; the lower five do not reach the sternum, and are named *a-sternal*, or *false*. . . . The ribs are by no means uniform in length ; they increase from the first to the 7th or eighth, and then diminish to the twelfth." [1] " The *costal cartilages* unite the ribs to the sternum. . . . Their length increases as far as the 7th, after which they become gradually shorter." [2] " The skull or skeleton of the head is composed of 22 bones, 8 of which form the skeleton of the cranium, 14 that of the face." [3] " The bones of the Tarsus, or ankle, are 7 in number." [4] " The *encephalon* [or brain] comprises (1) the medulla oblongata, (2) the cerebellum, with (3) the pons Varolii, (4) the mesencephalon, (5) the thalamencephalon, and (6 and 7) the cerebral hemispheres ; the three (4) parts last named being termed collectively the cerebrum." [5] The *medulla oblongata* " is the prolongation into the cranium of the spinal cord, so as to unite it with the brain. . . . The grey matter of the medulla is broken up by changes in the distribution of the white matter into [7] nuclei, or masses of nerve-cells. . . . The *pons Varolii* is above and in front of the *medulla oblongata*. . . . It consists of fibres. . . . Mixed up with these fibres are various nuclei of grey matter connected with the roots of cranial nerves. The most important of these nuclei are " 7 in number. [6]

" The *accessory* muscles [of the tongue] are the (1) stylo-hyoid, (2) digastric, (3) mylo-hyoid, (4) genio-hyoid, (5) omo-hyoid, (6) sterno-hyoid, and (7) thyro-hyoid." [7]

The fibres of the ventricles of the heart are said by Pettigrew to be arranged in 7 layers, three external, a fourth, or central, and three internal. [8]

[1] *Enc. Brit.*, xxv. 170, 171.
[2] *Quain's Anatomy*, 9th ed. i. 29.
[3] *Enc. Brit.*, xxv. 196. A later classification gives 15 to the cranium and 7 to the face.
[4] *Id.*, 177.
[5] *Quain's Anatomy*, i. 280.
[6] *Enc. Brit.*, 9th ed., art. " Physiology," xix. 35, 36.
[7] *Idem*, art. " Anatomy," i. 895.   [8] *Idem*, p. 901.

" The number of *voluntary* muscles to which distinct names have been given . . . amounts to (75 + 51 + 58 + 54 =) **238.**"[1]

" The interosseous muscles [of the hand] are **7** in number. . . . They are divided into two sets," *four* dorsal, and *three* palmar.[2] " The interosseous muscles of the foot, like those of the hand, are **7** in number, *three* plantar, and *four* dorsal."[3] The muscles of the eye are also **7** in number.[4] There are **7** bones in the orbit or socket of the eye.

The ciliary processes of the eye are some **70** triangular ridges.[5] The eye can be separated according to colour into **7** sufficiently distinct classes : (1) Pale or without pigment, (2) Yellow aureole, (3) Orange aureole, (4) Chestnut aureole, (5) Maroon aureole in a circle or disk around the pupil, (6) Maroon aureole covering the iris irregularly, (7) Maroon aureole covering the entire iris.[6]

Very widely distributed throughout the animal body there occur tissues which are grouped together under the name Connective Tissues. They comprise the following types : (1) areolar tissue, (2) adipose tissue, (3) reticular or lymphoid tissue, (4) white fibrous tissue, (5) elastic tissue, (6) cartilage, and (7) bone.[7]

The throat or pharynx contains **7** openings : larynx, œsophagus or gullet, two posterior nares or nostrils, two eustachian tubes, mouth.[8]

" The human being is composed chiefly of—Brain, Nerve, Bone, Muscle, Blood, Flesh, and Hair. The other tissues of anatomy are passive as regards *character*, and are merely connecting links to keep these **7** distinct ingredients in action, so that they may perform their proper functions."[9]

---

[1] *Quain's Anatomy*, i. 186.
[2] *Idem*, i. 227.
[3] *Idem*, i. 265.
[4] *Idem*, i. 281.
[5] *Enc. Brit.*, x. 92ª.
[6] Bertillon.
[7] *Enc. Brit.*, vi. 958ᵇ.
[8] *Harmsworth's Self-Educator*, i. 577.
[9] A. Oppenheim.

Proteids (an important class of substances which make up the greater part of living matter) are classified as follows : (1) Native Albumens, (2) Derived Albumens, (3) Globulins, (4) Fibrin, (5) Coagulated Proteids, (6) Peptons, (7) Lardacein.[1]

Dr. Carpenter observes that there are marked differences in the functional operations of Organic life, " which mark out the whole term of life into the various ' Ages,' which are commonly recognized as **7**, viz. Infancy, Childhood, Youth, Adolescence, Manhood, Decline, and Senility." [2] Similarly, Philo, in the first century after Christ, divided the periods of human life by *sevens*, as follows : [3]—

> " 1. Child (*paidion*)   up to **7** years.
> 2. Boy (*pais*)   „   **14**   „
> 3. Youth (*meirakion*)   „   **21**   „
> 4. Young Man (*neaniskos*)   „   **28**   „
> 5. Man (*anĕr*)   „   **49**   „
> 6. Elder (*presbutēs*)   „   **56**   „
> 7. Old Man (*gerōn*)   above **56**   „

" Every part of our body is . . . constantly throwing off old effete matter, and constantly receiving deposits of new and living matter. . . . In **7** years the whole structure is altered down to the minutest particles. It becomes essentially a different body, though the individual still retains his original form and his personal identity unimpaired." [4]

" The human voice is able to compass tones ranging from 100 to 1500 ' vibrations ' per second [giving a difference of **1400** vibrations between the lowest and highest tones], though no single voice could produce all these. . . . Trained violinists are said to be able to distinguish about **700** sounds in a single octave, or nearly 5000 [= **4900** ?] in all." [5]

[1] *Chambers' Ency.*, art. " Animal Chemistry."
[2] *Principles of Human Physiology*, 7th ed., p. 961, quoted in the *Speaker's Commentary*, Introd. to Rev., p. 473, note.
[3] Quoted in Smith's *N.T. Hist.*, p. 360, note.
[4] *Scientific Illustrations and Symbols*, pp. 72, 73.
[5] Hastings' *Atheism and Arithmetic*, pp. 38, 39.

Phrenologists tell us that there are **35** primitive faculties of the mind, **21** affective and **14** intellectual, each having a particular part of the brain for its organ, and, further, that the brain is double, each organ existing in both hemispheres of the brain.[1] They lay down **7** rules "by which to determine what mental powers are to be considered as primitive or original, and to have separate organs for their manifestation."[2]

Palmistry teaches that there are on the Hand **7** swellings or "mountains," and distinguishes **7** types of hand. The **14** swellings on the palmar faces of the phalanges of the fingers and thumb have each some quality ascribed to them.[3]

Finger-Prints have been classified in *four* types, styled arches, loops, whorls and composites. There are **7** sub-classes.[4]

Man is usually considered to possess five *senses*, though some would increase this number. These five —sight, hearing, taste, smell, touch—are also found in most animals, which is not the case with *speech* and *thought*, faculties which, indeed, can hardly be included in the definition commonly given of the word " senses," though they surely have some title to be classed along with the five above-named.[5]

With regard to the different **Races of Mankind,** the English editor of Cuvier's *Animal Kingdom*[6] writes : " Fischer, in his *Synopsis Mammalium,* indicates what he conceives to be **7** species of *Homo* [Man]. . . . His supposed *species* are as follows :—(1) *H. Japeticus* [=

---

[1] *Enc. Rel. Eth.*, art. " Phrenology." *Enc. Brit.*, id.

[2] Beeton's *Dict. of Universal Information*, art. " Phrenology."

[3] *Enc. Rel. Eth.*, art. " Palmistry." *Enc. Brit.*, id.

[4] *Enc. Brit.* x. 376°.

[5] So Ecclus. xvii. 5. To " be frightened out of one's seven senses," is an expression not unfrequently heard among " the common people." The-seven senses are said by Dr. Brewer to be—animation, feeling, speech, taste, sight, hearing, smelling (*Dictionary of Phrase and Fable,* art. " Seven Senses ").

[6] Bohn's edition (1863), pp. 39-41. The quotation is somewhat abridged.

Caucasian, *Cuvier*] ; (2) *H. Neptunianus* [Malays, etc.] ;
(3) *H. Scythicus* [= Mongolian, *Cuvier*] ; (4) *H.Ameri-
canus* [South Americans] ; (5) *H,. Columbicus* [the
ordinary Red Indian of America] ; (6) *H. Æthiopicus*
[Africans, etc.] ; (7) *H. Polynesius* [Australians, etc.].
Such is the arrangement of an able and accomplished
naturalist, published in 1829. . . . The most recent
authority, which is the third edition of Dr. Prichard's
elaborate *Researches into the Physical History of Mankind*, contends strenuously for unity of species in the
genus *Homo*.[1] . . . The following are the leading
varieties of Man, according to the opinion and arguments of Dr. Prichard. ' On comparing the principal
varieties of form and structure which distinguish the
inhabitants of different countries, we find that there
are 7 classes of nations which may be separated from
each other by strongly marked lines. . . . These 7
principal classes are, first, those nations which in the
form of their skulls and other physical characters
resemble Europeans, including many nations in Asia
and some in Africa. Secondly, races nearly similar in
figure and in the shape of the head to the Kalmucks,
Mongoles, and Chinese. These two first classes of
nations will be designated . . . Iranian and Turanian
nations, in preference to Caucasian and Mongolian.
. . . The third class are the native American nations,
excluding the Esquimaux and some tribes which
resemble them more than the majority of the inhabitants of the new world. The fourth class comprises
only the Hottentot and Bushman race. A fifth class
are the Negroes ; the sixth, the Papuas, or woolly-
haired nations of Polynesia ; the seventh, the Alfourou
and Australian races.' "

A man may have 7 relations (or classes of relations)
of the first degree : (1) father, (2) mother, (3) brother,
(4) sister, (5) wife, (6) son, (7) daughter.

[1] " Man may be regarded as specifically one." *Enc. Brit.*, viii.
850ᵇ. Believers in Scripture, of course, cannot recognize anything
else. See e.g. Acts xvii. 26.

Embryology. " In the life-history of a mammal it is possible to trace (1) how the germ at first lingers as it were among the Protozoa, (2) how it divides and passes through the transitional ' ball of cells ' stage, (3) how the embryo undergoes its first great differentiation like all other multicellular animals in becoming a two-layered gastrula, taking its place beside the ancestral Metazoa, (4) how it by and by acquires some of the characters of a young worm, and (5) then of a simple backboned animal like a primitive fish, (6) how with increasing complexity it ranks with reptilian embryos, and (7) lastly, how the foetus acquires mammalian features." [1]

Cytology. " The activities of living cells are manifested in four ways, viz. : (1) by movement, (2) by secretion, (3) by the transmission of stimuli, (4) by reproduction." [2]

The **Colours of Animals** have been divided, with reference to their uses and objects into *four* classes and 7 sub-classes, as follows :—

I. For Concealment.
   1. Procryptic : Colours which conceal as a defence.
   2. Anticryptic : Colours which conceal, enabling an enemy to catch its prey.
II. For Warning and Signalling.
   3. Aposematic : Colours which warn an enemy off.
   4. Episematic : Colours which enable individuals of same species to recognize and follow each other.
III. For Deception.
   5. Pseudaposematic : Colours which deceptively suggest something unpleasant or dangerous.
   6. Pseudepisematic : Colours which deceptively suggest something attractive to prey.
IV. For Courtship.
   7. Epigamic : Colours displayed in courtship. [3]

Colouring-matter of shells of birds' eggs. " Mr. Sorby (*Proc. Zool. Soc.*, 1875, p. 351), using the method of spectrum-analysis, has now ascertained the existence

[1] *Chambers' Ency.*, iv. 321 (from Von Baer).
[2] *Enc. Brit.*[12], xxx. 781[a].
[3] *Chambers' Ency.*, art. " Mimicry."

of 7 well-marked substances in the colouring-matter of eggs, to the admixture of which in certain proportions all their tints are due. These he names (1) Oorhodeine, (2) Oocyan, (3) Banded Oocyan, (4) Yellow Ooxanthine, (5) Rufous Ooxanthine, (6) a substance, giving narrow absorption-bands in the red, the true colour of which he has not yet been able to decide, and (7) lastly, Lichenoxanthine." [1]

"For the practical purposes of the dyer, colouring matters are classified under the following groups : (1) Acid, (2) Basic, (3) Direct, (4) Developed, (5) Mordant, (6) Miscellaneous, and (7) Mineral Colours." [2]

The number of colours known is about **700.**

Different meanings have been assigned to the word *Physics ;* it is defined as " the department of science that deals with (1) mechanics, (2) dynamics, (3) light, (4) heat, (5) sound, (6) electricity, and (7) magnetism." [3]

There were formerly said to be **7** sciences : thus Pope writes :—

> " Good sense, which only is the gift of heaven,
> And though no science, fairly worth the seven."

The **7** sciences are thus enumerated : (1) Grammar, (2) Rhetoric, (3) Logic, (4) Arithmetic, (5) Music, (6) Geometry, and (7) Astronomy. [4]

" Some writers upon Ethics sum up *all* the *circumstances* of the actions of men in the following terms, sometimes called *categories :* (1) *quis,* who ; (2) *quid,* what ; (3) *ubi,* where ; (4) *quibus auxiliis,* with what assistance ; (5) *cur,* why ; (6) *quomodo,* how ; (7) *quando,* when." [5]

Some further occurrences of **7** in Nature must be referred to very briefly.

[1] *Enc. Brit.,* 9th ed., iii. 774 ; 11th ed., ix. 13ᵈ.
[2] *Enc. Brit.,* viii. 745ᵈ.
[3] Annandale's *English Dict.,* s.v. " Physics."
[4] Webster's *Dictionary,* s.v. " Science," Also called the **7** liberal arts, *Enc. Brit.,* ix. 370ᶜ.
[5] Black's *Etymological Dict.,* s.v. " Circumstance," pp. 83, 84.

The following are from Professor Macalister's *Invertebrata :* " The eggs in earthworms are produced in two small ovaries in the thirteenth ring and opening on the 14th ring " (p. 73) ; " in the large anterior mass of the body [of a lobster, etc.], sheltered by the dorsal shield, there are 14 segments united, comprising the head, thorax, and abdomen " (p. 99) ; " the pincers of a lobster are made up of 7 joints " (p. 100) ; " the two succeeding pairs of abdominal limbs are also pincerlike at the extremity ; the two following are simply pointed, but still exhibit 7 joints " (p. 101) ; the mantis shrimps have 14 or 16 legs (p. 102) ; " in all the lower crustaceans the earliest stage of existence, after emission from the egg, is in the form of a minute oval body with three pairs of limbs and one central eye " = 7 organs (p. 104) ; the Crustacea are divided into 7 classes (p. 107) ; the antennæ of a centipede consist " rarely of 7, usually of 14 joints or more " (p. 113) ; " there are *more than twenty* segments in the body [of a centipede] (except in one little species), and each bears one or two pairs of legs, all with six or 7 joints, like those of a spider or crustacean " (p. 114) ; millipedes " have also small antennæ of 7 joints " (p. 114) ; " the larvæ [of fleas] are white footless grubs, which feed on animal matter for about twelve days, spin for themselves a cocoon, and pass to the pupa stage. After about 14 days' quiescence in this stage, the perfect insect emerges " (p. 128).

From Macalister's *Vertebrata* we learn that—the bones of the upper jaw arch of a fish are " sometimes 7 in number on each side " (p. 17) ; the large order *Passeres* " includes all our small birds [with certain exceptions]. They may be recognized by possessing short wing coverts, a tarsus covered in front with 7 large scales, etc. These birds are very numerous, and make up about 21 families " (p. 66). " The neck-region of the vertebral column, or backbone, in all mammals consists of 7 vertebræ, except in three cases " (p. 75). The number of teeth in the kangaroo rat is

28 or 29 (p. 83) ; in the "Tasmanian devil," 42 (p. 84) ; in the banded anteater, 28 in the upper jaw and 26 in the lower (p. 84) ; in the dog and bear families, 42 (p. 103) ; in the cat family 16 in the upper jaw and 14 in the lower (p. 103) the horse and pig families have 7 molars (including premolars) in each side of each jaw (pp. 91, 94), and so the mole, hyrax, hippopotamus, rhinoceros, and some marsupials ; whilst in the elephant "there is a constant succession of molars, 7 of which are developed during the life of the animal on each side of each jaw, but never more than two, or at most three, are on each side functional at one time " (p. 112). The hare and rabbit have 28 teeth, the tapir 42. Most of these animals whose dentition has been given are typical, it must be remembered, of many others.[1]

The number of teeth in mammals is, however, oftener a multiple of *four* than of seven ; as in the case of man, who has 32 teeth when full grown, 8 on each side of each jaw. An infant usually begins to cut its teeth at about the age of 7 months, the first set being only 20 in number. These begin to fall out during the 7th year, and are replaced by the adult or permanent teeth, which are 28 in number, or 7 on each side of each jaw. It is not until about the age of 18 or 20, or even later, that the four last, or " wisdom teeth," appear, and these are neither so strong nor so useful as the other molars.

In Cuvier's *Animal Kingdom* the number 7 is also frequently met with. Thus, in the section on Fishes, we read that the third family of the *Acanthopterygii* (*Sciænidæ*) is divided into genera with " 7 gill-rays " and " with less than 7 gill-rays ; " in the genus *Sciæna*, " there are 7 sub-genera " (p. 284) ; of the *Cyclostomata* there are two genera : *Petromyzon*, the Lampreys, have 7 gill-openings on each side ; the members of the other genus, *Myxine*, " are divided into sub-genera according to the number of their gill-openings ; *Hep-*

[1] See also *Enc. Brit.*, xxvi. 502–3.

tratremus has **7** on each side, like the Lampreys " (p. 322) ; the first and second divisions of the Perch family have **7** rays in the gills, other *Percidæ* " have more than 7 gill-rays and **7** soft rays, besides a spine in their ventrals " (p. 281). Again, the eighth order of Insects (*Neuroptera*), which includes the ant, dragon-fly, etc., has been divided by M. Rambur into **7** divisions (p. 652).

Respecting the order *Crocodilia*, Professor Huxley writes : " The body of each cervical rib, after the second and as far as the 7th or eighth, is short, . . . and the several ribs lie nearly parallel with the vertebral column. . . . The ribs of the eighth and ninth cervical vertebræ are longer. . . . From **7** to 9 of the anterior dorsal ribs are united with the sternum by sternal ribs. . . . From 5 to **7** pairs of sternal ribs are united with the prolongation [of the sternum] and its cornua. . . . In the ventral wall of the abdomen . . . lie **7** transverse series of membrane bones, which are termed ' abdominal ribs.' " [1]

" In the Lamprey there are **7** sacs upon each side, which open externally by as many distinct apertures." [2]

There are said to be " **7** artificial motions of a horse."[3] The rabbit breeds **7** times a year.[4]

" *Seven* appears as significant," says Dr. McCosh, " only in a single order of plants (*Heptandria*), but has an importance in the animal kingdom, where [as we have seen] it is the number of vertebræ in the neck of mammalia, and, according to M. Edwards, the typical number of rings in the head, in the thorax, and in the abdomen of crustacea." [5]

Coral. The skeleton or corallum of a typical solitary coral exhibits the following parts : (1) basal

---

[1] *Anatomy of Vert. Animals*, pp. 251, 253.
[2] *Idem*, p. 123.
[3] Webster's *English Dictionary*, s.v. " Demi-volt."
[4] Beeton's *Dictionary*, art. " Rabbit."
[5] *Typical Forms and Special Ends in Creation*, p. 520.

plate, (2) septa, (3) theca or wall, (4) columella, (5) costæ, (6) epitheca, (7) pali.[1]

It is said that the *oyster* continues growing until he reaches **7** years of age. After that time he may take a fresh growth and live **7** years longer. On completing that period he may take another growth and live **7** years more, and so on. Like horses they tell their own age up to **7** years, but after that time it becomes a difficult matter to tell what age they are.

" The properties of matter (says Bp. J. E. Mercer) rise up through various stages : (1) sensibility, (2) will, (3) consciousness, (4) intelligence, (5) reason, (6) conscience, (7) spiritual life. The universe is living, and moves in one vast harmonious sweep ever nearer to the throne of God." [2]

Another evolutionist, Bp. Arthur Chandler, traces **7** " ascending stages of existence " thus : (1) the in-organic world, (2) vegetable life, (3) " proteids," (4) animal life, (5) man, (6) God Incarnate, (7) God.[3]

Astronomy. There are **7** stars visible to the naked eye in each of the constellations Great Bear (*Ursa Major*) and Little Bear (*Ursa Minor*), both of which are noteworthy on account of their connection with the Pole-star, which being situated very close to the north pole is of incalculable service to navigators.

The Earth is the 7th planet in the solar system, counting from Neptune, and treating the Asteroids as one.

Jupiter has 9 satellites, of which **7** revolve round the planet in one direction, and two in another. Saturn has 9 or 10 satellites of which 8 (4 × 2) revolve in one direction. Uranus has *four* satellites.

The stars visible to the naked eye with the keenest sight are divided into **7** magnitudes.

Eclipses of the sun and moon cannot be less than two nor more than **7** in any one year, of both luminaries together.

---

[1] *Enc. Brit.*, art. " Anthozoa."   [2] *The Mystery of Life,* 45.

[3] *Scala Mundi.* The treatment of miracles in this book is especially noteworthy.

The first accurate day and month cycle is **49** lunar months, when the day and month agree within 1½ minutes.

49 years are a luni-solar cycle, being equal to 606 lunar months, with the slight excess of 1⅓ days nearly.

" The Earth has **7** motions in heaven : its three individual motions round the sun, round its own axis, and oscillation of the axis ; (4) motion of its perihelion point round the sun ; (5) vertical oscillation of the orbit ; (6) horizontal movement of the orbit tending to make it a circle ; (7) flight through space as a partaker of the sun's motion." [1]

The Constellations are divided into three groups, of which the Northern group contains **28** constellations and the Southern **49**. The Zodiacal group contains 12, to correspond with the months of the year.[2]

" There are **7** possible types of *Light :* common light, polarized light and partially polarized light ; the polarization in the two latter cases being elliptical, circular or plane." [3]

Nothing, perhaps, is more remarkable in connection with the Number Seven and Nature, however, than the fact that the period of **gestation** in a very large number of animals, and the corresponding period of **incubation** for many birds, etc., is an exact multiple of **7** days. Thus we have 3 *weeks* for the mouse, 3½ *weeks* for the marmot, 4 *weeks* for the hare, rabbit, hamster, squirrel, 5 *weeks* for the dormouse and weasel, **7** *weeks* for the hedgehog, 8 *weeks* for the cat and marten, 9 weeks for the dog, wolf, fox, lynx, polecat, otter, **14** weeks for the lion, 17 *weeks* for the pig, **21** *weeks* for the sheep, 40 *weeks* for the cow and many other mammals ; and among birds, 3 *weeks* for the common hen and raven, 3½ *weeks* for the peacock, 4 *weeks* for the duck, turkey, pheasant, guinea-fowl, 6 *weeks* for the ostrich and swan, and so on. In the elephant the period is said to be 90 *weeks* or **21** months ; in the

---

[1] W. A. Baker, *The Day and the Hour,* 130.
[2] *Enc. Brit.,* vii. 14[b].   [3] *Id.,* xxi. 934[b].

human species it is 40 *weeks*, or **280** days, a number remarkably compounded of 4 × 7, the two numbers we have met with so frequently in nature, multiplied by 10, the number of completeness, as is fitting when Man, the highest of earthly beings, is in question. Sometimes, however, it may be added, birth takes place at the end of **7** months.[1]

Now, the week of **7** days is not a *natural* division of time. Some philosophers and scientists tell us, indeed, that the weekly measure of time, which has been found amongst nearly all nations of the world, was adopted because it constitutes the fourth part of a lunar or natural month. Let those believe that who will; but, at any rate, Nature herself cannot have made the mistake of making **28** days a vital period when she meant 29½ days.

This whole subject, however, of heptadic periodicity in the life of animals and man has been so ably dealt with by Dr. H. Grattan Guinness, in his *Approaching End of the Age*, that I must refer the reader to that work for fuller details. I may be permitted to set forth briefly some of the facts which Dr. Guinness has collected, chiefly on the authority of Dr. Laycock and other medical men.

"The birth, growth, maturity, vital functions, healthy revolutions of change, diseases, decay and death, of insects, reptiles, fishes, birds, mammals, and even of man himself," says Dr. Guinness, "are more or less controlled by a law of *completion in* WEEKS." The *ova of insects* are hatched in periods varying considerably in length. The shortest is *half a week*, or 7 half-days, as in the wasp, the common bee, and ichneumon; in some, as the *cecidomia tritici*, the period is *one week*: in others it is 1¼ *weeks*, as, for example, the black caterpillar and the gooseberry grub. In the majority of insects, however, it is from two *weeks* to six *weeks*. The ova of the glow-worm occupy six *weeks*, of the mole cricket only four *weeks*, in hatching. The period passed by insects in the *larva* state is seldom less than 7 days. In the common bee it is 6¼ days, in the humble-bee 7 days exactly. In day *papiliones* it is four *weeks*, in moths six *weeks*. The larva of a new British wasp, of the genus *oplopus*,

---

[1] *Speaker's Commentary*, Introd. to Revelation, p. 473, note. *New Popular Encyclopedia*, art. "Gestation."

occupies twelve *weeks*: viz. from the period when its two first segments coalesced to the throwing off of its exuviæ was three *weeks*, and from the time of the latter change to its full development, nine *weeks*. The larva state of the common black caterpillar occupies 21 days; during which period it exuviates or changes its skin three times, at intervals of 7 days each. The wood piercer bee is in the larva state four *weeks*: of these four weeks it fasts exactly one, just before it enters the *pupa* state. The period spent in the *pupa* or *chrysalis* state is the most in accordance with the general law of limitation by *weeks*: thus in the *sphinx atropos* it is exactly eight *weeks*. If the pupa state is entered late in the summer, the perfect insect does not appear until the following spring. Larvæ and ova will also hybernate in the same way; but in all cases the period occupied is a *definite number of weeks*: some are 40, others 42, others 48 *weeks*. The vital actions of the perfect insect (*imago*) appear subject to the same general law. Thus 20 or 21 days after the queen bee has begun to lay the eggs of drones, the bees begin to construct royal cells. If the impregnation of the queen be retarded beyond the 21st day (Huber) or 28th (Kirby and Spence) of her whole existence, she lays only male eggs; and Huber states that after the 28th day, under these circumstances, she loses all feelings of jealousy towards the young queens in the nymphine state, and never attempts to injure them. Some insects attain puberty almost immediately after leaving the puparium; others are a considerable time before their organs acquire sufficient hardness, especially some of the beetle tribe. Thus the newly-disclosed *imago* of *cetonia aurata* remains two *weeks* under the earth, and that of the *lucanus cervus* not less than three *weeks*.

The pigeon sits two *weeks*, after having laid eggs also for two *weeks*. The seal calves on the rocks, and suckles its young for two *weeks*, when the calf casts its coat and goes into the water. The ova of salmon are hatched in 140 days, and those of the aquatic salamander in 14 or 15 days.

Dr. Laycock collected statistics of the period of gestation or incubation of 129 species of mammals and birds, and found that in 67 cases it was an exact number of weeks or months, in 24 it was so within a day, the others were too loosely stated to be of much value but there appeared to be only four exceptions to the general law; and he thinks it is impossible to come to any less general conclusion than this, that in animals changes occur every 8½, 7, 14, 21, or 28 days, or at *some definite number of weeks*.

In the human system, consciously to one sex, unconsciously but none the less really to the other, there is an alternate loss and gain of physical substance, *every four weeks*.

· And not only in health, but also in disease, 7 is a ruling number, for it has been observed that fevers, and intermittent attacks of ague, gout, and similar complaints, have an heptadic periodicity;

that the 7th, 14th, and 21st are critical days. Not only, however, is the *week* an evident measure in such fevers and intermittents, but the *half week* also. " We must start," says Dr. Laycock, " with the *half-day*, or day of 12 hours, as the *unit* which will comprise the phenomena of the best-marked class of periodic disease, the intermittents. Dr. Graves . . . observed that if this period were adopted, ' we should not count 3½ *days*, but 7 *half-days :* we would not say 7 days, but 14 half-days.' Reckoning thus, many of the anomalous critical effects, and critical terminations in continued fevers, would, I have no doubt, be found strictly conformable to some regular law of periodicity."

Dr. Laycock divides life into three great periods, the first and last each stretching over 21 years, and the central period, or prime of life, lasting 28 years. . The *first*, which extends from conception to full maturity at 21 years of age, he subdivides into 7 distinct stages, marked by well-defined physical characteristics. The *second* comprises three minor periods—(1) from 21 to 28 years of age ; (2) from 28 to 42 ; (3) from 42 to 49, after which age conception rarely takes place. The *third* great period comprises also three minor subdivisions—(1) from 49 to 63 years of age, (2) from 63 to 70, (3) from 70 to death.

Man's very pulse keeps time to the 7-day period. Dr. Stratton states, as the result of several series of observations, that, in health, the human pulse is more frequent in the morning than in the evening, for six days out of seven ; and that *on the 7th day it is slower.*

And man's life as a whole [concludes Dr. Guinness] is a week, a week of decades. " The days of our years are three score years and ten," and that by Divine appointment. Combining the testimony of all these facts, we are bound to admit that *there prevails in organic nature a law of septiform periodicity, a law of completion in weeks.*[1]

" There is a harmony of numbers in all nature. . . . We would refer to Professor Whewell's *Philosophy of the Inductive Sciences*, and to Mr. Hay's researches into the laws of harmonious colouring and form. From these it appears that the number 7 is distinguished in the laws regulating the harmonious perception of forms, colours, and sounds, and probably of taste also, if we could analyse our sensations of this kind with mathematical accuracy." [2]

[1] See *The Approaching End of the Age*, 9th ed., pp. 258–269, for the authorities for these statements, and for fuller details. The new ed. (1918) does not contain this matter.

[2] *The Approaching End of the Age*, p. 268 ; there quoted from the *Medical Review*, July, 1844.

In all departments of nature, then, the number 7 occupies a prominent place.   Prominent, yet not obtrusively so ; indeed, in most cases it is only through the investigations of modern science that its presence is revealed.   And in the Bible the number 7 is equally prominent, yet quite as unobtrusively.   It is like a rich vein of metal lying just underneath the surface of the ground, its presence unsuspected, though thousands have walked over it, until some circumstance, accidental or otherwise, causes the treasure to be laid bare. There has been, there can have been, no collusion here, no fraudulent attempt to make Scripture fit in with nature.   For then its authors would have taken care to proclaim the likeness, whereas it has remained unnoticed for well-nigh two thousand years.   There is but one alternative.   Nature is no thing of chance, it is a divine work, and the Bible proceeds from the same Hand.   This is confirmed even by the very differences which exist between the two with regard to the use of certain numbers.   *Seven* claims the first place in both.   In nature the second place undoubtedly belongs to *four*,[1] which, though it occupies a less important position in Scripture, generally signifies there, when used symbolically, the earth, the created world, or something in connection therewith.[2]   *Ten*, however, —the number which usually carries with it the idea of completeness—takes a higher place in Scripture than *four*, whilst it is found but sparingly in nature.   The importance of the number *three*, the numerical symbol of the Divine Being, is witnessed to by both the Bible and nature.   *Five* is also found in nature, and with the same signification of " incompleteness " which it bears in Scripture.   Thus it is prominent in the Vegetable Kingdom, where life exists, but a lower

---

[1] It is singular that the two chief Nature-numbers, 7 and 4, are considered by Dr. C. F. Burney to have been employed anciently as the names of gods.   Thus Beer-Sheba = Well of Number Seven God ; Kiriath-Arba = City of Number Four God.   (*J.T.S.*, xii. 118, Oct. 1910).

[2] See Chapter I for fuller notes on the Symbolism of Numbers.

kind of life than is possessed by animals in general, without the power of locomotion, and therefore "incomplete." So animals, as compared with man, are "incomplete ; " the more highly organized of them have *five* senses, but man, as before remarked, possesses in addition the faculties of thought and speech.

Thus the earth and all her inhabitants proclaim, and that with no uncertain voice, that their "builder and maker is God," the God of the Bible. The devout mind has seen this upon far less proof than is now available, and has been able to find—

> "Tongues in trees, books in the running brooks,
> Sermons in stones, and good in everything."

To it "the heavens declare the glory of God, and the firmament sheweth his handywork." [1] By it "the invisible things of [God] from the creation of the world are clearly seen, being understood by the things that are made." [2] The atheist looks on the same picture but to him it is a blank. It is the same now as of old : "The *fool* hath said in his heart, There is no God." [3]

Some may object to the ascription of such significance to certain numbers, because they do not occur *regularly*. In fact, we do not always know where to expect the number 7 until we actually find it. But is not this just what, both from the outward form of the Bible and from the appearance of the face of Nature, we might anticipate ? Is Nature symmetrical ? Do we find in her nothing but smooth plains, gently sloping hills, sandy shores, and even coast-lines ? And if we did find such, that is, if we found them everywhere should we admire them ? Are our conceptions of the beautiful, the grand, the magnificent in nature taken from the prairie and the sandy desert, or even from the fruitful plain, the gently flowing river, and the quiet calm of an almost waveless ocean ? or from the towering snow-capped peak, the majestic waterfall, the rugged cliff, the roaring torrent, and, in a word, from all that is "irregular" in nature ?

[1] Ps. xix. 1.   [2] Rom. i. 20.   [3] Ps. xiv. 1.

Part II

CHAPTER I

THE HEPTADIC OCCURRENCE OF WORDS AND PHRASES

IN *The Journal of Sacred Literature* for October, 1851, there appeared a remarkable article on "the Septenary Arrangement of Scripture," from which I extract the following :—

"The occurrence of WORDS seven times is also worthy of notice. This obtains especially in the Book of Revelation. As many of them have different renderings in our translation, they are given in the Greek below.[1] They are above forty in number. Beside which, there are not a few occurring as multiples of seven.

"In the First and Second Epistles to the Thessalonians the word 'coming' (παρουσία, more properly 'presence') occurs seven times ; four in the First Epistle, three in the last. It may be regarded as the characteristic word of the two letters."[2]

[1] "Αξιος. υπομονη. σαρξ. δεκα κερατα. μικρος. προφητεια. σημειον. ψυχη. καιρος. σεισμος. ετοιμαζω. βασιλεια. βασιλευω. ιματιον. δουλος αυτου. αβυσσος. εσχατος. φαγειν. εικοσι τεσσαρες. Ιησους Χριστος. πορνεια. νεφελη. τεταρτος. δρεπανον. τοπος. μακαριος. ακολουθεω. οξυς. ωδε. εκαστος. πιπτω, spoken of worship to God. Θυμος, spoken of God's wrath. πορνος and πορνη together. χρυσος and χρυσιον. βρονται, directly used, and not in comparison. κρισις and κριμα together. πενθος and πενθεω.' Jesus's coming seven times predicted."

[2] I have quoted the above simply to show that some of the matters treated of in this Part are not altogether new. Still, I think it right to add that I was acquainted with the heptadic occurrence of words in Scripture before I saw P. Q.'s paper.

It seems a pity that the writer of the article (whose identity is concealed under the letters " P. Q.") did not proceed further with his studies in this direction. Indeed, it is little less than marvellous how he and others [1] should have stopped short of discovering the full truth, after having come so near to it.

In this Chapter, then, I propose to deal with the occurrence of words and phrases an heptadic number of times, not simply in the separate books of Scripture, but also (and chiefly) in the sacred volume as a whole.

I must ask for the forbearance of some readers, in that it will be necessary to quote the words, and most of the phrases, in the original languages themselves. Still, I hope to make the subject intelligible, even to those who have no acquaintance whatever with those languages.

It will be convenient to illustrate the subject by examples, and to divide the examples into the following classes, which embrace all the different varieties of the heptadic occurrence of words and phrases, so far as my present observation extends, and as it will be seen that the classes are *seven* in number, I do not anticipate that any addition will need to be made to them.

I. Single words.
II. Phrases.
III. Words from the same root.
IV. Words from different roots, but of similar or allied meaning.
V. Cases where the plural is counted as equal to two words.
VI. Words used in a particular sense.
VII. Compound heptads, containing two or more heptadic series, each of which is destroyed by the formation of the other.

In each class I propose to give examples, first from

[1] By " others " I refer especially to Dr. E. Bertheau, author of *The Seven Groups of the Mosaic Law,* and to Dr. J. Forbes, author of *The Symmetrical Structure of Scripture.*

the Old Testament, and then from the New ; to express all Hebrew and Aramaic words first in the original characters, then in *italics*, followed by the meaning of them in English ; to express all Greek words, not in the original characters, but in *italics* only, followed as before by their English meaning, which will be given, in the case of both Hebrew and Greek words, in ordinary roman type between inverted commas ; to denote all Aramaic words by the abbreviation " Aram. ; " and, finally, to give all heptadic numbers, that is, all numbers which are exactly divisible by **7**, in thick type, in order to avoid continually calling attention to the fact of their being heptadic. The figures which follow each word or phrase denote the number of times it occurs in the *whole* of the Old or New Testament (as the case may be), unless otherwise stated.

A large number of additional examples of the more important classes are given in Part I, Ch. I.

CLASS I.—SINGLE WORDS.

(a) Old Testament.

1. אנפים *agappim*, " bands, hordes," **7** (all in Ezekiel).
2. אזור *ezor*, " a girdle," **14.**
3. אזכרה *azkarah*, " memorial," **7.**
4. אזל Aram., *azal*, " to go," **7.**
5. אחרנית *achorannith*, " backward," **7.**
6. אכל Aram., *akal*, " to eat." **7.**
7. אכר *ikkar*, " a husbandman," **7.**
8. אל *El* (3), and אלהים, *Elohim* (4), " God," **7** in Ezek. xxviii. 1–10.
9. אַלָּה *allah*, and אֵלָה, *elah*, " an oak," **14.**
10. אלך Aram., *illek*, " these," **14.**
11. אני *oni*, " a navy," **7.**
12. אנף *anaph*, " to be angry," **14.**
13. אספרנא Aram., *osparnah*, " speedily," **7.**
14. אָסָר *issar*, " a bond," **7** (all in Num. xxx.). See also Class V., No. 1.

15.   אֱסָר   Aram., *esar*, " a decree," **7** (all in Dan. vi.).

16.   אפק   *aphaq*, " to restrain," **7**.

17.   אפרים   " Ephraim," **7** in Samuel, **14** in Isaiah, **7** in Jeremiah.

18.   ארבע   Aram., *arba*, " four," **7** in Daniel.

19.   אש   *esh*, " fire," **7** in Ezek. i., **7** in Zech., **7** in Amos i. ii.

20.   אשה   *isshah*, " wife," 3, and plural נשים, *nashim*, " wives," 4, total **7**, in Nathan's address, 2 Sam. xii. 7–12.

21. אתה,אתא   *athah*, " to come," Heb. **21** ; Aram. **7** in conjugation P'al, and **7** in Aphel.

22.   בקר   *baqar*, " to search," **7**.

23.   בקשה   *baqqashah*, " a request. " **7** in Esther.

24.   בֹּר   *bōr*, " cleanness," **7**.

25.   בַּר   *bar*, " pure," **7**.

26.   בַּר and בָּר, *bar*, " corn," **14**.

27.   ברי   *b'ri*, and בריא, *bari*, " fat," **14**.

28.   ברית   *b'rith*, " covenant," **7** in Gen. ix. (of God's covenant with Noah) and **14** in Gen. xv., xvii. (of God's covenant with Abraham).

29.   גדף   *gadaph*, " to blaspheme," **7**.

30.   גולה   *golah*, " captivity," **42**, of which **7** are in the simple form, and **7** have the preposition ב, " into," prefixed.

31.   גזה   *gizzah*, " a fleece," **7** (all in Jud. vi. 37–40).

32.   גן   *gan*, " a garden," **14** in Genesis, **28** elsewhere ; total **42**.

33.   נפרית   *gophrith*, " brimstone," **7**.

34.   גת   " Gath," **7** in Chronicles.

35.   דוד   *dūd*, " a kettle *or* basket," **7**.

36.   דודי   *dudai*, " a mandrake. a basket," **7**.

37.   דור   Aram., *dūr*, " to inhabit," **7**.

38.   דשא   *desheh*, " grass," **14**.

39.   הדרעור   " Hadadezer," 9, and הדרעור, " Hadarezer," 12, total **21**. (Both names refer to same person.)

40.   היא   Aram., *hi*, 3rd personal pronoun feminine. **7**.

41. היִדד *hedad*, "a shouting," **7.**
42. הרן " Haran," **7.**
43. זקק *zaqaq*, " to refine," **7.**
44. חזיר *chazir*, " swine," **7.**
45. חח *chach*, " a hook," etc., **7.**
46. חי *chai*, " living," Aram. **7** ; Heb. **35** in Lev. **7** in Num., **21** in Deut., **49** in Sam., **56** in writings of Solomon (Prov., Eccles., and Song Sol.).
47. חל *chol*, " profane, common," **7.**
48. חלילה *chalilah*, " God forbid," etc., **21.**
49. חרב *chereb*, " a sword," **7** in Ezek. xxxiii.
50. טירה *tirah*, " an enclosure," **7**
51. טף *taph*, " little children," **7** in Deut., **21** in rest of Pentateuch, **14** elsewhere ; total **42.**
52. יהוד Aram., " Judah," **7.**
53. יהודי *y'hudi* (singular number only), = " Jehudi," **4** ; = " a Jew," **10** ; total **14.**
54. ילד *yalad*, " to beget," **28** in Gen. v.
55. יצחק and ישחק, " Isaac," **7** in Deut., **91** in rest of Pentateuch, **14** elsewhere ; total **112.**
56. ירשה *y'russhah*, " possession," **14.**
57. ישוע " Jeshua," **28** in Ezra and Neh. (Heb. and Aram.).
58. כהן *kohen*, " priest," **7** in Genesis.
59. כהנה *k'hunnah*, " priesthood," **14.**
60. כן *ken*, " a louse," and כנם, *kinnam*, " lice," **7** (including Isa. li. 6, " gnats," R.V. marg.).
61. לבונה *l'bonah*, " frankincense," **7** in Leviticus, **14** elsewhere ; total **21.**
62. לבנון " Lebanon," **7** in Song, **7** in Minor Prophets.
63. מאן Aram., *man*, " a vessel," **7.**
64. מורשה *morashah*, " a possession," **7** in Ezekiel.
65. מן *man*, " manna," **14.**
66. מסגר *masger*, " a smith, a prison," **7.**
67. מערב *maarab*, and מערבה, *maarabah*, " the west," **14.**

68. מצער *mits'ar*, and מצעירה, *mitsts'irah*, "little," **7.**
69. משלח *mishlach*, "a sending," **7.**
70. מתן *mattan*, מתנה, *mattanah*, and מתת, *mattath*, "a gift," **28.**
71. נא *na*, interjection, "I pray," or "now," **406.**
72. נגינה *n'ginah*, "a song," etc., **7** in titles of Psalms, **7** elsewhere; total **14.**
73. נגן *nagan*, "to play on a stringed instrument," **7** in I Sam. xvi.–xix. (all spoken of David).
74. נגף *negeph*, "plague," **7.**
75. נעם *noăm*, "pleasantness," **7.**
76. נתן Aram., *n'than*, "to give," **7.**
77. סוג *sug*, "to go back," **14.**
78. סרן *seren*, "a lord" (used only of the lords of the Philistines), **21.**
79. עבד Aram., *abad*, "servant," **7**; Heb. *ebed*, "servant," **7** in Esther.
80. עבדיהו "Obadiah" (Ahab's servant), **7.**
81. עדן "Eden," **7** in Ezekiel.
82. עזבון *izzabon*, A.V. "a fair," etc., **7** (all in Ezek. xxvii.).
83. עליז *alliz*, "joyous," **7.**
84. עמוס "Amos," **7** (all in the book of that name).
85. עש *ash*, "a moth," **7.**
86. פלג "Peleg," **7.**
87. פרש *peresh*, "dung," **7.**
88. פת *path*, "a morsel," **7** in simple form, **7** with suffixes; total **14.**
89. צאצאים *tseětsaïm*, "offspring," **7** in Isaiah.
90. צום *tsūm*, "to fast," **21.**
91. צפחת *tsappachath*, "a cruse," **7.**
92. צפיר Heb. *tsaphir*, and Aram., *ts'phir*, "a he-goat," **7.**
93. קהלת *qoheleth*, "a preacher," **7** (all in Ecclesiastes).
94. קטל Aram., *q'tal*, "to slay," **7.**
95. קל Aram., *qal*, "a voice," **7.**

96. קרח *qerach*, "ice," etc., **7.**
97. קרי *q'ri*, "contrary," **7** (all in Lev. xxvi.).
98. קרן Aram., *qeren*, "a horn," **14.**
99. רמה *rimmah*, "a worm," **7.**
100. רשם Aram., *r'sham*, "to sign," **7** (all in Dan. v., vi.).
101. שאגה *sh'agah*, "a roaring," **7.**
102. שאת *s'eth*, "a rising up," **7** in simple form, and **7** with prefixes and suffixes ; total **14.**
103. שבע *sheba*, "seven," **28** in Gen. xli.
104. שזר *shazar*, "to twine," **21.**
105. שטה "shittah," שטים *shittim* (a tree), **28.**
106. שטן "Satan," **14** in Job.
107. שרף *saraph*, "fiery serpent, seraph," **7.**
108. שרץ *sharats*, "to creep, to swarm," **14.**
109. תור *tōr*, "a turtledove," **14.**
110. תימן "Teman," **14.**
111. תנים *tannim*, "a dragon, dragons," **14.**
112. תנין *tannin*, "a serpent," etc. **14.**

(b) New Testament.

1. *Aganakteo*, "to be moved with indignation," **7.**
2. *Aēr*, "air," **7.**
3. *Akarpos*, "unfruitful," **7.**
4. *Anastasis*, "resurrection," **42** ; of which **21** have the article, and **7** are in the dative case.
5. *Anachōreo*, "to withdraw, to depart," **14.**
6. *Apeitheia*, "disobedience," **7.**
7. *Apeimi*, "to be absent," **7.**
8. *Apostello*, "to send," **7** in John xvii.
9. *Argurion*, "pieces of silver," Matt. ; "money," Mark, Luke ; **7** in connection with Judas.
10. *Astēr*, "a star," **14** in Rev.
11. *Atimia*, "dishonour," **7.**
12. *Aphthartos*, "incorruptible," **7.**
13. *Aphormē*, "occasion," **7** (all in St. Paul's Epistles).
14. *Basileuo*, "to reign," **7** in Rev., **14** elsewhere ; total **21.**

15. *Beelzeboul,*" " Beelzebub," **7.**
16. *Brecho,* " to rain," **7.**
17. *Brontai* (pl. nom.), " thunders," **7** (all in Rev.).
18. *Diastrepho,* " to pervert," **7.**
19. *Diatithemai,* " to appoint," etc., **7.**
20. *Doulos,* " servant," **14** in Rev.
21. *Dōma,* " the housetop," **7.**
22. *Epistamai,* " to know," **14.**
23. *Epistatēs,* " Master," **7** (all in Luke).
24. *Epitagē,* " commandment," **7.**
25. *Hēgeomai,* " to be chief," etc., **28.**
26. *Iatros,* " a physician," **7.**
27. *Isaak,* " Isaac," **7** in Luke and Acts ; **7** in St. Paul's Epistles and Hebrews.
28. *Israēlitai* (plural), " Israelites," **7.**
29. *Katapino,* " to swallow up," **7.**
30. *Kokkos,* " grain," **7.**
31. *Kurieuo,* " to have dominion over," **7.**
32. *Lampo,* " to shine," **7.**
33. *Luchnia,* " a candlestick," **7** in Rev.
34. *Makrothumia,* " longsuffering," **14.**
35. *Merizo,* " to divide," **14.**
36. *Mēketi,* " no longer," **21.**
37. *Mikron,* " a little while," **7** in John xvi.
38. *Periblepomai,* " to look round about," **7.**
39. *Peteinon,* " a bird," **14.**
40. *Prosphōneo,* " to call unto," **7.**
41. *Rhēgnumi,* or *Rhēsso,* " to break," **7.**
42. *Rhomphaia,* " a sword," **7.**
43. *Seismos,* " an earthquake," **7** in Rev., **7** elsewhere ; total **14.**
44. *Siōn,* " Sion," **7.**
45. *Speira,* " a band " (of soldiers), **7.**
46. *Stoicheia* (plural), "elements," **7.**
47. *Philēma,* " a kiss," **7.**
48. *Phlox,* " a flame," **7.**
49. *Ōdē,* " a song," **7.**

CLASS II.—PHRASES.

(a) Old Testament.

1. אל קנא, *El qanna*, and אל קנוא, *El qanno*, "a jealous God," **7**.

2. אני יהוה דברתי, *ani Y'hovah dibbarti*, "I the LORD have spoken," **14** in Ezekiel. (A.V. "said," in ch. xxi. 17).

3. אפסי ארץ, *aphse erets*, "the ends of the earth," **14**. (A.V. is different in Ps. ii. 8 ; xxii. 27.)

4. בך, *bak*, "in thee," and בתוכך, *b'thokēk*, "in the midst of thee," **14** in Ezek. xxii. 1–16.

5. דבר יום ביומו, *d'bar yōm b'yomo*, "daily" (lit. "a matter of a day in its day "), **14**.

6. הנה ימים באים, *Hinneh yamim baïm*, "Behold, the days come," **21** (rendered "Lo, the days come," Jer. xxx. 3, and "Lo, the days shall come," Amos iv. 2, both in A.V. and R.V.).

7. ויאמר, *Vaiyomer*, "And . . . said," **7** in Isa. xxxix.

8. ויתר דברי, *V'yether dibrē*, "And the rest of the acts of . . . ," **42**, all in Kings and Chron. (Two similar phrases each occur once, "And the rest of *all* the acts of," 1 Kings xv. 23, and "And the rest of *his* acts," 2 Chron. xxviii. 26).

9. ותחת כל עץ רענן, *V'thachath col ets raanan*, "And under every green tree," **7** (Deut. xii. 2 ; 1 Kings xiv. 23 ; 2 Kings xvi. 4 ; xvii. 10 ; 2 Chron. xxviii. 4 ; Jer. ii. 20 ; Ezek. vi. 13. (In Jer. iii. 6 occurs ואל תחת, etc., same translation in A.V. and R.V.)

10. טהור הוא, *Tahor hu*, "He *or* it (is) clean," **7** (all in Lev. xi., xiii.).

11. טמא הוא, *Tamē hu*, "He *or* it (is) unclean," **7** in Lev. xiii.

12. טמא הוא לכם, *Tamē hu lakem*, "He *or* it (is) unclean unto you," **7** (all in Lev. xi. and Deut. xiv.).

13. יברכך יהוה אלהיך, *Y'barek'ka Y'hovah Eloheka*, "The LORD thy God shall bless thee," **7** (Deut. xiv. 24, 29 ; xv. 10 ; xvi. 10. 15.; xxiii. 20 [21 Heb.] ; xxiv.

19) ; but not always translated as above either in A.V. or R.V.

14. יהוה צבאות, *Y'hovah Ts'baoth*, "The LORD of Hosts," **7** in Psalms ; **14** in Haggai.

15. כי יהוה דבר, *Ki Y'hovah dibber*, "For the LORD hath spoken " (as a complete phrase), **7** (1 Kings xiv. 11 ; Isa. i. 2 ; xxii. 25 ; xxv. 8 ; Jer. xiii. 15 ; Joel iv. 8 ; Obad. 18).

16. כה אמר אדני יהוה, *Koh amar Adonai Y'hovah*, "Thus saith the Lord JEHOVAH," 122, and כה אמר יהוה, *Koh amar Y'hovah*, "Thus saith JEHOVAH," 4 ; total **126** in Ezekiel. (In the A.V. the phrases are rendered, "Thus saith the Lord GOD," and "Thus saith the LORD," respectively.)

17. לעיניהם, *l'enehem*, "in their sight," **7** in Ezek. xii. 3–7.

18. מגור מסביב, *magor missabib*, "fear on every side," **7** (once in the plural).

19. מלא, *m'lo*, "fulness," joined with ארץ, *erets*, "earth *or* land," 12, and with תבל, *tebel*, "world," 2 ; total **14** (Deut. xxxiii. 16 ; Ps. xxiv. 1 ; l. 12 ; lxxxix. 11 [12 Heb.] ; Isa. vi. 3 ; viii. 8 ; xxxiv. 1 ; Jer. viii. 16 ; xlvii. 2 ; Ezek. xii. 19 ; xix. 7 ; xxx. 12 ; xxxii. 15 ; Micah i. 2).

20. נחל מצרים, *nachal Mitsrayim*, "the river [brook, R.V.] of Egypt," **7** (Num. xxxiv. 5 ; Josh. xv. 4, 47 ; 1 Kings viii. 65 ; 2 Kings xxiv. 7 ; 2 Chron. vii. 8 ; Isa. xxvii. 12. In Gen. xv. 18 the Heb. word for river is a different one, *nahar*).

21. עד אור הבקר, *ad ōr hab-boqer*, "until the morning light," **7** (Judg. xvi. 2 ; 1 Sam. xiv. 36 ; xxv. 22, 34, 36 ; 2 Sam. xvii. 22 ; 2 Kings vii. 9).

22. על פני כל הארץ, *al p'ne col ha-arets*, "upon the face of all the earth," **7** in Pent. (Gen. i. 29 ; vii. 3 ; viii. 9 ; xi. 4, 8, 9 ; Deut. xi. 25), besides Gen. xli. 56, "upon all the face of the earth."

23. רב טבחים, *rab tabbachim*, "captain of the guard," **7** in 2 Kings.

24. "Abraham, Isaac, and Jacob," **7** in Deut.

25. " All the words of this law," **7** in Deut. (xvii. 19 ;
xxvii. 3, 8 ; xxviii. 58 ; xxix. 29 ; xxxi. 12 ; xxxii. 46).
In ch. xxvii. 26, the word " all " is inserted in the A.V.
but it is not in the Heb., as is shown by its being
printed in italics. See also the R.V.

26. " And it shall come to pass in that day," **7** in
Zech. (So R.V., rightly, in ch. xii. 3 ; xiv. 8).

27. " And the children of Israel did evil in the sight
of the LORD," 3 (Judg. ii. 11 ; iii. 7 ; vi. 1) ; " And the
children of Israel again did evil in the sight of the
LORD," 4 (Judg. iii. 12 ; iv. 1 ; x. 6 ; xiii. 1) : total **7**
in Judges.

28. " And thou shalt know that I (am) the LORD,"
7 (1 Kings xx. 13 ; Isa. xlix. 23 ; Ezek. xvi. 62 ; xxii.
16 ; xxv. 7 ; xxxv. 4, 12. See also Isa. lx. 16).

29. " And thou shalt put away the evil from among
you," **7,** all in Deut. (In ch. xiii. 5 the A.V. reads, more
literally, " from the midst of thee." The R.V. in every
case renders, " So shalt thou [or thou shalt] put away
the evil from the midst of thee.")

30. " As I live, saith the Lord GOD," **14** (all in Ezek.).

31. " As I live " (spoken by God), **7** besides preceding
(Num. xiv. 28 ; Isa. xlix. 18 ; Jer. xxii. 24 ; xlvi. 18 ;
Ezek. xvii. 19 ; xxxiii. 27 ; Zeph. ii. 9. See also Num.
xiv. 21 ; Deut. xxxii. 40).

32. " Cherethites and Pelethites," **7.**

33. " Children of Asshur," i.e. Assyrians, 4 ; and
" Children of Babel," i.e. Babylonians, 3 : total **7** in
Ezek. xxiii.

34. " Cyrus king of Persia," **7** in Ezra ; " Cyrus the
king," 6 in Ezra ; and " Cyrus king of Babylon," 1 in
Ezra : total **14.**

35. " Daughter(s) of Jerusalem," **7** in the singular
and **7** in the plural.

36. " David my father," **7** in Solomon's prayer
(1 Kings viii. 15, 17, 18, 20, 24, 25, 26).

37. " From a month old and upward," **7** in Num. iii.

38. " From thirty years old and upward even unto
fifty years old," **7** (all in Num. iv.).

39. "From twenty years old and upward" ("above," A.V., in Exod. xxx. 14), **21** in Pentateuch.

40. "Hear thou from heaven," **7** in Solomon's prayer, 2 Chron. vi. 23, 25, (27), 30, 33, 35, 39. In ver. 27 the preposition is omitted, as it is in all the 7 instances in the parallel place, 1 Kings viii. 32, 34, 36, 39, 43, 45, 49, where the rendering is "Hear thou (in) heaven." (In 1 Kings viii. 30 and 49, the order of the words, both in the A.V. and the R.V., is not according to the Hebrew. It is given correctly in the parallel verses in Chron.)

41. "I lifted up my hand," **7** in Ezek. xx.

42. "Into the hand of the king of Babylon," **7** (excluding ch. xxxviii. 23) ; and "Into the hand of Nebuchadrezzar king of Babylon," **7** ; and "Into the hand of the Chaldeans," **7** ; all in Jeremiah.

43. "Man of God," used of Elijah **7** times.

44. "Master of the eunuchs," **1** ; and "Prince of the eunuchs" (referring to same person), **6** : total **7** in Dan. i.

45. "People, nations, and languages," **7** (all in Daniel; once in the singular).

46. "Plague of leprosy," **14.**

47. "Praise (thou) JEHOVAH," **1** ; "Praise (ye) JE-HOVAH," **4** ; "Praise (ye) the name of JEHOVAH," **2** ; total **7** (Ps. cxiii. 1 ; cxvii. 1 ; cxxxv. 1 ; cxlvi. 1 ; cxlviii. 1, 7 ; Jer. xx. 13 ; all with the objective particle *eth*).

48. "Rising up early and sending " (spoken of God), **7** (2 Chron. xxxvi. 15, and 6 times in Jeremiah).

49. "Shadrach, Meshach, and Abednego " (Aram.), **14** (Dan. ii. 49–iii. 30).

50. "The garden of God," **3** ; and "Eden," **4** : total **7** in Ezek. xxxi. (*cf.* ch. xxviii. 13).

51. "The glory of the LORD filled the house," **6** (1 Kings viii. 11 ; 2 Chron. v. 14 ; vii. 1, 2 ; Ezek. xliii. 5 ; xliv. 4) ; and "And I will fill this house with glory, saith the LORD of hosts," **1** (Hag. ii. 7) : total **7.**

52. "The land (*erets*, 6 ; *adamah*, 1) which the LORD

thy God giveth thee (for) an inheritance," **7** (all in Deut.).

53. " The land which [the LORD] sware unto . . . Abraham, to Isaac, and to Jacob," **7** (Gen. l. 24 ; Exod. xxxiii. 1 ; Num. xxxii. 11 ; Deut. i. 8 ; vi. 10 ; xxx. 20 ; xxxiv. 4).

54. " The tree of life," **7** (3 in Genesis and 4 in Proverbs).

55. " The voice of the LORD," **7** in Ps. xxix.

56. " These are the families of . . . according to those that were numbered of them," **7** in Num. xxvi.

57. " This (is) the law . . ." **14** in Lev., and **7** in Num. and Deut. including **2** " This (is) the ordinance of the law."

58. " To walk contrary to (me, you, them)," **7** (all in Lev. xxvi.).

59. " Two turtledoves or two young pigeons," **7.**

60. " Valley of Hinnom, *or* of the son *or* children of Hinnom," 13, besides Jer. ii. 23, where it is simply called, " the valley ; " total **14.**

61. " Written in the book of the chronicles," **85** (not including Est. ii. 23, where the Heb. is different) ; followed by " of the kings of Israel," 18 times ; " of the kings of Judah" 15 ; " of the kings of Media and Persia," 1 ; also found in Neh. xii. 23.

(b) New Testament.

1. *Anechōrēsen,* followed by *eis,* "withdrew *or* departed into," **7.**

2. *Apo katabolēs kosmou,* " from the foundation of the world," **7.**

3. *Hautē,* " this," followed by *hina,* " that," " in order that," **7** (John xv. 12 ; xvii. 3 ; 1 John iii. 11, 23 ; v. 3 ; 2 John 6, 6).

4. *Ei de mē* and *ei de mēgĕ,* " else," " if not," **14.**

5. *En gastri echō,* " to be with child," **7.**

6. *Heōs pŏtĕ,* " How long . . . ? " **7.**

7. *Hē hēmera tou sabbatou,* or *tōn sabbatōn,* " the sabbath day," **7.**

8. *Kata tēn taxin*, "after the order," **7** (all in Hebrews).

9. *Mia (tōn) sabbatōn*, "the first [day] of the week," **7**.

10. *Pistos*, "faithful," followed by *logos*, "word, saying," **7** (1 Tim. i. 15 ; iii. 1 ; iv. 9, 12 ; 2 Tim. ii. 11 ; Tit. i. 9 ; iii. 8).

11. *Tadĕ legei ho* . . . "These things saith," **7** in Revelation.

12. *Tris aparnēsē me*, "Thou shalt deny me thrice," **7** (the words are the same in every case, though the order of them is varied). [*arnēsē*, Jno. xiii. 38, Edd.]

13. "As it is written," *kathōs gegraptai*, 24, and *hōs gegraptai*, 4 ; total **28,** of which **7** are in the Gospels, and **14** in Romans.

14. "Children of Israel," **14.**

15. "Son of David," used of Christ **14** times, besides **7** places (Matt. xxii. 42 ; Luke i. 32 ; John vii. 42 ; Rom. i. 3 ; 2 Tim. ii. 8 ; Rev. v. 5 ; xxii. 16) where the wording is different, but to the same effect.

16. "There shall be weeping and gnashing of teeth," **7.**

CLASS III.—WORDS FROM THE SAME ROOT.

(a) Old Testament.

This class consists of root words, which, together with the whole of their derivatives, occur an heptadic number of times.

1. אבב *Abab*. (The root itself is not used, the following are its derivatives.) אב, *ēb*, "greenness, verdure," 2 ; אב, *ēb*, Aram. "fruit," 3 ; אביב, *abib*, "green ears of corn," 2 : total **7.** Also the following proper names—אביב, *Abib* (the name of a month), 6 ; *Tel-Abib* (a city), 1 : total **7.**

2. אל *el*, or אלה, *elleh*, 2 ; אילן, *illen*, 5 ; אלך, *illek*, 14 (all Aram. meaning "these") : total **21.**

3. אפס *aphes*, "to fail," 5 ; אפס, *ephes*, "end," etc., 41 ; אפסי, *aphsi*, "none besides," 3 : total **49.**

4. אשד *eshed*, "a stream," A.V., 1 ; אשדה, *ashedah*, "a spring," A.V., 6 : total **7.**

5. אשף *asshaph*, "an astrologer," A.V., Heb. 2 ; do. Aram. 6 ; אשפה, *ashpah*, "a quiver," 6 : total **14.**

6. גזל *gazal*, "to take by violence," 30 ; גזל, *gazel*, "robbery," 4 ; גזל, *gezel*, "violence," 2 ; גזלה, *g'zelah*, "spoil," 6 : total **42.**

7. גיח *giach*, "to break forth," Heb. 6 ; Aram. 1 : total **7.**

8. גלה *galah*, "to remove," 2, and גולה, *golah*, "removing *or* captivity," 5 ; total **7** in Ezek. xii. ("Captivity" in ver. 11 is a different word in the Heb.).

9. גנן *ganan*, "to defend," 4 ; גן, *gan*, 2, and גנה, *gannah*, 5, both meaning "garden," together **7** ; מגן, *magēn*, "a shield," 3 : total **14** in Isaiah.

10. גנז *genez*, "treasure," 3 ; גנז, *g'naz*, Aram., "treasure," 3 ; גנזך, *ganzak*, "a treasury," 1 : total **7.**

11. גף *gaph*, "a body," etc., 4 ; גף, *gaph*, Aram., "a wing," 3 : total **7.**

12. זן *zan*, "kind, species," Heb. 3 ; Aram. 4 : total **7.**

13. חוה *chavah*, "to show," 6 ; חות, *chavvoth*, "villages," **7** ; אחוה *achvah*, "declaration," 1 : total **14** (Heb. only).

14. טוח *tuach*, "to daub," 6, and טיח, *tiach*, "daubing," 1 ; total **7** in Ezek. xiii.

15. טפח *taphach*, "to spread out," etc., 2 ; טפח, *tephach*, "handbreadth," etc., 4 ; טפח, *tophach*, "handbreadth," 5; טפחים, *tippuchim*, "a nursing of children," 1 ; מטפחת, *mitpachath*, "a garment," 2 : total **14.**

16. יבל *yabal*, " to bring," Hiphil conjugation, 7 ;
Hophal, 11 ; יבל, *y'bal*, Aram., " to bring,"
3 : total verb 21 ; יבל, *yabal*, " a stream,"
2 ; יבל, *yabbal*, " running " (as a sore), 1 ;
אובל, *ubal*, " a river," 3 ; יובל, *yubal*, " a
river," 1 ; מבול, *mabbūl*, " flood," 13 ; יבול,
y'būl, " increase," 13 ; בול, *būl*, " produce,"
2 ; יובל, *yobel*, " horn *or* trumpet," 6 ; id.
" Jubilee," 21 ; תבל, *tebel*, " the world," 36 :
total **119.**

17. ירק *yaraq*, " an herb," 5 ; ירק, *yereq*, " greenness,"
6 ; ירוק, *yarōq*, " green herb," 1 ; ירקרק,
y'raqraq, " greenish," 3 ; ירקון, *yeraqōn*,
" mildew," 6 : total **21.**

18. כשב *keseb*, " a lamb," 13 ; כשבה, *kisbah*, " a ewe-
lamb," 1 : total **14.**

19. סוף *sūph*, " to have an end," Heb. 8, Aram. 2 ;
סוף, *soph*, " the end," Heb. 5, Aram. 5 ;
סופה, *suphah*, " a whirlwind," 15 : total Heb.
28, Aram. **7,** or **35** in all.

20. עבד *abad*, " to do," etc., 28 ; עבד, *abad*, " servant,"
7 ; אבידא, *abidah*, " work," 6 ; מעבד, *mabad*,
" work," 1 : all Aram., total **42.** The Heb.
words from the same root occur in the
history of Jacob and Laban as follows : עבד,
abad, " to serve," Kal conjugation, preterite tense, 7 ; future tense, 4 ; עבד, *ebed*,
" servant," 1 ; עבודה, *abodah*, " service," 2 :
total **14** in Gen. xxix.–xxxi.

21. ערג *arag*, " to desire," 3 ; ערוגה, *arugah*, " a gar-
den-bed," 4 ; total **7.**

22. צרע *tsara* (participle), " a leper," 3, and צרעת, *tsaraath*, " leprosy," 4 : total **7** in the history
of Naaman, 2 Kings v.

23. קמץ *qamats*, " to take in the hand," 3 ; קמץ,
qomets, " a handful," 4 : total **7.**

24. רבב *rabab*. The following words from this root all
have the same meaning, " ten thousand : "
רבבה, *r'babah*, Heb. 16 ; רבוא, *ribbo*, Heb.

10 ; רבו, *ribbo*, Aram. 2 : total **28.** There are other words usually considered to be from the same root as these, but these are all which have this meaning.

25. רען *ra'an*, " to be green," 2 ; רענן, *raanan*, " green, flourishing," 18 ; רענן, *raanan*, Aram., " flourishing," 1 : total **21.**

26. רקם *raqam*, " to embroider," 9 ; רקמה, *riqmah*, " broidered work," 12 : total **21.**

27. שוש *shush*. (Root not used ; probable meaning, " to be white.") שיש, *shayish*, " white marble," 1 ; שש, *shēsh*, " white marble," 3 ; שש, *shēsh*, " fine linen," 38 : total **42.** (From same root are sometimes derived שושן, " lily," etc., for which see Class V., No. 9.)

28. שמט *shamat*, " to release," etc., 9 ; שמטה, *sh'mittah*, " a release," 5 : total **14.**

29. שרק *sharaq*, " to hiss," preterite tense, 5 ; future, 7 ; שרקה, *sh'reqah*, " a hissing," 7 ; שריקה *sh'riqah*, " a hissing," etc., 2 : total **21.**

30. שרר *sharar* (participle), " enemy," 5 ; שר, *shōr*, " navel," 2 ; שרר, *shorer*, " navel," 1 ; שריר, *sharir*, "navel," 1 ; שרירות, *sh'riruth*, " stubbornness," 10 ; שרה, *sherah*, " a chain," 1 ; שרשה, *sharshah*, " a chain," 1 ; שרשרה, *sharsh'rah*, " a chain," 7 : total **28.**

(b) New Testament.

1. *Astēr*, " a star," 24 ; *astron*, " a star," 4 : total **28.**

2. *Basanos*, " torment," 3 ; *basanizō*, " to torment," 12 ; *basanismos*, " torment," 5 ; *basanistēs*, " a tormentor," 1 : total **21.**

3. *Bebēlos*, " profane," 5 ; *bebēloō*, " to profane," 2 ; total **7.** (From *Bēlos*, " a threshold," which does not occur in N.T.).

4. *Bradus*, " slow," 3 ; *bradunō*, " to be slack," 2 ; *bradutēs*, " slackness," 1 ; *bradu-ploeō*, " to sail slowly," 1 : total **7.**

5. *Brōma* and *brōsis*, "meat, food," **7** in I Cor. (From *Brōskō*, "to eat.")

6. *Galatia*, 4; *Galatai*, "Galatians," 1; *Galatikos*, "of Galatia," 2 : total **7.**

7. *Eleutheros*, "free," 23; *eleutheria*, "freedom," 11; *eleutheroō*, "to set free," **7**; *ap-eleutheros*, "a freedman," 1 : total **42,** of which **7** are in Romans and **7** in St. John's writings (Gospel and Rev.).

8. *Hēmisu*, "half," 5; *hēmi-thanēs*, "half-dead," 1; *hēmi-ōrion*, "half an hour," 1 : total **7.**

9. *Ēchos*, "a sound," 3; *ēcheō*, "to sound," 2; *ex-ēcheomai*, "to sound forth," 1; *kat-ēcheō*, "to teach by word of mouth," 8 : total **14.**

10. *Keirō*, "to shear," 4 : *keiriai*, "grave-clothes," 1; *kerma*, "money," 1; *kermatistēs*, "a money-changer," 1 : total **7.**

11. *Keramos*, "tiling," 1; *kerameus*, "a potter," 3; *keramikos*, "of a potter," 1; *keramion*, "a pitcher," 2 : total **7.**

12. *Keras*, "a horn," 11; *keration*, "a husk," 1; *keraia*, "a tittle," 2 : total **14.**

13. *Koniaō*, "to whiten," 2; *koni-ortis*, "dust," 5 : total **7.** (From *Konis*, "dust.")

14. *Krētē*, "Crete," 5; *Krētes*, "Cretans," 2 : total **7.**

15. *Kuklō*, "round about," 2, and *kuklothen*, "round about," 4, and *kukloō*, "to compass about," 1 : total **7** in Rev. (From *Kuklos*, "a circle.")

16. *Kurēnē*, "Cyrene," 1; *Kurēnaios*, "Cyrenian," 6 : total **7.**

17. *Lepis*, "a scale," 1; *lepra*, "leprosy," 4; *lepros*, "a leper," 9 : total **14.**

18. *Leui*, "Levi" (son of Jacob), 3; *Leuitēs*, "Levite," 3; *Leuitikos*, "Levitical," 1 : total **7.**

19. *Malakos*, "soft, effeminate," 4; *malakia*, "sickness," 3 : total **7.**

20. *Mastix*, "a scourge," 6; *mastizō*, "to scourge," 1; *mastigoō*, "to scourge," **7** : total **14.**

21. *Matēn*, "in vain," 2; *mataios*, "vain," 6;

mataiotēs, "vanity," 3 ; *mataioōmai*, "to become vain," 1 ; *mataiologos*, "a vain talker," 1 ; *mataio-logia*, "vain talking," 1 : total **14.**

22. *Naus*, "a ship," 1 ; *nautēs*, "a sailor," 3 ; *nauklēros*, "an owner of a ship," 1 ; *nau-ageō*, "to make *or* suffer shipwreck," 2 : total **7.**

23. *Odunē*, "sorrow," 2 ; *odunaomai*, "to be in anguish," 4 ; *ōdin*, "travail-pains," 4 ; *ōdinō*, "to travail," 3 ; *sun-ōdinō*, "to travail in pain together," 1 : total **14.**

24. *Petannumi*, "to expand" (root not used in N.T.); *ek-petannumi*, "to spread out," 1 ; *kata-petasma*, "a veil," 6 : total **7.**

25. *Pterux*, "wing," 5 ; *pterugion*, "pinnacle," 2 : total **7.** (From *Pteron*, "a wing.")

26. *Sabbaton*, "sabbath, week," 41 ; *sabbata* (plural), the same, 27 ; *sabbatismos*, "a sabbath-rest," 1 : *pro-sabbaton*, "the day before the sabbath," 1 : total **70.**

27. *Semnos*, "grave, honourable," 4 ; *semnotēs*, "gravity," 3 : total **7.** (Some derive these words from *Sebomai*, "to worship.")

28. *Tugchanō*, "common, it may be," etc., 6 ; do. with genitive, "to obtain," **7** ; *epi-tugchanō*, "to obtain," 5 ; *para-tugchanō*, "to meet with," 1 ; *sun-tugchanō*, "to meet with," 1 ; *en-tugchanō*, "to make intercession," 5 ; *huper-en-tugchanō*, "to make intercession for," 1 ; *en-teuxis*, "intercession," 2 : total **28.**

Sometimes two or more compound words, derived from the same two roots, occur together an heptadic number of times : as—

29. *Ana-lambano*, "to receive up," 13 ; *ana-lē(m)-psis*, "a receiving up," 1 : total **14.**

30. *Huper-ballo*, "to exceed," 5 ; *huper-bolē*, "exceeding greatness," 8 ; *huper-ballontōs*, "above measure," 1 : total **14.**

31. *Phil-adelphos*, "loving as brethren," 1 ; *phil-adelphia*, "love of the brethren," 6 : total **7.**

CLASS IV.—WORDS DERIVED FROM DIFFERENT ROOTS, BUT OF SIMILAR OR ALLIED MEANINGS.

(a) Old Testament.

1. ברוש, *b'rosh,* " fir," 20 ; ברות, *b'rōth,* " fir," 1 : total **21.**

2. גת, *gath,* " a wine-press," 5 ; יקב, *yeqeb,* " a wine-vat," 16 ; total **21.**

3. (*a*) יצק, *yatsaq,* " to pour out, to cast " (of metal), 53 ; יצקה, *y'tsuqah,* " a casting " (of metal), 1 ; מוצק, *mutsaq,* and מוצקת, *mūtseqeth,* the same, 3; מוצקה, *mūtsaqah,* " a funnel *or* pipe," 1 : total 58. (*b*) צוק, *tsūq,* " to pour out," 3 ; מצוק, *matsūq,* " a pillar," etc., 2 ; total, 5. Total from the two roots, **63.**

4. (*a*) כוה, *kavah,* Niphal, " to be burned," 2 ; כי, *ki,* " burning," 1 ; כויה, *k'viyah,* " burning," 2 ; מכוה, *mikvah,* " inflamed part " (A.V. and R.V. " burning "), 5 : total 10. (*b*) צרב, *tsarab,* Niphal, " to be burned," 1 ; צרבת, *tsarebeth,* " burning, inflammation," 3 : total 4. Total from the two roots, **14.**

5. (*a*) קרח, *qarach,* " to make bald," 5 ; קרח, *qereach,* " bald," 3 ; קרחה, *qorchah,* " baldness," 11 ; קרחת, *qarachath,* " a bald head," 4 : total 23, of which **7** are in Lev. (קרח, *qerach, qorach,* " ice," etc., occur **7** times, so that if they are included it makes no difference.) (*b*) גבח, *gibbeach,* " forehead bald," 1 ; גבחת, *gabbachath,* " a bald forehead," 4 : total 5. Total from the two roots, **28.**

6. (*a*) רבב, *rabab,* " to be many." From this root the following Aram. words are derived :—רב, *rab,* " great," 15 ; רברב, *rabrab,* " great," 8 ; רברבן, *rabr'-ban,* " a great man *or* prince," 8 : total 31. (*b*) רבה, *r'bah,* Aram., " to grow *or* become great," 6 ; רבו, *r'bu,* Aram., " greatness," 5 : total 11. Total from both roots (Aram. words only), **42,** not including רבו, *ribbo,* " ten thousand," which is therefore probably from a different root (see Class III. *a.* 24).

7. (*a*) שרת, *sharath,* " to serve, to minister," 97 ; שרת, *shareth,* " service," 2 : total 99. (*b*) שרד, *s'rad,* " ser-

vice (?)," 4 ; שֶׂרֶד, *sered* (meaning doubtful), 1 : total 5.
(c) שָׂרַד, *sarad*, "to flee, to escape," 1 ; שָׂרִיד, *sarid*, "one left *or* escaped," 28 : total 29. Total from the three roots, **133.** (The combination, however, is perhaps doubtful.)

(b) New Testament.

1. (*a*) *Arrēn* or *Arsēn*, "male," 9 ; *arseno-koitai*, "abusers of themselves with men," 2 : total 11. (*b*) *Thēleia, thēlu,* "female," 5 ; *thēlazo,* "to give suck," 5 (excluding Luke xxiii. 29, where the Revisers rightly read *trephō*) : total 10. Total from the two roots, **21.**

2. (*a*) *Amnos,* "a lamb," 4. (*b*) *Arēn,* "a lamb," 1 ; *arnion,* "a lamb," 30. Total from both roots, **35.**

3. (*a*) *Astrapē,* meaning "lightning," 8 ; *astraptō,* meaning "to lighten," 1. (*b*) *Brontē,* "thunder," 12. Total **21.**

4. (*a*) *Gelaō,* "to laugh," 2 ; *gelōs,* "laughter," 1 ; *kata-gelaō,* "to laugh to scorn," 3 : total 6. (*b*) *Muktērizō,* "to mock," 1 ; *ek-muktērizō,* "to scoff," 2 : total 3. (*c*) *Chleuazō* and *dia-chleuazō,* "to mock," 2. (*d*) *Empaizō,* "to mock" (from *pais,* "a boy"), 13 ; *empaigmos,* "mocking," 1 ; *em-paigmonē,* "mockery," 1 (1 Pet. iii. 3, R.V.) ; *em-paiktēs,* "a mocker," 2 : total 17. Total from the four roots, **28.**

5. *Onar,* "a dream," 6 ; *en-upnion,* "a dream," 1 : total **7.**

6. (*a*) *Horō,* "to excite" (root not used in the New Testament) ; *hormē,* "onset," 2 ; *hormaō,* "to rush," 5 ; *hormēma,* "a mighty fall," 1 ; *aph-ormē,* "occasion," 7 ; *koni-ortos,* "dust," 5 : total 20. (*b*) *Par-otrunō,* "to urge on" (from *otrunō ;* root not used), 1. Total from the two roots, **21.**

The following example is of a rather different kind from the preceding.

7. The Sea of Galilee is mentioned under the following names in N.T.: "Sea of Galilee," 4 ; "Sea of Tiberias," 1 ; "Sea of Galilee, which is (the sea) of Tiberias," 1 ; "Lake of Gennesaret," 1 : total **7.**

CLASS V.—WHERE THE PLURAL IS COUNTED AS EQUAL
TO TWO WORDS.

In Hurwitz's *Hebrew Tales*, under the head " The
Seven Ages," occurs the following : " Seven times in
one verse (said Rabbi Simon, the son of Eliezer) did the
author of Ecclesiastes make use of the word *vanity*, in
allusion to the seven stages of human life." And the
author adds in a foot-note, " Eccles. i. 2 [Vanity of
vanities, saith the Preacher, vanity of vanities, all is
vanity]. The word occurs twice in the plural, which
the Rabbi considered as equivalent to four, and three
times in the singular, making together *seven*." Nor is
this a mere Rabbinical conceit, as I think the following
examples will show :—

(a) *Old Testament.*

1. אֱסָר, *esar*, " a bond," 3 plural, 1 singular = **7** (all
in Num. xxx.).

2. גנה, *gannah*, " a garden," 9 pl., 3 sing. = **21.**

3. עבד, *ebed*, " servant," occurs in Eccles., 3 pl., 1
sing. = **7** ; and in Isaiah 16 pl. 24 sing. = **56.**

4. עין, *ayin*, " eye," occurs in connection with כהה,
kahah," to be dim," twice in pl. (Gen. xxvii. 1 ; 1 Sam.
iii. 2) and 3 times sing. (Deut. xxxiv. 7 ; Job. xvii. 7 ;
Zech. xi. 17) = **7.**

5. עריץ, *arits*, " terrible," 15 pl., 5 sing. = **35.**

6. ערל, *arēl*, " uncircumcised," 25 pl., 10 sing. ;
ערל, *arēl*, " to count as uncircumcised," 1 pl., 1 sing. ;
ערלה, *orlah*, " foreskin," 5 pl. (including Josh. v. 3),
11 sing. Total from root, 31 pl., 22 sing. = **84,** of
which **7** occur in Gen., **7** in Lev., and **14** in Samuel.
The form הערלים occurs **7** times.

7. פלס, *palas*, " to ponder," 1 pl., 5 sing. = **7.**

8. קן, *qēn*, " a nest," 1 pl., 12 sing. = **14.**

9. The three words שושן, *shoshan*, שושן, *shushan*,
and שושנה, *shoshannah*, all meaning " lily," occur in
Solomon's Song, 6 pl., 2 sing. = **14** ; in the titles of the
Psalms, 3 pl., 1 sing. = **7.**

10. תיש, *tayish*, " an he-goat," 3 pl., 1 sing. = **7.**

11. The phrase, " Daughter of Judah," occurs 3 times sing. and twice pl. = **7.**

12. " Virgin of Israel," 5 sing.; " virgins of Jerusalem," 1 pl. = **7.** (" Virgin " is not found joined to any other proper name, except in the phrase " virgin daughter.")

13. Coming under the same head, but of a different kind from the foregoing, are such passages as Neh. viii. 16, " Upon the *roof* of his house, and in their *courts*, and in the *courts* of the house of God, and in the *street* of the water gate, and in the *street* of the gate of Ephraim; " 2 pl. and 3 sing. = **7.** Instances of this kind are frequently met with, but the above example is noteworthy, on account of the peculiarity of the structure of the first two clauses, for it would have seemed more natural had the words " roof " and " court " been either both singular or both plural. But then the heptad would not have been made.

14. Sevens made up in this way will also be found in Ps. cxliv. 5, 6, " heavens, mountains, lightning, arrows ; " Ezek. xxxvii. 5, 6, " bones, sinews, flesh, skin, breath ; " Ezek. xxxix. 9, where the Hebrew reads, " shield, buckler, bow, arrows, handstave, spear " (" weapons " must not be taken in, as it is a general term meant to include the others, see ver. 10) ; Ezek. xxxviii. 22, " pestilence, blood, rain, hailstones, fire, brimstone ; " 2 Chron. xxix. 18 ; Ps. lxviii. 27 ; Jer. xxii. 25 ; xxvii. 19 ; xxix. 1 ; xxxi. 12 ; xxxv. 3 ; xxxvi. 12 ; xli. 16 ; 1 Kings i. 38, 44 ; Dan. v. 2, 3, 23 ; Hos. i. 7 ; ii. 19, 20 ; ii. 21, 22 ; Joel, i. 12 ; Hag. ii. 6, 7.

(b) *New Testament.*

1. *Aoratos,* " invisible," 2 pl., 3 sing. = **7.**
2. *Astron,* " a star," 3 pl., 1 sing. = **7.**
3. *Baros,* " weight," 1 pl., 5 sing. = **7.**
4. *Geōrgos,* " a husbandman," 16 pl., 3 sing. = **35.**
5. *Lepros,* " a leper," 5 pl., 4 sing. = **14.**
6. *Plateia,* " street," and *Rumē,* " street, lane " (together), 8 pl., 5 sing. = **21.**

7. Rev. viii. 5, " Voices, and thunderings, and light-nings, and an earthquake," 3 pl., 1 sing. = **7.**

CLASS VI.—WORDS WHICH HAVE TWO OR MORE MEANINGS, OR ARE USED IN DIFFERENT SENSES.

(a) Old Testament.

1. ברא *bara*, meaning " to create," 48 ; בריאה, *b'riah*, " a creation " (A.V. " a new thing "), 1 : total **49.** *Bara* occurs 6 times with other meanings.

2. גזרה *gizrah*, meaning " a separate place," **7** (all in Ezek. xli. and xlii.), besides once translated " polishing."

3. גלה *g'lah*, Aram., meaning " to reveal," **7** ; " to carry captive," 2,

4. כוס *kōs*, " a cup," used *figuratively* **21** times.

5. כן *kēn*, meaning " place, station," **7** (including Isa. xxxiii. 23), besides 10 times with other meanings.

6. מנצח *m'natstseach* (Piel participle from נצח), mean-ing " chief musician," **56** (including Hab. iii. 19, see R.V.). The verb also occurs 9 times with other meanings.

7. נזיר *nazir*, " Nazarite, separate," applied to man **14** times, to the vine twice.

8. עבד *ebed*, " servant," occurs in Isaiah, as applied to servants *of men*, **7** times (Isa. xiv. 2 ; xxiv. 2 ; xxxvi. 9, 11 ; xxxvii. 5, 24 ; xlix. 7), and to servants of God 33 times.

9 ערל *arēl*, adj., ערל, *arēl*, verb, and ערלה, *orlah*, " un-circumcised," etc., are used **14** times *figura-tively* (of the heart, lips, etc.), Exod. vi. 12, 30 ; Lev. xix. 23, 23, 23 ; xxvi. 41 ; Deut. x. 16 ; Isa. lii. 1 ; Jer. iv. 4 ; vi. 10 ; ix. 25, 26 ; Ezek. xliv. 7, 9.

10. שמר *shamar*, " to keep, preserve," occurs 12 times in the " Psalms of Degrees ; " **7** of the LORD keeping His people, and 5 otherwise.

(b) New Testament.

1. *Anatellō,* " to rise," and *anatolē,* " rising," used of the rising of the sun 7 times (*anatellō,* Matt. v. 45 ; xiii. 6 ; Mark iv. 6 ; xvi. 2 ; James i. 11 : *anatolē,* Rev. vii. 2 ; xvi. 12).

2. *Anatolē,* meaning " the east," 7 (Matt. ii. 1, 2, 9 ; viii. 11 ; xxiv. 27 ; Luke xiii. 29 ; Rev. xxi. 13).

3. *Apotithēmai,* " to put off," is used 7 times *figuratively* in the sense of putting away sin.

4. *Arnion,* " a lamb," is used 28 times of Christ in Rev.[1]

5. *Brōskō,* " to eat," 1 ; *brōsimos,* " eatable," 1 ; *brōma,* " food," 17 ; *brōsis,* meaning " food," 9 : total 28. *Brōsis* also occurs twice, meaning " rust ; " and *sētobrōtos,* " moth-eaten," and *skōlēkobrōtos,* " eaten of worms," each once.

6. *Brechō,* meaning " to rain," 5 ; *brochē,* " rain," 2 : total 7. *Brechō* is also twice translated " wash " (R.V. " wet ").

7. *Geuomai,* " to taste," occurs 7 times *literally,* with reference to food and drink, and 8 times figuratively.

8. *Duō* or *Dunō,* " to set " (of the sun), 2 ; *dusmē,* " the west " (lit. " setting [of the sun] "), 5 : total 7. Other derivatives occur, as *ekduō, enduō,* etc., but with different meanings.

9. *Koptō* occurs in the Middle voice, meaning " to lament," 6 times ; *kopetos,* " lamentation," 1 : total 7. *Kopto* also occurs twice in the Active voice, meaning " to cut."

10. *Plērōma,* " fulness," is used of God or of Christ 7 times (an incidental proof of the Deity of our Lord). The passages are John i. 16 ; Rom. xv. 29, Eph. i. 23 ; iii. 19 ; iv. 13 ; Col. i. 19 ; ii. 9.

11. *Potērion,* " cup," occurs 7 times in 1 Cor. (chs. x. xi.) with reference to the Lord's Supper, besides once in the phrase " the cup of devils."

12. *Sperma,* " seed," is used 35 times in the sense of " children, descendants," and 9 times besides.

[1] In Rev. xiii. 11 it does not refer to Christ, as is stated in Hudson's and apparently in Bruder's *Concordances.*

13. *Tupos*, "type, example," is **7** times applied to *men* (Rom. v. 14 ; Phil. iii. 17 ; 1 Thes. i. 7 ; 2 Thes. iii. 9 ; 1 Tim. iv. 12 ; Titus ii. 7 ; 1 Pet. v. 3).

14. *Tugchanō* has a variety of meanings ; it occurs with the genitive case, meaning "to obtain," **7** times.

CLASS VII.—COMPOUND HEPTADS, CONTAINING TWO OR MORE DIFFERENT HEPTADIC SERIES, EACH OF WHICH IS DESTROYED BY THE FORMATION OF THE OTHER.

This is the most peculiar and most interesting class of the seven, and I cannot perhaps better describe it than by relating how it first became known to me. I took up by chance the Greek word *Ouai*, "woe," which occurs in the N.T. 47 times, or rather, if we omit Matt. xxiii. 14, with the Revisers and other critics, 46 times, **14** of which are in Revelation. For a long time I could see no way of making this 46 into an heptadic number, when, turning again to Bruder's *Concordance*, I noticed that four of the texts were marked with an asterisk. Four from forty-six leaves **42** ! My hopes were excited, and I found that in the four places thus marked the word was used as a noun, while everywhere else it was an interjection. The four marked passages were all in Revelation (ix. 12, 12 ; xi. 14, 14). Here, then, were two entirely distinct, yet intermingled, heptadic series : (*a*) as noun and interjection the word occurred **14** times in Revelation ; (*b*) as interjection only it occurred **42** times in the whole of the N.T., including 10 in Revelation.

About the same time the familiar phrase "a land flowing with milk and honey" came under review. I found that it occurred in the Pentateuch 15 times, a number so near to **14** as at once to suggest a possible textual error. I therefore examined each of the 15 passages, but found no reason to doubt the genuineness of the phrase in any of them. Two things, however, I did find : (1) that in Num. xvi. 13 the words were applied by the rebellious Israelites to the land of Egypt, while

everywhere else they had reference to Canaan ; (2) that
in Deut. xxxi. 20 the Hebrew word for " land " is
adamah (literally " ground "), but everywhere else
erets. So that here, again, were two distinct heptadic
series : (*a*) in **14** passages out of the 15 the words
referred to the land of Canaan ; (*b*) in **14** passages (but
not the same 14) the Hebrew is " An *erets* flowing with
milk and honey," the fifteenth being " An *adamah*."
But we have not yet done with this phrase. It is found
five times in the O.T. outside the Pentateuch, or 20
times in all, the following being the various forms in
which it occurs, **7** in all :—

(1) " A land flowing with milk and honey," Exod. iii.
8, 17 ; xiii. 5 ; xxxiii. 3 ; Lev. xx. 24 ; Num. xvi. 14 ;
Deut. vi. 3 ; xi. 9 ; xxvi. 9, 15 ; xxvii. 3 ; Josh. v. 6 ;
Jer. xi. 5 ; xxxii. 22 (**14** times).

(2) " The land whither thou sentest us, and surely it
(is) flowing," etc., Num. xiii. 27.

(3) " A land which it (is) flowing," etc., Num. xiv. 8.

(4) " Out-of-a-land flowing," etc., Num. xvi. 13.

(5) " The land (*adamah*) which I sware unto their
fathers, flowing," etc., Deut. xxxi. 20.

(6) " A land which I had espied for them, flowing,"
etc., Ezek. xx. 6.

(7) " The land which I had given (them), flowing,"
etc., Ezek. xx. 15.

If No. (5) be taken away, on account of the Heb.
word for " land " being different from all the rest, then
the series of **7** phrases must be made up by dividing No.
(1) into two, as in four passages (Exod. iii. 8, 17 ;
xxxiii. 3 ; Num. xvi. 14) " land " is preceded by the
preposition " unto " (*el*). This reduces the **14** passages
in No. (1) to 10, so that again we have one heptadic
series destroyed by the formation of another. There
are **7** passages in all where *erets* " land," or *ha-arets* " the
land," is preceded by *el* " unto," viz. Exod. iii. 8, 17 ;
xxxiii. 3 ; Num. xiii. 27 ; xvi. 14 ; Ezek. xx. 6, 15.
I should, perhaps, add that while " unto a-land " is
two words in the Hebrew, " out-of-a-land " (Num. xvi.

13) is only one. By adding Sol. Song iv. 11 to the above 20 passages we have **21** where milk and honey are mentioned together.

Some other examples under this head must be given more briefly.

(a) Old Testament.

1. שנה, *shanah*, "year," occurs 16 times in Gen. xli. These may be reduced to **14** in two ways. (*a*) Two are in the singular number (vv. 46, 50), and **14** in the dual or plural (of which **7** are in the absolute state and **7** in the construct). (*b*) **14** refer to the years of famine and plenty, but of course not the same as the preceding 14, ver. 50 being literally "*year* of famine." The phrase "seven years" occurs 12 times in this chapter, of which **7** refer to the years of plenty, and 5 to the years of famine.

2. God's messages to Pharaoh were, (1) "Let my son go that he may serve me" (Exod. iv. 23) ; (2) "Let my people go that they may hold a feast unto me" (Exod. v. 1) ; then, 6 times, "Let my people go that they may serve me" (Exod. vii. 16 ; viii. 1, 20 ; ix. 1, 13 ; x. 3). Eight in all, but (*a*) **7** times saying "Let my *people* go," and (*b*) **7** times (but not the same 7), "that they [*or* he] may serve me."

3. "Skin of . . . flesh" occurs 9 times in Lev. xiii. (*a*) In **7** "skin" has the prefix "in" [בעור, *b'ōr* "in the skin of"], and (*b*) in **7**, but not the same 7, "flesh" has a pronominal suffix [בשרו, *b'sharo*, "his flesh," or בשרם, *b'sharam*, "their flesh"]. In ver. 43 neither word has either prefix or suffix, and "in" should be printed in italics in the A.V. This says much for the faithfulness of Jewish scribes, or perhaps we should rather say, for the Divine care for the integrity of the sacred text, however much appearances may tend to the contrary. The same remark will apply to many of the other examples in this class.

4. "They *or* these (are) unclean unto you" occurs 6 times ; "They-shall-be unclean unto you" (with the

verb expressed) once ; and " They (are) unclean " once.
So that (a) in 7 passages the plural adjective " unclean "
is found, followed by " unto you," and (b) in 7 the
same adjective with separate pronoun, but without a
verb. (c) 7 of the passages are in Lev. and one in
Deut. (In Lev. xi. 29, where the A.V. and R.V. have
" these," which indeed the sense requires, the Heb.
is " this.")

5. משחה, *mishchah*, " an anointing," occurs 23 times,
of which 16 are absolute, and (a) 7 construct. (b) In all
the 16 absolute and in 5 of the construct (total 21) it is
preceded by שמן, *shemen*, " oil " (" the anointing oil ").
In 7 of these, *shemen* has an inseparable particle prefixed.

6. In Deuteronomy the verb " remember " (זכר,
zakar) occurs 15 times. But (a) in ch. vii. 18 it is
doubled for emphasis (the Heb. being " Remembering
thou shalt remember "), making only 14 occasions on
which it was used. Again, (b) in ch. ix. 27 it is used in a
prayer to God, and in the other 14 in addressing the
children of Israel.

7. In 1 Kings xiii., which contains the history of the
disobedient prophet, " man of God " occurs 15 times :
(a) איש האלהים, *ish ha-Elohim*, lit. " man of the God,"
14; and איש אלהים, *ish Elohim*, " man of God," once (in
ver. 1). (b) The phrase occurs 7 times in vv. 1–8, the
narrative of the man of God and the king ; 7 times in
vv. 12–31, the story of the man of God and the old
prophet ; and once in ver. 11, which connects the two.

8. In the Books of Nehemiah and Esther the phrase
" If it please the king " occurs 9 times. (In Est. v. 4
it is translated, " If it seem good unto the king," but
the Heb. is the same.) (a) It occurs 7 times in Est.,
and twice in Neh. (b) Twice it is prefixed by " and,"
but not in the other 7 places. (c) In Esther viii. 5 ;
ix. 13, the word translated " please " is called an adjective by some authorities, and a verb in the other 7
passages, but the Heb. is the same in all the nine places.

9. נגינה, *N'ginah*, occurs (a) 7 times in the titles of

the Psalms, once in the singular (Ps. lxi., " To the chief Musician upon Neginah "), and 6 times in the plural (Pss. iv., vi., liv., lv., lxvii., lxx., " To the chief Musician on Neginoth "). (*b*) The same phrase occurs once elsewhere in the plural (Hab. iii. 19), or 7 times in all.

10. רעות, *r'ooth*, " vexation " occurs (*a*) **7** times, all in Eccles., and always as part of the phrase " vexation of spirit " (A.V.). (*b*) Six times this is part of the longer phrase " vanity and vexation of spirit," which also occurs in ch. iv. 16, where the Hebrew word for " vexation " is a different one, רעיון, *ra'yōn*.

11. " This . . . (is) vanity," occurs 15 times in Eccles. (*a*) In **14** the Heb. for " this " is זה, *zeh*, and in the other, ch. ii. 1, הוא, *hu*. (*b*) In **14** passages the phrase is " This *also* (is) vanity," *also* being omitted in ch. vi. 2. (*c*) In **7** instances it either forms a sentence in itself or ends one, being a complete sentence in ch. ii. 19 ; v. 10 ; vii. 6 ; viii. 10 ; and being preceded, but not followed, by other words in the same sentence in ch. ii. 1, 15 ; viii. 14. In other **7** instances it is followed by another phrase connected by *waw*, " and ; " these **7**, like the preceding, being again divisible into 4 and 3, as follows : In ch. ii. 26 ; iv. 4, 16 ; vi. 9 it is followed by " and vexation of spirit," and in ch. ii. 21 ; iv. 8 ; vi. 2 by other phrases. In the fifteenth passage, ch. ii. 23, it is followed by הוא, *hu*, " it," the Heb. being literally " This also vanity it." In the A.V. the word " is " here is not in italics, as in all the other **14** places, though there is no verb expressed in the Heb., but only the double pronoun. (*d*) In ch. iv. 16, " Surely this also (is) vanity and vexation of spirit," it neither begins nor ends the sentence ; in all the other **14** it does one or both.

12. " Daughters of Jerusalem " occurs (*a*) **7** times in Sol. Song. (*b*) But in ch. iii. 10 the form is different from the others (" for the daughters," etc.) ; in the other six it is a direct address, " O daughters," etc., to which add ch. iii. 11, " O daughters of Zion : " making **7**.

13. עָרֵל, *arēl*, " uncircumcised " occurs in Ezekiel 16 times. (*a*) Of these, **14** are in the singular number and 2 in the plural. (*b*) in **14** the word is used literally, and in 2 figuratively of the heart. But the two fourteens are not the same.

14. וְעַד בהמה, *v'ad b'hemah*, " and unto beast," occurs (*a*) **7** times : Exod. xi. 7 ; Jer. ix. 9 ; xxxiii. 12 ; li. 62 ; Exod. ix. 25 ; xii. 12 ; Jer. l. 3. (*b*) In the last three texts the words form part of the phrase מאדם ועד בהמה *meădam v'ad b'hemah*, " from man and unto beast," i.e. " both man and beast ; " and the almost identical phrase, מאדם עד בהמה, *meădam ad b'hemah*, " from man unto beast," identical in meaning, " both man and beast," is found 4 times : Gen. vi. 7 ; vii. 23 ; Num. iii. 13 ; Ps. cxxxv. 8, making **7** in all. (" Both man and beast " occurs also in Num. viii. 17 ; Jer. xxi. 6 : but the Heb. is different.)

(b) New Testament.

1. Antioch in Syria is mentioned by name 15 times. (*a*) The Greek word *Antiocheia*, " Antioch," occurs 13 times in Acts and once in Galatians, total **14.** (*b*) *Antiocheus*, " of Antioch," occurs once in Acts, making **14** in all in that book. (This city must be carefully distinguished from Antioch in Pisidia, which is mentioned four times.)

2. *Apeimi*, " to be absent," occurs (*a*) **7** times, and *apousia*, " absence," once, Phil. ii. 12. (*b*) In every case they are opposed to *pareimi*, " to be present," *parousia*, " presence," except in Col. ii. 5, where, however, the same idea of presence is expressed, but in different language, " with you."

3. *Theion*, and its derivative *theiōdēs*, both meaning " brimstone," occur 8 times. (*a*) Of these, **7** are in Revelation. (*b*) *Theion* alone occurs 6 times in Rev. and once in Luke, total **7.**

4. *Mē genoito* (lit. " Let it not be ") occurs 15 times, and is always translated " God forbid " in the A.V. (*a*) Of these, **14** are in St. Paul's Epistles. (*b*) The other

passage is Luke xx. 16, where, as in 13 other places (total **14**), they form a complete phrase. This is not the case in Gal. vi. 14, where the R.V. translates " Far be it from . . ."

5. *Hupakoē*, " obedience," occurs **7** times in Romans, **8** elsewhere, **15** in all. (a) *Hupakouō*, meaning " to obey," occurs **20** times. Total **35**. (b) *Hupakouō* also occurs in Acts xii. 13, where it means " to answer," making **21** occurrences of the word in all.

SUPPLEMENTARY CLASS—OLD AND NEW TESTAMENTS
COMBINED.

The seven classes already given might seem to have exhausted our subject, and indeed I believe they do ; but the examples hitherto given still leave something wanting. They prove, to my mind incontestably, that the Bible is the work of God, and that the Old Testament and the New proceed from the same Divine Source ; but they do not show that the two Testaments together form one complete Revelation, that they are parts of one homogeneous whole. And if this be the truth, as Christians hold it to be, we may expect that · it shall have some support in the heptadic occurrence of some words, phrases, etc., in the Old and New Testaments combined. And our expectations will not be disappointed, as the following examples will, I trust, sufficiently show. I would remark, however, that we must not look for a very large number of instances of this kind. For the Old and New Testaments, viewed in their literary aspect—and that is the only light in which we have to look at them at present—are entirely different from one another. The Old Testament is written (chiefly) in Hebrew, the New in Greek,—two languages radically and essentially different in genius, structure, and characteristics. The one language is Eastern, the other Western ; the one highly idiomatic, the other not more so than our own. In fact, the difference between Hebrew and Greek, which were both living languages together, is far greater than between the

Greek of two thousand years ago and the English of to-day.

1. *Hallelujah* ("Praise ye the LORD") occurs, as will be shown more fully in the next chapter, in 7 Psalms once each, in other 7 twice each, and in another three times, or 24 times in all in the O.T. It also occurs 4 times in the N.T., all in Rev., making a total of **28.**

2. קרבן, *qorban*, "an offering," 80 ; קרבן, *qurban*, the same, 2 : total 82 in the O.T. In the N.T. the same word *korban* occurs once, and *korbanas*, "the sacred treasury where offerings were received," once. This makes **84** in all.

3. אוי, pron. *oee*, "woe, alas," 24 in O.T. *Ouai*, same meaning, 46 in N.T. (excluding Matt. xxiii. 14, where it has no authority; see R.V.). Total **70.**

4. The Heb. for "milk" is חלב, *chalab :* the Greek *gala :* both evidently the same word, especially if the Hebrew be pronounced, as it perhaps should be, *ghalav.* The former occurs 44 times in the O.T. ; the latter 5 in the N.T. : total **49.**

5. The Heb. for "shepherd" is רעה, *roeh* (participle of רעה, "to feed"), and the Greek *poimēn.* The former is applied to God or Christ 12 times in the O.T., and the latter 9 times in the New ; total **21.** The following are the passages : Gen. xlix. 24 ; Ps xxiii. 1 ; lxxx. 1 ; Isa. xl. 11 ; Jer xxxi. 10 ; Ezek. xxxiv. 12, 23, 23 ; xxxvii. 24 ; Zech. xi. 16 ; xiii. 7, 7.—Matt. xxvi. 31 ; Mark xiv. 27 ; John x. 11, 11, 14, 16 ; Heb. xiii. 20 ; 1 Pet. ii. 25 ; v. 4. In Isa. lxiii. 11, the word refers to Moses, and in John x. 2, not to Christ specially, but to any true teacher. Matt. xxv. 32 is simply a similitude.

6. "Hosanna" occurs 6 times in N.T., being quoted from Ps. cxviii. 25 ; total **7.**

7. שטן, *satan*, "to be an adversary," 6 ; שטן, *satan*, "an adversary," without the article, 10, and with the article, "the adversary," i.e. Satan, 17, of which **14** are in Job ; שטנה, *sitnah*, "an accusation," 1 : total from root, **34.** In the N.T., Σατᾶν, *Satan*, occurs in

this the Heb. form once only (2 Cor. xii. 7), giving a total of **35**. (The Grecised form, *Satanas*, also occurs in the N.T. **35** times, if we exclude, with the Revisers and other editors, Luke iv. 8.)

8. "Sharon," the maritime plain south of Mount Carmel, is mentioned 5 times in the O.T., always with the article (1 Chron. xxvii. 29 ; Sol. Song ii. 1 ; Isa. xxxiii. 9 ; xxxv. 2 ; lxv. 10 ;) and once in the N.T. (Acts ix. 35). "Sharonite," i.e. inhabitant of Sharon, is found once (1 Chron. xxvii. 29), giving a total of **7**. (The Sharon mentioned in 1 Chron. v. 16, was east of Jordan, and the suggestion that Lassharon—so spelt in R.V., Josh. xii. 18—is the same as Sharon does not find favour with critics.)

9. "Man."—5 Heb. and 2 Greek words have this meaning, total **7**. (1) אדם, *adam ;* (2) איש, *ish ;* (3) אנוש, *enōsh ;* (4) גבר, *geber ;* (5) מתים, *m'thim* (plural only) ; (6) *anthrōpos* (Gr.) ; (7) *anēr* (Gr.). The Aram. terms having this meaning are identical with Nos. (3) and (4).

10. "Joshua " is the name of 4 persons mentioned in the O.T. : (1) the successor of Moses ; (2) a High Priest (Hag. i. 1) ; (3) a Bethshemite (1 Sam. vi. 14, 18) ; (4) a governor in Jerusalem (2 Kings xxiii. 8). The Greek form of the word, " Jesus," is the name of 3 persons mentioned in the N.T. (besides number (1) above) : (5) our Saviour ; (6) one of His ancestors (Luke iii. 29, R.V.) ; (7) Jesus surnamed Justus (Col. iv. 11). There are three or four persons named " Jeshua " mentioned in the O.T., (besides Nos. (1) and (2) above, who are also sometimes so called).

11. אבדון, *Abaddon,* " Destruction," occurs six times in the O.T., and once in the N.T. (Job xxvi. 6 ; xxviii. 22 ; xxxi. 12 ; Ps. lxxxviii. 11 ; Prov. xv. 11 ; xxvii. 20 ; Rev. ix. 11). See these passages in the R.V., where the Heb. word is always given as a proper name, either in the text or margin.

12. "The LORD of Hosts," " the God of Hosts," " the Lord GOD of Hosts," and " the LORD God of Hosts,"

occur, together, 285 times in the O.T., including 2
Kings xix. 31, where see R.V. marg. "The Lord of
Sabaoth" (Heb. word for "Hosts") is found twice in
the N.T. Total **287.**

13. The "Daughters of Jerusalem" are directly
addressed 6 times in the O.T. (see Class VII. *a.* 12),
and once in the N.T. (Luke xxiii. 28); total **7.**

14. "Tree of Life" occurs 3 times in Gen., 4 in
Prov., and 4 in Rev., including ch. xxii. 19 (see R.V.).
But the 4 in Prov. are obviously figurative, while in
the other **7** the phrase is used as of a literal tree.

15. "Uncircumcision of the heart" is spoken of 6
times in the O.T., and once in the New: (Lev. xxvi.
41; Deut. x. 16; Jer. iv. 4; ix. 26; Ezek. xliv. 7, 9;
Acts vii. 51): total **7.**

16. "Three and a half years." This well-known
prophetic period is mentioned **7** times in the Old and
New Testaments together, in five different forms and
in three different languages: Aram., "Time and times
and the dividing of time" (Dan. vii. 25); Heb.,
"Time, times and an half" (Dan. xii. 7); Greek,
"Time and times and half a time" (Rev. xii. 14);
"Forty and two months" (Rev. xi. 2; xiii. 5);
"Twelve hundred and sixty days" (Rev. xi. 3;
xii. 6).

17. Christ is spoken of as being, or to be, at the right
hand of God twice in the O.T. (Ps. cx. 1, 5) and 19
times in the N.T. (ἐν δεξιᾷ, 8, and ἐκ δεξιῶν, 11);
total **21.** In the N.T. τῇ δεξιᾷ also occurs twice (Acts
ii. 33; v. 31); and is translated in the R.V. "*by*"
and "*with* the right hand of God exalted," with
margin "*at.*"

18. "After the order of Melchizedek" occurs once
in the O.T., and six times in the N.T.; total **7.**

19. "The stone which the builders refused is become
the head of the corner," occurs once in the O.T. (Ps.
cxviii. 22), and is quoted six times in the N.T. (Matt.
xxi. 42; Mark xii. 10; Luke xx. 17; Acts iv. 11

¹ Ps. xvi. 8 has not this meaning.

I Pet. ii. 4, 7). Eph. ii. 20 does not refer to this text, but to Isa. xxviii. 16.

20. "Which (if) a man do, he shall live in them." These words occur 5 times in the O.T. (Lev. xviii. 5 ; Neh. ix. 29 ; Ezek. xx. 11, 13, 21) ; and are quoted twice in the New (Rom. x. 5 ; Gal. iii. 12) : total **7.** The Heb. and Greek are much nearer than would appear from the A.V.

21. "Thou shalt love thy neighbour as thyself" occurs once in the O.T. (Lev. xix. 18), and is fully quoted six times in the New (Matt. xix. 29 ; xxii. 39 ; Mark xii. 31 ; Rom. xiii. 9 ; Gal. v. 14 ; James ii. 8) : total **7.** It is also partly quoted in Matt. v. 43 ; Luke x. 27.

22. Palestine is called by **7** different names in Scripture : 2 in O.T. only, (1) " the Holy Land," Zech. ii. 12 ; (2) "the LORD's Land," Hos. ix. 3 : 2 in N.T. only, (3) "the Land of Promise," Heb. xi. 9 ; (4) " Judea," Luke i. 5 ; xxiii. 5 ; Matt. xix. 1 ; Acts xxviii. 21 : and 3 in both Old and New Tests., (5) " the Land," Ruth i. 1 ; Luke iv. 25 ; (6) " the Land of Israel," 1 Sam. xiii. 19 ; Matt. ii. 21 ; (7) " Canaan," Ps. cv. 11 ; Acts vii. 11 ; xiii. 19. (Kitto's *Bib. Cyc.* iii. 386, 387.) *Palestine* and *Palestina,* which occur 4 times in the A.V., refer only to Philistia, which the same Heb. word is elsewhere translated.

These examples do not constitute an eighth class, for it will be seen that the whole of them might have been included in one or other of the preceding seven classes. It seemed desirable, however, to place them together, on account of the important truth which they teach.

To bring my remarks in this chapter to a close, it would seem probable that almost every word found in the original text of Holy Scripture is capable of being placed in one or other of the foregoing seven classes. Difficulties there may be, and difficulties I admit there are, with regard to some words, especially in the present state of the text, but none, I believe, which will not yield in time to diligent study and prayerful research.

I have said *almost* every word, for I think this qualification must be made. For as all Scripture is not divided into heptads, but some sections contain ten, some five, divisions, etc., so it appears to be here. Ten especially is a number which should never be ignored in the study of Scripture, and I give therefore just a few instances where it, and not *seven*, governs the occurrence of words and phrases.

(a) Old Testament.

1. זר, *zēr*, " the crown " (of the ark of the covenant), 10.

2. כיור, *kiyor*, " laver," 10 in Exod. and Lev. (with reference to the laver in the tabernacle), and 10 in Kings and Chron. (with reference to the lavers in the temple).[1]

3. כן, *kēn*, A.V. " foot, base " (of the laver), 10.

4. על כל, *al col*, " upon all," 10 in Isa. ii. 12–16.

5. " And God said," 10 in Gen. i.

6. Hag. i. 11, " Upon the land, and upon the mountains, and upon the corn, and upon the new wine, and upon the oil, and upon that which the ground bringeth forth, and upon man, and upon beast, and upon all the labour of the hands ; " 8 singulars and 1 plural : = 10.

(b) New Testament.

1. *Pantokratōr*, " Almighty," 10.

2. *Katabolē kosmou*, " the foundation of the world," 10.

3. *Legei Kurios*, " Saith the Lord," as a complete phrase, 10 (Acts vii. 49 ; Rom. xii. 19 ; xiv. 14 ; 1 Cor. xiv. 21 ; 2 Cor. vi. 17 ; Heb. viii. 8, 9, 10 ; x. 16 ; Rev. i. 8. The R.V. omits it in Heb. x. 30).

(c) Old and New Testaments.

1. Twelve tribes, O.T. 5 ; N.T. 5 = 10.

[1] After Num. iv. 14, however, the Samaritan and Septuagint add a clause containing the word, which, if genuine, would make the total 21.

CHAPTER II

HEPTADIC DIVISION—FURTHER EXAMPLES

IT is here proposed to give a few chapters from the Old and New Testaments showing the heptadic or other divisions. They are selected in order to illustrate the different methods of division, the common text and the translation of the A.V. being generally followed, except that (as in Part I) in the O.T. *waw conversive* of the Heb. is always shown by " AND " in small capitals, and in the N.T. *καί* is shown in the same way by " AND " and *δέ* by " and " in ordinary type. No attempt is made to revise the original text, except in Luke xxii., unless it is needed to show the divisions more clearly. It is of the first importance that the correct sections and divisions be marked out before the revision of the text is attempted.

In *Seven the Sacred Number* one or more chapters from each book of the Bible were given in order to show that the heptadic arrangement was found throughout the whole of Scripture, but that is not necessary here.

We commence with Exodus xl., a rather long chapter, but one of the easiest to divide in the whole of Scripture.

EXODUS XL.—PART I. FIVE HEPTADS.

1, 2 (*1*) AND the Lord spake unto Moses, saying, On the first day of the first month shalt thou set up the tabernacle of the
3 tent of the congregation. (*2*) AND thou shalt put therein the ark of the testimony, (*3*) AND cover [i.e. "AND thou shalt cover : "
4 so throughout] the ark with the vail. (*4*) AND thou shalt bring in the table, (*5*) AND set in order the things that are to be set in

order upon it ; (*6*) AND thou shalt bring in the candlestick, (*7*) AND thou shalt light the lamps thereof. '

5   (*1*) AND thou shalt set the altar of gold for the incense before the ark of the testimony, (*2*) AND put the hanging of the door
6 to the tabernacle. (*3*) AND thou shalt set the altar of the burnt offering before the door of the tabernacle of the tent of the con-
7 gregation. (*4*) AND thou shalt set the laver between the tent of the congregation and the altar, (*5*) AND shalt put water
8 therein. (*6*) AND thou shalt set up the court round about, (*7*) AND hang up the hanging at the court gate.
9   (*1*) AND thou shalt take the anointing oil, (*2*) AND anoint the tabernacle, and all that is therein, (*3*) AND shalt sanctify it, and
10 all the vessels thereof : (*4*) AND it shall be holy. (*5*) AND thou shalt anoint the altar of the burnt offering, and all his vessels, (*6*) AND sanctify the altar : (*7*) AND it shall be an altar most holy.
11   (*1*) AND thou shalt anoint the laver and his foot, (*2*) AND
12 sanctify it. (*3*) AND thou shalt bring Aaron and his sons unto the door of the tabernacle of the congregation, (*4*) AND wash
13 them with water. (*5*) AND thou shalt put upon Aaron the holy garments, (*6*) AND anoint him ; . . . (*7*) AND he shall minister unto me in the priest's office.
14   (*1*) And-his-sons thou shalt bring, (*2*) AND thou shalt clothe
15 them with coats : (*3*) AND thou shalt anoint them, as thou didst anoint their father, (*4*) AND they shall minister unto me in the priest's office : (*5*) AND their anointing shall surely be an
16 everlasting priesthood throughout their generations. (*6*) AND Moses did according to all that the LORD commanded him, so
17 did he. (*7*) AND it was in the first month in the second year, on the first day of the month, that the tabernacle was reared up.

PART II.—FIVE HEPTADS.

18   (*1*) AND Moses reared up the tabernacle, (*2*) AND fastened his sockets, (*3*) AND set up the boards thereof, (*4*) AND put in
19 the bars thereof, (*5*) AND reared up his pillars, (*6*) AND spread abroad the tent over the tabernacle, (*7*) AND put the covering of the tent above upon it ; as the LORD commanded Moses.
20   (*1*) AND he took (*2*) AND put the testimony into the ark, (*3*) AND set the staves on the ark, (*4*) AND put the mercy seat above
21 upon the ark : (*5*) AND he brought the ark into the tabernacle, (*6*) AND set up the vail of the covering, (*7*) AND covered the ark of the testimony ; as the LORD commanded Moses.
22   (*1*) AND he put the table in the tent of the congregation, upon the side of the tabernacle northward, without the vail.
23 (*2*) AND he set the bread in order upon it before the LORD ; as
24 the LORD commanded Moses. (*3*) AND he put the candlestick in the tent of the congregation, over against the table, on the

25 side of the tabernacle southward. (*4*) AND he lighted the lamps
26 before the LORD ; as the LORD commanded Moses. (*5*) AND
he put the golden altar in the tent of the congregation before the
27 vail : (*6*) AND he burnt sweet incense thereon ; as the LORD
28 commanded Moses. (*7*) AND he set up the hanging at the door
of the tabernacle.

29 (*1*) And-the-altar of burnt offering he put by the door of the
tabernacle of the tent of the congregation, (*2*) AND he offered
upon it the burnt offering and the meat offering ; as the LORD
30 commanded Moses. (*3*) AND he set the laver between the tent
of the congregation and the altar. (*4*) AND he put water there,
31 to wash withal, and Moses and Aaron and his sons washed their
32 hands and their feet thereat : when they went into the tent of
the congregation, and when they came near unto the altar, they
33 washed ; as the LORD commanded Moses. (*5*) AND he reared up
the court round about the tabernacle and the altar, (*6*) AND set
up the hanging of the court gate. (*7*) AND Moses finished the
work.

34 (*1*) AND a cloud covered the tent of the congregation, (*2*)
35 and-the-glory of the LORD filled the tabernacle. (*3*) And Moses
was not able to enter into the tent of the congregation, because
the cloud abode thereon, (*4*) and-the-glory of the LORD filled the
36 tabernacle. (*5*) And-when the cloud was taken up from over
the tabernacle, the children of Israel went onward in all their
37 journeys. (*6*) And-if the cloud were not taken up, and they
38 journeyed not till the day that it was taken up, for the cloud of
the LORD was upon the tabernacle by day, (*7*) and-fire was on it
by night, in the sight of all the house of Israel, throughout all
their journeys.

A few remarks are necessary upon this chapter. It
is divided, it will be seen, into two parts, each containing five heptads : the first part giving the instructions
for the setting up of the tabernacle, etc., with a brief
note of its erection ; the second showing in detail how
the instructions were carried out, and relating how the
Lord came down and took possession of His " dwelling-
place." The dwelling-place, or tabernacle, was now
completed, and ready for its appointed use, and *ten*,
the number of completeness, is accordingly used to
denote the fact.

In ver. 13 the words " and sanctify him " are omitted,
as the heptad is complete without them. There is the
authority of two of Kennicott's MSS for the omission,

and they are probably an interpolation from vv. 9,
10, and 11. It will be noticed that Aaron's *sons* are
not said to be sanctified, ver. 15.

The phrase " as the LORD commanded Moses " occurs
7 times in the second part of the chapter. The A.V.
reads " *had* commanded " in ver. 23, but the original
is the same as in the other six places.

Up to ver. 33, where Moses and the people's part is
" finished," all the *waws* at the commencement of
the divisions are conversive except two, and they are
both at the beginning of heptads (vv. 14, 29), which is
not unusual.

From ver. 34 to the end of the chapter, which records
the Lord's approval of the work by sending the cloud,
the position is reversed ; the first *waw* is conversive
and the others simple, but each division contains a
complete sentence commencing with *waw*.

The 37th verse exhibits the peculiar structure
already met with in ch. xx. 25.

But we must not leave the Book of Exodus without
noticing a peculiarity found in the later chapters,
which is, probably, not to be met with elsewhere in
Scripture. In chapters xxv.–xxxi. we have the instructions given by God to Moses concerning the making of
the tabernacle, and matters connected therewith ;
which chapters contain apparently about 49 heptads,
though the division is not free from difficulty, and therefore the following should not be taken as patterns.[1]
In chapters xxxv.–xxxix., along with Lev. viii. and
Num. xxviii. 1–8, we have recorded in detail the carrying out of those instructions, and here most of the
sections appear to be not heptads but decads. This is,
of course, quite in accordance with the meaning we
have elsewhere found to be connected with the number
ten, as denoting completeness, or signifying the completion of anything.

[1] The position is complicated by the fact that the arrangement
of chh. xxxv.–xl. in the Sept. differs widely from the Heb. See
Swete, *Introd. to O.T. in Gk.*, 231–236.

For the first example we will take—

EXOD. XXVII. 9–17.

9 (*1*) AND thou shalt make the court of the tabernacle : for the south side southward hangings for the court of fine twined linen of an hundred cubits long for one

10 side : and the twenty pillars thereof and their twenty sockets of brass ; the hooks of the pillars and their fillets of silver.

11 (*2*) And likewise for the north side in length (there shall be) hangings of an hundred cubits long, and his twenty pillars and their twenty sockets of brass ; the hooks of the pillars and their fillets of silver.

12 (*3*) And for the breadth of the court on the west side (shall be) hangings of fifty cubits ; their pillars ten, and their sockets ten.

13 (*4*) And the breadth of the court on the east side eastward (shall be) fifty cubits.

14 (*5*) And [1] the hangings of one side (of the gate shall be) fifteen cubits ; their pillars three, and their sockets three.

15 (*6*) And on the other side (shall be) hangings fifteen cubits ; their pillars three, and their sockets three.

EXOD. XXXVIII. 9–20.

9 (*1*) AND he made the court : on the south side southward the hangings of the court of fine twined linen, an hundred cubits :

10 their pillars twenty and their brasen sockets twenty ; the hooks of the pillars and their fillets of silver.

11 (*2*) And for the north side (the hangings were) an hundred cubits, their pillars twenty, and their sockets of brass twenty ; the hooks of the pillars and their fillets of silver.

12 (*3*) And for the west side (were) hangings of fifty cubits, their pillars ten, and their sockets ten ; the hooks of the pillars and their fillets of silver.

13 (*4*) And for the east side eastward (they were) fifty cubits.

14 The hangings of the one side (of the gate were) fifteen cubits ; their pillars three, and their sockets three.

15 (*5*) And for the other side of the court gate, on this hand and that hand, (were) hangings of fifteen cubits ; their pillars three,

16 and their sockets three. All the hangings of the court round about (were) of fine twined linen.

---

[1] So in the Heb.

EXOD. XXVII. (contd.)
[See ver. 17.]

[See ver. 17.]

16 (7) And for the gate of the court (shall be) an hanging of twenty cubits, of blue, and purple, and scarlet, and fine twined linen, wrought with needlework;

their pillars four, and their 17 sockets four. All the pillars round about the court (shall be) filleted with silver; their hooks (shall be) of silver, and their sockets of brass.

EXOD. XXXVIII. (contd.)

17 (6) And the sockets for the pillars (were). of brass; the hooks of the pillars and their fillets of silver, and the overlaying of their chapiters of silver;

(7) And all the pillars of the court (were) filleted with silver.

18 (8) And the hanging for the gate of the court (was) needlework, of blue, and purple, and scarlet, and fine twined linen : and [1] twenty cubits the length, and the height in the breadth five cubits, answerable to the hangings of the court.

19 (9) And their pillars (were) four, and their sockets of brass four; their hooks of silver, and the overlaying of their chapiters and their fillets of silver.

20 (10) And all the pins of the tabernacle, and of the court round about, (were of) brass.

In the one passage *waw*, " and," occurs **21** times (3 × 7) in the common Hebrew text, and in the other 30 (3 × 10). It is noteworthy, also, how the word " and " is omitted in some places (as in ch. xxvii. 16, 17 ; xxxviii. 14, 16) so that the sections may not contain too many divisions.

In the foregoing example we have one heptad corresponding to one decad, but this is not usually the case, as will be seen from the following comparison of the parallel parts of chs. xxviii. and xxxix.

[1] " And " is omitted here in one MS and in the Sept.

EXOD. XXVIII.

1 (*1*) And take thou unto thee Aaron thy brother, and his sons with him, from among the children of Israel, that he may minister unto me in the priest's office, even Aaron, Nadab and Abihu, Eleazar and Ithamar, Aaron's sons.

2 (*2*) AND thou shalt make holy garments for Aaron thy brother for glory and for beauty.

3 (*3*) And thou shalt speak unto all that are wise hearted, whom I have filled with the spirit of wisdom.

(*4*) AND they shall make Aaron's garments to consecrate him, that he may minister unto me in the priest's office.

4 (*5*) And these (are) the garments which they shall make : a breastplate, and an ephod, and a robe, and a broidered coat [and[1]] a mitre, and a girdle.

(*6*) AND they shall make holy garments for Aaron thy brother, and his sons, that he may minister unto me in the priest's office.

5 (*7*) And they shall take gold, and blue, and purple, and scarlet, and fine linen.

[21 *waws* in above heptad, including the doubtful one.]

6 (*1*) AND they shall make the ephod of gold, blue, and purple, [and[2]] scarlet, and fine twined linen, with cun-

EXOD. XXXIX. 1–31.

[The first part of ver. 1 belongs to the preceding chapter.]

1 (*1*) AND they made the holy garments for Aaron ; as the LORD commanded Moses.

2 (*2*) AND he made the ephod of gold, blue, and purple, and scarlet, and fine twined linen.

---

[1] So some MSS and Sept.

[2] So many MSS and all the ancient versions.

Exod. xxviii. (contd.)

7 ning work. It shall have the two shoulderpieces thereof joined at the two edges thereof ;

(2) AND it shall be joined together.

8 (3) And the curious girdle of the ephod, which is upon it, shall be of the same, according to the work thereof ; of gold, blue, and purple, and scarlet, and fine twined linen.

9 (4) AND thou shalt take two onyx stones.

(5) AND thou shalt grave on them the names of the
10 children of Israel : six of their names on one stone, and the other six names of the rest on the other stone, according to their birth.
11 With the work of an engraver in stone, like the engravings of a signet, shalt thou engrave the two stones with the names of the children of Israel : thou shalt make them to be set in ouches of gold.
12 (6) AND thou shalt put the two stones upon the shoulders of the ephod for stones of memorial unto the children of Israel.

(7) AND Aaron shall bear their names before the LORD upon his two shoulders for a memorial.

[14 *waws* in above heptad, including the doubtful one].

Exod. xxxix. (contd.)

3 (3) AND they drew out [lit. " expanded "] the plates of gold . . . (into) wires, to work in the blue, and in the purple, and in the scarlet, and in the fine linen, with
4 cunning work. They made shoulderpieces for it, to couple it together : by the two edges was it coupled together.
5 (4) And the curious girdle of his ephod, that was upon it (was) of the same, according to the work thereof ; of gold, blue, and purple, and scarlet, and fine twined linen ; as the LORD commanded Moses.
6 (5) AND they wrought onyx stones inclosed in ouches of gold, graven, as signets are graven, with the names of the children of Israel.

7 (6) AND he put them on the shoulders of the ephod for stones of memorial unto the children of Israel ; as the LORD commanded Moses.

EXOD. XXVIII. (contd.)

13 (*1*) AND thou shalt make ouches of gold.

14 (*2*) And two chains of pure gold at the ends of wreathen work shalt thou make [them[1]].

(*3*) AND thou shalt fasten the wreathen chains to the ouches.

15 (*4*) AND thou shalt make the breastplate of judgment with cunning work; after the work of the ephod thou shalt make it; of gold, blue, and purple, and scarlet, and fine twined linen,

16 shalt thou make it. Foursquare it shall be being doubled; a span (shall be) the length thereof, and a span the breadth thereof.

17 (*5*) AND thou shalt set in it settings of stones, four rows of stones: a row of sardius, topaz, and carbuncle (shall be) the first

18 row; and the second row an emerald, a sapphire, and

19 a diamond, and the third row a ligure, an agate, and an

20 amethyst; and the fourth row a beryl, and an onyx, and a jasper: they shall be inclosed in gold in their settings.

21 (*6*) And the stones shall be with the names of the children of Israel, twelve, according to their names, like the engravings of a signet; every one with his name shall they be according to the twelve tribes.

EXOD. XXXIX. (contd.)
[See ver. 16.]

8 (*7*) AND he made the breastplate of cunning work, like the work of the ephod; of gold, blue, and purple, and scarlet, and fine twined

9 linen. It was foursquare; they made the breastplate double: a span (was) the length thereof, and a span the breadth thereof, being doubled.

10 (*8*) AND they set in it four rows of stones: a row of sardius, topaz, and carbuncle (was) the first row; and

11 the second row an emerald, a sapphire, and a diamond;

12 and the third row a ligure, an agate, and an amethyst;

13 and the fourth row a beryl, an onyx, and a jasper: (they were) inclosed in ouches of gold in their settings.

14 (*9*) And the stones (were) according to the names of the children of Israel, twelve, according to their names, like the engravings of a signet, every one with his name, according to the twelve tribes.

---

[1] Omitted by the Sept.

Exod. xxviii. (contd.)

22 (7) AND thou shalt make upon the breastplate chains at the ends of wreathen work of pure gold.

[See ver. 13.]

23 (1) AND thou shalt make upon the breastplate two rings of gold.

(2) AND thou shalt put the two rings on the two ends of the breastplate.

24 (3) AND thou shalt put the two wreathen chains of gold in the two rings on the ends of the breastplate.

25 (4) And the two ends of the two wreathen chains thou shalt fasten in the two ouches;

(5) AND thou shalt put them on the shoulderpieces of the ephod before it.

26 (6) AND thou shalt make two rings of gold ;

(7) AND thou shalt put them upon the two ends of the breastplate, in the border thereof, which is in the side of the ephod inward.

27 (1) AND two (other) rings of gold thou shalt make ;

(2) AND thou shalt put them on the two sides of the ephod underneath, toward the forepart thereof, over against the (other) coupling thereof, above the curious girdle of the ephod.

28 (3) And they shall bind the breastplate by the rings thereof unto the rings of the ephod with a lace of blue, that it may be above the curious girdle of the ephod, and that the breastplate be not loosed from the ephod.

Exod. xxxix. (contd.)

15 (10) AND they made upon the breastplate chains at the ends of wreathen work of pure gold.

16 (1) AND they made two ouches of gold, and two gold rings.

(2) AND they put the two rings on the two ends of the breastplate.

17 (3) AND they put the two wreathen chains of gold in the two rings on the ends of the breastplate.

18 (4) And the two ends of the two wreathen chains they fastened in the two ouches ;

(5) AND they put them on the shoulder pieces of the ephod before it.

19 (6) AND they made two rings of gold ;

(7) AND they put them on the two ends of the breastplate, upon the border of it, which was on the side of the ephod inward.

20 (8) AND they made two (other) golden rings ;

(9) AND they put them on the two sides of the ephod underneath, toward the forepart of it, over against the (other) coupling thereof, above the curious girdle of the ephod.

21 (10) AND they did bind the breastplate by his rings unto the rings of the ephod with a lace of blue, that it might be above the curious girdle of the ephod, and that the breastplate might not be loosed from the ephod ; as the Lord commanded Moses.

EXOD. XXVIII. (contd.)

29 (*4*) AND Aaron shall bear the names of the children of Israel in the breastplate of judgment upon his heart, when he goeth in unto the holy place, for a memorial before the LORD continually.

30 (*5*) AND thou shalt put in the breastplate of judgment the Urim and the Thummim ;

(*6*) AND they shall be upon Aaron's heart, when he goeth in before the LORD :

(*7*) AND Aaron shall bear the judgment of the children of Israel upon his heart before the LORD continually.

---

31 (*1*) AND thou shalt make the robe of the ephod all of blue.

32 (*2*) AND there shall be an hole in the top of it, in the midst thereof : it shall have a binding of woven work round about the hole of it, as it were the hole of an habergeon, that it be not rent.

33 (*3*) AND upon the hem of it thou shalt make pomegranates of blue, and purple, and scarlet, round about the hem thereof ;

(*4*) And (there shall be) bells of gold between them

34 round about : a golden bell and a pomegranate, a golden bell and a pomegranate, upon the hem of the robe round about.

35 (*5*) AND it shall be upon Aaron to minister :

EXOD. XXXIX. (contd.)

22 (*1*) AND he made the robe of the ephod of woven work, all of blue.

23 (*2*) And (there was) an hole in the midst of the robe as the hole of an habergeon, with a band round about the hole, that it should not rend.

24 (*3*) AND they made upon the hem of the robe pomegranates of blue, and purple, and scarlet, and twined linen.

25 (*4*) AND they made bells of pure gold ;

(*5*) AND they put the bells between the pomegranates upon the hem of the robe, round about between the

26 pomegranates ; a bell and a pomegranate, a bell and a pomegranate, round about the hem of the robe to minister (in) ; as the LORD commanded Moses.

EXOD. XXVIII. (contd.)

(6) AND his sound shall be heard when he goeth in unto the holy place before the LORD, and when he cometh out ;

(7) And he shall not die.

36   (1) AND thou shalt make a plate of pure gold ;

(2) AND thou shalt grave upon it, like the engravings of a signet, HOLINESS TO THE LORD.

37   (3) AND thou shalt put it on a blue lace ;

(4) AND it shall be upon the mitre ; upon the forefront of the mitre it shall be.

38   (5) AND it shall be upon Aaron's forehead ;

(6) AND Aaron shall bear the iniquity of the holy things, which the children of Israel shall hallow in all their holy gifts ;

(7) AND it shall be always upon his forehead, that they may be accepted before the LORD.

[7 *waws* in above heptad, all conversive.]

39   (1) AND thou shalt embroider the coat of fine linen.

(2) AND thou shalt make the mitre of fine linen.

(3) And thou shalt make the girdle of needlework.

40   (4) And for Aaron's sons thou shalt make coats ;

(5) AND thou shalt make for them girdles ;

(6) And bonnets shalt thou make for them, for glory and for beauty.

41   (7) AND thou shalt put them upon Aaron thy brother and his sons with him.

EXOD. XXXIX. (contd.)

[See vv. 30, 31.]

27   (6) AND they made coats of fine linen of woven work for Aaron, and for his sons :

28   (7) And a mitre of fine linen, and goodly bonnets of fine linen, and linen breeches

29 of fine twined linen, and a girdle of fine twined linen, and blue, and purple, and scarlet, of needlework ; as the LORD commanded Moses.

[7 *waws* in this division.]

EXOD. XXVIII. (contd.)

(*1*) AND thou shalt anoint them ;

(*2*) AND thou shalt consecrate them ;

(*3*) AND thou shalt sanctify them ;

(*4*) AND they shall minister unto me in the priest's office.

42 (*5*) And make them linen breeches to cover their nakedness ; from the loins even (*waw*) unto the thighs they shall reach :

43 (*6*) AND they shall be upon Aaron, and upon his sons, when they come in unto the tabernacle of the congregation, or when they come near unto the altar to minister in the holy place ;

(*7*) And they shall not bear iniquity, AND die ; it shall be a statute for ever unto him and his seed after him.

[See vv. 36, 37.]

EXOD. XXXIX. (contd.)

30 (*8*) AND they made the plate of the holy crown of pure gold ;

(*9*) AND they wrote upon it a writing, like the engravings of a signet, HOLINESS TO THE LORD.

31 (*10*) AND they tied unto it a lace of blue, to fasten it on high upon the mitre ; as the LORD commanded Moses.

Here, then, we have three decads corresponding to nine heptads, one decad being parallel with three, two, and four heptads respectively. A comparison of the two chapters affords many illustrations of the inconsistency of King James's translators, especially in the matter of words printed in italics, and such words are omitted, above, in the one chapter where they are not

found in the parallel place in the other.   In ch. xxxix.
3 an alteration in the text appears to be called for.   The
A.V. reads, "And they did beat the gold into thin
plates, and cut (it into) wires."   This, however, is
hardly a correct rendering of the Heb., which reads,
"AND-they-expanded [which might be either by beat-
ing or drawing out, the context must determine] the-
plates-of gold, and-*he*-cut wires."   But this would give
eleven divisions in the decad, and it is therefore probable that the word rendered "and-he-cut" is an
interpolation, which is practically confirmed by the
Septuagint.

It is worthy of note that in Exod. xxv.-xl. there are 7 lists of the
articles in the Tabernacle, in greater or less detail.   Leaving out
the smaller vessels there were 7 principal objects in the Tabernacle
and its court : (*1*) Ark, (*2*) Mercy seat (always spoken of as a separate thing from the Ark), (*3*) Altar of Incense, (*4*) Candlestick, (*5*)
Table of Shewbread, (*6*) Altar of Burnt-Offering, (*7*) Laver.

EZRA I.

1   (*1*) And in the first year of Cyrus king of Persia, that the
word of the LORD by the mouth of Jeremiah might be fulfilled,
the LORD stirred up the spirit of Cyrus king of Persia, (*2*) AND
he made a proclamation throughout all his kingdom, and also in
2 writing, saying, Thus saith Cyrus king of Persia, ¹The LORD
God of heaven hath given me all the kingdoms of the earth ;
²and he hath charged me to build him an house at Jerusalem,
3 which is in Judah.   ³Who is there among you of all his people ?
⁴his God be with him, ⁵and let him go up to Jerusalem, which
is in Judah, ⁶and let them build the house of the LORD God of
4 Israel, (he is the God,) which is in Jerusalem.   ⁷And whosoever
remaineth in any place where he sojourneth, let the men of his
place help him with silver, and with gold, and with goods, and
with beasts, beside the free will offering for the house of God that
5 is in Jerusalem.   (*3*) AND the chief of the fathers of Judah and
Benjamin rose up, and the priests, and the Levites, with all
them whose spirit God had raised, to go up to build the house
6 of the LORD which is in Jerusalem.   And all they that were
about them strengthened their hands with vessels of silver, with
gold, with goods, and with beasts, and with precious things,
7 beside all that was willingly offered.   (*4*) And Cyrus the king
brought forth the vessels of the house of the LORD, which Nebuchadnezzar had brought forth out of Jerusalem, AND had put

X

8 them in the house of his gods. (*5*) AND Cyrus king of Persia brought them forth, (*6*) [AND he delivered them] into the hand of Mithredath the treasurer, (*7*) AND he numbered them unto
9 Sheshbazzar, the prince of Judah. And this is the number of them, etc.

In this chapter, if we follow the *con. waws*, we shall only have six divisions, but there is reason to believe that a word has been lost from the Hebrew text in ver. 8. It now reads, " And Cyrus . . . brought them forth into the hand of the Mithredath,"[1] a phrase which is neither good Hebrew nor good English. If we turn, however, to the Greek translation of the chapter found in the Apocryphal Book of 1 Esdras (printed between the Old and New Tests. in some editions of the A.V.), we find there the words which I have inserted in brackets, and this reading is confirmed by three (somewhat late) manuscripts of the Sept.

In Cyrus's proclamation, vv. 2–4, the word " and " occurs 7 times, as it does also in the third division of the heptad, vv. 5, 6. It is instructive to notice how it is omitted or inserted so as to make up this number. Thus, in ver. 4, we read, " With silver, *and* with gold, *and* with goods, *and* with beasts," but, in ver. 6, " With vessels of silver, with gold, with goods, *and* with beasts, *and* with precious things."

The Book of Psalms is in the R.V. simply called The Psalms, for it is there, following the Jewish division, made to consist of five " books," as follows :—

Book	I.	Psalms	i.–xli.
„	II.	„	xlii.–lxxii.
„	III.	„	lxxiii.–lxxxix.
„	IV.	„	xc.–cvi.
„	V.	„	cvii.–cl.

That the Psalms were arranged in their present form by inspired hands, and that some subdivision into Parts was intended, is unquestionable ; and that the doxolo-

---

[1] The A.V. (which the R.V. follows) has " *by* the hand of," but the Heb. phrase *al yad*, though it occurs very frequently, nowhere else has this meaning. In Cheyne and Driver's *Variorum Bible* it is rendered " into " here.

gies found at the end of Psalms xli., lxxii., lxxxix., and cvi. are each meant to mark the close of a " Book,"[1] is equally undoubted. But why *five* " Books ? " Doubtless from a desire on the part of the Jews " to have as many parts in the Psalms as there are in the Law of Moses." But five, as we have seen, is the symbol of incompleteness, and, though rightly enough applied to the Law, which is incomplete as a revelation of God's will without the gospel, it does not seem appropriate when applied to the Psalms. For between the Law and the Psalms there is little in common. Thus, while the Law everywhere speaks of the necessity of sacrifice as a means of approach to God, the language of the Psalms is, " Sacrifice and offering thou didst not desire ; " " burnt offering and sin offering hast thou not required ; " " thou desirest not sacrifice, else would I give it ; thou delightest not in burnt offering." I therefore unhesitatingly agree with Dr. John Forbes,[2] that the true division of the Psalms is into SEVEN Books and not five, and that what is called in the Heb. Bible the fifth " book," should be divided into three, thus Pss. cvii.–cxvii. ; cxviii.–cxxxv. ; cxxxvi.–cl. We then find that Books I, II, III each end with " Blessed be the Lord, etc., Amen and Amen."

Book IV ends with " Blessed be the Lord, etc., Amen, Hallelujah."

Books V, VI, VII each begin with " O give thanks unto the Lord, for he is good ; for his mercy endureth for ever," and end with " Hallelujah."

So that there are

3 " Amen " Books ;

1 Central Book : " Amen, Hallelujah ; " and

3 " Hallelujah " Books ;

the 7 being divided into 3, 1, 3, like the Golden Candle-

[1] To avoid confusion, I retain " Book " as a title of the subdivisions of the Psalter though I think " Part " would be more appropriate.
[2] *Symmetrical Structure of Scripture*, p. 135.

stick which had a central stem with three branches on either side.[1]

As " Amen " is found nowhere else, it thus occurs 7 times in the Psalms. Take again the word "Hallelujah " which occurs *once* in 7 psalms either at the beginning or end (cxi., cxii., at the beginning ; and civ., cv., cxv., cxvi., cxvii., at the end) ; *twice* in 7 others, at both beginning and end (cvi., cxiii., cxlvi., cxlvii., cxlviii., cxlix., cl.) ; and three times in Psalm cxxxv., at the beginning, the end, and in ver. 3.[2] We have thus a total of 24 occurrences, a number not at all suggestive of 7 ; but it is also found 4 times in Rev., making 28 in the whole Bible. It will be noticed that the word only occurs in the last four Books of the Psalms : 7 times in the fifth Book, 7 times (4 and 3) in the fourth and sixth together, and 10 times in the seventh.

The number of the psalms is the point which next calls for consideration. " The number of separate psalms . . . is, by the concordant testimony of all ancient authorities, 150. . . . This total number," continues Mr. Thrupp, " commends itself by its internal probability as having proceeded from the last collector and editor of the Psalter."[3] Well reasoned, perhaps, if it were a human compilation we were dealing with ; but if the Book of Psalms consists of a series of inspired productions, then surely we may expect that the divine mark shall be stamped upon the total number of separate compositions contained in it. And in the number 150 I do not see this mark, but it is so near to 147 ($= 7 \times 7 \times 3$)—an odd number in man's eyes, but an even, a perfect number according to God's method of counting—that one is at once tempted to ask, " Is there

[1] Forbes : *Studies on the Bk. of Pss.*, p. 79. Forbes finds many 7's in the Pss., and also other numbers as 10, 12, etc.

[2] Why have the Revisers not put the marginal note, " Heb. *Hallelujah*," in this last case, as they have in every other ? They give the correct translation, however, " Praise ye the LORD," instead of the indefinite " Praise the LORD " of the Authorized Version.

[3] Smith's *Dict. Bib.*, art. " Psalms," vol. ii. p. 953.

any reason for believing that the number of psalms is now three more than it was originally ? " There is, and that without taking away a single verse from our present Psalter. For although nearly all ancient authorities give the number of separate psalms as 150,[1] yet they *do not arrive at that number in the same way.* Thus the Sept., which is followed by the Vulgate and other ancient versions, and partially by the Syriac, joins together Pss. ix. and x., and Pss. cxiv. and cxv., and divides into two each Ps. cxvi. and Ps. cxlvii.[2] That Pss. ix. and x. formed originally only one psalm can be easily proved. (1) They are joined together in four Heb. MSS, as well as in most of the ancient versions. (2) An imperfect alphabetical arrangement runs through the two, being continued from one to the other : seventeen out of the twenty-two letters of the Heb. alphabet being found at the commencement of successive, though not consecutive, lines : from *a* to *k* in Ps. ix., and from *l* to *tau*, the last letter of the Heb. alphabet, in Ps. x. They occur in regular order, but at irregular intervals, and therefore have evidently not been noticed by the early copyists who divided the psalm into two. (3) Ps. x. is without a title, a very rare thing in the first two Books of the Psalter. (4) The name JEHOVAH (" the LORD " A.V.) occurs 14 times in the two psalms together.

With regard to Pss. cxiv. and cxv., (1) no fewer than seventy-one Heb. MSS join them together, besides almost all the ancient versions. (2) Their separation destroys the sequence of Hallelujah psalms, the word Hallelujah not occurring in Ps. cxiv., though it is found in the three on either side of it (7 times in the 6 psalms). If the two are counted as one psalm, then the psalms containing Hallelujah either once or twice form three

---

[1] " The oldest Jewish tradition reckoned 147 Pss." *Enc. Bib.* iii. 3923. Swete, *Int. to O.T. in Gk.* 240 n. 3. Ginsburg, *Int. to Heb. Bib.* 777. *Expos. Times* xxii. 393.

[2] The numbering of the Psalms in the A.V. of course follows the Heb. ; that in the Douay Version, being taken from the Vulgate, follows the Sept.

groups : Pss. civ.–cvi. ; cxi.–cxvii. ; cxlvi.–cl. Ps. cxxxv., in which Hallelujah occurs three times, stands by itself. (3) This argument is strengthened if we examine all the psalms in the fifth Book or Part (Pss. cvii.–cxvii.). Of these the first begins with a doxology, the next three have titles, and the last six (counting cxiv. and cxv. as one) are Hallelujah Psalms. If we separate the two, this regularity is interfered with. (4) Ps. cxiv. ends too abruptly to be a complete composition.

We have now reduced the number of the Psalms to 148, and the Versions afford us no further help. But there need be no hesitation as to which other couple should be joined together, for modern critics are all but unanimous in the opinion that Pss. xlii. and xliii. formed originally but one. (1) They are so written in forty-six Heb. MSS, to which must be added the testimony of Eusebius (beginning of fourth century). (2) The refrain, " Why art thou cast down, O my soul," etc. (xlii. 5, 11 ; xliii. 5), shows them to be parts of the same composition. (3) Ps. xliii. is without a title, a most unusual thing, as before remarked, in the first and second Books (" the prayers of David the son of Jesse," Ps. lxxii. 20) of the Psalter. (4) " God " occurs 21 times in the two psalms together. (5) The division breaks in upon a group of psalms written by " the sons of Korah : " join the two together, and we have 7 consecutive psalms (Pss. xlii.–xlix.) bearing this title.

I borrow from Mr. Thrupp an argument which bears upon the whole three psalms, though by him used differently. In the article already quoted, he says, in order to show that the present Hebrew numbering is correct, " It is decisive against the Greek numbering that Ps. cxvi., being symmetrical in its construction, will not bear to be divided ; and against the Syriac, that it destroys the outward correspondence in numerical place between the three great triumphal psalms, Pss. xviii., lxviii., cxviii., as also between the two psalms containing the praise of the Law, Pss. xix., cxix."

Now, if the alterations be made which are proposed above, these psalms will be numbered—the first group xvii., lxvi., cxv., and the second xviii., cxvi., giving a difference of **49** (7 × 7) between the numbers of the first group, and **98** (7 × 7 × 2) between those of the second, more likely numbers, when it is God's book we are dealing with, than 50 and 100.

The true division of the Psalter, therefore, is as follows :—

Book	I. ctg.	40	Pss.	i.–xli.	⎫ Total **70** : " the prayers of David the son of Jesse." Ps. lxxii. 20.
	II. ,,	30	,,	xlii.–lxxii.	
	III. ,,	17	,,	lxxiii.–lxxxix.	
	IV. ,,	17	,,	xc.–cvi.	
	V. ,,	10	,,	cvii.–cxvii.	⎫ Total **28.**
	VI. ,,	18	,,	cxviii.–cxxxv.	
	VII. ,,	15	,,	cxxxvi.–cl.	

147

Let it be clearly understood that I do not propose to take away a single psalm from our present Psalter, but only to couple together three pairs of psalms, ix. and x. ; xlii. and xliii. ; cxiv. and cxv., and so reduce the total number by three. One hundred and forty-seven has been the original number, and in order to bring it up to the even number one hundred and fifty, three have been divided, but in such a way as to leave clear traces of where man has attempted to alter and improve God's perfect work.

Some further points of contact between the number **7** and the Psalter may here be noticed, without, however, attempting to exhaust the subject.

The **7** " penitential " psalms are well known ; they are Pss. vi., xxxii., xxxviii., li., cii., cxxx., cxliii.

There are **7** alphabetical or acrostic psalms. In Pss. xxv., xxxiv., xxxvii., cxi., cxii., cxlv., each line or verse [1] begins in the Hebrew with a different letter of the alphabet, in regular succession : in Ps. cxix. the same order is observed, but the psalm is divided into 22 groups (corresponding with the number of letters in the Hebrew alphabet), containing 8 verses each, every verse of a group beginning with the same letter.[2] But why 8 verses rather than 7 ? Because 7, instead of making a heptad, would have spoiled one. Thus in the six shorter psalms the alphabet is gone through 6 times (once in each), and in the 119th 8 times, giving a total of 14, or twice 7 in the 7 psalms.

As to the **titles of the psalms,** if we include Hallelujah as a title—as it undoubtedly is, see especially the alphabetical psalms, cxi. and cxii., and see the Sept. where it is left untranslated—then **126** psalms (7 × 18) have titles, and **21** [3] (7 × 3) are without them.[4]

The *design* of the titles is thus stated in Angus's *Bible Handbook.*[5] " These titles give either the (1) name of the author, or (2) directions to the musician, or (3) the historical occasion, or (4) the liturgical use, or (5) the style of the poetry, or (6) the instrument, or (7) the tune to which the Psalm is to be sung. Sometimes all these are combined, Ps. lx.''

The names of **7** *authors* are given in the titles: (1)

---

[1] In Ps. xxxvii., as a rule each alternate verse. In this Psalm, **7** verses begin with *waw*, " and," and **7** with *ki*, " for." An imperfect alphabetical arrangement also runs through Pss. ix., x., as stated above.

[2] In the A.V. and R.V. the name of the letter is given at the head of each group.

[3] 24 according to the common arrangement, but three of these, as shown above, are properly parts of the psalms preceding them.

[4] Dr. J. W. Thirtle has made the discovery (*The Titles of the Psalms*) that certain parts of the inscriptions belong to the end of the preceding psalm. Adopting this view there are

Pss. with both title and *subscription*	(including	63
Pss. with title only	Hallelujah	63
Pss. with no title		21

147

[5] Page 445. (So also Kitto's *Cyc. Bib. Lit.*, iii. 607.

David, (2) Asaph, (3) the sons of Korah, (4) Heman, (5) Ethan, (6) Solomon, (7) Moses.[1]

There are **7** different kinds of Pss. mentioned in the titles (1) Psalm, (2) Song, (3) Maschil, (4) Michtam, (5) Prayer, (6) Praise, (7) Shiggaion. The title of the whole book in Heb. is not " Psalms," but " Praises," although only one psalm (cxlv.) has this name in its inscription.

Psalm occurs **56** times in the titles, excluding Ps. lxxxviii.[2]

7 Pss. are ascribed to David in the N.T. : ii. xvi., xxxii., lxix., xcv., cix., cx.

There are **14** traditional " Royal Psalms ": ii., xviii., xx., xxi., xxviii., xlv., lxi., lxiii., lxxii., lxxxiv., lxxxix., ci., cx., cxxxii.[3] Another authority gives only **7** " Royal Pss.": ii., xviii., xx., xlv., lxi., lxxii., cx.[4]

The sequence of **7** Pss. xciii.–xcix. are also called " a series of Royal Pss. which celebrate the coming of JEHOVAH as King."[5]

There are other sequences of **7** psalms which have a connection running through them, e.g. ii.–viii., ix.–xv., xvi.–xxii., xx.–xxvi., xxvii.–xxxiii., xxxiv.–xl., (xx.–xxii. being in two heptades, and ix., x. counted as separate Pss.).[6]

" The Psalms are cited about **70** times in the New Testament."[7]

To turn, now, to the heptadic analysis of the Psalms themselves. As we have seen, the rule for dividing poetry is, briefly, that each division of a heptad con-

[1] Kitto's *Bib. Cyc.*, iii. 609, 610.

[2] Ps. lxxxviii. has two titles, and the first, " A Song, a Psalm of the sons of Korah " must be omitted ; it has doubtless been repeated from the preceding psalm. Further heptadic particulars respecting the Titles of the Pss. were given in *Seven the Sacred Number*, 325.

[3] Cheyne, *Bk. of Pss.*, v. 1, p. xxxii ; *Enc. Bib.* iii. 3950.

[4] Oxford *Helps*, p. 53.

[5] Perowne, *Bk. of Pss.*: Ps. xcix. So *Speaker's Comm.*, & Forbes, *Studies*, 130.

[6] Forbes, *Studies*, 264.

[7] Bp. Wordsworth's *Commentary*. Introd. to the Psalms, p. xiii., *note*.

sists of a single grammatical sentence, without regard to whether "and" or any other particle occurs in it or not.

PSALM I.

1   (*1*) Blessed (is) the man that walketh not in the counsel of the ungodly, (*2*) and he standeth not in the way of sinners,
2   (*3*) and he sitteth not in the seat of the scornful. (*4*) But his delight (is) in the law of the LORD ; (*5*) and in his law doth he
3 meditate day and night. (*6*) And he shall be like a tree planted by the rivers of water, that bringeth forth his fruit in his season ; (*7*) and his leaf shall not wither ; (*8*) and whatsoever he doeth
4 shall prosper. (*9*) The ungodly (are) not so : (*10*) but (they are)
5 like the chaff which the wind driveth away. (*11*) Therefore the ungodly shall not stand in the judgment, (*12*) and sinners (shall not stand) in the congregation of the righteous. (*13*)
6 For the LORD knoweth the way of the righteous : (*14*) and the way of the ungodly shall perish.

There is no difficulty in marking the fourteen divisions in this psalm, though they cannot well be made into two sevens. Division number 6 is lengthy, but perfectly regular. In number 12 the verb must be understood, as also in numbers 1, 4, 9, 10.

In some cases, however, it would appear that a clause only, and not a complete sentence, forms a division, for some of the psalms are so short that they do not contain seven sentences.

PSALM CXXXIV.

1   (*1*) Behold, bless ye the LORD, (*2*) all ye servants of the LORD,
2 (*3*) which by night stand in the house of the LORD. (*4*) Lift up your hands to the sanctuary, (*5*) and bless ye the LORD.
3 (*6*) The LORD bless thee out of Zion ; (*7*) even he that made heaven and earth.

I have followed the R.V. in this psalm, as it keeps more closely to the original in the last verse than the A.V.

Ps. cxvii. is shorter still, and the heptadic division can only be made out by including the "Hallelujah" at the end :—

1   (*1*) O praise the LORD, (*2*) all ye nations : (*3*) praise him, (*4*)
2 all ye people. (*5*) For his merciful kindness is great toward us :

(6) and the truth of the LORD (endureth) for ever. (7) Praise ye the LORD.

" The **Book of Proverbs** in like manner consists of **7** parts or sections, arranged as follows :—

I.   Ch. i.–ix.   Introductory Part.
II.   ,, x.–xxii. 16.   " The Proverbs of Solomon."
III.   ,, xxii. 17–xxiv.   " The words of the wise."
⎱ All written or collected by Solomon.

IV.   Ch. xxv.–xxix.   " Proverbs of Solomon which the men of Hezekiah king of Judah copied out."
V.   ,, xxx.   " The words of Agur."
VI.   ,, xxxi. 1–9.   " The words of king Lemuel."
VII.   ,, xxxi. 10–31.   An alphabetical poem—Description of a virtuous wife." [1]

In the second part, each verse contains a complete sense in itself, having no necessary connection with the context. The verses in this part have been carefully counted by critics, and found to number 375 in all. Every one of these 375 verses consists of two members except ch. xix. 7, and that, of course, has on this account been supposed to be defective. There is no need for any such supposition. Twice 375 = 750, the number of members which the critics think there should be. But as this one verse contains only a single member, the actual number in the Heb. text is 749, a number so eminently heptadic as at once to commend itself to us as the true one.

PROVERBS I.

1   (1) The proverbs of Solomon the son of David, king of Israel ;
2   [1]to know wisdom and instruction ; [2]to perceive the words of
3   understanding ; [3]to receive the instruction of wisdom, justice,
4   and judgment, and equity ; [4]to give subtility to the simple, to
5   the young man knowledge and discretion ; [5] that the wise may hear, and increase in learning ; [6] and that the man of under-
6   standing may attain unto wise counsels ; [7] to understand a proverb and the interpretation, the words of the wise and their

---

[1] Forbes' *Symmetrical Structure of Scripture*, p. 136.

7 dark sayings. (2) The fear of the LORD is the beginning of
8 knowledge : (3) fools despise wisdom and instruction. (4) My
son, hear the instruction of thy father, (5) and forsake not
9 the law of thy mother. (6) For they shall be an ornament of
10 grace unto thy head, and chains about thy neck. (7) My son,
11 if sinners entice thee, consent thou not. (8) If they say, Come
with us, let us lay wait for blood, let us lurk privily for the
12 innocent without cause, let us swallow them up alive as the
13 grave, and whole as those that go down into the pit ; we shall
find all precious substance, we shall fill our houses with spoil ;
14 cast in thy lot among us, let us all have one purse : my son,
15 walk not thou in the way with them ; (9) refrain thy foot
17 from their path : . . . (10) for in vain the net is spread in the
18 sight of any bird. (11) And they lay wait for their own blood ;
19 (12) they lurk privily for their own lives. (13) So (are) the ways
of every one that is greedy of gain ; (14) it taketh away the life
of the owners thereof.

20 (1) Wisdom crieth without ; (2) she uttereth her voice in the
21 streets : (3) she crieth in the chief place of concourse, in the
openings of the gates ; (4) in the city she uttereth her words :
22 (5) How long, ye simple ones, will ye love simplicity ? (6) and
will scorners delight in their scorning, (7) and will fools hate
knowledge ?

23 (1) Turn you at my reproof : (2) behold, I will pour out my
spirit upon you. (3) I will make known my words unto you.
24 (4) Because I have called, (5) AND ye refused ; (6) I have stretched
out my hand, (7) and no man regarded.

25 (1) AND ye have set at nought all my counsel, (2) and would
26 none of my reproof : (3) I also will laugh at your calamity ;
27 (4) I will mock when your fear cometh ; (5) When your fear
cometh as desolation, (6) and your destruction cometh as a
whirlwind ; (7) when distress and anguish cometh upon you.

28 (1) Then shall they call upon me, (2) and I will not answer ;
(3) they shall seek me early, (4) and they shall not find me :
29 (5) for that they hated knowledge, (6) and did not choose the
30 fear of the LORD : (7) they would none of my counsel.

31 (1) They despised all my reproof ; (2) and they shall eat of
the fruit of their own way, (3) and they shall be filled with their
32 own devices. (4) For the turning away of the simple shall slay
33 them, (5) and the prosperity of fools shall destroy them. (6)
And whoso hearkeneth unto me shall dwell safely, (7) and he
shall be quiet from fear of evil.

Ver. 16 is not found in the Sept.[1] nor Arabic versions, and does not appear to have formed part of the

[1] Codd. B., ℵ*, C and four cursives. It is in A.

original Heb. text, the heptad being complete without it. It has, doubtless, been inserted by an early transcriber from Isa. lix. 7, as a " gloss " upon the last clause of ver. 15.

ECCLESIASTES I.

1 2 3 4 (*1*) The words of the Preacher, the son of David, king in Jerusalem. (*2*) Vanity of vanities, saith the Preacher, vanity of vanities; (*3*) all is vanity. (*4*) What profit hath a man of all his labour which he taketh under the sun ? (*5*) One generation passeth away, (*6*) and another generation cometh: (*7*) and the earth abideth for ever.

5 6 (*1*) And the sun ariseth, (*2*) and the sun goeth down, (*3*) and he hasteth to his place where he arose. (*4*) The wind goeth toward the south, (*5*) and he turneth about unto the north ; (*6*) it whirleth about continually, (*7*) and the wind returneth again according to his circuits.

7 8 (*1*) All the rivers run into the sea ; (*2*) and the sea is not full ; (*3*) unto the place from whence the rivers come, thither they return again. (*4*) All things are full of labour ; (*5*) man cannot utter it : (*6*) the eye is not satisfied with seeing, (*7*) and the ear is not filled with hearing.

9 10 11 (*1*) The thing that hath been, it is that which shall be ; (*2*) and that which is done is that which shall be done : (*3*) and there is no new thing under the sun. (*4*) Is there anything whereof it may be said, See, this is new ? (*5*) it hath been already of old time which was before. (*6*) There is no remembrance of former things ; (*7*) and neither shall there be any remembrance of things that are to come with those that shall come after.

12 13 14 15 (*1*) I the Preacher was king over Israel in Jerusalem. (*2*) And I gave my heart to seek and search out by wisdom concerning all things that are done under heaven : (*3*) this sore travail hath God given to the sons of man to be exercised therewith. (*4*) I have seen all the works that are done under the sun ; (*5*) and, behold, all is vanity and vexation of spirit. (*6*) That which is crooked cannot be made straight ; (*7*) and that which is wanting cannot be numbered.

16 17 18 (*1*) I communed with mine own heart, saying, Lo, I am come to great estate, (*2*) and I have gotten more wisdom than all they that have been before me in Jerusalem : (*3*) and my heart had great experience of wisdom and knowledge. (*4*) AND I gave my heart to know wisdom, and to know madness and folly : (*5*) I perceived that this also is vexation of spirit. (*6*) For in much wisdom is much grief : (*7*) and he that increaseth knowledge increaseth sorrow.

This chapter divides very easily, on the poetic principle.

The Book of Lamentations is in one respect the most remarkably constructed in Scripture. Each of its five chapters contains 22 verses except the third, which has 66, or three times 22. In the first, second, and fourth chapters each verse begins with a different letter of the Hebrew alphabet, in regular succession. In the third chapter the first *three* verses each begin with A, the next three with B, and so on. In the fifth chapter there are again 22 verses, but the alphabetical arrangement is not followed. So that in the whole book the alphabet is gone through regularly 6 times, while there are 7 times 22 (the number of letters in the Hebrew alphabet), or 154 verses, in all. But why is the arrangement not regular in the fifth chapter, as it is in the others ? Is it a freak of the prophet ? There are no freaks in Scripture. What God does, He does designedly, though we may not always be able to trace the design. Here, however, we can, if I mistake not. We have seen that there are 7 acrostic psalms, in which the alphabet is gone through 14 times. We have also seen that the last 22 verses of the Book of Proverbs have the same alphabetical arrangement. Had the last chapter of Lamentations, therefore, been alphabetically arranged, the heptadic character of the acrostic or alphabetical poems of the Old Testament would have been spoiled. As it is, it is beautifully complete, the alphabet being gone through in all 21 times.[1]

LAMENTATIONS v.

1 (*1*) Remember, O LORD, what is come upon us : (*2*) consider,
2 (*3*) and behold our reproach. (*4*) Our inheritance is turned to
3 strangers, our houses to aliens. (*5*) We are orphans, (*6*) we
have no father, (*7*) our mothers are as widows.

---

[1] I have not thought it necessary to refer to the occasional deviations from the strict alphabetical order found in some of these poems. Some think that the order has not always been the same as at present.

4 (*1*) We have drunken our water for money ; (*2*) our wood is
5 sold unto us. (*3*) Our necks are under persecution : (*4*) we
6 labour, (*5*) we have no rest. (*6*) To Egypt we have given the
   hand, (*7*) to Assyria, to be satisfied with bread.

7 (*1*) Our fathers have sinned, (*2*) they are not ; (*3*) we have
8 borne their iniquities. (*4*) Servants have ruled over us : (*5*)
9 there is none that doth deliver us out of their hand. (*6*) We
   gat our bread with the peril of our lives because of the sword
10 of the wilderness. (*7*) Our skin was black like an oven because
   of the terrible famine.

11 (*1*) They ravished the women in Zion, the maids in the cities
12 of Judah. (*2*) Princes are hanged up by their hand : (*3*) the
13 faces of elders were not honoured. (*4*) They took the young
   men to grind, (*5*) and the children fell under the wood. (*6*)
14 The elders have ceased from the gate, (*7*) the young men have
   ceased [1] from their music.

15 (*1*) The joy of our heart is ceased ; (*2*) our dance is turned
16 into mourning. (*3*) The crown is fallen from our head : (*4*) woe
17 unto us, that we have sinned ! (*5*) For this our heart is faint ;
18 (*6*) for these things our eyes are dim. (*7*) Because of the mountain of Zion, which is desolate, the foxes walk upon it.

19 (*1*) Thou, O LORD, remainest for ever ; thy throne to genera-
20 tion and generation. (*2*) Wherefore dost thou forget us for
21 ever, dost thou forsake us so long time ? (*3*) Turn thou us
   unto thee, O LORD, (*4*) and we shall be turned ; (*5*) renew our
22 days as of old. (*6*) But thou hast utterly rejected us ; (*7*) thou
   art very wroth against us.

We have here again poetic divisions, consisting of
single sentences, and the only difficult verse in the
chapter is the sixth, though I cannot suggest any solution of the difficulty. The Sept. differs slightly from
the present Heb. text, but does not afford much help.

OBADIAH.

1 (*1*) The vision of Obadiah. (*2*) Thus saith the Lord GOD
   concerning Edom ; We have heard a rumour from the LORD,
   (*3*) and an ambassador is sent among the heathen, (*4*) Arise ye,
2 (*5*) and let us rise up against her in battle. (*6*) Behold, I have
   made thee small among the heathen : (*7*) thou art greatly
   despised.
3 (*1*) The pride of thine heart hath deceived thee ; (*2*) he that
   dwelleth in the clefts of the rock, the height of his habitation,[2]

---

[1] So the Sept.
[2] See Mr. Henley's note in the Eng. Trans. of Lowth's *Sacred
Poetry of the Hebrews*, p. 294.

hath said in his heart, Who shall bring me down to the ground ?

4 (3) Though thou exalt (thyself) as the eagle, and though thou set thy nest among the stars,[1] thence will I bring thee down,

5 saith the LORD. (4) If thieves come to thee, if robbers by night, (how art thou cut off !) would they not have stolen till they had enough ? (5) if the grapegatherers came to thee, would they

6 not leave some grapes ? (6) How are the things of Esau searched out ! (7) his hidden things are sought up !

7 (1) All the men of thy confederacy have brought thee even to the border : (2) the men that were at peace with thee have deceived thee, (3) they have prevailed against thee ; (4) they that eat thy bread have laid a wound under thee ; (5) there is

8 none understanding in him. (6) Surely in that day, saith the LORD, AND I will destroy the wise men out of Edom, and under-

9 standing out of the mount of Esau. (7) AND thy mighty men, O Teman, shall be dismayed, to the end that every one of the mount of Esau may be cut off by slaughter.

10 (1) For thy violence against thy brother Jacob shame shall

11 cover thee, (2) and thou wert cut off for ever in the day that thou stoodest on the other side, in the day that the strangers carried away captive His forces, and foreigners entered into his gates, and cast lots upon Jerusalem, thou also (being) as one of them.

12 (3) And thou shouldest not have looked on the day of thy brother in the day that he became a stranger ; (4) and thou shouldest not have rejoiced over the children of Judah in the day of their destruction ; (5) and thou shouldest not have spoken

13 proudly in the day of distress. (6) Thou shouldest not have entered into the gate of my people in the day of their calamity ; (7) yea, thou shouldest not have looked on their affliction in the day of their calamity ; (8) and thou shouldest not have laid

14 hands on their substance in the day of their calamity ; (9) and thou shouldest not have stood in the crossway, to cut off those of his that did escape ; (10) and thou shouldest not have deliv-ered up those of his that did remain in the day of distress.

15 (1) For the day of the LORD is near upon all the heathen : (2) as thou hast done, it shall be done unto thee : (3) thy reward

16 shall return upon thine own head. (4) For as ye have drunk upon my holy mountain, so shall all the heathen drink con-tinually, (5) AND they shall drink, (6) AND they shall swallow down, (7) AND they shall be as though they had not been.

17 (1) And upon mount Zion shall be deliverance, (2) AND there shall be holiness ; (3) AND the house of Jacob shall possess their

---

[1] Rather, " Though thou exalt thy nest as the eagle, and though thou set (it or thyself) among the stars " (Maurer, quoted in Fausset's *Commentary, in loc.*)

18 possessions. (4) AND the house of Jacob shall be a fire, and the house of Joseph a flame, and the house of Esau for stubble, (5) AND they shall kindle in them ; (6) AND they shall devour them ; (7) and there shall not be any remaining of the house of Esau.
19 (1) For the LORD hath spoken. (2) AND (they of) the South shall possess the mount of Esau, and (they of) the Plain the Philistines : (3) AND they shall possess the fields of Ephraim
20 and the fields of Samaria ; and Benjamin, Gilead : [1] (4) And the captivity of this host of the children of Israel shall possess the Canaanites, (even) unto Zarephath ; (5) and the captivity of Jerusalem, which is in Sepharad, shall possess the cities of the
21 South. (6) AND saviours shall come up on mount Zion to judge the mount of Esau ; (7) AND the kingdom shall be the LORD'S.

We have here not merely a chapter, but an entire book ; and its symmetrical construction is a sufficient answer to those who consider the prophecy of Obadiah, short though it be, a mere fragment. As will be seen above, it contains 7 sections : three heptads, a decad, 7 of whose divisions commence with "and," then three heptads more. I have, as usual, kept as closely as possible to the translation of the A.V., but have been obliged to depart from it in one or two places. In the last clause of ver. 10 the A.V. (which is followed by the R.V.) treats the *waw* as conversive, and trans-lates the verb as future, " Thou *shalt be* cut off." In the original, however, it is perfect or preterite, and I consider should be so rendered, " thou *wert* cut off," treating the *waw* as simple. Not that the cutting off was already past, save in the mind and purpose of God ; the language is similar to that in Gen. xvii. 20, " I have blessed him," meaning, " I have purposed to bless him : " so here, " I determined to cut thee off— thy doom was sealed—in the day that thou stoodest on the other side," etc., for ver. 11 forms part of the same sentence. With this alteration the book con-tains 14 *con. waws*. The first part of ver. 20 has puzzled critics ; the R.V. gives no fewer than three renderings of the passage. If, however, by a very

[1] The Sept. joins this to the preceding clause, reading, "and Benjamin and Gilead."

slight alteration of the Heb., we read ירשו *yirshu*, "shall possess," instead of אשר *asher*, "that (of)," all is clear. "The Canaanites" is, of course, put for the land of the Canaanites, in the same way as "the Philistines" is put for the land of the Philistines in the previous verse.

ZECHARIAH XIII.

1 (*1*) In that day there shall be a fountain opened to the house of David and to the inhabitants of Jerusalem for sin and for
2 uncleanness. (*2*) AND it shall come to pass in that day, saith the LORD of hosts, that I will cut off the names of the idols out of the land, (*3*) and they shall not more be remembered : (*4*) and also I will cause the prophets and the unclean spirit to pass
3 out of the land. (*5*) AND it shall come to pass when any shall yet prophesy, (*6*) AND his father and his mother that begat him shall say unto him, Thou shalt not live, for thou speakest lies in the name of the LORD : (*7*) AND his father and his mother that begat him shall thrust him through when he prophesieth.
4 (*1*) AND it shall come to pass in that day, that the prophets shall be ashamed every one of his vision, when he hath prophesied ; (*2*) and they shall not wear a rough garment to deceive,
5 (*3*) AND he shall say, I am no prophet, I am an husbandman ;
6 for man taught me to keep cattle from my youth. (*4*) AND one shall say unto him, What are these wounds in thine hands ? (*5*) AND he shall answer, Those with which I was wounded in the
7 house of my friends. (*6*) Awake, O sword, against my shepherd, and against the man that is my fellow, saith the LORD of hosts : smite the shepherd, and the sheep shall be scattered : (*7*) AND I will turn mine hand upon the little ones.
8 (*1*) AND it shall come to pass, that in all the land, saith the LORD, two parts therein shall be cut off, they shall die ; (*2*)
9 and the third shall be left therein. (*3*) AND I will bring the third part through the fire, (*4*) AND I will refine them as silver is refined, (*5*) AND I will try them as gold is tried : (*6*) they shall call on my name, and I will hear them : I will say, It is my people : (*7*) and they shall say, The LORD is my God.

This chapter is regular throughout : every division, except the first, contains a sentence commencing with "and," the "and" occurring always at the beginning of the division except in division 6 of the second heptad and division 6 of the third. The four occurrences of the word "and-it-shall-come-to-pass" (for this represents but one word in Heb.) are noteworthy : in ver. 3 it is followed by another " and," which would be accounted redundant in English ; but not in the other three places : any different arrangement of *waw* would spoil the heptad.

MALACHI IV.

1 (*1*) For behold the day cometh that shall burn as an oven ; (*2*) AND all the proud, yea, and all that do wickedly, shall be stubble : (*3*) AND the day that cometh shall burn them up, saith the LORD of hosts, that it shall not leave them root and
2 branch. (*4*) AND unto you that fear my name shall the Sun of righteousness arise, (*5*) and healing (is) in his wings ; (*6*) AND ye shall go forth, (*7*) and ye shall grow up as calves of the stall.
3 (*1*) AND ye shall tread down the wicked ; (*2*) for they shall be ashes under the soles of your feet in the day that I shall do
4 this, saith the LORD of hosts. (*3*) Remember ye the law of Moses my servant, which I commanded unto him in Horeb for
5 all Israel, with the statutes and judgments. (*4*) Behold, I will send you Elijah the prophet before the coming of the great
6 and dreadful day of the LORD : (*5*) AND he shall turn the heart of the fathers to the children, and the heart of the children to their fathers, (*6*) else I would come, (*7*) AND I would smite the earth with a curse.

Here each sentence forms a division, *waw* occurring at the beginning of each division except the first, in the first heptad, but not in the second. In verses 2 and 6 I have departed slightly from the A.V., the change in both cases, but especially in the second, being, I think, a gain to the sense. There are 14 *waws* in the chapter.

In the chapters which have been analysed, a few of the sections contain ten members, while one has only five, though the usual number is seven. But before taking leave of the Old Testament I desire to give one chapter more, in which some of the sections are of a different length from any we have hitherto met with.

GENESIS V.

1 (*1*) This is the book of the generations of Adam.
(*1*) In the day that God created man, in the likeness of God
2 made he him, male and female created he them ; (*2*) AND he blessed them, (*3*) AND called their name Adam [*or* Man], in the day when they were created.

3   (*1*) AND Adam lived an hundred and thirty years, (*2*) AND
begat a son in his own likeness, after his image ; (*3*) AND called
4 his name Seth.   (*4*) AND the days of Adam after he begat Seth
were eight hundred years : (*5*) AND he begat sons and daughters :
5 (*6*) AND all the days that Adam lived were nine hundred and
thirty years : (*7*) AND he died.
6   (*1*) AND Seth lived an hundred and five years (*2*) AND begat
7 Enos : (*3*) AND Seth lived after he begat Enos eight hundred
8 and seven years, (*4*) AND begat sons and daughters : (*5*) AND all
the days of Seth were nine hundred and twelve years : (*6*) AND
he died.
9   (*1*) AND Enos lived ninety years, (*2*) AND begat Cainan : (*3*)
10 AND Enos lived after he begat Cainan eight hundred and fifteen
11 years, (*4*) AND begat sons and daughters : (*5*) AND all the days
of Enos were nine hundred and five years : (*6*) AND he died.
12   (*1*) AND Cainan lived seventy years, (*2*) AND begat Mahalaleel :
13 (*3*) AND Cainan lived after he begat Mahalaleel eight hundred
14 and forty years, (*4*) AND begat sons and daughters : (*5*) AND all
the days of Cainan were nine hundred and ten years : (*6*) AND
he died.
15   (*1*) AND Mahalaleel lived sixty and five years, (*2*) AND begat
16 Jared : (*3*) AND Mahalaleel lived after he begat Jared eight
hundred and thirty years, (*4*) AND begat sons and daughters :
17 (*5*) AND all the days of Mahalaleel were eight hundred and ninety
and five years : (*6*) AND he died.
18   (*1*) AND Jared lived an hundred and sixty and two years,
19 (*2*) AND begat Enoch : (*3*) AND Jared lived after he begat Enoch
20 eight hundred years, (*4*) AND begat sons and daughters : (*5*)
AND all the days of Jared were nine hundred and sixty and two
years : (*6*) AND he died.
21   (*1*) AND Enoch lived sixty and five years, (*2*) AND begat
22 Methuselah : (*3*) AND Enoch walked with God after he begat
Methuselah three hundred years, (*4*) AND begat sons and daugh-
23 ters   (*5*) AND all the days of Enoch was [1] three hundred and
24 sixty and five years : (*6*) AND Enoch walked with God : (*7*)
and he was not ; for God took him.
25   (*1*) AND Methuselah lived an hundred and eighty and seven
26 years, (*2*) AND begat Lamech : (*3*) AND Methuselah lived after
he begat Lamech seven hundred and eighty and two years,
27 (*4*) AND begat sons and daughters : (*5*) AND all the days of Methuselah were nine hundred and sixty and nine years : (*6*) AND he died.
28   (*1*) AND Lamech lived an hundred and eighty and two years,
29 (*2*) AND begat a son : (*3*) AND he called his name Noah, saying,
This same shall comfort us concerning our work and toil of our
hands because of the ground which the LORD hath cursed.

[1] So in the Heb.

30 (*4*) AND Lamech lived after he begat Noah five hundred and
ninety and five years, (*5*) AND begat sons and daughters : (*6*)
31 AND all the days of Lamech was [1] seven hundred and seventy
and seven years : (*7*) AND he died.
32   (*1*) AND Noah was five hundred years old : (*2*) AND Noah begat
Shem, Ham, and Japheth.

There are several points worthy of notice in this
chapter. If the above divisions are right—and they
are too well marked to leave much room for doubt—
there are 12 sections in all, a number which has been
connected with 7 in the following manner, that " as
seven is made up of four and three *added* together,
so twelve is made up of four *multiplied* by three."
The first division stands alone, and forms a heading to
the chapter. Then there is one section of two divisions, one of three, six of six, and three of seven, giving
a total of 63 divisions, or 9 times 7, 9 being the number
of complete generations recorded in the chapter. The
ruling division of the chapter is, therefore, into sections
of six members, and as six is " man's number," [2] it is
what we might expect to find in " the book of the
generations of Man," as the first words of the chapter
may be translated. This is confirmed and emphasized
by there being *six* sections of this length. The section
relating to God's place in Man's genealogy properly
contains three divisions, for " in the record of Revelation *Three* is the numerical ' signature ' of the Divine
Being, and of all that stands in any real relation to
God." [3] The three heptads record the lives of Adam,
Enoch, and Lamech respectively. As Adam was the
first, so Lamech was the ninth and last complete
generation before the flood, and in each case the extra
division contains the words " and he called his name
. . . ," words almost the same as those used of God
in the second verse. That the record of Enoch's life
should form a heptad is not surprising. Being " the
seventh from Adam," [4] it is of him, if of any one, that

[1] So in the Heb.   [2] See page 39.
[3] See Appendix B.   [4] Jude 14.

we should expect to read that he " walked with God ; and he was not, for God took him," just as it is in entire accordance with the symbolical meaning attached to the number *ten* that God should wait until the tenth generation, before saying, " The end of all flesh is come before me ; for the earth is filled with violence through them ; and, behold, I will destroy them with the earth." There are other points of contact between the number 7 and this chapter. We find in it the names of 14 persons, if we include God and the three sons of Noah : I have spoken of " God's place in Man's genealogy," and although the expression may appear singular to some, the propriety of its use is shown by this fact. It is confirmed, too, by the genealogy of our Lord as given by St. Luke, which contains 77 names, including God's.[1] Nor must it be thought that St. Luke has strained a point, and improperly introduced the name of God in order to make up this mystical number. He has simply copied from the record before him in the fifth chapter of Genesis, which begins " the book of the generations of Adam," with his creation by God. St. Matthew's genealogy of our Lord supplies further confirmation of this.[2]

The phrase " and all the days . . . were " occurs nine times in the English version, but only 7 in the Hebrew, which, in the cases of Enoch and Lamech reads " and all the days . . . was." The ages of Enoch and Lamech are also noteworthy. Enoch lived on the earth 365 years, a number not heptadic, but remarkable as agreeing with the number of days in a year. Lamech lived 182 years and begat Noah ; after which he lived 595 years, and died aged 777 years ($7 \times 3 \times 37$) —all heptadic numbers, the latter eminently so.

The word " begat " occurs in this chapter 28 times.

Our next example differs from the others in this chapter, in that it rests upon an heptadically revised

---

[1] " Adam, the (son) of God," Lu. iii. 38.
[2] See Appendix D.

text. The R.V. is taken as a basis, and all differences
from the Revisers' Greek text are noted at the end of
each heptad, and are marked in the translation as
follows : omissions from the Revisers' text by a dotted
line . . . , additions to it by square brackets [ ] and
other changes as far as possible by the use of *italics*.
Kaì in the original is represented by AND or ALSO in
small capitals, and *δὲ* by " and " in ordinary type,
any exceptions being noted. Departures from the
R.V. not so marked are caused chiefly by the participles in the Greek being so translated, so as to avoid
the use of " and " where it is not expressed in the
original.

LUKE XXII. 1–53.

1 (*1*) And the feast of unleavened bread drew nigh, which is
2 called the Passover. (*2*) AND the chief priests AND the scribes
    sought how they might put him to death ; for they feared
3 the people. (*3*) And . . . Satan entered into Judas who was
4 *surnamed* Iscariot, being of the number of the twelve. (*4*)
    AND going away, he communed with the chief priests [AND the
    scribes] AND [the] captains, how he might deliver him unto them.
5 (*5*) AND they were glad. (*6*) AND they covenanted to give him
6 money . . . (*7*) AND he sought opportunity to deliver him
    unto them in the absence of the multitude.

> ver. 3 — δ. ἐπικαλούμενον for καλούμενον.
> ver. 4 + καὶ τοῖς γραμματεῦσι. + τοῖς bef. στρατηγοῖς.
> ver. 6 — καὶ ἐξωμολόγησε.

Revisers text	69 words	361 letters
True Text	70 ,,	371 ,,

7 (*1*) And the day of unleavened bread came, on which the
8 passover must be sacrificed. (*2*) AND he sent Peter AND John,
    saying, Go, make ready for us the passover, that we may eat.
9 (*3*) And they said unto him, Where wilt thou that we make
10 ready [for thee] ?   (*4*) And he said unto them, Behold, when ye
    are entered into the city, there shall meet you a man bearing
    a pitcher of water ; follow him into the house into which he
11 goeth. (*5*) AND ye shall say unto the goodman of the house,
    The Master saith unto thee, Where is the guest-chamber, where
12 I shall eat the passover with my disciples ?   And he (*kakeinos*)
    will shew you a large upper room furnished ; there make ready.
13 (*6*) And when they went they found as he had said unto them.
    (*7*) AND they made ready the passover.

ver. 8 Ἰωάνην for Ἰωάννην. ver. 9 + σοι. ver. 12 ἀνάγαιον for ἀνώγεον. κἀκεῖνος counted as two words.

Rev. text	.	.	.	.	97 words	494 letters.
True text	.	.	.	.	98 ,,	497 ,,

14 (1) AND when the hour was come, he sat down, AND the
15 apostles with him. (2) AND he said unto them, With desire I
16 have desired to eat this passover with you before I suffer : for
   I say unto you that I will not eat it until it be fulfilled in the
17 kingdom of God. (3) AND having received a cup, when he had
   given thanks, he said, Take this, (4) AND divide (it) among your-
18 selves : for I say unto you, that I will not drink from henceforth
   of the fruit of the vine until the kingdom of God shall come.
19 (5) AND taking bread, when he had given thanks, he brake (it).
   (6) AND he gave to them saying, This is my body which is given
20 for you ; this do in remembrance of me. Likewise ALSO the
   cup after supper, saying, This cup (is) the new covenant in my
21 blood, which is poured out for you. But behold, the hand of
22 him that betrayeth me (is) with me on the table. For the Son
   of man indeed goeth as it hath been determined : but woe unto
23 that man through whom he is betrayed ! (7) AND they began
   to question among themselves, which of them it was that should
   do this thing.

ver. 18 γενήματος for γεννήματος. ver. 20 ὡσαύτως bef. καί. ἐκχυννό-
μενον for ἐκχυνόμενον. ver. 23 συνζητεῖν for συζητεῖν.

Rev. text	.	.	.	.	168 words	769 letters.
True ,,	.	.	.	.	168 ,,	770 letters.

24 (1) And there arose ALSO a contention among them[selves], which
25 of them is accounted to be greatest. (2) And he said unto them,
   The kings of the Gentiles have lordship over them. (3) AND
26 they that have authority over them are called Benefactors. (4)
   And (δέ) ye (shall) not (be) so : but he that is the greater among
   you, let him become as the younger ; AND he that is chief as he
27 that doth serve. For whether is [the] greater, he that sitteth
   at meat or he that serveth ? is not he that sitteth at meat ? (5)
28 And (δέ) I am in the midst of you as he that serveth. (6) And
   ye are they which have continued with me in my temptations.
29 And-I (kago) appoint unto you a kingdom, as my Father
30 appointed unto me ; that ye may eat AND drink at my table in
   my kingdom. (7) AND ye shall sit on thrones judging the twelve
   tribes of Israel.

ver. 24 ἑαυτοῖς for αὐτοῖς. ver. 27 + δ after γαρ.
ver. 29 κἀγώ counted as two words.

Rev. text	.	.	.	.	111 words	509 letters.
True ,,	.	.	.	.	112 ,,	511 ,,

31   (*1*) Simon, Simon, behold, Satan asked to have you, that he
32 might sift you as wheat : (*2*) and (*δέ*) I made supplication for
    thee, that thy faith fail not : (*3*) *and* thou . . . *turn again,*
33 (*4*) [AND] stablish thy brethren.   (*5*) And he said unto him, Lord,
34 with Thee I am ready, (*6*) AND to prison AND to death to go.   (*7*)
    And he said, I tell thee, Peter, the cock shall not crow this day,
    until thou shalt thrice deny that thou knowest Me.

ver. 32 *ἐκλείπῃ* for *ἐκλίπῃ.*   *σὺ δὲ ἐπίστρεψον, καὶ* for *καὶ σύ ποτε
ἐπιστρέψας.*   ver. 34 + *μὴ* bef. *εἰδέναι.*

Rev. text	.	.	.	62 words 279 letters.
True ,,	.	.	.	63 ,, 280 ,,

35   (*1*) AND he said unto them, When I sent you forth without
    purse, AND wallet, AND shoes, lacked ye anything ?   (*2*) And
36 they said, Nothing. *Then* said he . . . But now, he that hath
    a purse, let him take it, AND likewise a wallet : (*3*) AND he that
37 hath none *shall* sell his cloke, (*4*) AND he shall buy a sword : for
    I say unto you, that this which is written must be fulfilled in
    me, AND he was reckoned with transgressors : (*5*) AND . . . that
38 which concerneth me hath an end.   (*6*) And they said, Lord,
    behold, here are two swords.   (*7*) And he said unto them, It is
    enough.

ver. 35 *βαλλαντίου* for *βαλαντίου.*   ver. 36 *εἶπεν οὖν* for *ὁ δὲ εἶπεν.*
— *αὐτοῖς. βαλλάντιον* for *βαλάντιον. πωλήσει, ἀγοράσει* for *πωλησάτω,
ἀγορασάτω.*   ver. 37 — *γαρ.*   ver. 38 *ἐστιν* for *ἐστι.*

Rev. text	.	.	.	80 words 358 letters.
True ,,	.	.	.	77 ,, 350

39   (*1*) AND going out, he went, as his custom was, unto the mount
    of Olives.   (*2*) And [his] disciples ALSO followed him.   (*3*)
40 And when he was at the place, he said unto them, Pray that ye
41 enter not into temptation.   (*4*) AND he *departed* from them about
42 a stone's cast.   (*5*) AND kneeling down, he prayed, saying,
    Father, if thou be willing, remove this cup from me : never-
43 theless not my will, but thine, be done.   (*6*) And there appeared
44 unto him an angel *from* heaven, strengthening him.   (*7*) AND
    being in an agony he prayed more earnestly.

ver. 39 + *αὐτοῦ* at end.   ver. 41 *ἀπεστάθη* for *ἀπεσπάσθη.*   ver. 43
ἀπὸ τοῦ for *ἀπ'.*

Rev. text	.	.	.	75 words 370 letters.
True ,,	.	.	.	77 ,, 378 ,,

44   (*1*) AND . . . his sweat became as it were great drops of blood
45 falling down upon the ground.   (*2*) AND when he rose up from
    the prayer, coming to the disciples, he found them sleeping
46 for sorrow.   (*3*) AND he said unto them, Why sleep ye ? rise,

47 pray that ye enter not into temptation. (*4*) [And] while he yet
spake, behold, a multitude. (*5*) AND he that was called Judas,
one of the twelve, went before *them*. (*6*) AND he drew near
48 unto Jesus to kiss him. (*7*) And . . . Jesus said unto him,
Judas, betrayest thou the Son of man with a kiss ?

ver. 44 *καί* for *δέ*. — *δ*. ver. 47 + *δέ* after *ἔτι*. *αὐτούς* for *αὐτῶν*.
ver. 48 — *δ*.

| Rev. text | . | . | . | . | . | 71 words | 369 letters. |
| True text | . | . | . | . | . | 70 ,, | 871 ,, |

49 (*1*) And when they that were about him saw what would
50 follow, they said, Lord, shall we smite with the sword ? (*2*)
AND a certain one of them smote the servant of the high priest,
51 (*3*) AND he struck off his right ear. (*4*) And . . . Jesus answering, said, Suffer ye thus far. (*5*) AND touching the ear he healed
52 him. (*6*) And *he* said unto the chief priests AND captains of the
temple AND elders which were come *to* him, Are ye come out,
53 as against a robber, with swords AND staves ? When I was
daily with you in the temple ye stretched not forth your hands
against me ; but this is your hour, (*7*) AND the power (is that)
of darkness.

ver. 51 — *δ*. ver. 52 — *ὁ* 'Ιησοῦς. *πρός* for *ἐπ'*. *ἐξεληλύθατε* for
ἐξήλθετε.

| Rev. text | . | . | . | . | . | 94 words | 430 letters. |
| True ,, | . | . | . | . | . | 91 ,, | 427 ,, |

This chapter is divided in the usual narrative style,
each division being marked by a sentence commencing
with " and " (*καί* or *δέ*). The exception in ver. 31
is only apparent, as it is not unusual for " and " to be
omitted at the commencement of a section. Ver. 33
is peculiar, but a similar construction is found elsewhere.[1] In ver. 38 *estin* is written with final *n* because
it is the end of a section.

All the changes made rest on good MS authority,
and the above represents in all probability the true
text, but it would be premature to say it does so
absolutely, until the Parts of Speech test has been
applied ; it may, however, be safely said that should
any differences be found they will be only in the orthography or other trifling matters not affecting the meaning. We may regard it as certain that vv. 43, 44 are

---

[1] E.g. Lu. i. 58 where there are three divisions in the verse.

an integral part of the Gospel, and should be printed without any qualifying marks or words either in text or margin.

Our next chapter will include some of St. Paul's long sentences, there being in it two of six verses each, and one of five, each sentence forming a division.

EPHESIANS III.

1 (1) For this cause I Paul (am) the prisoner of Jesus Christ,
2 (even) for you Gentiles. (2) Since indeed ye have heard of the dispensation of the grace of God which is given me to you-
3 ward : how that by revelation he made known unto me the
4 mystery : (as I wrote afore in few words, whereby, when ye read, ye may understand my knowledge in the mystery of
5 Christ) which in other ages was not made known unto the sons of men, as it is now revealed unto his holy apostles AND
6 prophets by the Spirit ; that the Gentiles should be fellow-heirs, AND of the same body, AND partakers of his promise
7 in Christ by the gospel, whereof I was made a minister, according to the gift of the grace of God given unto me by the
8 effectual working of his power. (3) Unto me, who am less than the least of all saints, is this grace given, that I should preach
9 among the Gentiles the unsearchable riches of Christ ; AND to make all men see what (is) the fellowship of the mystery, which from the beginning of the world hath been hid in God,
10 who created all things by Jesus Christ ; to the intent that now unto the principalities AND powers in heavenly places might
11 be known by the church the manifold wisdom of God, according to the eternal purpose which he purposed in Christ Jesus our
12 Lord ; in whom we have boldness AND access with confidence
13 by the faith of him. (4) Wherefore I desire that ye faint not
14 at my tribulations for you, which is your glory. (5) For this cause I bow my knees unto the Father of our Lord Jesus Christ,
15 of whom the whole family in heaven AND earth is named,
16 that he would grant you, according to the riches of his glory, to be strengthened with might by his Spirit in the inner man ;
17 that Christ may dwell in your hearts by faith ; that ye, being
18 rooted AND grounded in love, may be able to comprehend with all saints what (is) the breadth AND length AND depth AND height,
19 and to know the love of Christ, which passeth knowledge, that
20 ye might be filled with all the fulness of God. (6) And unto him that is able to do exceeding abundantly above all that we ask
21 or think, according to the power that worketh in us, unto him (be) glory in the church by Christ Jesus throughout all ages, world without end. (7) Amen.

It is usual to regard the first verse of this chapter as only the beginning of a sentence, which is continued in ver. 14, according to some, but in ch. iv. 1, according to others, the intervening verses forming a parenthesis. If this be so, I do not see how seven divisions are to be made out in the chapter. Nor does there seem any special relevancy in St. Paul speaking of himself as a " prisoner . . . for you Gentiles," if the words are supposed to be introduced thus casually. When the best Greek scholars differ even as to whether the Greek will admit of the translation given above, it is not for me to offer an opinion, further than to say that the heptadic structure of the chapter appears to require that the word " am " be understood, so making the verse form a complete sentence. And I would add that nothing is more common, both in Greek and Hebrew, than the omission of the verb " to be," as a glance at the *italics* in the Authorized Version will show.[1] The argument of the chapter, then, would appear to be, briefly, this :— Having declared that the purpose of God in Christ was to do away with the difference between Jew and Gentile, and to make both one (ch. ii.), he shows the vast importance of this doctrine : (1) by reminding them that for proclaiming it he had had to bear persecution and imprisonment, " for this cause I, Paul, (am) the prisoner of Jesus Christ, (even) for you Gen-

---

[1] I cannot help expressing my regret that the Revisers should have chosen to depart from the system to which we have been accustomed with regard to the use of *italics*. Without going so far as to say, as some have done, that by printing in common type words which are not in the original, " words have been attributed to God which He never spoke," I may say that I have found the italics of the Authorized Version of great use in my study of the original languages of Scripture. And they are useful in other ways. Thus, without any knowledge of Hebrew, one can follow, with the A.V. in hand, the argument of Dr. Pusey (*Lectures on Daniel*, third ed., pref., p. xviii.), where he attempts to prove, from the presence of " was " in the first clause, and its absence in the second clause of Gen. i. 2, that an indefinite interval of time separates the first verse of Genesis from the second. But with only the R.V. to depend upon, one would have to take this argument entirely on trust.

tiles," i.e. for asserting your equal rights with the Jews ; and (2) by telling them, what, however, they knew already (" *seeing that* ye have heard," etc., ver. 2, not " if," as the A.V. and practically the R.V.), that it was a doctrine which had been made known to him by special revelation, ver. 3. But he does not regret having preached a doctrine which had brought imprisonment upon him, nay, he glories in the fact that " unto *me*, who am less than the least of all saints, is this grace given, that I should preach among the Gentiles the unsearchable riches of Christ," ver. 8. And lest they should still think that he was *reproaching* them as being in some measure the cause of his imprisonment, he beseeches them " not to be dispirited in my tribulations for you, seeing that they are your glory."[1] Then follows the eloquent prayer which occupies the remainder of the chapter, drawn forth " for this cause," ver. 14, i.e. because Jews and Gentiles now constitute one family, or rather one branch of God's greater family, and therefore addressed to " the Father, of whom the whole family in heaven and earth is named."

2 TIMOTHY III.

1 2 (*1*) And this know, that in the last days perilous times shall come. (*2*) For men shall be lovers of their own selves, covetous,
3 boasters, proud, blasphemers, disobedient to parents, unthankful, unholy, without natural affection, trucebreakers, false
4 5 accusers, incontinent, fierce, despisers of those that are good, traitors, heady, highminded, lovers of pleasures more than
6 lovers of God ; having a form of godliness. and denying the power thereof : (*3*) AND from such turn away. (*4*) For of this sort are
7 they which creep into houses, AND lead captive silly women laden with sins, led away with divers lusts, ever learning, AND
8 never able to come to the knowledge of the truth. (*5*) And as Jannes AND Jambres withstood Moses, so do these ALSO resist
9 the truth ; men of corrupt minds, reprobate concerning the faith. (*6*) But they shall proceed no further : (*7*) for their folly
10 shall be manifest unto all men, as theirs ALSO was. (*1*) But (δὲ) thou hast fully known my doctrine, manner
11 of life, purpose, faith, longsuffering, charity, patience. per-

---

[1] So Alford translates.

secutions, afflictions; what things befell me at Antioch, at
Iconium, at Lystra; what persecutions I endured: (2) AND
12 out of them all the Lord delivered me. (3) Yea (δέ), AND all
that will live godly in Christ Jesus shall suffer persecution.
13 (4) And evil men AND seducers shall make progress for the worse,
14 deceiving AND being deceived. (5) But (δέ) continue thou in
the things which thou hast learned AND hast been assured of,
15 knowing of whom thou hast learned them; AND that from a
child thou hast known the holy scriptures, which are able to make
thee wise unto salvation through faith which is in Christ Jesus.
16 (6) All scripture (is) given by inspiration of God, (7) AND (it is)
profitable for doctrine, for reproof, for correction, for instruc-
17 tion in righteousness; that the man of God may be perfect,
throughly furnished unto all good works.

I JOHN I.

1 (1) That which was from the beginning, which we have heard,
which we have seen with our eyes, which we have looked upon,
2 AND our hands have handled, of the Word of life; (AND the life
was manifested, AND we have seen it, AND bear witness, AND
shew unto you that eternal life, which was with the Father, AND
3 was manifested unto us;) that which we have seen AND heard
declare we unto you, that ye ALSO may have fellowship with us:
(2) yea (δέ), AND our fellowship (is) with the Father, AND with
4 his Son Jesus Christ. (3) AND these things write we unto you
5 that your joy may be full. (4) AND this is the message which
we have heard of him, AND declare unto you, that God is light,
6 (5) AND in him is no darkness at all. (6) If we say we have
fellowship with him, AND walk in darkness. we lie, (7) AND we
do not the truth.
7 (1) But (δέ) if we walk in the light, as he is in the light, we
have fellowship one with another, (2) AND the blood of Jesus
8 Christ his Son cleanseth us from all sin. (3) If we say that we
have no sin, we deceive ourselves, (4) AND the truth is not in us.
9 (5) If we confess our sins, he is faithful AND just to forgive us
our sins, AND to cleanse us from all unrighteousness. (6)
10 If we say that we have not sinned, we make him a liar, (7) AND
his word is not in us.

This chapter is exceptionally easy: nowhere, perhaps, in the New Testament, can we find a chapter
where the divisions can be made out with less difficulty.

REVELATION XXII.

1 (1) AND he shewed me a pure river of water of life, clear as
crystal, proceeding out of the throne of God AND of the Lamb.

2 (2) In the midst of the street of it, AND on this side of the river
AND on that, (was) the tree of life, bearing twelve manner of
fruits, yielding her fruit every month : (3) AND the leaves of
3 the tree (are) for the healing of the nations. (4) AND there shall
be no more curse : (5) AND the throne of God AND of the Lamb
4 shall be in it ; (6) AND his servants shall serve him : (7) AND
they shall see his face ; (8) AND his name (shall be) in their
5 foreheads. (9) AND there shall be no night there ; (10) AND
they need no candle, AND light of the sun ; (11) for the Lord
God giveth them light ; (12) AND they shall reign for evermore.
6 (13) AND he said unto me, These sayings (are) faithful AND true ;
(14) AND the Lord God of the holy prophets sent his angel to
shew unto his servants the things which must shortly be done.
7 (1) AND [1] behold, I come quickly : (2) blessed (is) he that
8 keepeth the sayings of the prophecy of this book. (3) AND I
John saw AND heard these things. (4) AND when I had heard
AND seen, I fell down to worship before the feet of the angel
9 which shewed me these things. (5) AND he saith unto me, See
thou do it not ; (6) for I am thy fellowservant, AND of thy
brethren the prophets, AND of them which keep the sayings
of this book : (7) worship God.
10 (1) AND he saith unto me, Seal not the sayings of the pro-
11 phecy of this book ; (2) for the time is at hand. (3) He that is
unjust, let him be unjust still ; (4) AND he which is filthy, let
him be filthy still ; (5) AND he that is righteous, let him be
righteous still ; (6) AND he that is holy, let him be holy still.
12 (7) Behold,[1] I come quickly. (8) AND my reward (is) with me,
13 to give every man according as his work shall be. (9) I (am)
Alpha AND Omega, (10) (I am) the beginning AND the end, (11)
14 (I am) the first AND the last. (12) Blessed are they that do his
commandments, that they shall [2] have right to the tree of life ;
(13) AND they may [3] enter in through the gates into the city.
15 (14) Without [3] (are) dogs AND sorcerers, AND whoremongers,
AND murderers, AND idolaters, AND whosoever loveth AND
maketh a lie.
16 .(1) I Jesus have sent mine angel to testify unto you these
things in the churches. (2) I am the root AND offspring of David,
17 (3) (I am) the bright, the [3] morning star. (4) AND the Spirit
AND the bride say, Come. (5) AND let him that heareth say,
Come. (6) AND let him that is athirst come. (7) Whosoever [3]
will, let him take the water of life freely.
18 (1) For I testify unto every man that heareth the words of

---

[1] So the true reading ; see R.V.
[2] So in the Greek ; compare ch. xxi. 27, " And in no wise *may*
enter into it any thing that defileth."
[3] So the true reading ; see R.V.

the prophecy of this book, If any man shall add unto these things, God shall add unto him the plagues that are written 19 in this book : (2) AND if any man shall take away from the words of the book of this prophecy, God shall take away his part out of the book of life, AND out of the holy city, (even from) the things 20 which are written in this book. (3) He which testifieth these things saith, Surely, I come quickly. (4) Amen : (5) come,[1] 21 Lord Jesus. (6) The grace of our Lord Jesus Christ (be) with you all. (7) Amen.

A chapter might have been chosen from this book in which the heptads are more plainly marked than in this, still there is little difficulty about it. I have taken it simply because it is the last, in order that it might be seen that throughout the whole Bible unequivocal testimony is borne to the Heptadic Structure of Scripture.

[1] So the true reading ; see R.V.

CHAPTER III. CONCLUSION

THE INSPIRATION OF SCRIPTURE

THUS far we have dealt mainly with facts, leaving them to tell their own story. But our work would be incomplete if we did not say at least a few words as to the significance of those facts and the value to be attached to them.

What then do we gain by the study of the Heptadic Structure of Scripture ? Much every way, but chiefly, in two directions.

First, it is of the greatest assistance in ascertaining the true text. We would not for a moment underrate the work of such illustrious scholars as (to take the New Testament only) Tischendorf, Tregelles, Westcott & Hort and others, without whose zealous and indefatigable labours and investigations the Heptadic Structure could not have been established. But they themselves admit, by the use of brackets, alternative readings and other marks, " the present impossibility of arriving everywhere at uniformly certain conclusions." [1] Here, then, the Heptadic Structure steps in, and offers a means of judging between alternative readings and of discovering the apostolic text.

Secondly, we gain clearer views as to the meaning of Inspiration. To whose agency must we ascribe this Heptadic Structure ?

Let us illustrate again what is meant by the phrase from a passage not hitherto dealt with, the xviith ch. of St. John's Gospel. This chapter—not the prayer only, but the whole chapter—contains, when the true

[1] WH, *Introd.* par. 376.

text has been restored by being purified from the errors of scribes, **49** sentences (**7 × 7**), **490** words (**70 × 7**) and **2079** letters (**77 × 27** or **3 × 3 × 3**). All these three numbers are exactly divisible by **7**, and by no other number. By sentence we mean the shortest complete sentence which the laws of grammar will allow, and being so divided, we find the chapter contains **7** paragraphs or " sections," each section containing **7** sentences or " divisions," the number of words in each section being a multiple of **7**, and also the number of letters a multiple of **7**. Taking the Parts of Speech in the whole chapter, we find that the number of

Verbs and Participles is a multiple of		**7**
Nouns (Subst. and Adj.)	,, .	**7**
Pronouns	,, .	**7**
Conjunctions	,, .	**7**
Articles and Adverbs	,, .	**7**
Prepositions and Adverbs	,, .	**7**

(The Adverbs are counted twice because there are three pairs of words, 'Ιησοῦν Χριστόν, ὦσιν ἡγιασμένοι, and ὦσι τετελιωμένοι, each pair being counted as two words, but as only one item in the Parts of Speech.) [1]

Again, the number of

Consonants in the chapter is a multiple of	.	**7**
Long and short vowels	,, .	**7**
Doubtful vowels	,, .	**7**

The number of Nouns and Pronouns relating to the Father and the Son are together a multiple of 7 and they may be further heptadically divided. (The Holy Spirit is not mentioned in the chapter.) The Pronouns relating to the Disciples of Jesus (taking the word in its widest sense) is a multiple of 7. There are a great many other verbal *sevens* in the chapter which

[1] In Mat. i. ii. even the letters in the Parts of Speech are heptadic, but not here. So in Mat. the name Jesus Christ is counted as two nouns, but here only one.

we need not particularize here. And not only in the chapter by itself, but as part of the Gospel and also as part of the New Testament, many *sevens* may be traced, showing that the heptadic arrangement runs through the whole of the New Testament. The same may be said of the Old Testament. And more remarkable still, many phrases, and even words, are found 7 times in the Old and New Testaments combined.

Thus take the word " Passover " which occurs 49 times in O.T. and 28 in N.T. (omg. Jno. vi. 4, where we have shown that it is an interpolation) ; total 77. The root is the Heb. *pasach* "to pass over," etc., which occurs 7 times, and the only other derivative is *pisseach*, "lame," 14 times, making a total of 98 for root and derivatives in the whole Bible.[1] Then we have

"eat the passover "   .   .   O.T. 1, N.T. 6 = 7
" sacrifice (of) the passover " .   ,,   4,   ,,   3 = 7
" kill(ing) the passover "   .   ,,   7,   ,,   none,

" kill " in Mk. xiv. 12, Lu. xxii. 7 A.V. being rightly rendered " sacrifice " in R.V. " (To) keep the passover " (active) O.T. 19, N.T. 2 = 21, of which 7 are in Numbers, 7 in Chronicles, and in 7 other books once each ; 7 are plural (O.T.), 7 sing. (O.T. 5, N.T. 2) and 7 Infinitive (O.T.). פסח, *pesach*, " passover," uninflected, 14, of which 7 are in " keep passover to the Lord," and with sign of accusative *eth happesach* 7. In the N.T. πάσχα and τὸ πάσχα, *to pascha*, " the passover " (nom. and acc.) 21, τοῦ and τῷ π. (gen. and dat.) 7. " Passover " occurs 7 in Exod. and 7 in Luke ; and in immediate connection with a verb 34 in O.T. (keep 23, kill 6, sacrifice 3, eat 1, roast 1) and 15 in N.T. (keep 2, sacrifice 3, eat 6, make ready 4), total 49. The word is found in 7 different books of the N.T.

How are we to account for these remarkable figures and the similar ones given in more detail in the first and second chapters of this work ? Are they acciden-

[1] For the Etymology, see p. 156.

tal ? Such a suggestion is absurd. By whom then were they designed ? Are we to suppose that St. Matthew, St. Luke, St. John went to the infinite pains which would be needed, even if it were possible, and they were clever enough with all the pains, to produce such results ? And not these three only, but all the N.T. writers, not only individually, but collectively. And not the N.T. writers only, but those of the O.T. also. Must we not conclude, are we not indeed driven to the conclusion, that it is not the unaided work of man, but that " holy men of God spake " and wrote " as they were moved by the Holy Ghost ? " [1]

The Jewish Rabbis called the Massorah " the Hedge of the Law," but unfortunately the text had suffered before this hedge was planted. The Heptadic Structure is a hedge placed by God Himself round the Sacred Scriptures, and though man in his ignorance, and sometimes in his conceit; has marred its symmetry somewhat, happily the hedge is so constructed and so intertwined as to provide the means for its own reconstruction, so that in most cases, especially in the N.T., the mischief is not irreparable.

A recent writer says " We turn to Nature and find evidence of order, system, rationality, and attribute those qualities to God. We find more : we find aim and purpose, for both scientists and philosophers seem to have given back to us the teleology which some feared had been lost with the coming of evolution. . . . So with the fact of the beauty of the world. I often wonder that more use is not made of the æsthetic argument in apologetics." [2]

Why may we not expect to find this " order, system and beauty " in the Word as well as in the Works of God ? Or at least why should we be surprised when we do find them ? Some may think it beneath the dignity and greatness of God to give such care and

[1] 2 Pet. i. 21.
[2] Canon R. B. Tollinton, D.D., at the Modern Churchmen's Conference, in *The Modern Churchman* for Sept. 1921, p. 238.

attention to such minute details. But (a principle too often forgotten) " My thoughts are not your thoughts, neither are your ways my ways, saith the Lord." God is the God not only of the infinitely great, but of the infinitely little, and some of His most wonderful works are seen only through the microscope. Why has He bestowed such care and pains (if we may predicate these things of the Almighty) to the designing and making so beautifully the wings of a small insect, or the eye of a fly, or a thousand other things which were hidden from the eyes of man until the microscope was invented a few hundred years ago ? " Hast thou entered the treasury of the snow ? " asked the Lord of Job, to see how the snowflakes are made so that they fall, not in shapeless masses, but in crystals of the most exquisite beauty ? " The physical universe has perhaps no more general law than this, its laws are mathematical relations." [1] Is it any marvel then if we find the same in the Sacred Scriptures, or something akin to it ?

Upon the belief in the Inspiration of the Bible rests its authority. That authority is being undermined and lowered, and I would urge all who are jealous for the honour of God's Word to give diligent study to its Heptadic Structure, in order that by this and other means its authority may be re-established, and that it may be accepted, even as St. Paul " thanked God without ceasing " that his Thessalonian converts " accepted it, not as the word of men, but as it is in truth, THE WORD OF GOD."

[1] McCook : *The Gospel in Nature : God as Geometer*, 109.

APPENDIX A

THE HEBREW AND GREEK LANGUAGES

THE following is the Hebrew alphabet :—

Character.	Name.	Sound.	Numerical Value.
א	Aleph	—	I
ב	Beth	B	2
ג	Gimel	G hard	3
ד	Daleth	D	4
ה	He	H	5
ו	Waw	W or V	6
ז	Zayin	Z	7
ח	Cheth	Ch hard	8
ט	Teth	T	9
י	Yod or Jod	Y	10
ד כ	Kaph	K	20
ל	Lamed	L	30
ם מ	Mem	M	40
ן נ	Nun	N	50
ס	Samech	S	60
ע	Ayin	—	70
ף פ	Pe	P or Ph	80
ץ צ	Tsa-de	Ts	90
ק	Qoph	Q (K)	100
ר	Resh	R	200
שׂ	Sin	S }These count as one }	
שׁ	Shin	Sh} letter only. }	300
ת	Taw	T or Th	400

There are thus 22 letters, but counting the final forms of Kaph, Mem, Nun, Pe, Tsa-de, and the double forms שׂ, שׁ, 28 different forms in all. Each letter is now considered as a consonant, the true sounds of א and ע being lost, or being at least doubtful.

Vowels are expressed by small dashes and dots, termed

points, appended to the letters. There are in all 14 vowels, 10 of which are sometimes termed *perfect* and 4 *imperfect* or indistinct.

There is also an intricate system of somewhat similar marks called *accents*. Of these Professor Lee counts 35,[1] making with the vowel-points 49 characters used in Hebrew writing in addition to the actual letters of the alphabet.

There are in Hebrew 7 inseparable particles, i.e. single letters representing separate words, but always prefixed to other words, and never standing alone : these are ב, *b*, " in ; " ה, *h*, " the ; " ו, *v* or *w*, " and ; " כ, *k*, " as ; " ל, *l*, " to ; " מ, *m*, " from ; " שׁ, *sh*, " which." The above are their most usual meanings, but some of them are used in a variety of senses ; thus ו, *waw*, the most remarkable of them all, is translated in the A.V. in the following different ways : *again, also, although, and, as, as for, as soon as, beside, both, but, either, even, for, furthermore, howbeit, if, likewise, moreover, nevertheless, nor, notwithstanding, now, or, otherwise, seeing, so, so that, that, then, therefore, though, thus, to* (infinitive), *together* (*with*), *when, wherefore, whereupon, which, while, with, yea, yet.* This list is probably not exhaustive.

7 letters are used as suffixes, תכונסדיה. There are **seven** conjugations of the verb in common use.

The 7 letters האמנתיו, forming the memorial word *heĕmantiv*, are used in the formation of nouns from verbal roots.[2]

The following is the Greek alphabet :—

Character.		Name.	Sound.	Numerical Value.
A	α	Alpha	A	1
B	β	Beta	B	2
Γ	γ	Gamma	G hard	3
Δ	δ	Delta	D	4
E	ε	Epsilon	E short	5
Z	ζ	Zeta	Z	7

[1] *Grammar of the Hebrew Language*, pp. 24–26.
[2] Tregelles' *Heads of Hebrew Grammar*, p. 14. Of a different nature from the above are the following :—The Talmud specifies 7 letters, each of which must be ornamented on the top with certain ornaments, viz. שׁעטנזגץ (Dr. Ginsburg, in Kitto's *Cyc. Bib. Lit.*, art. "Jot and Tittle ") ; the Kabbalists count 7 double consonants, בגדכפרת, called double because they have a double pronunciation (Ginsburg's *Kabbalah*, p. 70).

H	*η*	Eta	E long	8
Θ	*θ*	Theta	Th	9
I	*ι*	Iota	I	10
K	*κ*	Kappa	K	20
Λ	*λ*	Lambda	L	30
M	*μ*	Mu	M	40
N	*ν*	Nu	N	50
Ξ	*ξ*	Xi	X	60
O	*o*	Omicron	O short	70
Π	*π*	Pi	P	80
P	*ϱ*	Rho	R	100
Σ	*σ ς*	Sigma	S	200
T	*τ*	Tau	T	300
Y	*υ*	Upsilon	U	400
Φ	*φ*	Phi	Ph	500
X	*χ*	Chi	Ch hard	600
Ψ	*ψ*	Psi	Ps	700
Ω	*ω*	Omega	O long	800

There are thus **49** characters, viz. **24** capitals and **25** small letters, counting the final form of Sigma.

The Greek verb has **7** tenses : Present, Imperfect, Future, Aorist, Perfect, Pluperfect, Future-perfect.[1]

The Greek language has **7** vowels, *α, ε, η, ι, o, υ, ω.* In the Greek verb there are **7** Conjugation classes.[2] The Greek noun has **7** cases : Nominative, Genitive, Ablative, Dative, Locative, Instrumental, Accusative.[3] Others include Vocative as a case, but exclude Instrumental, still making **7**.[4]

In the Roman notation, **7** letters only were used to represent numerals I V X L C D M.

[1] S. G. Green's *Handbook to the Grammar of the Greek Test.*, p. 60.
[2] J. H. Moulton : *Gram.* ii. 184.
[3] *Id.* i. 61. Robertson : *Gram.* 249.
[4] Nunn : *Syntax N.T. Greek,* 34.

APPENDIX B

THE NUMBER *THREE*

I HAVE sought to confine myself as much as possible in this volume to the number *seven*, but the occasional mention of other numbers has been unavoidable. Next to seven, the two most important numbers in Scripture are *three* and *ten*, and upon each of these a few remarks are offered in this and the following note.

" Among the heathen, if at all civilized," says Archdeacon Lee, " every type and image of Deity, all that stands in immediate relation to It,—all, in short, in which the Divine completes itself, has the stamp of *Three*. This idea almost forces itself on the mind when man contemplates Creation : there are *three* dimensions of Space ; Time is *past, present, future ;* the Universe offers to the view Sky, Earth, Sea. . . . It is but natural indeed that the essential character of the Triune GOD, as He has revealed Himself, should be impressed upon His works. And so, in the record of Revelation, *Three* is the numerical ' signature ' of the Divine Being, and of all that stands in any real relation to God." [1]

At the same conclusion almost all writers on the symbolism of numbers arrive, and Prof. Moses Stuart, after giving several illustrations of the use of the number *Three* in Scripture, in nature, and in heathen theology, remarks, " It would appear now, from the view which has thus been taken, that the doctrine of a *Trinity* in the Godhead lies much deeper than the New Platonic philosophy, to which so many have been accustomed to refer it. An original impression of the character in question plainly overspread all the ancient oriental world ; and whence could this come but from earlier tradition, which flowed from a revealed and patriarchal religion ? " [2]

---

[1] *Speaker's Commentary*, Introduction to Revelation, p. 474.
[2] *Commentary on the Apocalypse*, Excursus II. (1).

The number *Three* is very fully and ably dealt with in Dr. T. A. G. Balfour's little work, *The Typical Character of Nature*, from which I extract the following : " The whole world, from its foundation, seems to have been designed to proclaim a Tripersonal God, but only in the threefold constitution of man was the whole realized in one nature. Body, soul, and spirit are the *three* constituents of man, as he comes perfect from the hands of his Creator, and each was, in my opinion, designed to symbolize or represent a distinct person in the Godhead.

" Again, every one conversant with human embryology knows that the whole structures of the human body are developed from *three* laminæ, or layers, viz. the serous or animal, the vascular, and the mucous or vegetative layer. . . . If we take the vertebra, whose importance is seen in classification, and also in the fact that it is the first formed portion of the osseous system, we shall discover *three* essential portions, and only three, which have been styled the *body*, the *neurapophysis*, and the *hæmapophysis*, and these three, when modified in various ways, contain the whole internal organs.

" The doctrine of the Trinity, therefore," proceeds Dr. Balfour, " is not one which is peculiar to Scripture, but which is inwoven in the very constitution of man, and to which all Nature bears its willing testimony.

" I have said it is inwoven in man's very constitution,—how otherwise can we account for the circumstance that the doctrine of a *Trinity* should appear in the religious tenets of so many nations,—how otherwise can the fact be explained that the greatest thinkers of antiquity admitted a *trinity* of *persons* as the highest of their gods,—and, as reason and speech ($\lambda\delta\gamma o\varsigma$ $\dot{\varepsilon}\nu\delta\iota\dot{\alpha}\theta\varepsilon\tau o\varsigma$ and $\lambda\delta\gamma o\varsigma$ $\pi\varrho o\varphi o\varrho\iota\varkappa\dot{o}\varsigma$) are the distinctive peculiarities of man, how can we, on other principles, account for the fact, that in his speech he is limited to a *three*-fold mode of expressing his thoughts, and that *three persons in grammar express all the relationships among mankind*, and that there are but *three* degrees of comparison of qualities ? Again, we find that *three* things, viz. a subject, a predicate, and a copula, are indispensably necessary for even the simplest proposition, and also that *three* propositions are necessary to constitute a syllogism, which, in the process of reasoning, we so constantly employ ; these are the major and minor premises, and the conclusion, which, again, contain only three terms, viz., major, minor, and middle.

" I said, also, that all Nature bears her willing testimony to the same glorious truth, as appears in the *three* great kingdoms, viz. mineral, vegetable, and animal, which matter, as unorganized and organized, presents to our view ; and in the *three* [1] only forms which that matter can assume, viz. solid, liquid, and aëriform.   Hath not God, who commanded the light to shine out of darkness, also thereby shined into our hearts to give a knowledge of His Tripersonality ? for in the one ray we have the *three* colours, red, yellow, and blue ; or, viewing them in another relation, we are still limited to the *three*, calorific, luminous, and actinic." [2]

So Archdeacon Basil Wilberforce wrote : " Prof. Tyndall discovered, by experiments with the spectrum, that an intensely heated body emits at the same time three rays, producing entirely different results, whilst this trinity of rays form such a unity as to be inseparable.   There is, first, the ' heat ray,' which is felt but not seen ; secondly, the ' light-ray ' which is seen but not felt ; thirdly the ' actinic ray,' which is neither felt nor seen but is only known by its effects, such as its chemical action in the operations of photography.   These are all one, all in an inseparable unity, and yet one is not the other, and not one can exist except in conjunction with the others.   So in the Holy Trinity we have The Father, felt but not seen, ' No man hath seen God at any time,' The Son, the light ray, ' I am the light of the world,' seen but not felt, not touched except by the touch of faith—' though the multitudes thronged him.'   The Holy Ghost, neither felt nor seen, but known by His effects in conversion, renewal and sanctification ; sensitising the heart of man to receive the photograph of its God when the Light of the World is poured into it.   Thus even a superficial study of the analogies of nature forbids me to allow that ' threeness in unity ' is either absurd or unphilosophical." [3]

Dr. John Forbes follows another line of argument, based upon the tripartite nature of man as consisting of body, soul, and spirit.   "*Threefold*," he says, " are the temptations of man, ' the lust of the flesh, the lust of the eyes, and the pride of life ' (1 John ii. 16), the threefold temptations by which the first Adam fell, and over which the second Adam triumphed. . . . *Threefold* are the enemies of human nature, ' the flesh,

---

[1] But see *supra*, p. 250.

[2] See *The Typical Character of Nature*, pp. 23–28 ; and Appendix, Notes II. and III., pp. 94–129.

[3] From a sermon on " The Holy Trinity " in *Following on to know the Lord*, 37.   Also in *Spiritual Consciousness*, 80.

the world, and the devil,' each part having its more peculiar tempter ; the flesh being the tempter of the body, the world, of the soul or heart, and the devil, of the spirit. '. . . But *threefold* are the offices which the Saviour holds to meet the wants of each part of our nature—Prophet, Priest, and King :— to impart, as need requires, ' wisdom,—righteousness and sanctification (δικαιοσύνη τε καὶ ἁγιασμός),—and redemption ' [1] (compare Rom. viii. 23, ' the redemption of our *body* '), until His people be fully renewed again after the image of Him that created them in *knowledge—righteousness* and *holiness*—with *dominion over the creatures.* *Threefold* therefore is the nature of man, because made after the image of God ; and *threefold* consequently must be the essential attributes of Deity, *wisdom, goodness,* and *power.* Is not then," asks Dr. Forbes, " this very triplicity of nature in man, wherein he so far resembles his Creator, another of those analogies intended to facilitate our faith in the higher verity of a Trinity in the Divine nature ? If man consists of *three* distinct parts, *spirit, soul,* and *body,* which yet are so indissolubly united as to form one being, why may not a similar distinction consist with perfect unity in the Godhead ? Or to put the argument in a different form : There is an absolute distinct difference in the three essential attributes of God. . . . Yet no one will for a moment contend that this distinction destroys the unity of His nature. . . . God, therefore, is not one in such a sense as to exclude all distinction and diversity. And if in one respect there exists such a distinction in the Godhead, entirely compatible with His unity, why not in another, which we cannot better understand, nor more clearly define, than by the Scriptural representations and expressions—' Father, Son, and Holy Spirit.' " [2]

Three things are predicated of God in Scripture : (1) " God is Love ; " [3] (2) " God is Light ; " [4] (3) " God is Spirit." [5] Each of these is, of course, true of the three Persons of the Trinity, but each, probably, is also specially true of one particular Person. Thus (1) Love refers specially to the Father ; *cf.* 2 Cor. xiii. 14, " The grace of the Lord Jesus Christ, and the *love of God* [i.e. the Father], and the communion of the Holy Ghost ; " John iii. 16, " God [i.e. the Father] so *loved* the world, that he gave his only begotten Son ; " 1 John iii. 1, " Behold, what manner of *love* the Father hath bestowed upon us ; " 1

---

[1] 1 Cor. i. 30, see R.V.
[2] *Symmetrical Structure of Scripture,* pp. 194, 195.
[3] 1 John iv. 8, 16.   [4] 1 John i. 5.   [5] John iv. 24, R.V. *marg.*

John iv. 10, " Herein is *love*, not that we loved God, but that he [i.e. the Father] *loved* us, and sent his Son to be the propitiation for our sins." So (2) Light is specially connected with the Son, who testified of Himself, " I am the *light* of the world " (John viii. 12 ; ix. 5 ; xii. 46) ; and of whom it is said that " in him was life, and the life was the *light* of men " (John i. 4) ; He is called " the Sun of righteousness " (Mal. iv. 2), and " a *light* to lighten the Gentiles " (Luke ii. 32) ; He came " to give *light* to them that sit in darkness and in the shadow of death " (Luke i. 79) ; lastly, " the kingdom of [God's] dear Son " is set forth as the opposite of " the power of *darkness* " (Col. i. 13). (3) Nothing need be said about the Third Person of the Trinity ; He is connected by His very name with Spirit.

With regard to the number *Three* in the animal world, the following example is taken from a letter headed " Number Three and the Honey Bee," which appeared in the *Baptist* newspaper for March 28, 1884 : " The number *three* plays a prominent part in the economy of the bee. In *three* days after the queen has deposited the egg the young grub is hatched, which is fed up to the *ninth* day (3 × 3). The queen grub reaches maturity in *fifteen* days (5 × 3) ; the worker in 21 days (7 × 3), and is at work in *three* days after leaving the cell ; and the drone in *twenty-four* (8 × 3). The antennæ, or feelers, are composed of *nine* sections (3 × 3). The two eyes, which are compound, are made up, it is believed, of about *three* thousand exceedingly small eyes, each eye, like the cell in the comb, being *six*-sided (3 × 2). On the top of its head are *three* distinct eyes, forming the angles of a triangle. . . . Beneath the body are secreted *six* (3 × 2) small wax scales, with which the comb is made. The bee has *six* legs (3 × 2). Underneath, or rather inside the hind leg, are *nine* (3 × 3) fine rows of hairs which serve as a clothes-brush. The leg itself also is composed of *three* sections. Between the third, or lower section, and the claws, are *three tri*angular sections, forming the foot. The sting, which is flattish, has *nine* (3 × 3) barbs on each side. . . . As to their weight, there are about *three* hundred [bees] to an ounce. . . . The bee itself is composed of *three* sections —*first*, the head ; *second*, the first stomach ; *third*, the second stomach. In the first stomach the nectar from the flowers is transformed into honey, and thence deposited into the cells."

Science maintains the unity of the physical universe. But the man of science also finds that this unity is really triunity. He tells us that the physical universe exists as a trinity of ether, matter and energy. He cannot separate them, but together they form the whole physical universe.[1]

" As in the body there are three systems, that of the nerves and senses, that of the circulation of the blood, and that of the digestion ; so in the social world, there are three systems, the economic, the political, and the spiritual or individual . . . The three elements correspond to the three watch-words, Fraternity, Equality, Liberty." [2]

In an interesting article on *Triangular Numbers in the N.T.* by F. H. Colson,[3] it is pointed out that there are in the whole of the N.T. only **7** definite numbers above 100 (exclusive of thousands and excluding 430 as a chronological datum derived from the O.T.)—four of which are triangular numbers (120, 153, 276, 666), two square numbers (144, 1600), and one " oblong " number (1260). 120 and 666 are doubly triangular. 666 is the " triangle " of 36, which is the sum of the first three cubes $= 1 + 8 + 27$, and it also possesses the rare if not unique property of being both square and triangular. It is also the 36th triangular number. 28, the " triangle " of **7**, is the number of beings round the throne $= 24$ Elders and 4 living creatures (beasts, A.V.). 28 is also in Pythagorean arithmetic a " perfect number," as being the sum of its factors, $1 + 2 + 4 + 7 + 14 = 28$.

See further on Three, and other numbers, in *Enc. Rel. Eth.* art. " Numbers," and in Hastings' Biblical Dicts.

[1] *The Witness of Physical Science to the Triune God ;* Lecture by A. T. Wilkinson, M.D., p. 9.

[2] *Expos. Times* xxxi. 448 ; review of Steiner's *Threefold State.*

[3] *J.T.S.,* Oct. 1914. A triangular number is the sum of a series of successive numbers commencing with 1 which may be arranged in the form of an equilateral triangle. It is half the product of two consecutive numbers.

APPENDIX C

THE NUMBER *TEN*

It is strange that Fairbairn, in his *Typology of Scripture*, has so little to say respecting numbers. The number *seven* he does not mention, so far as I have noticed, so that he cannot be charged with seeing types and symbols where none really exist. Concerning the number *Ten*, however, he has something to say, and his remarks upon it are, on the whole, so judicious as to leave little further to add. Speaking of the Commandments, he says, " *Ten*, the symbol of completeness, indicates that they formed by themselves an entire whole, made up of the necessary, and no more than the necessary, complement of parts. . . . There are certain points [regarding the symbolic import of numbers] which may be considered to have been thoroughly established respecting them ; and none more so than the symbolic import of *ten* as indicating completeness. The ascribing of such an import to this number appears to have been of very ancient origin ; for traces are to be found of it in the earliest and most distant nations ; and even Spencer, who never admits a symbol where he can possibly avoid it, is constrained to allow a symbolical import here. ' The *ten*,' to use the words of Bähr, ' by virtue of the general laws of thought, shuts up the series of primary numbers, and comprehends all in itself. Now, since the whole numeral system consists of so many decades (*tens*), and the first decade is the type of this endlessly repeating series, the nature of number in general is in this last fully developed, and the entire course comprised in its idea. Hence the first decade, and, of course, also the number *ten*, is the representative of the whole numeral system. And as number is employed to symbolize being in general, *ten* must denote the complete perfect being—that is, a number of particulars necessarily connected together and combined into one whole. So that *ten* is the natural symbol of perfection and completeness itself—a definite whole, to which nothing is wanting.' It is on account of this symbolical import of the number *ten* that the plagues of Egypt were precisely of that number—forming, as such, a complete round of judgments); [1] and it was for the same reason that the transgressions of the people in the wilderness were allowed to proceed till the same number had been reached—when they had ' sinned *ten* times ' they had filled up the measure of their iniquities. [2] Hence also the consecration of the *tenths* or tithes, which had grown into an established usage so early as the days of Abraham. [3] The whole increase was represented by *ten*, and one of these was set apart to the Lord in token of all being derived from Him and held of Him. So this revelation of law from Sinai, which was to serve for all coming ages as the grand expression of God's holiness and the summation of man's duty, was comprised in the number *ten* to indicate its perfection as one complete and comprehensive whole. . . . As further examples of the Scriptural import of *ten*, we might have mentioned the *ten* men, in Zech. viii. 23, laying hold of the skirt of a Jew, the parable of the *ten* virgins, and the *ten* horns or kingdoms in Revelation (ch. xvii. 12)." [4]

Archdeacon Lee, in the *Speaker's Commentary* (Introd. to Revelation), has also some excellent remarks upon this number.)

[1] Exod. ix. 14.　　　[2] Num. xiv. 22.　　　[3] Gen. xiv. 20.
[4] Fairbairn's *Typology of Scripture*, 6th ed., vol. ii., pp. 91–93.

APPENDIX D

THE CONNECTION BETWEEN *SIX* AND *SEVEN*

THERE is occasionally noticeable in Scripture a certain connection between the numbers *six* and *seven*, of which a few examples may be given.

Perhaps the most remarkable is in connection with the two genealogies of our Lord, which are given by St. Matthew and St. Luke respectively. That in Luke iii. contains 77 names, and though some have suggested that one or two names should be struck out, there is no textual authority for this being done, and 77 must certainly stand as the correct number of generations, including GOD at the one end, and Jesus at the other. St. Matthew, on the other hand, does not give the complete genealogy, but only from Abraham onwards, enumerating 42 names (6 × 7), but omitting three in one place in order to arrive at this number. If we complete the genealogy by adding these three, the twenty patriarchs from Adam to Terah the father of Abraham, and the name of GOD, as in St. Luke's genealogy, we have *sixty-six* names in all. The following is a list of them :—

1. GOD.	17. Peleg.	33. Obed.
2. Adam.	18. Reu.	34. Jesse.
3. Seth.	19. Serug.	35. David.
4. Enos.	20. Nahor.	36. Solomon.
5. Cainan.	21. Terah.	37. Rehoboam.
6. Mahalaleel.	22. Abraham.	38. Abijah.
7. Jared.	23. Isaac.	39. Asa.
8. Enoch.	24. Jacob.	40. Jehoshaphat.
9. Methuselah.	25. Judah.	41. Jehoram.
10. Lamech.	26. Pharez.	42. Ahaziah.
11. Noah.	27. Hezron.	43. Joash.
12. Shem.	28. Ram.	44. Amaziah.
13. Arphaxad.	29. Amminadab.	45. Uzziah.
14. Cainan.	30. Nahshon.	46. Jotham.
15. Salah.	31. Salmon.	47. Ahaz.
16. Eber.	32. Boaz.	48. Hezekiah.

49. Manasseh.	55. Zerubbabel.	61. Eliud.
50. Amon.	56. Abiud.	62. Eleazar.
51. Josiah.	57. Eliakim.	63. Matthan.
52. Jehoiakim.	58. Azor.	64. Jacob.
53. Jeconiah.	59. Sadoc.	65. Joseph.
54. Salathiel.	60. Achim.	66. JESUS.

It can be by no accident that our Lord is the sixty-sixth in descent from God through Adam in one line, and seventy-seventh in another. What, then, does it mean? *Six* is " man's number," [1] as *seven* is God's ; and the two numbers being used here, doubtless point to the fact that our Lord was at once both Son of man and Son of God. So in His very name, Ἰησοῦς Χριστός, " Jesus Christ," the human name, Ἰησοῦς, " Jesus," contains *six* letters, and the official title Χριστός, " Christ," signifying the Anointed of God, *seven*. And, in accordance with this, it is generally agreed that the genealogy given by St. Matthew is that of Joseph " as legal successor to the throne of David, i.e. it exhibits the successive heirs of the kingdom ending with Christ as Joseph's reputed son." [2] Connecting him, therefore, with a long line of kings, St. Matthew's genealogy was one of which Jesus, *as man*, might well be proud ; but, on the other hand, it contains the names of many who were noted for their wickedness—a stain from which St. Luke's genealogy may be said to be free. [3]

If, as many have supposed, St. Matthew gives the genealogy of Joseph, and St. Luke that of Mary, [4] then there were *thirty-six* men (6 × 6), who were the common ancestors of both, viz. from Adam to David (34), Salathiel, and Zerubbabel.

Six and *Seven* are also found connected with regard to the sons of Noah, the three names, Shem, Ham, and Japheth, being found in immediate connection *six* times, but Shem and Japheth (including these) *seven*. The two who received their father's prophetic blessing are thus associated with the sacred number 7, and the one whose posterity was cursed, with " man's number " *six*.

---

[1] See *supra*, p. 39.

[2] Smith's *Dict. Bib.*, i., 666. Murray's *Illust. B.D.*, 300.

[3] Judah and David are the only two in St. Luke's list of whom any gross sins are recorded. and there is good evidence that both afterwards repented.

[4] See Kitto's *Cyc. Bib. Lit.*, art. " Genealogy of Jesus Christ," for a defence of this theory.

Of Cain, also, the first of the human race upon whom the curse of God fell,[1] we find that the names of his descendants are given only as far as the *sixth* generation.

So Israel's lovers are represented as giving to her *six* things —" My bread and my water, my wool and my flax, mine oil and my drink ; " but God tells her that He gave her 7—corn and wine and oil, silver and gold, wool and flax.[2]

In Matt. xvii. 1 ; Mark ix. 2, *six* appears to be used for *seven ;* compare the parallel passage, Luke ix. 28, where " eight days " doubtless includes the first and last days, while the " six days " of the two former passages excludes both.

In Ezekiel's vision, the measure used was a " reed of six great cubits," " of a [common] cubit and an handbreadth each,"[3] so that the length of the reed was *six* great cubits, or *seven* common cubits, there being six handbreadths to the cubit.[4]

We frequently find in Scripture *one* general term followed by *six* explanatory ones, = 7 in all :—

2 Kings xviii. 32 : " A land like your own land, a land of corn and wine, a land of bread and vineyards, a land of oil olive and of honey."

Ps. viii. 6–8 : " Thou hast put all things under his feet : all sheep and oxen, yea and the beasts of the field ; the fowl of the air and the fish of the sea, and whatsoever passeth through the paths of the seas."

Isa. xi. 2 : " The spirit of the LORD shall rest upon him, the spirit of wisdom and understanding, the spirit of counsel and might, the spirit of knowledge and of the fear of the LORD."

Joel ii. 28, 29 : " I will pour out my spirit upon all flesh ; your sons and your daughters, . . . your old men, . . . your young men, . . . the servants and the handmaids."

Rom. ix. 4 : " Who are Israelites ; to whom pertaineth the adoption, and the glory, and the covenants, and the giving of the law, and the service of God, and the promises."

So the Golden Candlestick had 7 lamps, of which one was on the main stem, and the others on the six branches, which were fixed three on each side.

According to both St. Matthew and St. John, who, however,

---

[1] Adam and Eve were not themselves cursed.
[2] Hos. ii. 5, 8, 9.
[3] Ezek. xl. 5 ; xli. 8, R.V.   [4] Kitto's *Cyc. Bib. Lit.,* iii., 1098.

give the words differently, the Title on the Cross contained 7 words, and *thirty-six* (6 × 6) letters.

There were six cities of Refuge, but the horns of the Altar of Burnt-offering provided a 7th sanctuary, 1 Ki. i. 50.

Ezek. ix. 2. Six men with slaughter weapons, and one man in the midst of them with an inkhorn.

APPENDIX E

THE CONNECTION BETWEEN *SEVEN* AND *EIGHT*

As Six and Seven are sometimes found connected together in
Scripture, so also, but much more frequently and more closely,
are Seven and Eight, as the following instances will show :—

Exod. xxi. 23–25 : " (1) Life for life, (2) eye for eye, (3) tooth
for tooth, (4) hand for hand, (5) foot for foot, (6) burning for
burning, (7) wound for wound, (8) stripe for stripe." Here the
first stands in quite a different category from the other 7 :
a man might suffer any or all of *them*, but if his life was for-
feited he was beyond the reach of further punishment.

Exod. xl. In this chapter the phrase, " as the LORD commanded Moses," occurs 7 times,[1] and the very similar sentence,
" Thus did Moses : according to all that the LORD commanded
him, so did he," *once*, ver. 16. So also ch. xxxix. 1–32.

Lev. xxiii. 39 : " On the fifteenth day of the seventh month,
when ye have gathered in the fruits of the land, ye shall keep the
feast of the LORD 7 days : on the first day shall be a solemn rest,
and on the *eighth* day shall be a solemn rest " (Revised Version).
So vv. 34–36 ; Num. xxix. 39 ; Neh. viii. 18. It is the Feast
of Tabernacles which is thus called " the feast of the LORD," or,
more simply still, " the feast," 1 Kings viii. 2 ; 2 Chron. v.
3 ; vii. 8, 9, " because," says Dr. Ginsburg, " of its importance, and of its being the most joyful of all festivals."[2] As it
is the only one of the three great feasts which may be said to
have lasted eight days, so it is the only one which, as a type,
still remains unfulfilled.

2 Sam. xx. 23–26 : " Now Joab was over all the host of
Israel ; and Benaiah . . . was over the Cherethites and over
the Pelethites ; and Adoram was over the tribute ; and
Jehoshaphat . . . was recorder ; and Sheva was scribe ;

[1] In ver. 23, the A.V. reads " had commanded," but the Heb. is
the same as in the other cases ; see R.V.
[2] Kitto's *Cyc. Bib. Lit.*, iii., 927.

and *Zadok and Abiathar* were the priests; and Ira also the Jairite was a chief ruler about David." Here **7** offices are named, but *eight* men.

1 Kings xviii. 43 : " And [Elijah] said to his servant, Go up now, look toward the sea. And he went up, and looked, and said, There is nothing. And he said, Go again **7** times." This would appear to mean *eight* times in all, though this is perhaps doubtful.

1 Chron. xxvi. 2–8 : Meshelemiah had **7** sons, Obed-edom had *eight*, " for God blessed him." (Obed-edom's immediate descendants were 62, making with himself **68**.)

2 Chron. vi. : " Hear thou from heaven." These words occur **7** times in Solomon's prayer, vv. 23–39, sometimes followed by " from thy dwelling place." The similar phrase, " Hear thou from thy dwelling place, from heaven," occurs *once*, v. 21. Similarly in the parallel passage, 1 Kings viii.

There are **7** Alphabetical Psalms, and an *eighth* (Ps. ix. x., which originally formed but one psalm), where the alphabetical arrangement is *partly* followed.

Isa. v. 1, 2 : " (1) My wellbeloved hath a vineyard in a very fruitful hill ; (2) and he fenced it, (3) and gathered out the stones thereof, (4) and planted it with the choicest vine, (5) and built a tower in the midst of it, (6) and also made a winepress therein ; (7) and he looked that it should bring forth grapes. (8) And it brought forth wild grapes." The first **7** sentences describe the vineyard, what was done for it, and what was expected of it ; the *eighth* gives the result.

Ezek. xxvi.–xxviii. In these three chapters **7** judgments are pronounced upon Tyre, each being marked by the use of the phrase, " Thus saith the Lord GOD," and commencing respectively at ch. xxvi. 1, 7, 15, 19 ; xxvii. 1 ; xxviii. 1, 11. The same phrase also occurs ch. xxviii. 6, but it does not here mark a separate judgment, as is shown by the words " because," ver. 2, and "therefore," ver. 6.

In Ezekiel's Temple, **7** steps led into the outer court, and *eight* from the outer to the inner (Ezek. xl. 22, 26, 31, 34, 37). Special sacrifices were to be offered on the sabbath day and on the day of the new moon, the burnt offering on the former comprehending **7** animals and on the latter *eight* (Ezek. xlvi. 4, 6).

In Amos i., ii., judgment is pronounced on **7** nations, if Israel and Judah be counted as one, but upon *eight* if they are counted separately.

Micah v. 5 : " And this man shall be our peace : when the Assyrian shall come into our land, and when he shall tread in our palaces, then shall we raise against him 7 shepherds and *eight* principal men " (R.V.).

Matt. vi. 9–13. The Lord's Prayer contains an invocation, and 7 petitions.

Matt. xix. 29 (R.V.) : " (1) Houses, (2) or brethren, (3) or sisters, (4) or father, (5) or mother, (6) or children, (7) or lands." So in Mark x. 29 (R.V.) ; but in Luke xviii. 29, an *eighth*, " or wife," is introduced, though the other seven are not all given.

Our Lord claimed to be greater than (1) Abraham, Jno. viii. 58 ; (2) Jacob, Jno. iv. 12 ; (3) Moses, Jno. vi. 32, 48–51 ; (4) David, Mt. xxii. 43 ; (5) Solomon, Mt. xii. 42 ; (6) Jonah, Mt. xii. 41 ; (7) the Temple, Mt. xii. 6 ; and also to be (8) Lord of the Sabbath Day, Mt. xii. 8.

Eph. iv. 4–6 : " (1) One body, (2) and one Spirit, even as ye are called in (3) one hope of your calling ; (4) one Lord, (5) one faith, (6) one baptism, (7) one God and Father of all." Here are 7 unities, but two titles are given to the last.

Col. iii. 12, 13. The Christian is here exhorted to " put on " 7 graces : " (1) bowels of mercies, (2) kindness, (3) humbleness of mind, (4) meekness, (5) longsuffering, (6) forbearing one another, and (7) forgiving one another." Ver. 14 : " But over all these [he must put on] *love*, which is the *bond* of *perfectness*," an upper garment (says Fausset) which *completes* and keeps together the rest, which, without it, would be loose and disconnected.

This last passage, perhaps, furnishes a clue which may help to explain the numerical symbolism in our Lord's answer to the rich young ruler : " If thou wilt enter into life, keep the commandments. . . . (1) Thou shalt do no murder, (2) Thou shalt not commit adultery, (3) Thou shalt not steal, (4) Thou shalt not bear false witness, (5) Honour thy father and thy mother : and (6) Thou shalt love thy neighbour as thyself. The young man saith unto him, All these things have I kept from my youth up ; what lack I yet ? Jesus said unto him, *If thou wilt be perfect*, go and sell that thou hast, and give to the poor, and thou shalt have treasure in heaven ; and come and follow me." This is St. Matthew's account (ch. xix. 17–21). St. Mark's is as follows : " Thou knowest the commandments, (1) Do not commit adultery, (2) Do not kill, (3) Do not steal, (4) Do not bear false witness, (5) Defraud not, (6) Honour thy father and mother. And he answered and said unto him, Master, all these have I observed from my youth. Then Jesus beholding him loved him, and said unto him, *One thing thou lackest;* go thy way, sell whatsoever thou hast, and give to the poor, and thou shalt have treasure in heaven; and come, follow me " (Mark x. 19–21). So, then, the young man lacked *one* thing to make him *perfect.* Each of the two Evangelists enumerates six commandments which he said he had kept; therefore one added would make 7, and it may be that this is as far as we have a right to go. But considering that St. Luke in his account only gives five commandments, and that in the passage we have just been considering (Col. iii. 14) an *eighth* grace, and not a seventh, is said to be " the bond of *perfectness,*" it may be that we should take the *combined* testimony of the Evangelists here. This would give 7 commands which he said he had observed from his youth—for Matthew and Mark each have one which the other omits—to which our Lord added " one thing " more (i.e. an *eighth*), to make him " perfect."

The above, however, is perhaps open to doubt, and is merely offered as a suggestion.

James iii. 17 : " The wisdom that is from above is first (1) pure, then (2) peaceable, (3) gentle, (4) easy to be intreated, (5) full of mercy and good fruits, (6) without partiality, and (7) without hypocrisy." Here number 5 is double, so that the 7 might easily be made into *eight.*

Circumcision was performed upon a male child when it was what we should term 7 days old, but the day is invariably spoken of in Scripture as the *eighth* day.

Abraham had *eight* sons, 7 of whom were " born after the flesh," and the other was " by promise."

At the consecration of Aaron and his sons they were commanded to " abide at the door of the tabernacle of the congregation day and night 7 days," and on the *eighth* they were fully installed in their office (Lev. viii. 35; ix. 1). See also Ezek. xliii. 26, 27.

In the Tabernacle and its court there were 7 chief articles: (1) Ark; (2) Mercy-seat (which is always spoken of as a separate thing from the ark); (3) Altar of Incense; (4) Golden Candlestick; (5) Table of Shewbread; (6) Altar of Burnt-offering; (7) Laver. Against these there were in Solomon's Temple 35 articles, which fall into *eight* groups: (1) Ark; (2) Mercy-seat; (3) Altar of Incense; (4) Ten Candlesticks; (5)

Ten Tables of Shewbread ; (6) Altar of Burnt-offering ; (7) Brasen Sea ; (8) Ten Lavers.

Eight times in the Pentateuch is the Sabbath commanded to be kept holy : 7 times by God directly (Exod. xx. 8 ; xxiii. 12 ; xxxi. 13 ; xxxiv. 21 ; Lev. xix. 3 ; xix. 30 ; xxiii. 3) ; and once by Moses (Exod. xxxv. 2). Deut. v. 12 is only a repetition of the fourth commandment.

It is rather remarkable that David should in one place (1 Chron. ii. 15) be called the 7th son of Jesse, and elsewhere (1 Sam. xvi. 10, 11 ; xvii. 12) the *eighth*.

Our Lord spoke 7 times when he was on the cross ; but one of the sayings was a double one : ": Woman, behold thy son ; " " Behold thy mother."

Eight is sometimes put for 7, as in John xx. 26, " after eight days ; " and Luke ix. 28; " about eight days after." [1]

Lastly, as evil sometimes tries to imitate good (for like as Christ is called a Lion,[2] so " the devil, *as* a roaring lion, walketh about ; " [3] and again, as Christ is called a Lamb, so the beast whose number was 666 " had two horns *like* a lamb "[4]), so we read that " the beast that was, and is not, is himself also an *eighth*, and is of the 7." [5]

The inquiry suggests itself, What is the meaning of this close connection between the numbers Seven and Eight ? The connection itself is too obvious to have escaped notice, and I will not attempt to do more than quote the reasons which some have assigned for it.

Dr. John Forbes, speaking of the Beatitudes in the Sermon on the Mount, says : " The tenth verse—*Blessed are they which are persecuted for righteousness' sake ; for theirs is the kingdom of heaven*—though resembling in form the 7 Beatitudes, is yet clearly distinguishable from them, since it describes no additional *grace* essential to the Christian character. . . . If it be asked, Is, then, this verse, which so exactly coincides in form with the preceding seven verses, no eighth Beatitude ? We answer, It is, and it is not. *Seven* in itself, like *three*, is a complete and perfect number : yet at times, even when the climax has been reached, the full heart will overflow, and pass the

---

[1] So to the present day " eight-days " is the common colloquial expression for " a week " in Scotland ; thus, where an Englishman would speak of (say) " Tuesday week," a Scotsman would probably use the phrase " Tuesday eight-days." So also, in England, a clock made to run 7 days only is invariably called an eight-day clock.

[2] Rev. v. 5.
[3] 1 Pet. v. 8 ; cf. Rev. xiii. 2.
[4] Rev. xiii. 11.
[5] Rev. xvii. 11.

prescribed measure in its anxiety to express the feelings with which it is fraught. ' Give a portion to *seven*—yea, even to *eight*,' Eccles. xi. 2. . . . Our Lord had already pronounced a complete sevenfold blessing upon His disciples, but in His anxiety to comfort them under the trials which He foresaw awaiting them, He would add one more still, beyond the perfect number : ' Blessed are they which are persecuted for righteousness' sake,' etc. *Theoretically*, the Christian, if possessed of the seven dispositions described, would be in all things ' perfect, wanting nothing ; ' but *practically*, for the exercise and development of these graces, conflict with an evil world is requisite, and, like his Master, the disciple of Christ must be made ' perfect through sufferings.' " [1]

To a somewhat similar conclusion, though for a different reason, came that learned lady Mrs. Mary Anne Schimmelpenninck. " The word שבעה [*shib'ah*], ' seven,' comes," she says, " from the root שבע [*shaba*], ' he filled, satisfied, *or* completed.' Thus seven means the complete number, probably because the world was created in six days, and on the seventh was the sabbath of rest. In many natural objects, too, the number seven seems to prevail, as in that of the colours in the rainbow, and the notes in the musical scale ; in both which instances the colour or note succeeding the seventh, or, in other words, the octave, is always a reduplication of the first. Hence, in Hebrew, not only the word שבעה [*shib'ah*], ' seven,' means the *satisfying* or *complete* number, but the word ' eight ' denotes the *superabundant* or *overflowing* number. The word שמנה [*sh'monah*], ' eight,' being derived from שמן [*shaman*], ' he superabounded.' . . . Thus the number *seven* is always used in Scripture to denote the totality or completeness of a thing ; and the number *eight* is, again, continually applied to signify an overflowing abundance or multitude ; because in the instances of days, of colours, of notes, etc., the octave, by exceeding seven, which is the complete number, only becomes a reduplication of the first." [2]

---

[1] *Symmetrical Structure of Scripture*, pp. 208, 209. Dr. Forbes shows clearly that while apparently eight (some reckon nine) Beatitudes, there are really only 7 : " for while a new and distinctive promise is attached to each of the seven Christian graces, this, by some considered an eighth Beatitude, returns back, as it were, upon the first, having the same promise repeated, ' For theirs is the kingdom of heaven,' " p. 168.

[2] *Biblical Fragments*, i., 253, 254. The etymologies on which these remarks are founded are those given by Parkhurst, who, however, is not followed by the more modern school of Hebraists.

Others assign an entirely different meaning to the number *eight*, based, not upon the etymology of the Hebrew word, but upon the use of the number in Scripture. From the time of St. Augustine, if not earlier, it has been considered the numerical symbol for Resurrection. Thus our own Venerable Bede writes : " Not only the etymology of this very sacred name of Jesus, but also the very number which is contained in the letters, comprehend the mysteries of our salvation ; for it is written according to the Greeks with six letters, the numbers of which are—

$$I = 10$$
$$\eta = 8$$
$$\sigma = 200$$
$$o = 70$$
$$v = 400$$
$$\varsigma = 200$$

These together make 888 ; and it is an illustrious type of the resurrection. For the eighth number in the Sacred Scriptures is adapted to the glory of the resurrection ; because the Lord rose from the dead on the eighth day, that is to say, on the day after the Sabbath. And we, after the lapse of six ages, and also of the seventh, which is the Sabbath of the souls in a separate state of existence, shall be raised, as it were, in the eighth time."

And so Mr. Andrew Jukes : " *The eighth day* is always typical of resurrection. The eighth day, the day after the seventh, or Sabbath, answers to ' the first day of the week ' on which Christ rose ; it is, however, ' the first day ' in reference to seven having gone before. Seven days include the periods proper to the first creation. The eighth day, as it takes us beyond and out of these—that is, beyond the limits of the old creation—brings us in type into a new order of things and times ; in a word, into the new creation or resurrection." [1]

So also Bp. Chr. Wordsworth : " The *first Sabbath*, on which God rested from His works, was a type of the *last Sabbath*, on which Christ rested from His works in the grave. . . . *But on the first day* of the week [He rose from the dead], i.e. the day after the *Sabbath* or Seventh Day, and therefore the *Eighth* Day ; and therefore it is observed by the Fathers that our Lord *arose* on the *Eighth* Day. . . . *Seven* is expressive of *rest* in Christ ; *Eight* is expressive of *Resurrection* to *new life* and *glory* in Him.

[1] *The Law of the Offerings*, 11th ed., p. 30. See also *The Types of Genesis*, p. 226.

In accordance with this number the *Eighth* day was the Day of *Circumcision*—the type of Christian Baptism, the sacrament of Resurrection, in which we *rise* from the death of sin to newness of Life in Him. Our Lord received the name JESUS on the *eighth* day (Luke ii. 21) ; He as our *Jesus, Joshua, Saviour,* brings us to the heavenly Canaan—to the glory of the Resurrection. . . . Hence also we find that the Transfiguration—which was a figure and a glimpse of the future glory of the bodies of the Saints after the resurrection—is mentioned as having taken place *eight* days after our Lord had said, ' There be some standing here which shall not taste of death till they shall see the Kingdom of God ' (Luke ix. 27)." [1]

And again : " The *Eighth* day is the Day of Resurrection after the sabbath of the grave. In Ezekiel's Temple there are 7 steps to the outer court (xl. 22, 26), and *eight* steps from it into the Temple [2] (xl. 31, 34, 37). The former symbolizes the transition from labour to rest ; the latter symbolizes the transition from rest to glory." [3]

There are 7 miracles recorded in St. John's Gospel, and an *eighth* after the resurrection.

As bearing upon this, it may be added that *eight* resurrections are recorded in Scripture, beside those of our Lord and of the " saints " who arose with Him, viz. (1) the widow of Zarephath's son, (2) the Shunammite's son, (3) the man whose body was thrown into Elisha's tomb, (4) Jairus's daughter, (5) the widow of Nain's son, (6) Lazarus, (7) Dorcas, (8) Eutychus. [4]

---

[1] *Commentary*, on Luke xxiii. 56 ; xxiv. 1.

[2] This is not strictly correct ; the *eight* steps led from the outer to the inner court, from which, again, other steps led into the Temple. How many there were here the Hebrew text does not say ; it merely has " and by the steps whereby they went up to it " [i.e. to the porch of the Temple]. But the Sept. reads, "and by *ten* steps they went up to it " (see Ezek. xl. 49, text and margin, in R.V.). This, if correct, gives the following instructive gradation : There were *seven* steps from the street into the outer court, *eight* from the outer to the inner, and *ten* from the inner court (in which was placed the altar of burnt offering), into the Temple itself. Compare the reading of Cod. D in Acts xii. 10, that when the Angel delivered Peter from prison, " they went down the seven steps," which Bp. Chase believes comes from this passage in Ezek. (*Old Syriac Element in Cod. Bezæ*, p. 86).

[3] *Commentary*, on Ezekiel, *Retrospect*, p. 279.

[4] If we compare the three resurrections of the Old Testament with the three of the Gospels, we find that in each case one was of the son of a widow, one of the child of a rich person, and one of a full-grown man. In each case, too, the man was raised from the tomb, whilst the children had not been buried.

So, when the earth was wrapped in death by the Flood, *eight* persons were saved alive in the ark. ·

Dr. H. Grattan Guinness writes: " The septiform divisions of time in the O.T. run on constantly to an octave, and give a glad and glorious prominence to the 8th day and the 50th day [7 × 7 + 1] in connection with observances intimating that a new and better economy was destined to succeed the Jewish ; that in a New Creation to follow the Old, and in that alone, would full purity and peace, perfect joy and liberty be found." [1]

To quote one writer more : " See what is written concerning the Queen of Sheba, the type of every faithful soul when it shall enter into the New Jerusalem. There are *eight* distinct steps of her astonishment set down. . . . Those *seven* things ['all Solomon's wisdom, and the house that he had built, and the meat of his table, and the sitting of his servants, and the attendance of his ministers, and their apparel, and his cup-bearers ']—the types in the palace of the earthly Solomon—the Queen of Sheba saw, and she yet desired to see more ; but when she came to the *eighth*—' his ascent, by which he went up to the house of the Lord '—then, ' there was no more spirit in her.' And so of us. When we have seen all these—when we come to the *eighth* thing, which speaks of the New Creation as accomplished, to the octave which fills up the measure of that perfect harmony, the ascent by which we fully, and for ever, ourselves, enter into the very Holy of Holies—when that Head which for us bowed down upon the cross shall then, in the Beatific Vision, kiss us with the kisses of His mouth,—then, indeed, there will be no more spirit in us. Beyond this we cannot go. Every power of love will be filled. Every capacity for delight will be contented. That is the knowing even as we are known." [2]

Nor is it only in Scripture that the numbers Seven and Eight are found connected together. In the Apostles' Creed 7 sections may be counted, but one of them (" The holy Catholic Church ; The Communion of Saints ") is double, and has the appearance of two. [3]

There are 7 notes in music, but an *eighth* is required to complete the harmony, and an " octave " (from *octo*, eight, *octavus*,

[1] *Approaching End of the Age*, 9th ed., p. 468.
[2] J. M. Neale's *Sermons on the Song of Songs*, pp. 13–16.
[3] See Appendix G, p. 388.

eighth) is defined as being in music " an interval of 7 degrees or *twelve* semitones." [1]

The number of permanent teeth in man is 32, or eight on each side of each jaw ; of these 7 make their appearance early in life, and the *eighth*, or " wisdom tooth," not until many years later.

If we consider the whole body as the " organ " of the sense of touch, then the five senses may be said to have either 7 organs or *eight*, according as the sense of smell be treated as having one organ (the nose), or two (the nostrils).

[1] Annandale's *English Dictionary*.

APPENDIX F

CONCORDANCES TO THE SCRIPTURES

A FEW words respecting concordances may, perhaps, be useful to some readers.

In seeking to ascertain the number of occurrences of words and phrases in Scripture, of course a purely English concordance, such as Cruden's, is of little or no use, for the same Hebrew or Greek word is often translated by several English ones, and, on the other hand, the same English word may represent different words in the original. Concordances in or based upon the original languages of Scripture, are, therefore, a necessity. Of these I have no hesitation in assigning the first place (as regards the *Old Testament*) to—

The Hebraist's Vade Mecum, now called *A Handy Hebrew Concordance,* both for its completeness and accuracy. It gives every occurrence of every word in the Hebrew and Aramaic Scriptures, arranged according to grammar (the inseparable particles, however, only being given in connection with the words to which they are joined) ; it is, therefore, most useful for ascertaining the number of occurrences of a word, or inflection of a word, where the meaning and context are not required to be taken into account. Considering the sea of figures which this book presents, it is a marvel of accuracy.

The Englishman's Hebrew and Chaldee Concordance of the Old Testament is a work of a different nature. It gives every occurrence of every Hebrew and Aramaic word (except the verb *to be,* and the frequently recurring particles), with the context in English, and is specially designed for the use of those who have little or no knowledge of the original languages. It is a very accurate work, and, so far as my use of it has extended, I have only noticed one error.[1]

[1] 1 Chron. xv. 22 is omitted under יְסֹר, p. 545. The writer of the article " Divination," in Kitto's *Cyc. Bib. Lit.*, calls attention to two *supposed* omissions of the word אִשֶּׁה ; had he looked a little more closely, however, he would have found the two passages under the heading אִשִּׁים (*Hebrew plural*).

For the proper study of Phrases in the Old Testament, however, a Heb. concordance is necessary, such as Fürst's, B. Davidson's or the ponderous and expensive one of S. Mandelkern (Leipzig, 1896). The late Prof. Driver compared the three thus: "B. Davidson's Concordance pub. by Bagsters (my copy bears date 1876) is both far more convenient than Fürst's, and decidedly more accurate. . . . Since I first learnt of Davidson's Concordance I have entirely discarded Fürst, and I still use the former for all ordinary purposes, merely employing Mandelkern for the particles and proper names." [1] Davidson's is the handiest and best arranged, but where strict accuracy is required it should be compared with the *Hebraist's Vade Mecum* or the *Englishman's Heb. Conc.*, or in the case of phrases by reference to other words in the phrase.

A supplement showing the various readings and emendations given by Kittel and others would be a most valuable aid to the study of the O.T. text. The *Oxf. Heb. Lex.* gives much help in this direction.

For the *New Testament*, the *Englishman's Greek Concordance* is the most reliable, but it gives the received text only. *A Concordance of Various Readings occurring in the Greek N.T.* forms an admirable Supplement to it, and is also useful in other ways.

Of purely Greek Concordances there are two good ones :

(1) Bruder's, which gives full occurrences of all words except δ, δς, καί, with the variations of WH and earlier edd., also many various readings of the principal MSS. Its chief drawbacks are that it is based on Griesbach's text and gives only a short context.

(2) Moulton & Geden's (2nd edn.) is an excellent work, being based on WH, with the variations of Tisch. and the Revisers, and giving a fuller context than Bruder. While it may generally be relied upon, it is not wholly free from error, and should be checked by the *Englishman's* and its Supplement where strict accuracy is desired.

A valuable feature in both Bruder and Geden is that different forms and significations of certain words are noted.

Dr. Robert Young's *Concordance to the Greek N.T.* aims at giving the occurrences of each inflection of the words in the rec. text without the context, but it cannot be relied upon for accuracy.

---

[1] *Expos. Times*, vii., 431.

Young's *Analytical Concordance to the Bible* is based on the English version, and is therefore not suitable for our purpose. but it has the Proper Names with context, and in the Appendix it gives the number of occurrences of most words in the original as does also (for the O.T.) the *Oxf. Heb. Lex.*   The latter is the more reliable of the two.

For the *Septuagint*, Hatch & Redpath's Concordance is an excellent one.   Messrs. Bagster have also published *A Handy Concordance to the Septuagint*, without the context.

APPENDIX G

THE NUMBER SEVEN AND THE PRAYER-BOOK

A FEW words on this subject will not, I trust, be deemed out of place, though I have not made it a very special object of study.

Certain Church of England writers have given expression to very high views respecting the Church and her formularies. Thus Dean Goulburn says, " It may be very much questioned whether there is such another uninspired book [as the Book of Common Prayer] in the world." [1] And he quotes the following from Professor Blunt : " The Prayer-Book is a book *sui generis*. We have no other of the same kind or like it. . . . It is the voice of the ancient Church expressed upon the highest matters ; and so, not improbably, that of the Founder of that Church." [2]

" That liturgy," writes Bishop Jebb, " which was not compiled and preserved without the special inspiration of God's Spirit, and the almost unexampled care of His providence, . . . [is an] easy, artless, and unfettered exhibition of divine truth, not as it is mutilated or perverted in any system of human manufacture, but as it is diffused over the rich expanse of Scripture, with a *noble negligence of rule*, such as, probably, appeared in the paradise of God." [3]

" Thus was our excellent Liturgy," says Wheatly, " compiled by martyrs and confessors, together with divers other learned bishops and divines ; and being revised and approved by the archbishops, bishops, and clergy of both the provinces of Canterbury and York, was then confirmed by the King and the three estates in parliament, A.D. 1548, who gave it this just encomium, viz. *which at this time* BY THE AID OF THE HOLY GHOST *with uniform agreement is of them concluded, set forth*," etc. [4]

[1] *The Holy Catholic Church*, p. 313.　　　　[2] Idem, p. 315.
[3] Jebb's *Pastoral Instructions*, pp. 56, 57.
[4] Wheatly on *The Book of Common Prayer*, p. 25.　(Ed. 1848.)

To quote one writer more: "She [the Church Catholic]," says Mr. Jukes, "may have been teaching far more than some of her sons as yet have learnt from her." [1] He speaks with approbation of "those . . . who believe that the Church was divinely guided in the order and appointment of the Christian Year," [2] and elsewhere says, "How much is there in the order of the Christian Year far beyond the thought of the Church herself which ordained and arranged this order? . . . The Creeds . . . not only may confess far more than the Church's children apprehend, but confess it for reasons, and in relation to matters, which as yet they have not thought of." [3]

This is strong language, even though we admit, as we must admit, that the inspiration, the divine guidance spoken of, is something of a very much lower nature than that vouchsafed to the writers of Holy Scripture, and it is not for me to express either approval or disapproval of it. But can the HEPTAD TEST be applied to it, and, if so, what does it say?

In the Service-books of the pre-Reformation Church, and of the Roman Catholic Church of the present day, the number 7 is of frequent occurrence. Thus there are said to be 7 works of mercy (bodily) and 7 works of mercy (ghostly); 7 deadly sins and 7 contrary virtues; also 7 (other) virtues, 3 theological and 4 cardinal. Then we have the 7 gifts of the Holy Ghost, and the 7 penitential psalms. "The mediæval Church held 7 festivals in honour of the Virgin Mary." [4] There are 7 orders in the Roman Church, 3 holy or greater and 4 lesser; [5] 7 sacraments; 7 offices for daily prayer, sometimes called the "Canonical Hours;" 14 stations of the Cross.

Also 7 Dolours or Sorrows of the Virgin; and 7 Joys of Mary. There were 7 Antiphons addressed to Christ sung during Advent (the great O's—O Sapientia, etc.). [6]

All these—which evidently point to some special sanctity being supposed to reside in the number 7—our Reformers swept away when they compiled the Book of Common Prayer, the only vestige remaining being in those words of the ancient Hymn to the Holy Ghost used in the Ordination Services—

[1] Jukes's *Restitution of All Things*, p. 45.   [2] Idem, p. 53.
[3] Jukes's "*Catholic Eschatology*" *Examined*, p. 4. Also Jukes's *Order and Connexion of the Church's Teaching*, preface.
[4] Procter's *History of the Book of Common Prayer*, 12th ed., p. 302.
[5] Idem, p. 440, note.
[6] See Rendel Harris: *Testimonies*, II. p. 99.

" Thou the anointing Spirit art,
Who dost Thy seven-fold gifts impart."

The 7 penitential psalms, it is true, are appointed to be used on Ash Wednesday, but they are so divided that few would be aware of the fact were not their attention called to it. Beyond this one place, I am not aware that the compilers have anywhere used the word *seven*, except in the casual remark in the Preface, that " the ancient Fathers have divided the Psalms into 7 portions." [1]

It is clear, then, that the compilers of the Liturgy attached no special importance to the number seven ; and if we still find traces of it in the Prayer-Book, it can hardly be because they intentionally placed them there.

To commence with the Creeds. Of these there are *three*—a number at once suggestive of that Triune God whom they so clearly teach. The Romish Church destroys the symbolism by adding a fourth, that non-Catholic formulary called the " Creed of Pope Pius IV."

In the Apostles' Creed, the shortest and most ancient of all, 7 professions of faith are made :—

(1) I believe in God the Father Almighty, . . .
(2) And in Jesus Christ His only Son our Lord. . . .
(3) I believe in the Holy Ghost ;
(4) { The holy Catholic Church ;
     { The Communion of Saints ;
(5) The Forgiveness of sins ;
(6) The Resurrection of the body ;
(7) And the life everlasting.

It will be seen that the central article is a double one ; for that the two parts of it have the same meaning, or, at least, that one is included in the other, I need not stop to prove.

---

[1] So far as I can gather from the Concordances of Mr. Green and of the Christian Knowledge Society, the word *seven* and its derivatives occur in the Prayer-Book (omitting the Commandments and other portions of Scripture) only in the following places :—(1) Preface, as above ; (2) Ordination Service for Priests, and (3) for Bishops, as above ; (4) Rubrics to Proper Prefaces for Christmas Day, (5) Easter Day, and (6) Ascension Day. The word *seventh*, of course, occurs at the head of the Collect, etc., for the Seventh Sunday after Trinity. The word *fourteen* occurs in the third rubric at the beginning of the Communion Service. Compare the first rubric in the Office of Baptism for such as are of Riper Years, where " a week " is used, not " seven days."

In the Nicene Creed the same 7 doctrines are taught :—
(1) I believe in one God the Father Almighty, . . .
(2) And in one Lord Jesus Christ . . .
(3) And I believe in the Holy Ghost. . . .
(4) And I believe one Catholic and Apostolic Church.
(5) I acknowledge one Baptism for the remission of sins,
(6) And I look for the Resurrection of the dead,
(7) And the life of the world to come.

These 7 articles of the Apostles' and Nicene Creeds exactly correspond with the 7 unities of Eph. iv. 4–6 : " There is one body, and one Spirit, even as ye are called in one hope of your calling ; one Lord, one faith, one baptism, one God and Father of all." I do not know whether this has ever been pointed out before, but, as I have never seen it, it may be well to show it in detail.

(1) " One God and Father " = " God the Father Almighty."
(2) " One Lord " = " Jesus Christ."
(3) " One Spirit " = " The Holy Ghost."
(4) " One Body " = " The Holy Catholic Church, the Communion of Saints," Eph. i. 22, 23.

(5) " One Baptism " = " The forgiveness of sins ; " or, as the Nicene Creed expresses it more fully, " One Baptism for the remission of sins."

(6) " One Faith " = " The Resurrection of the Dead," which is the chief article as well as ground of our faith, for, " if there be no resurrection of the dead, then is Christ not risen ; and if Christ be not risen, . . . your *faith* is vain " (I Cor. xv. 13, 14). This is followed (I Pet. i. 3, 4) by—

(7) " One Hope " = " The Life Everlasting " (Titus i. 2 ; Col. i. 5).

The Athanasian Creed is not so easy to deal with, but it will probably be admitted that the following 7 verses contain a fair summary of the whole :—

(1) " The Catholic Faith is this : That we worship one God in Trinity, and Trinity in Unity."

(2) " The Father is made of none : neither created, nor begotten."

(3) " The Son is of the Father alone : not made, nor created, but begotten."

(4) " The Holy Ghost is of the Father and of the Son : neither made, nor created, nor begotten, but proceeding."

(5) " Furthermore, it is necessary to eternal salvation,

that he also believe rightly the Incarnation of our Lord Jesus Christ. For the right Faith is, that we believe and confess that our Lord Jesus Christ, the Son of God, is God and Man."

(6) " At whose coming all men shall rise again with their bodies ; and shall give account for their own works."

(7) " And they that have done good shall go into life eternal : and they that have done evil into eternal fire."

The Athanasian Creed contains **42** verses, and is appointed to be said on **13** days in the year : on 6 days dedicated to **7** of the Apostles, St. Simon and St. Jude's being one, and on **7** days not connected with the Apostles.

" The Feasts that are to be observed in the Church of England throughout the year " are, according to the Table at the beginning of the Prayer-Book, **77** in number, viz. " all Sundays in the year," and twenty-five other days. But that our Reformers did not set this number before them in selecting these from the Saints' Days of the pre-Reformation Church, is evident, for they actually add four other days of quite a different character, raising the total number to eighty-one. These are Monday and Tuesday in Easter Week, and Monday and Tuesday in Whitsun Week, days which commemorate nothing, have no special collects, as all the others have, and are simply appointed to add dignity to the two great Festivals of Easter Day and Whitsun Day.[1]

The Feasts or Holy Days appointed in commemoration of persons other than our Lord, i.e. of created beings, are **21** in number, as may be seen from the same Table.

There are **91** days for which Epistles and Gospels are provided, viz., Sundays 53 ; Holy Days with Collects 28 (= Feasts as above 25, Ash Wednesday, Good Friday and Easter Even) ; King's Accession, 1 ; Days without special Collects 9 (= Sunday after Christmas Day, Monday and Tuesday in Easter Week, Monday and Tuesday in Whitsun Week, and four days in Holy Week). Good Friday has three Collects, so that the number of Collects for special days is **84**.

---

[1] There is perhaps, however, a reason for the appointment of these four extra days as Feasts, for it will always happen that one or more of the twenty-five other days will fall on Sunday, which would reduce the total below **77** were not their places supplied by these. For although one, two, three, or four of the twenty-five may fall on Sunday, neither five nor six ever can. Seven and even eight may, in which cases the total number of separate days must be taken as **70**.

7 events in the Life of Christ are commemorated by Holy Days: (1) Christmas Day; (2) The Circumcision; (3) The Epiphany; (4) Ash Wednesday; (5) Good Friday; (6) Easter Day; (7) Ascension Day. And though we have also "The Presentation of Christ in the Temple," the proper name for this day, and the *only* one given in the Calendar, the Table of Feasts, and the Table of Proper Lessons, is "The Purification of the Virgin Mary," showing that it is the latter event, rather than the former, which is commemorated. And for a very obvious reason; for as Christ submitted to circumcision, thus putting Himself in the sinner's place, and becoming "a debtor to do the whole law," so must His mother offer a sin-offering and be purified, although she had contracted no defilement. Her purification, therefore, was an event of deep significance to us, and is deservedly commemorated by the Church, showing, as it does, that from His very birth our Lord, who knew no sin, was treated as a sinner, and bore the shame attaching thereto. Yet, as we sometimes find the number 7 expanding into 10 in connection with our Lord (as in the case of the angelic manifestations, 3 of which took place before His birth and 7 after), so it is here. For in addition to the 7 events above mentioned, there are 3 others which, if we may so say, primarily relate to others, but in a secondary sense also concern Him. These are (1) His Incarnation (the Annunciation of the Virgin Mary); (2) His Presentation in the Temple (the Purification of the Virgin Mary); and (3) His sending the promised Comforter (Whitsun Day).

Though it is certain that to some Holy Days a greater importance must be attached than to others, the Church nowhere gives any list of how many, or which, these days are. We are not, however, left without a guide, and there are 7 days which may be denominated Holy Days of the First Class. These are nowhere mentioned together in the Prayer-Book, but all of them have one or two marks of distinction possessed by no other days, six of them having Proper Psalms appointed, and five Proper Prefaces in the Communion Service. (1) Christmas Day, (2) Easter Day, (3) Ascension Day, and (4) Whitsun Day, have both; (5) Trinity Sunday, the latter only; and (6) Ash Wednesday, and (7) Good Friday, being "Fasts," the former only.

To turn now from the beginning of the Prayer-Book to the end, we find there "A Table of Kindred and Affinity," which gives a list of 30 (3 × 10) possible female relations whom "a man may not marry." These 30, however, are really reducible to 7, viz. (1) Grandmother, (2) Mother, (3) Aunt, (4) Daughter, (5) Sister, (6) Niece, (7) Granddaughter. The others are simply varieties of these.[1]

The Services for Morning and Evening Prayer each include 14 prayers, which may be divided into two *sevens :* (1) the Confession, (2) the Absolution, (3) the Lord's Prayer, (4) the same, (5, 6, and 7) the three Collects. Then follows the " Anthem," which marks a distinct break in the service. After this we have (1) the Prayer for the King, (2) the Prayer for the Royal Family, (3) the Prayer for the Clergy and People, (4) the Prayer for All Conditions of Men, (5) the General Thanksgiving, (6) the Prayer of St. Chrysostom, (7) the Apostolic Benediction. This last is expressly called a Prayer, both in the rubric before the Prayer for the King, which speaks of " these five Prayers following " (of which it is one), and in the rubric at the beginning of the " Prayers and Thanksgivings." [2] The Absolution is not usually considered a prayer, and indeed is rather spoken *of* God than addressed *to* Him, but it is expressly called a Prayer in the rubric at the end of it, which says, " The people shall answer here, and at the end of all *other prayers*, Amen."

The first definite act of worship, both at Morning and at Evening Prayer, is the repeating of the General Confession. This contains 14 clauses, which naturally divide themselves into two portions of 7 each ; the first portion dealing (after the Invocation) solely with confession of sin, the second portion with prayer for pardon and restoration. In the first portion, the subtle connection between seven and eight [3] may be noticed, for if we leave out the Invocation ("Almighty and most merciful Father "), the confession of sin still embraces 7 particulars, one clause being a double one, " (1) We have erred, (2) and (we have) strayed from Thy ways like lost sheep," for only " strayed " and not " erred " is connected with the concluding phrase, "like lost sheep." The Confession then proceeds, " (3) We have followed too much the devices and desires of our own hearts. (4) We have offended against Thy holy laws. (5) We have left undone those things which we

---

[1] See *The Prayer-Book Interleaved*, p. 399.

[2] So Wheatly observes that it " is rather a *prayer* than a blessing ; since . . . the minister . . . is directed to pronounce it *kneeling*, and to include himself as well as the people." Chap. III., sec. xxvi.

[3] See Appendix E.

ought to have done ; (6) And we have done those things which we ought not to have done ; (7) And there is no health in us." Here confession ends, and now petition begins : " (1) But Thou, O Lord, have mercy upon us, miserable offenders. (2) Spare Thou them, O God, which confess their faults. (3) Restore Thou them that are penitent ; (4) According to Thy promises declared unto mankind in Christ Jesu our Lord. (5) And grant, O most merciful Father, for His sake ; (6) That we may hereafter live a godly, righteous, and sober life ; (7) To the glory of Thy holy name. Amen."

The word " and " occurs **7** times in the Confession, and *ten* times in the Absolution.

At Morning Prayer on Sundays—the ante-Communion Office being used—**7** portions of Scripture are appointed to be either read or sung : (1) Ps. xcv. ; (2) the Psalms for the Day ; (3) the First Lesson ; (4) the Second Lesson ; (5) the Song of Zacharias, *or* Ps. c. ; (6) the Epistle ; (7) the Gospel.

Evening Prayer also includes **7** portions of Scripture, but as two of them are alternatives, not more than *five* can be used on the same day : (1) the Psalms for the Day ; (2) the First Lesson ; (3) the Song of Mary *or* (4) Ps. xcviii. ; (5) the Second Lesson ; (6) the Song of Simeon *or* (7) Ps. lxvii.

The Prayer for the King's Majesty contains **7** petitions.

When Morning Prayer and the Communion Office are used together, **7** opportunities for singing are provided by the Prayer-Book : (1) the *Venite*, Ps. xcv. ; (2) the Psalms for the Day ; (3) the *Te Deum* or *Benedicite ;* (4) the Song of Zacharias (*Benedictus*) or *Jubilate*, Ps. c. ; (5) the Anthem after the Third Collect ; (6) the Thanksgiving or *Sanctus* (" Therefore with Angels and Archangels," etc.) ; (7) the *Gloria in Excelsis.* It is true that two of the Creeds are also appointed to be " sung or said," but they can hardly be classed with the foregoing, being neither Hymns, Psalms, nor Anthems. The same may be said of the Litany.

Again, if we exclude the Psalms, which are placed in a different part of the Prayer-Book, and vary day by day, there are **7** portions of Scripture appointed to be sung at Morning and Evening Prayer together : (1) Ps. xcv. ; (2) the Song of Zacharias *or* (3) Ps. c. ; (4) the Song of Mary *or* (5) Ps. xcviii. ; (6) the Song of Simeon *or* (7) Ps. lxvii. Three of these, it will be seen, are alternatives, so that only four can be used on the same day.

The Psalter is divided into thirty daily portions, but as **7** months of the year have each thirty-one days, the portion for the thirtieth day is repeated on the last day of these months. This portion includes 7 psalms, which are therefore 7 times each year sung or read over twice.

In the Litany, 14 events connected with our Lord are mentioned : (1) Incarnation, (2) Nativity, (3) Circumcision, (4) Baptism, (5) Fasting, (6) Temptation, (7) Agony, (8) Bloody Sweat, (9) Cross, (10) Passion, (11) Death, (12) Burial, (13) Resurrection, (14) Ascension. These are contained in 7 clauses :—

(1) By the Mystery of Thy Holy Incarnation ;
(2) By Thy Holy Nativity and Circumcision ;
(3) By Thy Baptism, Fasting and Temptation ;
(4) By Thine Agony and Bloody Sweat ;
(5) By Thy Cross and Passion ;
(6) By Thy precious Death and Burial ;
(7) By Thy Glorious Resurrection and Ascension ; to which an 8th clause is added : And by the coming of the Holy Ghost.

14 petitions of the Litany are addressed *directly* to Christ : (1) " O God the Son, Redeemer of the world," etc. ; (2) " Spare Thy people, whom Thou hast redeemed with Thy most precious blood," etc. ; (3) " By the mystery of Thy holy Incarnation," etc. ; (4) " By Thine Agony and Bloody Sweat," etc. ; (5) " Son of God, we beseech Thee to hear us ; " (6) " O Lamb of God, . . . grant us Thy peace ; " (7) " O Lamb of God, . . . have mercy upon us ; " (8) " O Christ, hear us ; " (9) " Christ, have mercy upon us ; " (10) " From our enemies defend us, O Christ ; " (11) " O Son of David, have mercy upon us ; " (12) " Both now and ever vouchsafe to hear us, O Christ ; " (13) " Graciously hear us, O Christ," etc. ; (14) the Prayer of St. Chrysostom.

" We beseech Thee to hear us, good Lord," is repeated 21 times in the Litany, of which 7 are after petitions for our governors and teachers in Church and State.

The Communion Office contains 14 prayers : (1) the Lord's Prayer ; (2) the Collect for Purity ; (3) the Responses to the Commandments ; (4) the Collect for the King ; (5) the Collect of the Day ; (6) the Prayer for the Church Militant ; (7) the Confession ; (8) the Absolution ; (9) the Thanksgiving ; (10) the Prayer of Humble Access ; (11) the Prayer of Consecration ; (12) the Lord's Prayer ; (13) one of the two alternative prayers following ; (14) the *Gloria in Excelsis*. The Absolution is here included, as, if the form in the Order for Morning and Evening Prayer may be counted among the prayers, much more may this.[1] The final Blessing, however, is not included, for it differs essentially from the Benediction at the close of Morning and Evening Prayer, in which the first person is used, but here the second ; and it is nowhere called a prayer, as is the other.

When there is no Communion, and merely the ante-Communion Office is used, only the first *six* of the above prayers are said, but in this case the 7 is made up by the use of one of the Collects specially provided at the end of the Communion Office, agreeably to the rubric, which runs : " Upon the Sundays and other Holy Days (if there be no Communion) shall be said all that is appointed at the Communion, until the end of the general Prayer [For the whole state of Christ's Church militant here in earth] together with one or more [2] of these Collects last before rehearsed, concluding with the Blessing."

There are 7 Occasional Offices in the Prayer Book : (1) Baptism ; (2) Confirmation ; (3) Matrimony ; (4) Visitation of the Sick ; (5) Burial of the Dead ; (6) Churching of Women ; (7) Commination.

In the Ordination Services 7 Questions are put to those about to be made Deacons, 8 to Priests, and 7 to Bishops.[3]

It is not necessary to go further. If members of the Church of England consider that in their Prayer-Book they possess a treasure, let them take heed that they use it circumspectly. To think that membership of the Church, or the use of her Liturgy, will save them, is to repeat the error of the Israelites in the days of Eli, when they trusted in the ark of God—which

---

[1] So Dean Comber, speaking of the three forms of Absolution in the Prayer-Book, says, " The second form is *Petitionary* in the *Communion Service*, where the minister lays down the promise, and on that ground, by virtue of his own office, *begs of God* to make that promise good " (*Companion to the Temple*, pt. i. sec. iv., §1).

[2] It is, however, a very rare thing to find more than one used at the same time.

[3] It is difficult, in the absence of a really complete Concordance, to deal with the number of occurrences of words and phrases in the Prayer-Book, but the following may probably be depended on :—*Angel-s*, 7 times, and *Archangels*, 1 ; *Blood*, 14 in Communion Office ; *Catholic*, 7 (excluding Preface) ; *Holy Communion*, 13 in Communion Office, and 8 elsewhere, total 21 ; *Lord's Supper*, 7 ; *Lord's Table*, 7 in Communion Office ; *Mystery-ies*, 7 ; *Mystical*, 7 (counting Services for Infant and Adult Baptism separately) ; *Passion* (of Christ), 7 ; *Pastors*, 7 ; *Sacrament-s*, 7 in Communion Office ; *Virgin*, 7 ; *Inspire-ation*, 7.

was undoubtedly the symbol of God's presence in their midst—
and not in God Himself, and defeat instead of victory was their
portion.   It is to say, with the Jews of a later date, " We be
Abraham's seed ; " forgetting that it is " they which are of
faith, the same are the children of Abraham ; " that " they
which be of faith are blessed with faithful Abraham ; " and
that " if ye be Christ's, *then* are ye Abraham's seed, and heirs
according to the promise." [1]

[1] Gal. iii. 7, 9, 29.

INDEX I

TEXTS

397

INDEX II

SUBJECTS AND AUTHORS

Printed in the United States
96097LV00001B/226/A